RELIGIOUS REVIVALS
IN BRITAIN AND IRELAND
1859–1905

Religious Revivals
in Britain and Ireland
1859–1905

JANICE HOLMES

IRISH ACADEMIC PRESS
DUBLIN • PORTLAND, OR

First published in 2000 by
IRISH ACADEMIC PRESS
44, Northumberland Road,
Dublin 4, Ireland

and in the United States of America by
IRISH ACADEMIC PRESS
c/o ISBS, 5824 NE Hassalo Street,
Portland, OR 97213-3644

Website: www.iap.ie

British Library Cataloguing in Publication Data

Holmes, Janice
  Religious revivals in Britain and Ireland, 1859–1905. –
  (New directions in Irish history)
  1. Revivals – Great Britain – History – 19th century
  2. Revivals – Ireland – History – 19th century
  I. Title
  269.2'4'0941
  ISBN 0716526921

Library of Congress Cataloging-in-Publication Data

Holmes, Janice Evelyn, 1967–
  Religious revivals in Britain and Ireland, 1859–1905/Janice Holmes.
    p. cm.
  Includes bibliographical references and index.
  ISBN 0-7165-2692-1
  1. Revivals–Great Britain–History–19th century. 2. Great Britain–Church
history–19th century. 3. Revivals–Ireland–History–19th century. 4. Ireland–Church
history–19th century. I. Title.

BV3777.G6 H64 2000
269'.24'094109034–dc21

00-053971

Typeset by Vitaset, Paddock Wood, Kent
Printed by
Creative Print and Design (Wales), Ebbw Vale

For my father and mother
Thomas Holmes and Susan Lapsley Holmes

Contents

List of Illustrations

Acknowledgements

In the course of researching and writing this book I have had more than enough time to accumulate some debts of gratitude. The International Liaison Committee of Queen's University Belfast provided the initial funding for my PhD, upon which this book is based. A grant from the Royal Historical Society financed a research trip and a Faculty of Arts Fellowship from University College Dublin provided me with the financial security in which to complete. More recently, the University of Ulster has been extremely generous in the provision of research funding. I am grateful to all of them for their financial commitment to this project.

With a topic that straddles two countries and touches on a third, a wide range of archives and institutions are owed a word of thanks. In England I would to thank the archivists and staff of the British Library, the British Library Newspaper Library Colindale, Cliff College Calver, Lambeth Palace Library, Salvation Army International Heritage Centre, Christian Brethren Archives and Methodist Archives and Research Centre. In America, the staff at Oberlin College, Oberlin Ohio and the Moody Bible Institute, Chicago were extremely helpful. In Ireland, I am grateful to the staff at the Linen Hall Library, Presbyterian Historical Society Belfast, Union Theological College Library and the Public Records Office Northern Ireland, many of whom struggled with unwieldy catalogues in order to facilitate my progress. Special thanks goes to Ulster Television for permission to use 'The Street Meeting' as the cover illustration. I would like to particularly thank Dr Peter Nockles, Mr Michael Smallman and Mr Robert Bonar for their kind assistance. I am also very grateful to Kay Ballantine at my home university, the University of Ulster at Coleraine.

No acknowledgement page would be complete without a recognition of the debts I owe to professional colleagues. Dr Louis Billington deserves a special note of thanks for putting me on the trail of the Reverend Thomas Champness and *Joyful News*, as does the Reverend Stephen Hatcher, who very kindly made available to me a number of rare working-class autobiographies from his own personal collection. Professor Sheridan Gilley and Professor Ken Brown made valuable comments and suggestions for improvement. Professor Keith Jeffrey, Professor T.G. Fraser and Professor Alan Sharp have all been knowledgeable, and determined, guides to the publishing process. Gillian Coward, on very short notice, prepared the illustrations for publication. Linda Longmore and the staff at Irish Academic Press warrant a special thanks for their patience and tolerance. Finally, I must thank Professor David Hempton, who supervised my original research and has provided me with much valuable advice ever since. I have learnt a great deal from him about the nature of popular evangelicalism and am deeply grateful to him for the time he took out of an increasingly busy schedule to discuss my research.

On a more personal level I would like to acknowledge the debt I owe to Jenny McConnell, Andrew McConkey, Mike Cronin, Sara Jan and Steve and Jane Ickringill, all of whom gave generously of their spare living space in order to make my numerous London research trips both affordable and enjoyable. Peter Gray, Cathy McKeown and John McCafferty assisted me with a multitude of 'small details', while my colleagues at the University of Ulster have provided me with a constant stream of coffee breaks. David Roberts supplied some structural incentive when it was greatly needed. Pól Ó Dochartaigh, Katy Radford, and Donette Murray have been good friends in times of trouble, and I greatly appreciate their various acts of kindness. Above all, I would like to thank my parents, Thomas and Susan Holmes, who, although they live far away, have always been near in spirit. Because they, at least, have never doubted my abilities, this work is dedicated to them.

Introduction

OVER THE past thirty-five years there has been an explosion of interest in and writing on the role of religion in nineteenth-century Britain. Beginning with E.R. Wickham's analysis of the churches in Sheffield in 1957,[1] much of this work has ordered itself around the interpretative framework of decline. Wickham, along with other historians such as K.S. Inglis and Hugh McLeod,[2] felt the 'weakness and collapse of the churches in the urbanised and industrialised areas of the country'[3] was a patently obvious historical development. Part of this collapse was the result of the widespread alienation of the labouring classes from institutionalised religion, and much of the debate has involved a class interpretation of this decline. In important books written in the 1970s, James Obelkevich, Alan Gilbert and Stephen Yeo[4] developed this interpretation, arguing that the forces of modernisation, secularisation and industrialisation had a fundamental influence on the nature of British religion. They all accepted the inevitability of decline, although their work involved explaining this process in more depth and greater detail. Obelkevich felt the growing prosperity, respectability and individualism of many churchgoers, resulting from the shift to a class-based society, challenged the communal base of religious denominations. According to Gilbert, although the onset of industrialisation stimulated an increase in religious institutions, over the long term it heralded 'the gradual emergence of external societal and internal religious-cultural and organisational conditions essentially antithetical to the Churches'.[5] Stephen Yeo put forward a slightly different argument in his discussion of religious institutions in Reading, explaining their decline in terms of an emerging capitalism. The work of these historians revealed the complexities of religious decline, but did not challenge its fundamental existence.

As with all good historical debates, there has been the inevitable revision. The work of Jeffrey Cox and Callum Brown has questioned the inevitability of religious decline and working-class alienation from the churches, arguing that Victorian churches were relatively successful, that working-class religiosity was much more extensive than previously believed, and that the advent of modern secular society did not automatically signal a decline in faith.[6] In the past few years several more contributions to the secularisation debate have appeared.[7]

The example of Ireland has also served as a counterweight to the interpretation of decline. Unlike Britain, approximately 80 per cent of the population was Catholic. Thus, the established Church of Ireland represented only about 10 per cent of the population. These Irish Protestants, along with their Presbyterian and Methodist counterparts, were heavily concentrated in the north of the island, mainly in counties Antrim and Down, where they formed the largest religious group.[8] Over the course of the nineteenth century, all religious groups in Ireland experienced a period of renewed vitality. This process of revitalisation contributed to the growth of sectarian tensions, as Irish denominations battled for control of educational facilities and sought to prevent the other from overt acts of proselytism. The association of the religious terms 'Protestant' and 'Catholic' with the political aspirations of 'Unionism' and 'Nationalism' has promoted a high level of religious commitment amongst Ireland's religious groupings which has lasted well into the twentieth century.

A fundamental component of religion in nineteenth-century Britain and Ireland is the role of evangelicalism, a movement which emerged during the early decades of the eighteenth century and permeated elements of the established Church, transformed the old dissent of Congregationalists and Baptists and spawned Methodism.[9] David Bebbington has pointed out that despite its widespread influence in the nineteenth century, many aspects of this movement remain in obscurity, and the development of the movement as a whole has been sorely neglected.[10] The theological components of evangelicalism, which Bebbington defines as conversionism, activism, biblicism and the central role of the cross, came to dominate the bulk of Victorian nonconformity and had a substantial following within the established churches in England and Ireland. The values and concerns of its adherents set the agenda for much of the social and political developments in society and gave the nineteenth century much of its distinctive aura.[11] With such a pervasive influence, David Hempton and Myrtle Hill are correct to point out, in their analysis of evangelicalism in Ulster, that 'denominational studies of Protestantism limit the perception of how important evangelicalism actually was as it proceeded from splinter groups and voluntary societies to infiltrate every aspect of institutionalised religion'.[12] Therefore, when historians discuss the decline of Victorian religion, they are primarily discussing the decline of evangelicalism.

Although it is easy to characterise the Victorian period as a 'crisis of faith', with falling levels of church attendance and the growth of secular attitudes, it is also possible, paradoxically, to see it as a time of religious revival. Efforts on the part of the Oxford movement brought about a renewed interest in the sacraments, liturgy and ritual of the Church of England. The Catholic Church was also undergoing a period of renewal as a growing number of committed clergy worked to spread a new, ultramontane piety amongst the increasingly large numbers of Irish Catholics who were flooding into England and Scotland's major cities.[13] The methods which these groups were using – such as special services and emotional preaching – borrowed heavily from the evangelical Protestant tradition of revivalism which can be traced back to the closing years of the seventeenth century.

According to W.R. Ward, the basic characteristics of eighteenth and nineteenth-century revivalism were initially developed by Protestant minorities in central and eastern Europe. At this time, many Protestants were concerned about the growing threat to religious tolerance which had been established at Westphalia in 1648. The Hapsburgs in particular had adopted a harsh, assimilationist policy against Protestants within the Holy Roman Empire and many were forced to convert or flee as refugees. Of those who adopted the latter strategy, many ended up in Prussia, where religious tolerance was enshrined in law. Here, these refugees sought to transform what they considered to be the cold, formal and theologically moribund Protestant orthodoxy with their own emotional and personal version. While under the threat of persecution, these 'pietist' groups had developed a more vibrant religious practice which stressed the importance of a direct relationship with God and the need for a 'New Birth' to cement that relationship. A wide range of informal methods were developed to sustain and spread these views and they included private devotions and Bible reading, house meetings, field preaching and the dissemination of devotional literature.[14] This form of religious expression was particularly common in Silesia, where the orthodox Protestant religious system had collapsed in the wake of the Hapsburg take-over in the 1630s. Protestants were now forced to meet in private homes, often in isolation from their co-religionists. As a result, the Silesians developed 'an inwardness of faith, [and] a tenderness of piety' which manifested itself publicly after 1707 (when rights to Protestants were restored) in a number of mass awakenings and camp meetings.[15]

The vitality of this new approach to Protestant belief spread very quickly throughout Europe and the wider transatlantic community. Part of the reason was the existence of a flourishing print culture within pietist circles, which produced vast quantities of devotional works, Bibles and catechisms for popular consumption. The distribution of this printed material was facilitated by the networks of personal contacts which had sprung up as pietists were forced into exile or chose to go out as missionaries. In this way, John Wesley, an English clergyman and the founder of Methodism, while returning to England from America, met a group of Moravians on board his ship. Impressed by their pietism, he began to look for a similar religious experience and eventually experienced a 'new birth' in 1738. Through a variety of different means, then, European pietist ideas spread to Britain, Ireland and beyond. And along with this theology went the methodology which European Protestants had developed to sustain their beliefs. In the late seventeenth and early eighteenth century, religious revivals – in the form of emotional conversions, outdoor meetings and itinerant preaching – functioned as a mechanism for the sustenance of a religious community under threat. Over time, it would come to operate, within the wider transatlantic evangelical community, as a means for the spread of those beliefs to those considered to be 'unsaved'.

To examine only the European context for the 'Evangelical Revival' as it is known, is to ignore the importance of national, regional and local factors in the spread of evangelicalism and the occurrence of revival. In Britain, John Walsh has identified what he considers to be the 'taproots' of the religious awakening when he suggests that there was an existing tradition of Anglican and Dissenting piety upon which new ideas and young activists could draw.[16] Historians like David Hempton have pointed out that the growth of Methodism was crucial to the spread of evangelical ideas and revivalist fervour.[17] Regional characteristics, however, must also be taken into consideration. In Wales, it was the activities of the Anglican laity, in particular the efforts of Howell Harris and Daniel Rowland, which popularised evangelical ideas and promoted the widespread use of revival strategies like itinerant preaching and class meetings.[18] In Scotland, evangelical notions spread because of a pre-existing tradition of revival enthusiasm which revolved around the communion season.[19] Thus, it was in the lowland areas of Kilsyth and Cambuslang where two of the most spectacular eighteenth-century revivals took place.

In Britain, evangelical ideas spread rapidly throughout the eighteenth century due to the combination of an existing tradition of piety, the growth of Methodism and distinct regional characteristics. In Ireland, the spread of evangelicalism was more complicated. Because the majority of the population was Catholic, it remained relatively impervious, if not downright hostile, to the efforts of John Wesley and other itinerant preachers. The established church was also opposed to the disorderly nature of outdoor meetings. As well, existing groups of Protestant minorities, such as the Baptists, Palatines and Huguenots, did not feel that they were under threat of state persecution. As a result, 'the threat of assimilation by powerful states and established churches, which fanned the flames of religious revivalism in central Europe, simply did not operate with the required urgency in eighteenth-century Ireland'.[20] The Presbyterians, who were the largest of the nonconformist groups, were also resistant to evangelicalism during the eighteenth century. They were more interested in the finer points of theological disputation and in maintaining themselves as a distinct religious and political entity.[21] The growth of Methodism, which in England was spreading rapidly, was much more limited in Ireland because it could only draw on the existing Protestant community for potential recruits. As well, it was increasingly finding its success restricted to the northern part of the country, where competition for land had exacerbated sectarian tensions and prompted a short-term outburst of millenarian excitement.[22] The spectacular growth of Irish Methodism which occurred between 1770–1830 was not sustained, however. High levels of emigration and a reluctance to erode Protestant unity meant that Methodists in Ireland remained a small minority. 'Only in Ulster, and at a much later date, was evangelical religion able to exercise the kind of cultural dominance that crowned its efforts in Wales, the highlands of Scotland, and parts of North America, and that was because evangelicalism had ceased to be the preserve of powerless minorities and had made substantial inroads into the Established and Presbyterian churches.'[23]

Eighteenth-century evangelicalism, therefore, had complex roots. In Britain, at least, it was increasingly popular and grew strongly. Throughout the century this growth was manifested in the spontaneous revivals which sprang up, particularly in the north and the far south-west of the country. However, by the second quarter of the nineteenth century, it was clear that these traditional methods were in decline and that evangelicals were adopting a series of 'new measures' to promote their religious beliefs. In short, revivals were increasingly being 'planned'. Charles Finney, an American evangelist, was the greatest proponent of this trend and outlined his ideas in the hugely influential *Lectures on revivals of religion* published in England in 1835. A liberal Calvinist, Finney argued that Christians could influence the work of the Holy Spirit through their prayers and actions. Thus, it was possible to employ a variety of techniques in order to promote the outbreak of a revival. Some of the more popular methods designed to prompt people to conversion included the use of a professional revivalist, who adopted a very direct and highly emotional style, and the 'pro-traction' of services over several days or weeks. 'Anxious seats' and 'penitent forms' were also used. These were small benches or pews located at the front of the church to which potential converts were directed during the service so that they could be addressed more directly, either by the preacher or by a helper. These methods were already standard practice in many Methodist churches and were increasingly adopted within Calvinist circles as well.[24] The definition of a revival as a spontaneous outpouring of the Holy Spirit was increasingly under threat.

The historiography of revivalism in the nineteenth century has been domin-ated by the attempt to determine causation. J.E. Orr was reiterating contem-porary opinions rather than predicting future historical trends when he claimed, 'any explanation of the Revival other than that of an outpouring of the [Holy] Spirit is considered inadequate'.[25] In the two decades after Orr's work was published, historical analyses of revivals rejected his theological interpretation in favour of explanations which relied on external factors such as economic depression, political instability and ideas of 'modernisation'.[26] E.P. Thompson's 'chiliasm of despair' was a controversial but well-argued example. Most histor-ians now recognise that there is no direct correlation between the outbreak of a revival and either economic depression or the failure of political radicalism. Twentieth-century revivals have also changed assumptions about the impact of modernity on popular religious enthusiasm. New interpretations of revivalism are at pains to stress the importance of community, regional identities and social factors like the threat of cholera, mining disasters or the influence of American revivalists.[27] In a remark which Thompson rarely gets credit for, even he observed that 'revivalism is not a phenomenon which admits of a single hold-all explanation'.[28]

There are several studies which deal with nineteenth-century revivalism in a more extensive fashion. Richard Carwardine's *Transatlantic revivalism* (1978) is a sympathetic account of revivalism in Britain and America in the years between

1790 and 1865. Carwardine points to the influence that each religious tradition had on the other's experience of revivalism. British contributions – in the form of itinerant preachers, revival literature and a polished platform style – shaped the emergence of a 'new' revivalism in the urban centres around New York state. This revivalism loosened the strictures which Calvinism placed on the possibility of conversion and allowed specific measures, such as protracted meetings and an 'anxious seat' to facilitate it. In return, the visits of various American revivalists influenced British denominations to adopt these new measures, albeit in a quieter and less extreme form. It is in the context of this transformation that the Ulster revival is placed. Describing 1859 as 'one of the most extraordinary of nineteenth-century revivals', Carwardine is correct to point out its limitations, especially its failure to make a significant impact on the British evangelical community. Carwardine's analysis ends in 1865, and he has presented the revival in Ulster as the climax to the developments of the preceding decades. However, he has pointed out that 1859 also initiated a 'new era' in which American influences on British and Irish religion featured even more prominently than before.[29] This book will explore this 'new era' of revivalism in the years between the events in Ulster in 1859 and the outbreak of a similar revival in Wales in 1904–5.

In order to gain a proper understanding of our starting point, the work of David Hempton and Myrtle Hill is required reading.[30] They examine the controversial events in Ulster during the summer of 1859 with reference to geographical setting and religious history. Developments within the Presbyterian community, its tradition of revival and the influence of events in America in 1857–8 set the stage for the outbreak of 'one of the last great folk revivals in the history of the British Isles'.[31] Placed within the context of its locality and distinctive heritage, the revival is explained as a collective response of the Protestant community to a resurgent Catholicism. Concerned primarily with the revival's place in Ulster's tradition of evangelical Protestantism, Hempton and Hill do not examine its role in the wider British context. This study will attempt to do just that.

John Kent has provided the most comprehensive account of revivalism in the Victorian period, beginning with the tradition of American revivalism and 1859, and moving on to discuss Moody and Sankey, as well as holiness and Anglo-Catholic varieties of revivalism. His book, however, is difficult to assess. At one point Kent argues that '[t]echniques of persuasion, menace and group intoxication have characterised Revivalism throughout its history' and that in the late Victorian period it had become 'an aspect of that anti-modernist, anti-materialist, anti-democratic and often anti-intellectual movement ... which might in religious terms be labelled the cult of "Christ against Western culture"'.[32] Revivals have no doubt contained at various points of their existence elements of psychological manipulation and anti-intellectualism, but such a categorisation does not do justice either to the personal motivation of the revived or to the social contexts within which revivalism operated. Referring to the revival of 1859, he states, 'there is no serious question of anything like a Second Evangelical Awakening having taken place in the Anglo-Saxon world in these years'.[33] On one level Kent's analysis is a perceptive one. Although English evangelicals desired a revival along the lines of the one which swept England and America in the eighteenth century, such a widespread, international movement did not take place. On another level, Kent's blunt dismissal of British revival hopes fails to consider the contemporary controversies and popular perceptions surrounding those events and reflects an essential distrust of popular religious enthusiasm of any kind. Once again, this book will consider the phenomenon of religious revivalism, and the people who participated in it, in a sympathetic and sensitive manner.

The high quality of the various analyses of revival characteristics and causation forms an intimidating corpus of scholarship. This study relies to a large extent on many of the ideas suggested by these texts but develops them in a rather different fashion. Apart from Kent, nobody has studied late nineteenth-century revivalism comprehensively.[34] Moody and Sankey have merited passing reference in numerous studies, but an extensive examination of their British activities is confined to the thesis literature.[35] The Welsh revival and the evangelistic crusades of Torrey and Alexander also lack critical monographs.[36] It is only in recent years that the American revival of 1857–8 has received its own particular study.[37] For most historians, 1859 represented the last manifestation of traditional folk religion, with its spontaneity and emotionalism. Subsequent manifestations of revivalism have been slotted into the interpretative framework which sees the shift from spontaneous to planned revivalism as part of an overall decline in Victorian religion. The relationship between revivalism and the evangelical community, however, was more complex than one of simple decline. Great outbursts of folk revivalism did largely disappear in the latter part of the nineteenth century on a national scale, but single churches or isolated circuits, especially in rural areas, continued to experience smaller and more limited local revivals. The concept of revival as a divine outpouring of God's grace was still vigorously defended and actively promoted. Although the actual occurrence of revivalism declined, its promise of changed individuals and an improved society continued to make it a desirable intellectual and spiritual aspiration. Local attempts to recreate this experience, dismissed by most historians as mere human constructions, actually show the ongoing importance of revival to the evangelical frame of mind.

The complexity of Victorian revivalism emerges when a more personal approach is taken. This book focuses not so much on the character and distribution of revivals, but on the individuals involved and seeks to examine their attitudes, beliefs and responses to the phenomenon. They include ministers and clergymen, lay evangelists and secular commentators, women and men. The attitudes of revival audiences are, unfortunately, more difficult to establish. The depth, colour and variety of revivalism which an approach of this kind reveals challenges Kent's rather impersonal and detached analysis of revival motivation.

The people who preached at evangelical services and attended revival meetings do not feature prominently in his analysis. According to him, the working classes rejected organised religion in favour of their own political institutions, such as trade unions, because of the non-political nature of revivalism and its lack of relevance to their daily lives.[38] Although a large proportion of the working classes did indeed reject many of the outward forms of organised religion, this account tries to portray, in a sensitive manner, those working people who found in religion, and especially its revivalistic elements, an arena for the exercise of their spiritual and personal goals.

Historians have been more than willing to admit women formed a majority within Victorian congregations and that they adhered to religious beliefs longer than men.[39] At last, research is being devoted to the explanation of this trend and the female experience of religion is being explored.[40] Women have played a distinct role in the context of revivalism, not only as the largest component of revival audiences and apparently especially predisposed to physical mani-festations, but also as active promoters of the evangelical message. Accepted interpretations argue that female preaching to mixed audiences declined in the decade after the 1859 revival.[41] I would like to argue here that female partici-pation in public preaching was a regular feature of revival activity, even in the latter stages of the Victorian period and among denominations, like the Wesleyan Methodists, who had formally prohibited such female endeavour. Despite clerical prohibitions and cultural expectations, women continued to participate in public evangelical activity such as preaching throughout the nineteenth century. Leading revival meetings gave women an opportunity to fill personal spiritual goals as well as leadership aspirations.

As David Bebbington has pointed out, an emphasis on personal conversion was one of the fundamental defining characteristics of nineteenth-century evangelicals. This was an internal process by which sinful individuals recognised their lost spiritual condition and through the work of the Holy Spirit were restored to their original relationship with God. For evangelical nonconformists, such an experience was often a requirement for church membership. Based as congregations were on the voluntary system, it was important to encourage this conversion process if they wanted to maintain the strength of their denomi-nations. Revivals enjoyed the reputation of being one of the best ways to gain such conversions and thereby promote church membership. By definition, a revival indicated a large number of conversions over a short period of time, with an accompanying renewal of religious life, which set it apart from the day-to-day work of 'proclaiming the gospel'. The events at Pentecost (Acts 2), where 3,000 people were converted under the preaching of the apostle Peter, were seen as the New Testament model of all subsequent revivals. As we have seen, from the early days of the evangelical awakening, revivals took place spontaneously, with little regard for time or place. Over the course of the nineteenth century, however, as the character of the denominations which promoted revival changed, what previously had been viewed as a spontaneous 'outpouring' of the Holy

Spirit, was institutionalised as a regular mechanism of church growth. W.R. Ward, the eminent authority in this field, has recently pinpointed the funda-mental paradox which lay behind this development. Referring to the evangelical revival he states:

> ... the missionary Church was a purposive organisation, a 'rational' one in Weberian terms, and ... turned on analysing the purpose to be achieved and contriving an organisation which would bring to bear the manpower and other resources necessary to achieve it. The churches assumed their modern shape of vast and rambling machines, capable of being assessed in terms of their efficiency for their policy objectives, but not reasonably to be discussed in terms of symbols ... This in turn set a theological problem. For those who most beat the drum about the depravity of mankind and the all sufficiency of grace were now the most committed to hectic pro-grammes of works and to the construction of rational organisations for their accomplishment. Works-righteousness might in the jargon of that day be filthy rags, but that is what the religious community was being adapted and devoted to. In this respect the Great Awakening bequeathed a problem in theology and pastoral psychology which is still with us.[42]

Revivalism is a classic example of this contradiction. Traditional forms of revivalism had occurred seemingly without recourse to human ingenuity, but over the course of the nineteenth century, they were becoming more planned and organised. Although evangelicals were committed theologically to a position which only recognised the divine origin of a spiritual transformation, their entire denominational machinery was devoted to achieving conversions by an elaborate process of works. Late nineteenth-century revivalism in Britain and Ireland provides a case study of the encounter between these two contradictory percep-tions. With the knowledge that 'true' revivals were the result of the Holy Spirit's intervention, evangelicals, confronted with their failure to reach the working classes, sought to reproduce a spontaneous revivalism which promised numer-ous conversions and church growth through a variety of different means.

By the turn of the century, therefore, 'revivalism' was a familiar concept which reflected significantly diverse origins and traditions. Thus, it would be well to establish just what is meant by 'revivalism'. Discussion of definitions of the term has been an enduring feature of the historiography, both contemporary and modern, and will be discussed in greater detail in chapter six.[43] For clarity's sake, a revival will be taken to mean an apparently spontaneous outbreak of religious excitement in a region (ideally a nation, but more than likely a circuit or locality) which results in a large number of conversions over a relatively short period of time and is characterised by protracted meetings, lay activity and physical manifestations of conversion. This describes the events in Ulster in 1859 and Wales in 1904, but not the so-called revival activity in between. For the annual evangelical meetings conducted by single congregations and the itinerant travels of lay evangelists like D.L. Moody, the terms 'revival meeting', 'mission' or 'special services' will be used to distinguish these regular, planned and localised results from those of their more elusive cousin. Some would argue that the latter activity is in no way revivalistic. It was, however, distinctly evangelistic and these meetings were organised with the intention of promoting the likelihood of a revival.

Using Ward's interpretation as a starting point, this book intends to demonstrate that such a theological and pastoral contradiction within evangelical perceptions of revival was reflected in the controversies and tensions surrounding its late nineteenth-century manifestations. Although the form and conduct of revivals changed greatly during this period, its reception did not. Revivalism caused as much controversy in 1874 and 1904 as it did in 1859. Therefore, this book attempts to chart the progress and development of revivalism in late nineteenth-century Britain and Ireland, and to explore the impact it had on the evangelical community in both countries. It is not primarily an in-depth account of revivals or revival meetings during this period, nor is it a specifically denominational survey of revival attitudes. Rather, it is a study of how evangelicals from a number of different traditions and with widely differing agendas perceived revivalism, how they responded to it and the implications that has for the study of evangelicalism as a whole. The first section sets the scene with an analysis of the Ulster revival of 1859 as an example of the popular folk revivalism that had been so prevalent in the eighteenth and early nineteenth centuries. It was, as its most recent historians have suggested, 'a pivotal event within popular Protestantism itself. Before it happened it was longingly anticipated, after it happened it was nostalgically remembered, and ever after it became a litmus test of the spiritual vigour of evangelical religion.'[44] With this standard of religiosity established, Chapter Two moves on to discuss the impact such a revival had on popular Protestantism in Britain. The ambivalent, and often contradictory, responses of the British evangelical community to the events in Ireland should serve as an accurate reflection of the 'theological problem' outlined by W.R. Ward.

These first two chapters establish the foundation upon which the rest of the book is based. The next section is concerned with analysing those who were involved in the promotion of revivals and religious conversions. Chapter Three takes a broad look at the American influence on British and Irish revivalism, particularly the visit of D.L. Moody to both countries in 1873–5. Although the transatlantic connection was well established, and news of American religious developments was common knowledge, the blatantly mechanistic methods of this middle-class American caused difficulties for Christians throughout the British isles on a number of different levels. The concern expressed over Ira D. Sankey's use of a harmonium and Moody's reliance on inquiry rooms echoed similar sentiments about other groups of revival participants which had long caused problems for the evangelical community – women and working-class men. Chapter Four contends that a significant number of both middle-class and working-class women continued their involvement in public revival activity long after they were thought to have vanished. Although denominations formally rejected such female activity, evangelical pragmatism in reality offered women the opportunity to fulfil personal goals and religious aspirations. Similar arguments are put forward in Chapter Five when the prevalence of popular working-class evangelists is examined. Despite claims that the working classes were lost to organised religion, a considerable number of men from working-class backgrounds gave themselves over to full-time religious work throughout the century. These men challenged established denominational rituals like ordination and clerical control of public preaching and contributed to the tensions surrounding revival activity.

With a picture of the responses to revivalism in place, Chapter Six moves the focus away from the promoters of revival to examine the definition and practice of revivalism within the broad context of continuity and change. Evangelicals altered definitions of revival to suit changing needs and objectives. Under the influence of a growing denominationalism and of 'modern thought', revivalism became more of an ideal than a reality. Why revival remained a valid concept for evangelicals despite the tensions and divisions it created amongst them are questions which will be discussed here. A conclusion which endorses the evolution of revivalism, rather than its extinction, will hopefully contribute to recent efforts to re-examine traditional theories of religious decline.

This book is based for the most part on an extensive use of printed sources such as newspapers, pamphlets and biographies. Relevant manuscript sources, where they existed, rarely mention revivalism in any detail. Only the controversy surrounding Moody and Sankey's London campaign yielded a significant collection of letters, written to the Archbishop of Canterbury.[45] The resulting reliance on printed material has opened up new avenues of exploration. Although biography was a popular form in Victorian Britain, it has been underestimated as a source in the secondary writing on religion.[46] Over 180 biographies were examined for this book, including ones of prominent ministers and laymen, working-class evangelists, local preachers and women. The extent of this genre reflects the existence of a subculture which found revivals and those who promoted them worthy of commemoration. The experiences which they relate, reflecting a variety of different denominations, places and social classes, have allowed for an in-depth evaluation of individual motives.

At certain times interest was high enough to sustain periodicals specifically devoted to the promulgation of revival news. Based in London, *The Revival* was the most influential and longest running magazine of several started in the 1850s. Its early coverage of the Ulster revival soon expanded to include more straightforward accounts of travelling preachers and evangelistic services. The interest which sustained a non-denominational magazine like *The Revival* was also seen in the numerous denominational periodicals and newspapers, many of which had sections devoted to evangelical activity or featured articles on revivalism. The numerous books and pamphlets published on similar topics indicated the continued relevance of revivalism to the evangelical community throughout the nineteenth century.

On one level, revivalism was a theme of the evangelical subculture. On another level, it was, at certain times, a newsworthy phenomenon. Metropolitan newspapers and journals periodically reported on revival activity. The Ulster revival was often mentioned in national British newspapers like *The Times* and the *Daily Telegraph*. During 1873–5 the Glasgow, Dublin and London dailies all gave extensive coverage to Moody and Sankey's urban campaigns. Editorial comments and letters to the editor offer a more sceptical view of revivalism and expose the often bitter controversies between different segments of the evangelical community. The debate which such controversies generated shows that revivalism was an emotive topic, both inside and outside the religious communities which sustained it. It also shows that a religious revival, often regarded by evangelicals then and now as the purest form of divine initiative, was more of a human event *and* more of a contested ideological construction, than some have been prepared to admit.[47]

Janice Holmes
Coleraine, 2000

PART I
FOUNDATIONS

Connor Presbyterian Church, Connor, Co. Antrim

CHAPTER ONE

The Ulster revival of 1859

T HE ULSTER revival of 1859 was a sudden and powerful explosion of intense religious excitement which took place primarily within the Protestant communities of Antrim and Down and to a lesser extent in Londonderry, Tyrone, Fermanagh and Armagh. Although the Established Church, Methodists and Baptists did support and participate in the revival effort, the majority of those actively involved were Presbyterians, primarily because they formed such a large proportion of the Protestant population. In the largely Catholic counties of Donegal, Cavan and Monaghan the revival, predictably, had proportionately less success.[1] In essence, the revival was an extraordinary increase of interest in religion, which manifested itself in a large number of conversions over a short period of time and was characterised by a high level of lay participation, the occurrence of unusual physical manifestations and the temporary moral transformation of society. Over the course of the summer months, various types of religious meeting were held at frequent intervals and in numerous locations. Individuals were exhorted to 'turn away from their sins in repentance and to Christ in faith', a process of sudden change which involved intense feelings of agony, guilt and eventual relief.[2] The emotional intensity of these crowded meetings caused many people to give in to their spiritual anguish in physical ways – from moaning and hysterical sobbing to fits and shaking and to even more ecstatic phenomena such as visions, clairvoyance, trances and the appearance of stigmata-like markings. The resulting chaos and confusion gave ordinary men and women an opportunity to exercise their leadership abilities – conducting prayer meetings, assisting with conversions and preaching in public. Religious leaders had reservations about this development and tried to emphasise the revival's more pragmatic goals of church growth and reinvigorated denominations.

Such an outburst of religious fervour put the Protestant community under a great deal of stress. Lay preaching and other forms of lay initiative challenged clerical ideas of religious propriety and threatened the spiritual leadership of clergymen. The physical manifestations of conversion quickly became the subject of public controversy, as widely differing opinions concerning their origin, effect and result were debated in printed pamphlets and the secular press. That these differing perceptions would clash was almost inevitable.

The revival has not always been portrayed in this manner. Early accounts took a very uncritical approach, describing 1859 as 'an extraordinary religious Revival' which 'equalled in magnitude the famed eighteenth-century Evangelical Revival'.[3] In response to this, subsequent analysis has concentrated its attention on an explanation of revival origins, often relying on socio–economic processes of rural decline and 'modernisation'.[4] Unfortunately, these arguments have excluded the possibility of an internal religious dynamic. Other interpretations have been concerned to emphasise the revival's Presbyterian character,[5] its transatlantic influences[6] and its British dimension.[7] The most recent research has sought to place the revival within its unique cultural context as well as to give equal weight to the many internal factors which contributed to it.[8] This growing body of research is an indication of the significant place the revival holds in Ulster's religious history. Indeed, as the revival's most recent historians point out, the revival was a turning point for the evangelical community. Over time, in the Ulster Protestant psychology, it became 'both a historical event and a supernatural encounter invested with almost mythical significance'.[9] With these developments in mind, this chapter aims to give an overview of the revival's basic context and character, to outline the role of the participants and how they perceived the proceedings and to discuss the major controversies and their impact on the evangelical community in Ulster.

Some historians have portrayed the revival as a sudden outburst of religious fervour, which followed a period of religious decline and formalism.[10] The accepted view, however, generally portrays the revival against the background of the growing influence of evangelical religion within Ulster Protestantism. Among Presbyterians, the expulsion of Arianism from the Synod of Ulster allowed it to unite with the more orthodox and evangelical Secession Synod in 1840. This unity allowed the denomination to concentrate more on its outward mission to the wider society through devices such as tract distribution and Sunday schools. The growing influence of evangelical theology led to an interest in conversion and the licensing of open-air preachers in 1853. Throughout the 1850s there were continued prayers for revival at meetings of the General Assembly.[11] Denominational magazines, like the *Irish Presbyterian*, regularly published articles on the need for a revival.[12] Ulster also had a tradition of revivalism which stretched back to the Six Mile Water revival of 1625 and included Methodist outbreaks in the late eighteenth century. Thus, when news reached the province that a revival had broken out in America in 1857, it was received by a populace which understood the concept of revival and desired its manifestation among them.

When the revival did spread to Ulster it began in an area outside Ballymena, a market town in the middle of county Antrim, in the villages of Kells, Connor and Ahoghill. Prayer meetings had been established in Connor several years previously and had proved to be extremely popular among the local Presbyterians.[13] The first real manifestations of unusual excitement, however, were noticed in Ahoghill, when 'unexpected and instantaneous "conversions", accompanied by the physical and spiritual operations of some overwhelming power upon the minds and bodies of the parties so converted' occurred in the wake of lectures and sermons describing the revival in America. Religious meetings were subsequently transformed. At a public meeting in the village, assembled to discuss recent developments, a massive crowd gathered, with many hundreds unable to gain admittance.

> Soon after commencement of the services an impulse to address the audience fell suddenly, and apparently with all the power of prophetic inspiration, upon one of the 'converted' brethren. Every attempt to silence or restrain him was found utterly impossible. He declared that a revelation had been committed to him, and that he spoke by the command of a power superior to any ministerial authority. Defying every effort at control he proceeded to vociferate religious phrases with a rapidity and fluency which excited the most intense astonishment, and created a panic of very serious alarm among the audience. A rush was made towards the front of the galleries, and under an apprehension that they might possibly break down, the presiding clergyman gave a peremptory order that the house should forthwith be vacated. A scene of terrible confusion immediately ensued; and, when the premises were ultimately cleared, the streets of Ahoghill presented another scene which baffles all powers of description, and such as the older inhabitants had never witnessed. The leading 'Convert' – who is a comfortable farmer and a member of the congregation – assisted by several other speakers of the 'confirmed' class, addressed the people, then numbering about 3,000, and comprising persons of every creed from the Episcopalian to the Roman-catholic [sic]. The chief speaker vehemently proclaimed pardon to all sinners, inviting them to come forward and receive the spirit of adoption, which he declared himself commissioned to impart – occasionally holding up his hands, and bidding the people to receive the Holy Ghost. The immense assemblage appeared to be thoroughly paralysed. Amid a chilling rain, and on streets covered with mud, fresh 'converts', moved by the fervency and apostolic language of the speaker, fell upon their knees in the attitude of prayer; a spark of electricity appeared to have animated and impressed a large number of the audience … Their meetings are multiplied in number; and the 'new births' … are daily upon the increase.[14]

This account illustrates several of the various components and characteristics of the Ulster revival. In rural areas, participants tended to be members of the agricultural workforce, such as the farmer addressing this meeting, or weavers and agricultural labourers. In urban areas like Belfast, mill workers and factory operatives employed in the growing linen and shipbuilding industries comprised a large proportion of revival supporters. Much attention was given to the conversion of drunkards, prostitutes and other reprobates, but these formed only a minority of revival participants.[15] It is also significant that the main speaker at the Ahoghill meeting was already a church member. This was probably the case for a large number of those caught up in the revival. Revival accounts reveal that many converts either attended church regularly or had some familiarity with the Bible and other basic tenets of the Christian faith.[16] The conduct of the meeting also conformed to a pattern which became familiar over the succeeding months. Revival meetings were often organised by clergy and held in local churches. Frequently, normal proceedings would be interrupted by a member of the congregation who wanted to speak or who cried out under the influence of the Holy Spirit. The clergy were usually powerless to prevent the confusion which subsequently arose, and the meeting would normally be abandoned in favour of spontaneous prayers, testimonies and ministering to those under conviction of sin.[17] The possibilities for lay preaching were consistently taken up by both men and women throughout the revival, in spite of clerical concerns about the spread of false doctrine and increased opportunities for excessive emotionalism. The message which these Ahoghill converts preached was consistent with revival meetings elsewhere. Dry, arid sermons arguing the finer points of Calvinist theology were abandoned in favour of extempore, emotional appeals based on the gospel message of repentance and salvation. Audiences were urged to confess their sins to Christ and to receive the Holy Spirit, a process which revival preachers claimed was sudden and instantaneous. During the revival, this conversion experience was often accompanied by physical manifestations – from outward expressions of piety to cries, fits, shaking, visions and clairvoyance. The popular interest, which was evident in the numbers of people turned away from this Ahoghill meeting, was evident throughout all the Protestant areas of Ulster. Meetings for prayer and exhortation were held every night and were protracted, some lasting well into the early morning hours. The locations of these meetings expanded in size to suit the growing demand. As a result, fields and factories, as well as front rooms and street corners, became potential venues for spontaneous gatherings. Apart from the spiritual transformation taking place within individuals, the revival was credited with bringing about social improvements, such as the closure of public houses, a decline in crime and improved personal morality. While these changes were no doubt given extra impetus by the revival, it is important that they are seen as the result of a growing ideology of respectability, which was already eroding elements of popular culture such as cock fighting and excessive drunkenness.[18]

Unlike the American revival of the same period, the clergy were very active in the administration of the religious awakening in Ulster. Although more and more ministers took an active interest in their pastoral duties, they did not view their church members as equals, nor did they have much appreciation of church members' daily concerns. Well-established frameworks of class, manners and religious practice caused ministers to see their congregations, for the most part, as ignorant, prone to ill-mannered behaviour, such as the revival's physical manifestations, and susceptible to dubious innovations like lay preaching. The laity, on the other hand, viewed the clergy with a mixture of deference and disdain. Although lay people had a great deal of respect for the clerical position, during the revival they increasingly ignored ministerial concerns about the length and size of meetings, the spread of physical manifestations and the proliferation of lay preaching. This often led to public controversies over the issues of lay leadership and the appearance of ecstatic phenomena. Clergy and laity saw the revival from two very different perspectives. The laity sought to expand their spiritual roles during the chaos and upheaval of the revival while the clergy were concerned to maintain religious propriety and respectability. The success which the laity experienced was, however, only a temporary development. Once the excitement had died down, the traditional religious forms, which largely excluded lay involvement, quickly reasserted themselves.

For the clergy, the general ignorance of the laity was only to be expected and therefore nothing to be ashamed of. They spoke openly about the poor speech, bad grammar and ill manners of their congregations, and publicly admitted that the revival had taken place primarily among the lower or working classes. Those ministers who most supported the revival saw it on the one hand as miraculously converting lay ignorance into wisdom, and on the other as glorifying the simple, humble and ignorant over the wise and intelligent. Ministers did not give the laity any credit for this because the transformation of lay ignorance was seen to be the work of the Holy Spirit and proof of His involvement in the genesis of the revival. Reverend David Adams (Ahoghill) claimed that one result of the revival was an improvement in the converts' intellectual abilities. The 'powers of the mind are enlarged, so that the memory remembers long-forgotten facts; and the judgment, even of the uneducated, judges rightly'.[19] For others, conversion had enabled formerly ignorant people to pray with extraordinary fluency. One observer at a revival meeting commented:

> My attention was drawn to a woman whose prayer would have done credit to a distinguished Divine. I remarked to my friend how appropriately she applied the several quotations of Scriptures – how eloquent the language and not one word improperly placed.[20]

This did not convince everyone. Opponents of the revival, such as the Reverend Francis King, belittled this extraordinary change by saying that 'loud ejaculations, and eloquent words, are no essential part of prayer'.[21] For him the laity remained ignorant and ill-spoken, even under supposedly divine influence.

It was, however, the glorification of lay ignorance which truly characterised clerical attitudes to the laity. Supporters claimed that the revival was a genuine work of the Holy Spirit *because* it was being promoted by the poor and illiterate. Such an inversion was most evident in the area of public speaking. Success – defined in terms of large audiences and numerous conversions – was now more likely to come from the ignorant and uncouth preacher than from an eloquent and ordained minister. One observer stated:

In the present religious awakening the converts, in their public addresses, derive success from their very weakness! They are *constrained* by their feelings, and *confined* by their limited education to concentrate their burning, earnest, persuasion on a small surface, – and thus the light of Christianity, concentrated, as it were, through a burning glass, falls on the religious feelings, and melts down insane indifference.[22]

And thus, revivalists inverted the 'natural' or 'acceptable' forms of preaching. This process, however, did not indicate that the clergy were giving up the power which they wielded in their churches (via ordination) and in society (through a class hierarchy). Lay endeavour of this sort was justified on the basis of the chaos surrounding the revival. Therefore, irregularities were not considered to be an indication of a redrawing of traditional social boundaries, but a temporary method used by God to reinforce them.

Even those ministers who staunchly defended the revival proved reluctant to grant lay preaching a full endorsement. Only if the layman was an elder, or the individual had been officially sanctioned by church officers, would it be acceptable.[23] Some defended it on the basis of its good results. Reverend John Baillie cited the case of a mill mechanic who had been preaching in Belfast and converting entire neighbourhoods. Although there was some concern about using 'so humble an instrumentality', the obvious success of his efforts legitimised his practice.[24] Others, however, saw such preaching as an unregulated activity, and were convinced that young, untrained converts would preach bad doctrine and lead entire congregations astray.[25] Reverend Charles Seaver (Belfast) hinted that many people had already left the Church of Ireland because of its refusal to encourage lay involvement.[26] For many ministers the reduction in congregational size, the loss of clerical authority and the abandonment of the ministerial office was becoming more and more of a possibility.

The clerical response to this perceived lay aggression was to assert control over revival proceedings and thereby maintain the clergy's position and the standards of the Christian faith.[27] Reverend J. Kennedy (Newtonlimavady) believed that 'great practical wisdom and caution are necessary to guide the movement aright, and prevent extravagances and mistakes'.[28] He stressed how important it was for ministers to curtail lay preaching, long meetings and the tendency to equate physical manifestations with conversion. Ministers should confine young converts 'to an account of what God has done in them and for them, without attempting to teach' in case 'from ignorance and inexperience' they may render their public speaking 'contemptible to others'.[29] Clergymen hoped the revival would provide them with church members who were enthusiastic and diligent and would adopt their ideas of morality and social conduct. In actuality, the revival was a threat to their position. Lay preaching represented a loss of ministerial authority and a challenge to the clergyman's position as spiritual leader of the community.

Although conversion promoted an acceptance of clerical guidelines of behaviour, the most prevalent attitude among the laity during the revival was a resistance to clerical leadership, guidance and control. Lay people were unwilling to restrict themselves to a passive role in their religious instruction and exerted their independence on a number of different levels. Conversions, for example, took place without the presence of an ordained minister. One young girl, a warehouse worker in Belfast, was convicted of sin and taken to her home where she requested the presence of her minister. While awaiting his arrival, a layman prayed with her, and 'while singing a verse of a hymn, she became happy, and, with joyousness beaming in her countenance, told them her soul had been set at liberty ...'[30] It was only later that the minister arrived and was told the good news. A poor widow who had doubts about her spiritual condition sought advice from her minister, the Reverend James Morgan of Fisherwick Presbyterian, Belfast, who was unable to assist. 'I gave her the best counsel I could,' said Morgan. 'I dwelt especially on the truth, that the blood of Jesus Christ, God's Son, cleanseth us from all sin.' This seemed to quiet her fears somewhat, but it was not until she had conversed with his maidservants, whom she knew well, that she became 'filled with the joy and peace in believing'.[31] It is apparent that for this widow, discussing her fears with friends was more conducive to conversion than the doctrinal exhortations of her minister.

The laity exhibited a surprising amount of resistance to clerical attempts to fashion guidelines concerning proper religious conduct. Ministers feared that the length and size of revival meetings could result in extravagances such as sexual immorality, and the aforementioned lay preaching and physical manifestations.[32] Attempts to limit the length of prayer meetings often met with disastrous results. Reverend Thomas Watters of Newtownards was described as a 'regular living man' who normally retired at an early hour. At one of his revival prayer meetings, some strangers addressed the audience and as a result the meeting went on until well after its normal closing time of ten o'clock. At the next meeting he issued a warning that 'it would be desirable – nay, the proper thing –' to end before ten o'clock. But well into the service, John Colville, an elder, got up to pray and 'made several allusions to the request in his prayer, telling God "if the clock strike ten, let it strike there," they would not be influenced by clocks, but wait for the blessing. And so he continued.'[33] It was obvious that Colville had heard his minister's admonition and simply chose to ignore it.

Despite their warnings and prohibitions regarding lay preaching, the clergy were aware of how popular it was. They remarked that the revival meetings conducted by laymen were much better attended than those led by local clergymen.[34] One Belfast commentator pointed out that 'people are far more impressed with the unpolished, simple, solemn address of one from their own ranks than with the most eloquent sermon from one of our best clergymen'.[35] Although this argument attracted some clerical support, most ministers felt that lay preaching was being foisted upon them by an increasingly aggressive laity.[36] At one meeting two clergymen went so far as to interrupt the proceedings and order the platform to be cleared in order to prevent several laymen from speaking, 'alleging that it was *only* the work of the ministry'. This peremptory behaviour so angered members of their own congregations that 'had not a few wise men interfered the work of revival would have been greatly injured in that neighbourhood'.[37] Revival enthusiasm, so often desired for its ability to unite clergy and laity in a common cause, also had the power to divide congregations when perceptions of acceptable behaviour differed.

Despite clerical concerns about lay preaching, most of the converts who did address public meetings did not expound Scripture, but shared their testimony or preached a gospel message. Before a revival meeting in Antrim, several members of the Reverend Mr Morrison's church approached him about the possibility of allowing their visiting friends from Ballymena to address the congregation. Morrison discouraged the idea, suggesting they address the Sunday school children instead. While Morrison was closing the service, however, 'two of the boys, not able to restrain their religious ardour, presented themselves on the precentor's platform, told what the Lord had done for their souls, and poured forth two successive prayers'.[38] The desire for public expressions of religious enthusiasm was evidently intense and often proved impossible to prevent.

Similar feelings were expressed among female converts. Women had even fewer opportunities to share their religious experiences in a public manner than men. Although they were the most active participants in the revival movement, their leadership roles were confined for the most part to counselling on an individual basis, to all-female gatherings, such as prayer meetings in the workplace or to the numerous informal gatherings held in homes. In the latter, considered to be their rightful sphere, women often led converts in singing or prayer.[39] Clerical opinion was firmly opposed to any formal manifestation of female preaching and critics of the revival used female preaching as evidence to condemn the entire movement, denouncing it as

> in contradiction to Scripture, but also in direct contrariety to that gentleness and modesty which render [women] the ornament as well as blessing in every department of social life, and which, when they depart from, they become lowered in proportion to their former excellence, and the Scripture emblem of a lovely but indiscreet woman forces itself on the mind in its painful associations.[40]

The power of a conversion experience was often strong enough to overcome these social and cultural prohibitions. Upon her conversion, a woman known only as R___ went around the area of Crumlin exhorting people to repent. '"The Lord," said she to all the people in these houses, "has sent me to bring you to Him. He is waiting for you. 'Arise, and follow me.'"' And many of them did so, leaving their work behind them 'while she marched at their head like a general'. At this point she met her minister, the Reverend William Magill, who advised her to be quiet and not to excite herself, lest people would think she was deranged. In an account of this event, Magill recalled her response:

> She drew herself up in the most commanding manner, and measuring me from head to foot, exclaimed, 'I am astonished at you, Mr M.; did you not teach me in your Sunday-school and Bible class? Oh, I can teach the children now. I will bring them to Jesus. Must I not do the will of my heavenly Father? Oh, I have a Father *now*. ... I cannot hold my peace. It is not I, but the Spirit of the Lord, that is speaking.'[41]

Magill was awed into silence at this 'young Deborah', fell in behind her and became one of her followers. The nature of R___'s experience was such that she could not help but speak out and exhort those around her. Like many female preachers in England, she claimed the sanction of the Holy Spirit for her actions, thus shielding her from criticism at her apparent violation of the feminine ideal. The fact that a man, and a Presbyterian minister at that, followed her, conferred legitimacy on her activities. Most importantly, however, R___'s unusual abilities were only temporary. Magill relates that after a few days she settled down as a consistent follower of Jesus, 'her work' completed. 'She roused the country, and then retired into private life, and in the quiet home of the family circle she and her sisters are adorning the doctrine of the gospel by a becoming walk and conversation.'[42]

For both men and women, the revival offered a short-lived opportunity to exercise leadership aspirations. The implications this had for regular standards of religious behaviour caused much alarm among the clerical community. Although a majority of Protestant ministers were in favour of the revival and were pleased with its moral and spiritual results, the occurrence of unusual manifestations among the laity had given many of them grave doubts about its short-term desirability. Similar feelings were expressed about the physical manifestations of the revival. One of the earliest recorded instances of such excitement took place in Laymore, just north of Ballymena:

> On that occasion a deputation of the converted, from Ahoghill, conducted open air services of prayer and exhortations at an immense assemblage of the neighbouring people; and in the course of these services some of the audience were very suddenly and remarkably impressed. Before the following morning ten persons who had attended the meeting exhibited all the symptoms heretofore described as peculiar to the visitation – they were suddenly 'struck' with great pain and weakness of body, a nervous twitching or quivering of the muscles, fearful agony of mind, and a torturing sense of sin – as indicated by loud impulsive cries of pardon, and earnest supplications for reconciliation with God. The duration of this paroxysm is more or less lengthened – in some cases it extends over three days, but it is always succeeded by peace of mind and reformation of character.[43]

These rather unusual experiences were eventually supplanted with even more ecstatic phenomena which included visions, usually involving heaven or hell;

trances, in which the individual became deaf and dumb for predicted amounts of time; and the appearance of 'marks' resembling stigmata and supposedly of divine origin. The explanations of these occurrences have been numerous and have varied according to the perspective of the commentator. Contemporaries who were in favour of the revival interpreted the physical manifestations as the work of the Holy Spirit. Reverend Adam Magill (Boveva) felt that some individuals had become so hardened in sin 'that God saw that an extraordinary remedy was necessary for an extraordinary emergency; … And, therefore, regarding the physical features of the revival here, I feel constrained to bow, and say, "It is the Lord, let him do as it seemeth him good."'[44] Some felt that the Holy Spirit did not cause these features but simply used them to suit his own ends.[45] Others were more critical, saying they were the work of Satan, who was trying to bring the truly spiritual elements of the revival into disrepute.[46] Medical opinion, as expressed in the British journal *The Lancet*, believed 'that the violent physical "manifestations" which have accompanied the "revivals" in the north of Ireland, are morbid and injurious phenomena' and could be attributable to hysteria, at that time considered a psychological disease.[47] A large component of these criticisms involved a fear that the revival was increasing the numbers of the insane. In July 1859 the *Northern Whig*, a Belfast newspaper known for its anti-revival stance, claimed that the Belfast District Lunatic Asylum had admitted seven people suffering from religious excitement. These figures were quickly disputed by the *Banner of Ulster*, a paper sympathetic to the revival. The debate was soon taken up by *The Times* and other English papers.[48] Even more controversial was the appearance in September of women claiming to have been marked by the Holy Spirit. At a meeting in Belfast, a woman in her mid-thirties had fallen into a trance and when she awoke discovered she had 'a large red fiery cross' imprinted on one breast, along with the words 'Jesus' and 'Christ', and on her arm she had the phrase 'Seek ye the Lord'.[49] The campaign to expose these 'impostures' was led by the Reverend William Breakey, who discovered that hundreds of people were travelling great distances to view these women, and that admission was being charged for the privilege. Apparently, some words were spelt incorrectly and others were easily rubbed off, 'yet in the minds of the diseased and infatuated multitude it is nothing short of a revelation'.[50] Popular controversies like this reveal the gap between clerical expectations and the unorthodox manifestations of lay enthusiasm.

Women played a predominant role in all of these controversies because they were the ones who experienced the physical phenomena most frequently. Although crowded, stuffy churches and prolonged meetings with emotional preaching were believed to contribute to ecstatic outbursts, contemporary opinion still considered women more vulnerable to visions and prostrations because of their weak and excitable nature.[51] Women who gave in to such prostrations were accused of abandoning their modesty and exposing themselves to dangerous influences. Reverend E.A. Stopford, a prominent critic of the revival, asked the mothers of Belfast '[d]o you desire your daughters to be exhibited, struggling under hysterical affection, in the rude and brawny embrace of young men, who experience a depraved delight in thus violating female modesty? Is not such conduct a foul outrage on woman's nature?'[52] Despite the dire warnings of religious leaders, women continued to embrace the wilder aspects of the revival with a startling enthusiasm. A close examination of the motives behind this behaviour reveals that it was not just the result of a vulnerable constitution. Physical manifestations of religious excitement enabled women to move from the wings to the centre of the religious stage and to be influential agents in the transmission of revival enthusiasm rather than passive victims. In the economy of revivalism notoriety conferred power, even on the otherwise powerless.

Ecstatic behaviour was considered to be an outward sign of the internal spiritual transformation known as conversion. Women experienced the agonising conviction of sin, which expressed itself in cries, groans and even physical self-abuse. For many women, the standard revival conversion was not the extent of their religious experience. Some women claimed to have visions; others were prostrated or fell into trances that lasted for days; while others professed the ability to predict the future and to be clairvoyant. Examining the content of these visions offers an insight into female perceptions of religion and what women found to be meaningful forms of spiritual expression.

A large number of visions took place in the setting of heaven or hell and indicated a certain level of familiarity with religious concepts and metaphors. A___ S___ was stricken at a factory prayer meeting in Portadown, where she had a vision of hell 'as a burning lake' and when she passed by 'the gates flew open, and she beheld burning mountains of fire'.[53] Such a picture, no doubt influenced by vivid sermons on the nature of hell, often involved confrontations between Satan, who had a hold of the woman or placed chains on her, and Jesus, who, in the words of a woman from Newtonlimavady, 'held out His pierced hands to receive me – I could resist no longer – I leaped into His arms'.[54] Jesus not only offered salvation, but also granted status and recognition. In visions about heaven, women often saw themselves conversing with Jesus, he showing them his wounds and they receiving gifts from him. One woman described how, in her vision, heaven opened and Christ came towards her. 'I see Him now,' she said,

> and He is beautiful; and, look! the angels open out, and He comes forward, and He comes to me; and what has He in His hand? Oh, it is a gown! and how beautiful it is! What a beautiful gown! And it is a gown of glory. And it is for me. And, look! He comes straight to me! What is He going to do now? He is going to put it on me Himself. And now He puts it on ... Where am I now? What a beautiful seat! No, no, it's not a seat. I am sitting on the throne of God, and Jesus sitting beside me![55]

In a similar vision another woman received a 'robe of righteousness', while another was promised 'a crown and a kingdom ... in the skies'.[56] Others were granted the privilege of sitting beside Christ and watching him remove their sins from the book of life.[57]

Other visions exhibited a more literary tone. At the meeting in Laymore cited earlier, a middle-aged woman was stricken and remained prostrate for nearly three days. She had never been taught to read but during this time 'she maintained that a Bible, traced in characters of light, was open before her, and that, although unable to read, a spiritual power had endowed her with [the] capacity to comprehend the meaning of every word in it'. She repeated a large number of quotations from both the Old and New Testaments and used them in connection with the various prayers and hymns she was constantly uttering. This ability faded as time went on and as she was restored to good health.[58] Such visions could be interpreted as the natural outcome of a religious tradition which placed strong emphasis on the Bible as the source of truth. They could also reflect a general longing for education and literacy. In the wake of the revival, numerous Sunday schools and literacy classes were established, some with the intention of maintaining religious interest[59] and others devoted to reading and writing.[60]

Of all the factors contributing to revival, the threat of death was one of the most consistent.[61] Visions recorded during the revival indicate the close proximity of death and how women attempted to deal with it. One young girl, described as shy, intelligent and well instructed in religion, had been prostrated one day while getting ready for school. She remained in a trance for about five hours, after which she sat up and claimed

> she had been in the company of superhuman beings in a world of light and blessedness; and, to the utter amazement of her parents, she affirmed that she had there intuitively recognised her infant brother, who had died eleven months after his birth, and *five years before she was born*![62]

Mary Sarah Buchanan was a member of the Kilwarlin Moravian Church. On 11 September 1859 she was struck with a vision and professed to see departed loved ones, including Kilwarlin's former minister, the Reverend Mr Zula, and his wife.[63] Looking beyond the literal possibility of such events, there lies a picture of women and children struggling to cope with the nature of death in all its complexity. Visions of deceased loved ones offered the potential to comfort and encourage those who remained alive.

Even more sensational were the 'sleeping cases', which were situations where women predicted when they would fall into a trance and lose the use of their faculties. Mary Ann H___ was an 18-year-old girl who lived in Drummaul, Co. Antrim. She was a Presbyterian and regularly attended Sunday school. On 30 June 1859 she was struck down, whereupon she began to pray in a deeply earnest fashion for half an hour. When completed she rose, stating

> 'I know I will be deprived of sight, speech, and hearing, till twelve o'clock tomorrow; but, Oh God, Thou wilt be with me! – Thou wilt never leave

me! – Thou wilt pour Thy grace into my heart!' She then explained to her parents that she would have the power of speech only for a few minutes on Sunday at twelve o'clock. ... Immediately after giving this intimation her eyes closed, her teeth went together with an audible snap, and she was found motionless!

Hearing of this extraordinary occurrence, hundreds of people crowded around her, convinced she was caught up in some sort of spiritual vision. When she did awake, those gathered were most interested in what she had seen. Mary Ann rebuked them for their curiosity and told them nothing.[64]

Apart from anything else, these visions, and others like them, reflected the capacity women had to believe in the direct interaction of the supernatural with their finite lives. Women exhibited the bruises from their encounters with evil angels,[65] they felt Satan trying to push them from the narrow path[66] and they could see fire-balls appear out of heaven and hover over them.[67] These experiences reflected a mixture of beliefs that included Christian concepts, popular folklore and magic. Visions allowed women to express themselves in ways that would not have normally been available. Spectacular visitations could fulfil an internal spiritual need. They could also increase the status of these women among other working people. Although they were condemned by the clergy, it is obvious from the crowds surrounding the stricken that they were considered to be recipients of a special spiritual power. Mary Ann H___ was automatically endowed with a certain status as a result of her vision. Because of her experience, which no one could challenge, she obtained a level of authority and leadership she never could have hoped to achieve elsewhere. The revival provided both the opportunity and the context for that experience by legitimating it as a special blessing from God. For women, these manifestations acted as a means of attracting the kind of attention normally denied them. The clergy had always been the traditional interpreters of God's will for society, via their sermons and their control of congregational discipline. Through the ecstatic visions, women bypassed this system, eliminating the clergy from any sort of power they derived from their role as religious mediators.

The position which men and women occupied in the Ulster revival was influenced by two contradictory forces: the liberating force of conversion which stressed a spiritual equality based on a shared religious experience; and the restrictive force of a society and an established denominational system which was preoccupied with respectability, propriety and control. The differences between these two positions created tension and discord. The revival was not the idyllic paradise of revitalised religion that subsequent evangelicals and religious traditions have tried to portray. It was a time of chaos and confusion, when traditional standards of religious practice were temporarily abandoned. Lay preaching and ecstatic visions, embraced by a predominantly working-class grouping, challenged accepted standards of middle-class religiosity. This created problems for the clergy. They desired the positive results that a revival promised, such as increased interest in religion, renewed vitality among their congregations and church growth, but they frowned upon the excesses and sought to channel any enthusiasm into denominational frameworks. The clergy who had preached revival found themselves left behind when they were visited with one. By the end of the nineteenth century, members of the evangelical community had forgotten most of the controversy surrounding the events of 1859. They were by then more comfortable with their hopes for a repetition than they would have been with its reality.

In the fifty years after 1859, revivalism of the Ulster variety would rarely be seen in either Britain or Ireland. The spontaneous and uncontrollable proliferation of religious meetings over a wide area, combined with physical manifestations and enhanced leadership roles for the laity, was never seen on a national scale, although it was reproduced in a more limited fashion in certain localities. It was not until 1905, when a widespread and 'ecstatic' revival broke out in Wales, that such phenomena would be seen again. While such outbursts of spontaneous revival were now largely a thing of the past, revivalism as a concept within evangelical ideology was still important. Even though it did not happen, British and Irish evangelicals still avidly sought a revival along the lines of the 1859 revival in Ulster. Much of their denominational machinery in the late nineteenth century was geared towards the promotion of such an event, and revival missions and special services were an important and regular part of evangelical church life.

In fact, the promotion of a 'spontaneous' revival had become, by the end of the nineteenth century, a familiar, if institutionalised, process within many evangelical denominations. Most churches would have held, during the winter, an annual revival mission, which would have lasted for up to a month. A time of preparation, in which prayer meetings would be held, homes visited and handbills distributed, would then be followed by the arrival of a professional evangelist, who would have been invited to come and conduct the services. He (or she) would often be accompanied by an organist or a singer, and would be responsible for conducting a gospel service each night, as well as holding specialist services for mothers, children and young people during the day. At the end of the gospel service, members of the audience would be invited to come forward and give their lives to Christ. An after-meeting would sometimes be held to celebrate the conversion of these individuals and to pray for the future of their Christian lives. Although the aspiration continued to be the conversion of those outside of the Church, those deemed to be lost to organised religion, increasingly these mission services functioned simply to revive those already in contact with the local church, or to convert their as-yet unsaved children. Even though revival missions had much more restricted ambitions than a full-blown revival, evangelicals still held out the hope that an authentic revival would break out among them. Therefore, the idea of revival as represented by the events in Ulster continued to cause tension and discord within the evangelical community well into the final decades of the nineteenth century.

Back in 1859, however, the Ulster revival not only posed problems of religious control within the province, but also opened up, in quite a remarkable way, debates throughout the British Isles about the place of popular revivalism within the conventional denominational structure of mid-Victorian religion. It is to that story that we must now turn.

THE REVIVAL:

OR,

WHAT I SAW IN IRELAND;

WITH THOUGHTS SUGGESTED
BY THE SAME.

THE RESULT OF TWO PERSONAL VISITS.

BY

THE REV. JOHN BAILLIE,
COPY. AND CAIUS COLL., CAMBRIDGE,
AUTHOR OF "MEMOIRS OF HEWITSON," ETC.

"Then tidings of these things came unto the ears of the church which was in Jerusalem; and they sent forth Barnabas, that he should go as far as Antioch: Who, when he came, and had seen the grace of God, was glad. . . . . For he was a good man, and full of the Holy Ghost and of faith."—Acts xi. 22-24.

LONDON:

JAMES NISBET AND CO., 21 BERNERS STREET.

M.DCCCLX.

IRISH REVIVALS.

THE ULSTER AWAKENING:

Its Origin, Progress, and Fruit.

WITH

NOTES OF A TOUR OF PERSONAL OBSERVATION
AND INQUIRY.

BY THE REV. JOHN WEIR, D.D.,
MINISTER OF THE PRESBYTERIAN CHURCH, ISLINGTON, AND AUTHOR OF "CARNARVON" LECTURES FOR THE YOUNG.

WITH

A PREFACE BY THE HON. AND REV. B. W. NOEL, M.A.

LONDON:

ARTHUR HALL, VIRTUE, & CO.,
25 PATERNOSTER ROW.
1860.

Frontispieces from two English accounts of the 1859 revival

CHAPTER TWO

The British response to 1859

ALTHOUGH THE Ulster revival was largely the product of local factors and its wilder characteristics had only a regional influence, the events of 1859 had a much wider significance throughout Britain as a whole. From the early days of the revival the ecstatic manifestations had attracted the attention of newspapers across the country, including *The Times, Manchester Guardian* and the *North British Daily Mail*. Soon they attracted to Ulster a steady stream of curiosity seekers, social observers, religious 'tourists' and hopeful participants who reflected the full range of responses – from hostility and scepticism to gratitude and belief. Even within the evangelical community there were mixed opinions.

The graphic accounts of physical manifestations intrigued, but at the same time frightened, evangelicals in Britain. Suddenly, the religious revival which so many of them had been praying for was virtually on their doorstep. Although many were expectant, the transfer of religious enthusiasm to England never took place to any significant degree. As a spontaneous outpouring, the 1859 revival failed to take root in all but a few areas, such as the isolated region of Cornwall and the western lowlands of Scotland. To leave the story at this point, however, is to tell only half the tale. For British evangelicals, the revival's true importance lay in its function as a symbol of an ideal state of spirituality and church growth. The response of the evangelical community, and to a certain extent society at large, to the events in Ulster revealed their contradictory attitudes about the nature of revivalism, the status of Irish Protestants and their hopes for their own churches. The physical manifestations reminded these individuals that revivals could be quite disorderly and distasteful affairs, despite the promise they provided of rapid church growth and improved morality. Changing perceptions of what constituted proper church behaviour propelled many evangelicals towards a fundamental alteration of the accepted meaning of 'revivalism', allowing them to abandon the traditional, yet embarrassing, features in favour of a quieter and more sedate version. The Ulster revival was of crucial importance in the metamorphosis of revival definitions.

REVIVALISM IN A PERIOD OF CHANGE

By the middle of the nineteenth century, British Christians were well acquainted with the concept of revivalism, although its practice had been much more restrained than in America. Revivals had accompanied the origin and growth of Methodism in the early eighteenth century, but as the movement became more formalised and hierarchical it increasingly distanced itself from revivalism and other folk customs, such as female preaching. The numerous splits within Methodism in the late eighteenth and early nineteenth centuries nevertheless reflected the continued importance of these practices for a substantial minority. Groups of Bible Christians and Primitive Methodists maintained camp meetings and other elements of popular religious practice until well into the 1830s, if not later.[1] The Wesleyan Methodists, from whom these sects had separated, remained the largest group of Methodists. They were more middle class in composition and had become more concerned with respectability, rejecting the enthusiasm which had characterised many of the revivals that had contributed to their growth as a denomination. The disruption caused by the American revivalist Lorenzo Dow when he came to England in 1805 made Wesleyans wary of a movement which threatened their church discipline and control.[2] Another constraint on the occurrence of revivalism in Britain was the institutional nature of religious worship. The Church of England had a long history of suspicion of popular religious enthusiasm, which was regarded as theologically undesirable, pastorally inconvenient and socially unacceptable.[3] The other nonconformist denominations such as the Baptists and Congregationalists, though substantially affected by the evangelical revival and by county associations for itinerant evangelism, were also lukewarm about uncontrolled religious enthusiasm.

Fresh developments in the theory and practice of American revivals nevertheless contributed to a growing willingness to experiment with this form of church growth in England. The moderate Calvinism of Charles Grandison Finney, which was so influential among American Presbyterians, was experiencing similar popularity among English Baptists and Congregationalists. In his book *Lectures on revivals of religion*, Finney argued that it was possible for 'human instrumentality' to create an environment favourable to revival.[4] This approach was cautiously introduced among nonconformist groups in the form of special services for working men and evangelistic meetings in unconsecrated buildings. Evangelical Anglicans adopted similar methods, some even venturing so far as to conduct preaching services in the open air.[5] Despite the decline in spontaneous revivals in the early years of the nineteenth century, these planned efforts testify to continued interest in the rewards of revival activity.

The changes taking place in America led, by the 1850s, to a growing acceptance among British Christians of this new type of revivalism. In 1857–8 reports arrived from America of a revival breaking out among the businessmen of New York, many of whom had suffered during a recent financial crisis. Several features distinguished it from previous revivals and contributed to its general acceptance among the evangelical community in Britain. Its urban origins and the respectability of the participants meant it was largely free of the physical manifestations and other unsavoury behaviour so typical of other American revivals. Instead, this religious movement was promoted through the mechanism of nondenominational prayer meetings held during the lunch hour.[6] Such a positive reception was an indication of the shift in British attitudes as well as of the changes in the nature of revivalism itself. The opinion of the Reverend John Angell James, one of the most prominent mid-century evangelicals, is a good example. In keeping with tradition, James emphasised his dislike of the physical displays and emotional extravagance to which American revivals were prone. At the same time, he also expressed his disapproval of the trend towards 'new measures', or what he called a 'bustling, organised, and all but mechanical means to obtain' a revival.[7] Reports from America alleviated these fears. Rather than excitement, the revival had been based on habitual prayer, and instead of elaborately organised preaching services, the movement was spreading through a network of small prayer meetings. By using this model of revival activity (albeit with several qualifications) James claimed 'we may have, if we seek it, an extraordinary work of grace in this land'.[8] When the church showed evidence of brotherly love, solemnity, a spirit of prayer and a large number of conversions it could be said to be experiencing a revival of religion. Such 'eminent godliness', however, did involve some effort on the part of ministers and their congregations. Such an admission placed James in an awkward position. Although in essence opposed to the use of 'mechanical means', he now appeared to be arguing in favour of them. This was not the case. His perception of what was acceptable behaviour lay firmly in the spiritual realm, with faith, prayer and gospel sermons comprising the extent of his methodology. The admission of a legitimate role for human agency, however, opened the door for other commentators, like Professor J.G. Lorimer, to go even further. In an effort to promote a revival, ministers were encouraged to endorse the doctrine of sudden conversions and to adopt American procedures in their prayer meetings.[9]

James' and Lorimer's positive response to the American revival revealed an increasing openness to the concept of respectable revivalism and the emergence of a spirit of expectation among British evangelicals. Lorimer remarked 'what an unspeakable advantage it would be to the British, and indeed, the European churches, were they blessed with a true, large, continuous revival'.[10] The links of shared language and religion between America and Britain, it seemed, were the result of Divine Providence and had been established to promote true religion. As a result, '[was] there not to British Christians special ground for rejoicing in such a glorious effusion of the Spirit of God upon the American Churches?'[11] There was also evidence of a growing willingness to promote revival on a practical level. Apart from the efforts of the nonconformists and evangelical Anglicans mentioned earlier, there was the decision of the Church of England to open cathedrals for public preaching.[12] Among Methodists, the visit of James Caughey, while causing numerous difficulties for more conservative members, proved a remarkable success among a responsive laity.[13] The visit of this American revivalist coincided with the emergence of native lay evangelists like Brownlow North, Reginald Radcliffe and Baptist Noel, who began long and profitable careers in this period. In light of these developments, some British evangelicals believed the American revival would spread to England next. When news of a revival in Ulster was announced, these evangelicals were forced to reformulate some of their basic assumptions about the nature of their faith. Prepared for a repeat of the orderly American prayer meetings, cases of physical prostration in Ulster caused them even more soul searching.

A SENSE OF EXPECTANCY

English opinions of Ireland and Irish religious life prior to the revival were a confused mixture of fear, ignorance and mockery. The Irish people, it was felt, were dominated by a superstitious religion which contributed to the backward economic and social condition of the country. Some commentators were aware of a Protestant minority in the northern part of the island, but felt that for the most part, these communities were religiously lethargic and practised only a formal, dead religion.[14] A religious awakening in Ulster, as reported in English and Scottish national papers, therefore, was something of a surprise. The earliest accounts came from local Irish papers like the *Ballymena Observer*, *Londonderry Standard*, *Belfast News-Letter* and *Banner of Ulster* and spared nothing in their descriptions of the intense outburst of religious fervour in their areas. The desire to verify these reports, along with the threat of unsubstantiated rumour, combined with natural curiosity to motivate a number of British ministers and laymen to visit the scenes of revival for themselves and to report back to their friends, fellow church members and parishioners. Thus, between the months of June and October 1859 a large number of English and Scottish clergymen, and a smaller number of laymen, made the journey to Ulster.

One hundred and twenty-three of these clergymen have been identified from various printed sources, and they represent a fair cross-section of the religious geography of Britain. A little more than fifty per cent came from England, although five of these men were originally from Ulster.[15] Scotland supplied another forty per cent and the remainder came from Wales, North America and other parts of Ireland. Denominationally, Free Church of Scotland (Presbyterian) ministers were the most numerous visitors, followed by the Church of England, Methodists (Wesleyan, New Connexion and United Methodist Free Church), Baptists, Independents and English Presbyterians respectively, together with ten clergymen whose denominational affiliations remain unknown. These clerical visitors were a prominent feature of the Ulster revival and at times they threatened to outnumber the actual participants.[16] Most ministers, upon their arrival, stayed with people they knew or associated themselves with their local denominational representative. Some came to assist clerical friends, or to substitute for a colleague, especially if they belonged to one of the smaller denominations like the Baptists or Methodists. These latter denominations were keen to take advantage of the rapid church growth the revival was stimulating and encouraged their English members to give up holiday time to assist their Irish brethren.[17] Most 'observers' visited several localities in Ulster over the course of a two to six-week tour, relying on the willingness of the local minister to familiarise them with the locality, take them to meetings and allow them to interview people who had experienced physical prostrations. For the five Ulster natives who returned to Ulster, the revival was of obvious interest. Reverend John Graham, who had emigrated to London when he was thirty, still had family and friends in Antrim, Derry and Tyrone and as a result felt that his impressions of the revival and its impact on society were more accurate than the average English 'tourist'.[18]

Not all visitors to the north of Ireland in 1859 were clerical. The revival attracted, in the words of one critical newspaper, large numbers of 'summer tourists', who were 'flocking hither to see what capital can be got out of it'; inveterate explorers in search of titillating material for their travelogues.[19] This was no doubt a slight exaggeration. Lay visitors were in evidence, but it is difficult to establish their actual numbers. Only forty-one have been identified in the available sources, and most of these were from the middle to upper echelons of society. Presumably, only individuals with the time and money could afford to embark on a trip of this nature. Prominent men, such as the Chamberlain of the City of London, Benjamin Scott, the editor of the *Morning Advertiser*, James Grant, and military officers, such as Captain Orr and Captain Hawes, were members of this group, which also included interested gentlemen, mission and Bible society representatives, newspaper correspondents and church elders.

Whether clerical or lay, both sets of men, when they returned to their home towns, took their impressions of the revival with them, often publishing them as open letters to national newspapers, as small pamphlets or as articles in religious periodicals. They were not afraid to admit that before they witnessed the revival at first-hand, they had entertained doubts about its supposed impact on Irish society. Benjamin Scott had found the reports of physical manifestations 'perplexing and humbling', and refused to make a decision about their origin until he visited Ulster himself. Observing the unusually large number of individual conversions and the moral transformation of society, he concluded that the events were indeed God's handiwork.[20] These two issues constituted the fundamental arguments in almost all British evangelical justifications of the revival. Mr Budgett, the son of a successful Bristol merchant, had been 'more than once staggered by attempts in England at getting up Revival excitement as a part of machinery and means – well intended, but dubious in their character and results'.[21] After his visit to Coleraine, however, he was convinced that the revival was not the result of 'human appliances', but of God's will. Those visitors, like Scott and Budgett, who returned with favourable impressions, formed the centre of an active group within the evangelical community which sought to promote revival in England. Although there may have been varying degrees of support for the revival, and several interpretations of its more controversial elements, there was complete unanimity on what these observers considered to be the most pressing question – what was the cause of this revival? Reverend William Chalmers, of the English Presbyterian Church, summed up the general feeling of most observers when he stated, 'To my mind there is not a doubt that the work called the Revival is of God; [and] that a very special Divine influence has for some months been accompanying the ordinary means of grace in Ulster.'[22]

With memories of crowded churches, penitent and tearful congregations, monster prayer meetings in the open air, empty pubs and declining crime statistics, these spiritual tourists returned to their homes convinced of the revival's beneficial impact on Ireland's social and spiritual life, and assured that a similar event would produce similar results in England. The confidence of this assumption reflected a widespread sense of expectancy among many British evangelicals. Conflicting explanations for this expectancy were given. Some Christians claimed it was the superiority of British religious, social and political structures that made a revival in their country inevitable. Alternatively, they were keen to stress British parallels to countries like America and Ireland, which had already experienced revival.

In some respects, such expectations were only natural. Reverend F.A. West, speaking at a public meeting in Aldershot, expressed his confidence 'that the wave of salvation which had visited America, and had wafted across to Ireland, is already extending to our own shores'.[23] Other commentators noted that 'there is doubtless an influence from the Revival in Ireland on the minds and expectations of a large number of Christian people'.[24] What that influence involved, however, was rarely elaborated on. Reports of revival in America and Ireland certainly made one English Christian hopeful. '[F]rom hearing and reading of the American, Irish and Scotch Revivals, I am encouraged to pray and labour now for the power of the Holy Ghost to be exhibited amongst the teeming population of the east of London.'[25] The image of revived churches in other countries helped English Christians to persevere in their efforts for a corresponding result at home. It was the similarities between themselves and countries experiencing revival, like America and Ireland, which fuelled their own national expectations. One element of this was geographical proximity. Reverend Dr Buchanan, speaking at the Free Church Synod of Glasgow and Ayr, believed Scottish Christians would have been greatly disappointed if the revival which visited America had bypassed them. When they heard of the Irish revival, he explained, their expectations rose dramatically. With Ireland 'being so near us, multitudes could go and see the work, and have their own hearts and minds stirred up by the manifestation of the Lord's blessing'.[26] In this instance, it was felt that the closer a revival was, the greater the opportunity for it to spread to one's own locality.

Likewise, some evangelicals were prepared to concede that England's need for a religious revival was at least as great as that of Ireland. The immorality and social destitution of English cities were compared with the baleful effects of Roman Catholicism and economic impoverishment in Ireland. There was a growing conviction that English society was becoming more wicked and that the urban working classes were sinking further and further into religious apathy. Therefore, the Anglican Reverend Samuel Garratt expected a revival because, to his mind, no city needed a revival more than London. God wanted to send his blessings where they were needed, Garratt claimed, and because London was so full of sin, he was confident a revival was imminent.[27] Similar ideas were expressed in Scotland also, where one newspaper correspondent wrote, '[s]urely Scotland is not less in need of a revival of religion than Ireland, and surely there is abundant encouragement to expect that the prayer of faith will ascend as speedily to heaven from our own land as from the sister island'.[28] Scottish Christians could also claim the numerous ties of religion and nationality between themselves and the Presbyterians in Ulster as a basis for expecting the revival's appearance in their country. These attempts at establishing a common ground between Ireland and Britain were not, however, the most common approach. The comparisons of mutual sinfulness challenged a popular conception of British society (that it was already pious) by comparing it to a society (Irish) that was traditionally viewed as corrupt.

Other sources of revival expectation were the arguments from inevitability, which claimed that the very character of God and the behaviour of British Christians virtually guaranteed the spread of religious excitement to English and Scottish shores. For all their protestations that revivals were the work of the Holy Spirit and could not be engineered, British evangelicals actually had quite mechanistic views of revival causation. Because a revival had broken out in a neighbouring country, they felt they had a right to expect one themselves. And because British society needed an improved spiritual life as much as Ireland, they logically assumed a revival was imminent. Other reasons, similarly mechanistic, were proposed. Looking at the number of people already converted in England, the Irish Methodist William Arthur stated that if individual Christians were 'zealous and believing' in their efforts to spread the gospel, then 'the conversion of all their neighbours may be looked for.'[29] The earnest Samuel Garratt believed that the prayers of the Ulster converts, specifically for the conversion of London, were powerful indications that a 'great outpouring' could be expected in the metropolis.[30] The patience and faith of believing Christians combined with the proliferation of prayer meetings to promote this sense of inevitability. In part the sense of expectation was created by the idea that God had promised a revival. A resolution signed by twenty-eight Anglican clergymen in London stated,

> We are convinced, moreover, that God has made promises with reference to the gift of the Holy Spirit, which never yet received their full accomplishment, and that the Church of Christ is warranted in expecting, in answer to special and united prayer, a special and abundant blessing.[31]

In this sense, a revival was the inevitable reward British Christians would receive if they fulfilled their part of a spiritual contract. Prayer gave them a right to expect positive results, and supplied the bridge with which to connect divine power with human instrumentality.

Reverend John Weir offered other reasons for this attitude of expectancy. In his book, *The Ulster awakening: its origin, progress and fruit* (1860), he argued, using the analogy of nature, that revivals of the Church were to be expected. Just as:

> the fading flower, the drooping plant, the parched cereals, by the gentle shower and the gladsome sunshine, are resuscitated into fresh life – so, by the fresh communications of his heavenly grace, the Holy Ghost restores from a languishing condition that inner life which he had previously bestowed.[32]

Typical among evangelicals, Weir believed that the events at Pentecost signalled the beginning of a new 'dispensation', or a new set of rules under which God dealt with mankind, which he termed the 'apostolic age'. The characteristics of Pentecost – speaking in tongues, numerous conversions resulting in the rapid spread of the New Testament Church – became the model for revival activity in the nineteenth century. Thus, Weir argued:

> we are warranted to expect that what took place in apostolic times, and in connection with the first successes of Christianity, shall again and again be realised in the history of the Church; and this by periodic, special, and abundant visitations of heavenly influence, until Christianity shall become the dominant power in the world.[33]

The revival origins of the early Christian Church provided a biblical standard of religious vitality that, with a cyclical perception of history, made the present expectations of British evangelicals fairly reasonable. In fact, periodic revivals indicated the Church was in the process of moving inexorably towards its goal of world dominion.

These images of the cyclical nature of progress towards the goal of religious supremacy reflected the influence of British evangelical thinking of the mid-nineteenth century. Encouraged by the growth of Britain's colonial empire, some evangelicals imposed this model of political dominance on to their hopes of extensive church growth. As a result, imperial arguments justifying the expectation of revival appeared in evangelical literature. The *British Standard*, in an article concerning the beginnings of revival in Newcastle-upon-Tyne, boldly stated:

> that the arm of the Lord is being made bare in Ireland, Scotland, and Wales, is now clear beyond all rational contradiction. We do trust that the blessing will not be denied to the seat of Empire, England. There lies the head, the heart, the moral might of the Evangelical world. Everything short of this

will in its nature and position be introductory. Revival here will be revival
everywhere.[34]

The growing wickedness of society was reducing England's moral influence on
the world stage. The beginning of a revival promised to restore society to its
former moral purity and to eliminate vice and apathy. At that point 'the mission
of England [would] be well fulfilled among the nations, and, cleansed from her
iniquities at home, she would go forth to carry the best blessings of earth and
heaven to all the countries over which she exercises influence"[35] England's
position of political and moral leadership made a revival appear inevitable.
Evangelicals, however, introduced the idea of national purity to the equation.

WAYS TO PROMOTE A REVIVAL

Even with a mental framework which saw the coming of revival as a certainty,
British evangelicals did not rest on their laurels, but worked hard to create an
environment receptive to its imminent arrival. Two methods, mentioned
previously, were the most effective: the published reports and public lectures of
British visitors upon their return. Letters to the editors of local and national
newspapers narrating first-hand observations of revival in the north of Ireland
were the most prevalent forms of publicity and achieved the widest coverage.
Letters frequently appeared in religious papers like the *British Standard*, *The
Record*, *Wesleyan Times* and *The Revival*. Accounts were also sent to the *Daily
News*, *Morning Advertiser*, *Morning Star* and *Scottish Guardian*, secular papers
which had relatively positive editorial policies on the revival. Correspondence
was also conducted with *The Times*, *The Spectator* and the *Daily Telegraph*, all
of which were very critical of this religious awakening. Most letters either gave
narrative accounts of individuals' experiences while in Ireland, or contributed
to debates, such as the debate on the veracity of accounts relating to the physical
manifestations. Letters of a positive nature invariably concluded with an
affirmation of the revival's divine origins and an exhortation to British Christians
to pray for revival blessings in their localities. During the months of September
and October 1859, revival news featured prominently in these national papers
and was reported almost daily. The extent of the coverage guaranteed the
revival's exposure to a broad cross-section of the British population, even if this
exposure was only temporary. Evangelicals who desired to spread news of the
revival could not have chosen a more effective method.

Not content with press reports, interested evangelicals conducted a series of
public lectures and addresses in their attempts to disseminate positive information about the Irish revival. One of the earliest of these meetings was held at
the Free Trade Hall in Manchester on 6 September 1859. Mr John Montgomery,
a corn dealer from Portadown, Co. Armagh, organised and financed the meeting
because he wanted to see the revival spread from 'his country to England'.[36] As

with many other of these events, the laity occupied a prominent position. Montgomery not only organised the Manchester meeting but also delivered the main address, describing what he had seen in Ireland and justifying the physical manifestations. Benjamin Scott, the Chamberlain of the City of London, spoke at several meetings in and around London. Robert Baxter, a lawyer from Doncaster who was active within the growing circle of evangelical Anglicans, had visited Ulster and returned to address a meeting of the Church of England Young Men's Society in London.[37] Captain Andrew Orr, born in Coleraine and serving in the British Army at Woolwich Arsenal, had led meetings while visiting Ulster and upon his return gave several lectures describing his experiences. Other military personnel involved included Captain Hawes, a representative for the Religious Tract Society, Captain Fishbourne and General Alexander, all of whom went on to pursue more active preaching careers.

The conduct of these meetings followed a format and style which was to gain in popularity as the century wore on. Borrowing from the American model, both the planning and conduct of the meetings involved a number of clergy and laity from different denominations. As a result, non–religious buildings, such as town halls, assize courts, YMCA rooms and local schools, were the preferred locations; in one instance even a tavern was used. The proceedings followed a standard combination of prayers, hymns, scripture readings and address. The content of the message also followed a standard form, with speakers generally confessing to their doubts about the revival prior to their visit, relating cases of physical manifestations they had seen, explaining their true nature and defending their occurrence. The confession of doubt and the focus on the physical manifestations was an obvious choice for the content of a promotional lecture. While stories of wild conversions would attract the curious, admitting one's own doubts and how they had been alleviated would persuade others with similar hesitations to believe more fully and to promote the revival in their own localities.

Although this sounded like a simple process, evangelical support soon clashed with more traditional religious opinion. A meeting in Woolwich Town Hall brought this conflict into the open. On that occasion, two speakers, the Reverend John Baillie, minister of All Soul's, Marylebone and General Alexander of Black-heath, had been asked to give an account of their recent 'tours of observation' in the north of Ireland. They both concentrated on the issues of physical manifestations and the long-term status of converts, reaching favourable conclusions on both counts. The number of people desiring admission was so large that a second meeting had to be scheduled directly after the first. At the conclusion of the meeting the assemblage left the hall 'deeply impressed with the conviction that "the kingdom of God was come nigh unto them"'.[38] This positive endorsement of the revival in Ulster provoked a series of critical responses. In a letter to the editor of the *Daily Telegraph*, Richard Hibbs, who had attended the Woolwich meeting, claimed that Baillie and Alexander's description of the physical manifestations had given the impression that the

Holy Spirit 'was supposed to display some ocular proofs of his existence and power' and that English Christians should desire the same. 'Now, Sir, "England with all her faults," I firmly believe is really too pious, as well as too honest, for such exhibitions.' English converts, he added:

> are, indubitably, as much more exalted by true religion above these Ulster mimics of the loud-professing, but really mammon-worshipping Americans, as they are incapable of, to say the least, such a manifest got-up display of the so-called miraculous and supernatural.[39]

The faith in the piety of the English population revealed a racial snobbery, which underlaid much of the critical opinion concerning the revival as a whole. Unlike the people of America and Ulster, some commentators felt the 'true religion' which the English already possessed rendered irrelevant the cheap carnival tricks of physical manifestations in Ulster.

The parallels between a religious revival and a three-ring circus were more than obvious to some critics. One editorial compared the Woolwich meeting to one of Mr Barnum's ploys to attract those fascinated with 'the marvellous'. It accused Baillie and Alexander of misleading the 'English masses' who were present by telling them that 'through the instrumentality of these painful hysterical exhibitions, "God had visited his people."' This constituted the preaching of:

> humbug – and very dangerous humbug too – to a class of people who, from the position they occupy in the social scale, have a tendency at all times to be attracted by the prodigious, and much more so when it is offered to them through the mouths of people whom they think ought to possess a higher order of intelligence than themselves.[40]

Evangelicals believed public lectures were an effective way to spread the news about revival to a wide cross-section of the ministerial and lay community, and thus promote interest in launching revival work in England. For their critics, however, such meetings were a threat to an established way of viewing English society. Attempts to publicise England's need of revival were interpreted as efforts to promote ecstatic religious behaviour, and challenged the accepted notion of England's religious superiority. In doing so, it threatened to subvert the traditional means of promoting religion. When evangelicals urged the working classes to promote revival themselves, they were bypassing the clergy and the ordinary functions of the church as the source of religious leadership and authority.

Public lectures like the ones held in Woolwich and Manchester's Free Trade Hall rarely marked the end of interest in revival in a locality. They were essentially promotional meetings, using the appeal of a visiting speaker to spark local interest into establishing regular work of some similar nature. For example, at the meeting in Manchester it was decided to hold another such gathering during the following week to allow those interested in promoting a local revival to meet for fasting and prayer.[41] In Penkhall, Stoke-on-Trent, the local vicar and one of his church members had visited Ireland, and upon their return gave a public lecture in the local schoolroom. At that meeting, one person was 'stricken', as in Ireland, with conviction of sin to the point of physical collapse. The fervour exhibited at this meeting prompted the vicar to establish regular prayer meetings, at which three more people were stricken and many others revived.[42] Evangelical concerns about using mechanistic means to promote revivals tended to limit their efforts to overtly spiritual ones like faith and prayer. The success of the recent American revival, with its numerous prayer meetings, encouraged British Christians to do the same and hope for similar results.[43]

Thus, if anything spread over the country during 1859, it was the phenomenon of prayer meetings. Meetings such as these could be found all over England, in places like Devon and Cornwall, Kent and the Midlands, Liverpool and Lancashire.[44] Evangelicals, especially those behind *The Revival*, misinterpreted these meetings as evidence of a revival taking place,[45] when in actual fact they were never more than preparatory in nature, designed to stimulate English Christians to renewed efforts at revival. After the visit of the Reverend J.W. Massie, interested ministers and laity in Penley, Ellsmere started a Wednesday evening prayer meeting in the Church of England schoolroom, where they heard reports of the revival and prayed for its outpouring on them.[46] Similarly, the local Christians in Bedford had heard of God's work in Ireland and were 'stirred up in the Spirit' to hope for an awakening in their town. Prompted to action, leading laity and clergy organised local prayer meetings and preached revival sermons in the various churches. For all their efforts, the organisers could only admit there was an increasing desire among local Christians for the 'blessing of the Holy Spirit to descend upon them'.[47] This was not a revival, but an awakened desire for the outbreak of one. As hopeful evangelicals were soon to realise, events in England would rarely progress beyond this preparatory stage.

Before this reality set in, British efforts to instigate a national revival went unchecked throughout the latter part of 1859. Another weapon in evangelicals' arsenal of publicity was a logical outcome of the widespread use of public meetings and lectures: Irish ministers and lay converts were invited to come to England and Scotland to give their testimony. As actual participants in the revival excitement, these individuals had an authority and credibility above that of mere British visitors. In some respects, listening to these men was like looking at the revival itself, and this was obviously a leading motive behind their participation. In evangelical circles, where personal experience of religious events was placed at a premium, there could be no better witnesses than these Irish converts.

Unlike travel in the other direction, the number of Irish laymen visiting England was greater than the number of clergymen. At least fifteen converts have been traced, while evidence of only eight ministers has been found. Two of these laymen are worth considering in more detail. James McQuilkin was a handloom linen weaver living in Connor, Co. Antrim when he experienced conversion in 1856. Along with three other young men, he started to meet for prayer in the nearby village of Kells, praying specifically for a revival to take place in Ulster. Within twelve months the gathering had become a public one and the growing level of interest led them to establish an adult Sunday School. According to most commentators, these humble beginnings formed the origins of the Ulster revival.[48] As the supposed 'first convert' of the revival McQuilkin's role in its origin – now semi-mythologised – has hidden his subsequent activity from view. British visitors, however, were quick to recognise his significance and were keen to have him address their churches. Reverend J.P. Wallis of Birmingham had met McQuilkin while on a tour of observation in Ulster and was impressed with the weaver's revival credentials. He persuaded McQuilkin to come to Birmingham and speak at a meeting in the Town Hall to give an account of several cases of conversion which he had witnessed. The meeting was declared a complete success.[49] McQuilkin is also known to have visited other towns, like Port Glasgow in Scotland, on the same trip.[50]

McQuilkin's connections to the beginnings of revival, and his reputation as the first convert, made him an attractive means of bringing revival enthusiasm home to British audiences. In a similar fashion, David Cresswell travelled to England as an example of the revival's ability to convert Catholics. With the internal revitalisation of both Protestant and Catholic churches in nineteenth-century Ireland, the previous uneasy accommodation and cooperation which had existed between two denominations was increasingly replaced with suspicion and intolerance. As churches became more confident, they adopted more rigid and combative attitudes. The efforts of Protestant missionaries to win converts among the Catholic Irish in the 1830s and 1840s, known as the 'Second Reformation', seriously damaged relations between the true denominations.[51] In the 1850s, sensitivity to any threat of proselytism remained high. During the revival, even though several Protestant ministers had been charged with abduction and illegal proselytising to minors, evangelicals remained undeterred from what they believed to be one of the most important results of the revival – the conversion of Catholics. Despite claims to the contrary, the revival in the north of Ireland had little impact on the Catholic community. Thus, when David Cresswell's conversion experience was publicised on the front page of the *Ballymena Observer*, it was something of a novelty.[52] Cresswell was eighteen years old and a stonemason from Derry working in Moneymore. Since birth he had been plagued with a severe speech defect that made him difficult to understand. While at Moneymore, he attended several of the revival services 'to hang about the outskirts, and mock at the people'. One day he passed a house in the town and heard the local Presbyterian minister say some words which spoke to his soul. He was induced to go in, and subsequently experienced the conviction of sin and some slight physical manifestations. Two weeks later he was 'struck again', and after six hours 'blessed be God, I found that the power of perfect speech had been bestowed on me, and that I, who had never before spoken a plain word in all my life, could now praise His holy name without impediment'. 'I was a Roman Catholic,' Cresswell went on to say, 'I am not one now, nor ever shall be again'. Cresswell was soon addressing meetings throughout Ulster. An invitation was issued to Cresswell to speak and conduct evangelistic work in Devon, and he spent several weeks there, which suggests that he may have been trying to avoid family members or an angry parish priest.[53] With a conversion involving not only a Catholic but also a miraculous healing, Cresswell's story had an obvious appeal. English Christians hoped the presence of Irish converts would attract people to revival meetings. After the visit of two such converts to Preston, prostrations, increased church attendance and pub closures were evident, but never developed into a full-scale revival.[54] The whiff of sensationalism which Irish converts supplied was never enough to fan local revival fires into a national conflagration.

Clerical visits to Britain were more structured and organised than their lay counterparts, but still relied heavily on personal contacts. Clerics' motives, as members of denominations, reflect their concern to consolidate gains made during the revival and to solicit financial support for their churches. The General Assembly of the Irish Presbyterian Church sent a formal delegation to the Free Church of Scotland Assembly to report on the progress of the revival and its potential spread to Scotland.[55] Individual ministers, like the Reverend J.S. Moore, travelled in England to publicise the situation in Ireland. He enlisted the support of Benjamin Scott to advertise his availability and organise his preaching schedule. Besides informing people about the progress of the revival, he wanted to plead for the 700 Irish converts in his area who still had not been able to find church accommodation.[56] Moore's ill-concealed attempts at fund raising provoked several critical letters in the *British Standard*.[57]

INSTITUTIONAL AND DENOMINATIONAL RESPONSES

The initiative British evangelicals showed in setting up interdenominational prayer meetings and public lectures was matched by the efforts of churches and voluntary religious societies who responded to the revival on an institutional and a denominational level. As part of the general wave of curiosity, a number of London-based missionary organisations sent representatives over to Ireland to observe the revival's progress. Reverend J.W. Massie travelled to Ulster as a representative of the Irish Evangelical Society, as did the Reverend Mr Andrews in his capacity as secretary of the Irish Church Missions Society in the south of Ireland. The interest of the Evangelical Alliance in the Irish revival was manifest in the decision to stage its 13th annual conference in Belfast during the summer of 1859. Established in 1845, one of the primary objectives of this organisation was 'to enable Christians of different denominations to realise to themselves, and to exhibit to others, that living and essential UNION which binds all true believers together in the fellowship of Christ'.[58] Membership was based on allegiance to a general statement of evangelical doctrines, which included the divine inspiration of Scripture, the Trinity, the incarnation and atonement and justification by faith alone.[59] As one of a number of Protestant organisations that were formed during this period, the Evangelical Alliance's desire for unity was seen not only as a spiritual desire but also as a political necessity, arising 'from the mighty efforts of Popery and Infidelity within the visible Churches, and the vast extent of untouched idolatry and Mohammedanism'.[60] When news of the revival became known, many Alliance members expressed their desire to observe it on a firsthand basis.[61] To them, the revival's 'total disregard of the ecclesiastical divisions of the Church'[62] embodied the Alliances's central principle of Christian unity.[63] At the conference itself, reports on the progress of the revival dominated the proceedings. Of the six formal papers, four concerned themselves directly with accounts of the revival.[64] Reverend Charles Seaver, an Irish Anglican, was chosen to tour England as the Alliance's representative and spread the word about the revival. Over the course of two weeks he spoke twenty-one times in eleven towns in the London and Hertfordshire areas, and conducted informal meetings with the Archbishop of Canterbury and the Bishop of London, as well as attending a conference for metropolitan clergy.[65] During the conference, one evening was specially reserved for a public debate on pre-circulated questions like 'What spiritual benefit can Irish brethren confer on Britain as the result of the great revival?' and 'In what way may British Christians best cooperate with their Irish brethren in promoting the advancement of evangelical truth and godliness in Ireland?'[66] The discussion, however, quickly degenerated into bitter disputation when the Reverend William McIlwaine, a Belfast Presbyterian and known opponent of the revival, rose to address the audience. The physical phenomena, he declared, along with lay preaching, were 'new things', unscriptural innovations which could not be condoned. He maintained that conversion was a result of hearing the Word of God, and he denounced the appearance of 'visions' and other abuses of the revival, urging caution on all members of the assembly. Although Alliance supporters tried to camouflage the audience's reaction, it was apparent that McIlwaine's speech was frequently interrupted by hissing and shouts of 'Are you converted yourself?'[67] This obvious lack of unity did not go unnoticed. The *Daily News*, generally positive in its outlook on the revival, noted that McIlwaine's 'announcement of dissent was not received with the courtesy and patience which might have been expected of the Evangelical Alliance ... Common propriety should have forbidden the manifestations with which [McIlwaine] was received, since his objects were those which his hearers professed'.[68] Although the revival was portrayed as a visible manifestation of Christian unity, Alliance members found such an example difficult to follow.

Despite the obviously newsworthy nature of the revival, it was only one of many issues competing for the attention of the British populace. The war in Italy, religious riots in the east end of London, the progress of the Nine Hours Bill,

the wreck of the Royal Charter and the account of Blondin going over Niagara
Falls in a barrel occupied space in the national newspapers alongside reports
from Ballymena describing all night prayer meetings and cases of conversion.
What was true for the newspapers also held good for the major Protestant
denominations. Methodist and Anglican, Congregational and Presbyterian all
had a variety of concerns which needed their attention, such as church building,
training clergy, fund raising and mission activity. Yet each one of them was
influenced on an official level to respond to the revival in Ulster. When the
Wesleyan Methodist conference convened in Manchester, an entire day was set
aside for a public meeting on the revival. With about 4,000 people in attendance,
the Reverend Mr Jones, the Irish representative, and the Reverend F.A. West
gave personal narratives of such a stirring nature that one reporter was moved
to comment, '[t]his revival in Ulster! Why, it is Old Methodism renewing its
youth in a Presbyterian Church!' and to declare 'that the most triumphant days
of Christianity and of Methodism are close at hand'.[69] In his comments, West
exhorted British Wesleyans to work hard, consecrate themselves and continually
plead with God for the 'outpouring of the Holy Spirit'.[70] The prayers 'that went
up on that memorable occasion from thousands of God's elect will yet issue,
doubtless, in widespread blessing'.[71] Other denominational responses were
similarly enthusiastic. The Methodist New Connexion, which had seven mission
stations in Ireland at this time, issued a series of suggestions to assist individual
circuits to 'bring down a mighty effusion of the Holy Spirit, and thereby secure
a genuine and a general revival of the work of God'.[72] The Congregationalists
delivered speeches at their annual conference of 1859 concerning the progress
of the revival in Ireland and England. In 1860 they passed a resolution expressing
their thankfulness for the revival and recommending 'renewed liberality and
prayer on behalf of the Irish Evangelical Society'.[73]

The revival also occupied a prominent position within the proceedings of the
General Assembly of the Free Church of Scotland. It heard the reports of both
Irish and Scottish ministers and issued an official circular which was to be read
from all pulpits concerning the work of God in Ireland. Expressing thankfulness
to God for the revival, it concluded by saying that 'the sovereign power of the
Holy Spirit, and the efficacy of believing prayer, ought to encourage us to
"attempt great things for God, and expect great things from God".'[74] The outbreak of revival in certain parts of western Scotland no doubt stimulated this
institutional interest. Even synods within the Church of Scotland had passed
resolutions encouraging their ministers to pray 'for wisdom to direct this
religious movement aright, and for the spiritual benefits which, by the Divine
blessing, it may be instrumental in producing'.[75]

For the most part, religious institutions and denominations reacted to the
Irish revival in a positive, thankful and expectant fashion. To them, the revival
was more than just a fringe phenomenon. The mainline denominations made
special allowances to discuss the issue and make pronouncements upon it. The
Evangelical Alliance went so far as to choose their conference location on the

basis of it. Such reactions indicated that the revival had made a substantial impact on the official levels of denominational and institutional evangelicalism.

THE 1859 REVIVAL AND WALES

So far, the Welsh response to the Irish revival has been conspicuous by its absence, especially since it also experienced a substantial revival during 1859. Several factors conspired to keep these two movements relatively separate. Most contemporary accounts of the Welsh revival place its origins in an American rather than an Irish context. Through emigrant letters and religious newspapers,[76] news of the American revival had reached the province by 1858, where it spread among an audience with a pre-existing history of interest in American religious developments. Charles Finney's *Lectures on revivals of religion* (1835) had been immensely popular in Wales and were a major force behind a series of local revivals which occurred between 1839 and 1843.[77] Printed accounts of American developments in 1857–8 were reinforced by the preaching of Humphrey Jones, a Welsh minister who had been active on the American revival scene and had returned to spread the gospel in his native country. Under the stimulus of his preaching, the Welsh people responded enthusiastically. Jones was also credited with the conversion of the Reverend David Morgan, a Calvinistic Methodist minister, who went on to become one of the leading lights of the revival movement.[78]

There were obvious similarities between the revivals in Ulster and Wales. Neither of them had prominent leaders. In Ulster, no single individual emerged to lead the movement. In Wales, while Jones and Morgan are credited with the initial stages of promotion, they were quickly joined in their efforts by numerous other clergymen. Similar techniques, such as the nondenominational prayer meetings, were used, signifying the importance of the American influence on both movements. Welsh supporters and their counterparts in Ulster claimed, in the wake of their respective revivals, that there had been a radical transformation of social morals. J.E. Orr, although at pains to stress the individuality of the Welsh revival, was willing to admit that it 'displayed many features of spiritual kinship with the contemporary movements in Ireland and Scotland, and all three derived inspiration from the American movement of 1858'.[79]

However, the Welsh revival was very much its own movement and remained largely separate from the events in Ulster. Part of this was due to the existence of a strong indigenous chapel-based culture which continued to emphasise the importance of revivals. Strong links between rural and industrial regions in Wales meant that the growing urban population had maintained much of its traditional religious beliefs. When Jones and Morgan began to itinerate throughout the country, they preached to a population which still found meaning in a revival-oriented religion.[80] As a spark to the Welsh revival, the events in Ulster were marginal in comparison to indigenous factors.

Welsh ministers, like the Reverend Thomas Phillips, were aware of the events in Ulster and drew comparisons, but never made a causal connection between the two.[81] For one thing, although Wales had a well-established tradition of revival enthusiasm, it did not experience physical manifestations as Ulster had. Welsh cultural and geographic isolation erected other hurdles. The prevalence of the Welsh language made the spread of revival news from Ulster difficult, as did the poor communication links between the two regions.[82] The historical consensus concerning the insular nature of the Welsh revival is supported for the most part by contemporary sources. English evangelicals were apparently interested in Wales, but there is little evidence that they exercised their curiosity in tours of observation. In return, Welsh ministers were aware of the revival in Ulster, but very few of them appear to have journeyed to the province. The only known visit was from a group of Congregational ministers led by the Reverend Thomas Rees. Prior to their visit they appeared ignorant about Ulster's social background and critical about the progress of revival there.[83]

CONTESTED TERRAIN

British evangelicals, as has been shown, had gone to enormous lengths to promote the revival in England and Scotland. They had visited Ulster, held public lectures, established regular prayer meetings, brought in visiting speakers and imported Irish converts. They had made resolutions, published papers and even started a periodical devoted entirely to revival news.[84] According to the revival formula, all this enthusiasm, prayer and hard work should have triggered a 'shower of the Holy Spirit' as in Ireland. As 1859 wore on into 1860 it became increasingly obvious that a 'spontaneous' religious awakening was not going to occur. That is not to say there was no revival activity in Britain. The proliferation of revival prayer meetings and evidence of a few local revivals points to widespread interest in the Irish phenomenon. However, journals like *The Revival* felt these few instances meant a general awakening was underway. Stories of Staffordshire miners conducting prayer meetings during their dinner hour were reported by a religious press eager for early signs of an indigenous revival movement.[85] The arrival of the American evangelists Walter and Phoebe Palmer to Newcastle in September also raised hopes. The *Newcastle Guardian* saw the local excitement which their meetings had generated as a direct inheritance from the revivals in America, which had spread to Ireland and on into Scotland.[86] Even *The Times* seemed impressed, remarking that the revival in Newcastle 'bids fair to rival anything of the kind which has yet occurred either in America or in the North of Ireland'.[87] By October, public interest in the revival was spreading. Reverend 'Roaring' Hugh Hanna, a Presbyterian minister from Belfast, had preached in Trinity Presbyterian Church to overflowing crowds[88] and according to a local Methodist minister, all of the three daily prayer meetings were regularly forced to turn people away.[89] Such enthusiasm, however, remained a local phenomenon, never spreading beyond the Shields region or Gateshead.[90] With the departure of the Palmers in mid-November, religious life returned to its normal levels. The events in Newcastle nevertheless convinced many expectant evangelicals that an actual revival, in the 'Irish' sense of the word, was still possible in England.

Localised outbursts of this nature occurred in other parts of England,[91] but historians are in agreement that a revival comparable to the events in Ireland never took place. Circumstances in England were much different. John Kent has attributed part of the difficulty to the influence of the Church of England, which had no history of revivals or any experience of them. He also points to the growing divisions between urban and rural England that made revivals difficult to engineer. Large conurbations, with their secular populations, lacked the social coherence and religious identity which had made revivals so successful in a rural Irish context.[92] Carwardine and Bebbington both agree that the Ulster revival never successfully spread to England. However, they are at pains to stress that the significance of the revival operated on other levels besides numerical success. Even if the revival never really altered the broad patterns of religious life in England, for a short time it did capture the popular imagination on a wide scale.[93] More importantly, the revival exposed underlying tensions and differences within the English evangelical community.

In fact, many evangelicals were unsure how to respond when they experienced a 'real' revival. In the Congregational chapel in Bicester, the Reverend W. Ferguson conducted a prayer meeting at which several young women from the local boarding school were stricken down. Other members of the congregation seemed paralysed and were unable to leave when the service concluded. Reverend John Fogg, who was present at the time, remarked 'we did not know what to make of it. It was so strange – so new – we never expected it, and yet we were praying for the outpouring of the Holy Spirit.'[94] Here, Fogg neatly summarised the contradictory attitudes of many British evangelicals towards revivalism. On the one hand, they desired a revival and had been praying for one to occur. On the other hand, when a revival did occur, many Christians simply 'did not know what to make of it'. The ecstatic phenomena in Ulster and their unusual innovations contradicted preconceived notions about proper religious behaviour. The revival, therefore, exposed a deep-seated contradiction within British evangelical thought between revival as a spiritual ideal and its actual occurrence. When evidence of the desired spiritual awakening became apparent in Ulster, the response of British Christians reflected their commitment to revival as a method of church growth. Some evangelicals, like the ones seen in previous pages of this chapter, responded to the revival without hesitation or doubt. It was undoubtedly the work of the Holy Spirit, sent to revitalise the Church and convert the ungodly. Reverend F.A. West believed that nothing short of a miracle, accompanied with 'glorious signs ... would have arrested attention and aroused a slumbering church; and so, in England, men must be deeply impressed by some extraordinary means'.[95] This enthusiastic and uncritical response was not possible for everyone. Other evangelicals, particularly members of the clergy, discovered that revivals challenged many of their perceptions about the theory and practice of religious conduct. The physical phenomena, lay preaching and other so-called excesses convinced some clergymen that a revival was not worth the disruption it created, and that it was a dangerous phenomenon which should be criticised and controlled.

One area that illustrates the clerical dilemma particularly well was the tendency of a revival to promote lay preaching. Reports from Ulster indicated that lay converts were initiating and leading a large number of revival meetings. Some of this was only the result of sheer necessity. The desire for Bible classes, open-air meetings and individual counselling was so great that ministers could not have supplied these services on their own. Many lay men and even a few women, however, were preaching, not out of expediency, but because they felt called to do so by the Spirit of God or through their own desire for self-expression.[96] The range of clerical responses indicates the ambivalent attitudes the revival provoked. Some clerics condemned the revival outright, claiming that lay preaching was a dangerous innovation which could inadvertently promote wrong doctrine and uncontrollable excitement.[97] Others held positive views on the revival as a whole, but found lay preaching unacceptable. Reverend John Williams of Glasgow felt:

> the cause of God and truth may suffer much at the hands of incompetent advocates; and I am afraid that the practice of pushing converts forward to speak at revival meetings will be found to be hurtful, both to themselves, in filling them with pride and vanity, and to the people, in fostering among them a very unhealthy excitement and fanaticism.[98]

Such altruistic concerns could not entirely mask the threat which such lay activity posed to clerical authority. The excitement which generated a demand for lay testimonies suggested the loss of clerical control and potentially, the rejection of an ordained ministry altogether. Ministers who supported the revival were forced to walk an intellectual tightrope, admitting, like the Reverend Charles Seaver, that although the revival had spawned a number of hot-headed and injudicious preachers, 'on the whole, the testimony of sober-minded men, lay and clerical, has been borne to the soundness of their views, the discretion and wisdom with which they acted, and, in many instances, the unction and power that accompanied their services'.[99] Such preaching, Seaver reassured his readers, had not lessened the esteem in which ministers were held; in fact, 'the ministerial office was never more highly honoured'.[100]

Direct clerical control was also threatened by the disruption of regular church services. Revival meetings in Ulster were notorious for their crowded and excited atmosphere, where people could not be persuaded to leave and where the regular liturgy broke down in the face of sobbing, shouting, convulsions and other spontaneous interruptions. Some British observers found such reports disturbing,[101] but evangelical clergymen who supported the revival offered two separate lines of defence. On the one hand, they argued that revivals reinvigorated regular church worship, that God used the unusual methods of lay converts and 'certain stunning "manifestations"' in order to 'disturb the clerical martinet out of his propriety by certain invasions of his neat theories of order and of quiet decorum'.[102] On the other hand, they maintained that the revival had left church order and the liturgy undisturbed. Converts had by no means been compelled to abandon their order of worship; in fact, 'the accustomed forms were more to be prized than ever' and they 'spoke of the Liturgy with joy, as breathing forth most fitly their confessions and thanksgivings'.[103] The desire for a revival to come and renew church life, to 'stir up the dry bones' and unsettle a dead formalism battled with the clerical desire for decorum and order.

Without a doubt, the most controversial element of the Ulster revival, according to both clerical and secular opinion, was its unusual physical manifestations. Secular opinion in England was extremely critical of these phenomena and focused on the medical impact such prostrations could have upon the Irish population.[104] Dismissing them as no more than 'hysteria',[105] *The Lancet*, a prestigious medical journal, described them as 'morbid and injurious phenomena' with symptoms of insensibility, prolonged convulsions, rolling eyes, wild dreams and mad ravings.[106] It was commonly assumed that these phenomena, if prolonged, could cause permanent insanity. The fear of insanity was a constant theme in secular criticism. One newspaper remarked:

We believe this union of a spiritual awakening with a bodily paralysis to be most injurious in its results. Yet these Revivalist preachers are troubled with no doubts. They evidently consider that they are possessed of gifts little short of miraculous. They are not far behind the Apostles. Nay, in some respects they excel them. The Apostles were wont to heal sickness. The Revivalists have hitherto devoted themselves principally to producing it. The former used to cast out devils. The latter, it appears, do just the reverse. We fear it cannot be denied that many of these subjects of conversion have become insane, and have been removed to lunatic asylums. They have gained doubtless a 'sense of sin', but the sense of everything else they have lost, perhaps for ever. To the discovery of the need of 'saving grace' has succeeded the need of a strait-waistcoat. Here the case passes from the hands of the preacher to those of the physician. The latter is requested to repair the mischief which the former has produced.[107]

These fears were further substantiated when the *Northern Whig*, a Belfast newspaper hostile to the revival, published statistics which showed an increase in committals to Belfast asylums from 1858 to 1859. When published in *The Times*, these statistics provoked an extensive controversy.[108] Newspaper editorials and letters merely reflected the fears of the reading public, which quite understandably found it difficult to interpret such phenomena. Some people thought that like any other disease, they 'aggravate[d] the nervous debility of invalids, ... ruin[ed] the health of thousands, ... [shook] the mind and vitiate[d] the constitution'.[109]

Secular critics feared that such physical outbursts threatened more than just the spread of epidemic disease. They were also concerned for the future of British civilisation and the 'true religion' it represented. 'True religion' was defined as a calm and rational pursuit, 'a rule of life, a beacon set up by the highest wisdom to guide the human race into the haven of happiness, by teaching them how they ought to act in every condition and circumstance of life'.[110] The recent outburst of ecstatic religious phenomena threatened this standard and degraded it into a 'necromantic superstition'.[111] The revival glorified the abandonment of rationality, a characteristic which British Christians felt set them apart from the rest of the world. It shocked them to discover what they felt to be a return to pre-modern forms of religious behaviour. 'Let [revival excitement] be countenanced by the public, and there will be a second deluge of Unknown Tongues, of Southcotism [sic], and every species of sensual heresy.'[112] The loss of reason was also feared because it upset proper gender roles. Men no longer acted in a rational fashion and women were no longer the modest creatures society assumed them to be.[113] Revival excitement threatened what many people believed were the foundations of British society – rational men, modest women and calm religion.

In the debate over the physical manifestations, it was not a clear-cut case of secular newspapers opposing evangelicals. There were members of the clergy who were equally critical. Reverend E.A. Stopford, the Archdeacon of Meath, provided critics with the most ammunition in his widely circulated pamphlet *The work and the counterwork: or, the religious revival in Belfast* (1859). In it he condemned all physical aspects of the revival, saying it was actually a 'counterwork' of Satan to try to bring the revival into disrepute. Stopford's construction of this interpretive model typified the struggle almost all ministers had when it came to revival manifestations. Stopford wanted to support the revival, but could not endorse the prostrations that he found so distasteful. He resolved the ambivalence this created by separating the prostrations and other physical phenomena from the rest of the revival work, attributing the former to Satan and leaving himself free to support the aspects of the revival which he had deemed acceptable.

Other evangelical ministers were more favourably disposed toward the revival's ecstatic outbursts. Secular and religious criticism, however, forced them to adopt positions they were unsure of and to use arguments which stretched the limits of logic. A common defence was the claim that the prostrations and visions served a higher purpose. Reverend J.P. Wallis of Birmingham expressed his opinion that 'in many instances, the cases of bodily prostration were the direct work of the Spirit of God, having especial purpose to draw the attention of the world to the reality of the work'.[114] Thus, prostrations occurred to publicise the revival and encourage its spread. Other arguments stated that such physical manifestations were the natural response of the body to strong mental emotion. The testimony of eminent evangelical theologians, such as Dr Merle D'Aubigné, from the Geneva School of Theology, were solicited to verify this.[115] The analogy of being trapped inside a burning house was often quoted in this context. Surely, in this situation, it was only natural to cry out for help. Evangelicals argued that the same held true for the conviction of sin. How could individuals who had come to the terrible realisation that they were going to hell resist crying out for help?[116] Still other supporters refuted criticisms on the basis of personal observation. Reverend Charles Kirtland attended a monster revival meeting in Armagh in September and from what he witnessed, he believed there was no attempt to create artificial excitement. While he did see some prostrations, there were no fits or convulsions as he had been led to believe would be present. He could not believe this was what E.A. Stopford had described as 'the morbid action of disease' because he found the spiritual tone of the meeting perfectly acceptable.[117] Reverend G.V. Chichester also rejected Stopford's comments based on his own experiences in Ireland.[118]

These examples show evangelicals defending the existence of physical phenomena as a central part of the revival experience. Other British evangelicals, however, made no secret of their dissatisfaction with the physical concomitants of the Irish revival. Those who wished to endorse the revival's positive results frequently adopted a position which sought to distance the ecstatic behaviour from the rest of the movement. For example, the Reverend G.V. Chichester, in his defence of the revival, rejected the importance of prostrations when he stressed the predominance of conversions which had taken place without any such visible signs. Evangelical ministers, generally more concerned about propriety and proper conduct than their congregations, were initiating a process which resulted in the eventual elimination of physical manifestations from the accepted definition of revival. In doing so, British evangelicals resolved their dilemma by creating a new definition of revival which was acceptable to them. If physical prostrations were no longer characteristic of a revival, then it was perfectly logical for *Evangelical Christendom* to say concerning the progress of revival in England that 'the same power is at work as in Ireland, though manifested in a more settled and quiet manner'.[119] The power was the same, but the manifestation was different.

A similar alteration of perception occurred in the area of the revival's claimed social reforms. Again, based on statistics from the *Northern Whig*, *The Times* published what it considered to be proof that the revival had not reformed society in any substantial fashion. In fact, the revival had 'increased to a very considerable extent the ratio of drunkenness, criminal offences, and personal misconduct' in Ulster.[120] Such accusations were vigorously refuted in a dispute which raged off and on over the following six months. As with the debate over physical prostration, the critics had the advantage. Unlike their evangelical opponents, they had no vested interest in seeing the revival succeed and were not implicated if it failed. British Christians who had associated themselves with the revival were once again forced to defend a position which they most certainly had doubts about themselves. Their first reaction was to refute the *Whig's* statistics and offer their own tabulations of criminal incidents and cases of drunkenness.[121] As one minister boldly pointed out

> even were these figures correct they would not warrant such a conclusion, [that the revival had increased crime] for the frequenters of the police-courts, were not, to any extent, affected by the movement, and until it can be shown either that the religious revival produced this drunkenness, or that the drunkards had been brought under its influence, the argument is of no value.[122]

Expostulations of this nature, however, were in direct contradiction to countless claims made by evangelicals that, in fact, the revival had deeply affected even the most wicked members of the community, including drunkards and other reprobates. The need to defend the revival had its supporters running in circles. Like the physical manifestations, personal testimony was used as a weapon of defence. In this case, *The Revival* formally urged its readers to compile their own statistics on the revival's moral results, to write them down, along with their personal impressions and have them validated by a magistrate, police official or clergyman.[123] These testimonies flooded in to British newspapers over the succeeding months. Benjamin Scott's book, *The revival in Ulster: its moral and social results* (1859) was a compilation of testimonies from a range of eminent individuals with the one intention of proving the good results of the revival. The most common reaction of revival supporters was to blame the increasing crime levels on the growing proportion of Catholics in Belfast, saying they had been relatively unaffected by the revival.[124] The response of the *British Standard* was more blatantly sectarian. Referring to the increase in gaol committals in 1859, it declared 'How far the priests themselves may have contributed to bring this about – which is an easy matter – we cannot tell; but it may have proceeded from other causes.'[125]

Evangelicals were also sensitive to criticisms about the long-term status of revival converts. During the course of the revival, there had been grand claims about the considerable number of individuals who had experienced conversion at the various revival meetings and gatherings. Indeed, numerous conversions were one of the indicators a real revival was in progress. Those critical of revival excitement believed conversions obtained under such circumstances would not be permanent and would not last. Evangelicals, of course, were stung into a response. Some clergymen, like the Reverend John Venn of Hereford, made a second trip to the north of Ireland to satisfy themselves and others that the conversions they had witnessed during their previous first visit were still faithful to their original commitment. As a result of conversations with local ministers, Venn returned to England satisfied that the conversions were indeed permanent ones.[126] Several years later *The Revival* once again urged its readers to send them verified reports on the progress of converts in their areas, so they could refute such criticisms.[127] As time went on, however, evangelicals were forced to admit that some converts had fallen by the wayside. This admission involved new defences and justifications of the revival's success. Backsliders were categorised as 'false' converts who had been only superficially influenced by the physical manifestations and never truly saved. Other converts were excused on the grounds that they had not received the saving influence long enough for it to make a permanent impression on their lives.[128]

When it came to the moral reform of society, the revival's efficacy was determined only by its results. The means used to achieve a revival were very controversial, so the results were an important justification of their use. If the moral improvement and conversion of sinners was determined to be false, then the entire revival could be interpreted as a hoax. Evangelicals, unwilling to accept the extremity of this position, engaged in a frantic refutation of criticism, which forced them to adopt various contradictory positions. Because of their vested interest in seeing the revival succeed, the exposure of any of its flaws created doubts and divisions among its supporters. The lack of an enthusiastic and uncritical ministry no doubt contributed to the revival's failure to make much progress in England. Evangelicals wanted a revival to operate within their preconceived notions of acceptable religious behaviour.

THE 'IRISH' DIMENSION

Because the essential character of the 1859 revival was so unusual, evangelicals were suddenly unsure if it really was the best means to promote church growth. They had a similar dilemma with regards to the location of the revival. Because it had emerged in Ireland first, it challenged their views on British national, racial and religious superiority. Their mid-Victorian perceptions of Ireland, the Irish and Catholicism created a deep-seated ambivalence about the efficacy of revivalism.

The 1850s witnessed the convergence of several strands of thought concerning Ireland and the Irish. The widespread belief in Britain that the Irish were racially inferior combined with a growing anti-Catholicism and the emergence of ethnology as a reputable science. It is against this background that the revival must be considered. The evangelical aversion to 'popery', as they called it, was a characteristic in evidence from the very beginning of the movement. In the early nineteenth century, this tendency, which had become quiet and unassuming, was stirred into action by several developments. The granting of full emancipation to Catholics in 1829 returned anti-Catholic arguments to the forefront of political debate. The growing influx of Irish immigrants to Britain stirred up fears of revolutionary tendencies, barbarism and poverty. The decision of the British government in 1845 to increase their annual grant to Maynooth College, an Irish-based training college for priests, angered many evangelicals. Even more were disturbed by the decision of Pope Pius IX to restore the Catholic hierarchy in England and Wales in 1850. This 'papal aggression', as it was known, provoked widespread public disorder and forced Lord John Russell, the then prime minister, to take action in the form of the Ecclesiastical Titles Act.[129] This anti-Catholic feeling combined with a growing interest in ethnology – the explanation of national traits on the basis of race – which was to become an increasingly acceptable part of nineteenth-century thought. Early proponents of ethnology supported the traditional view of the Irish Celt as barbaric, lawless and incurably lazy. Thomas Carlyle felt the Irish were an 'unmethodic, headlong, violent, mendacious' race, driven by the famine to emigrate to England, which they threatened to bring down to their level.[130] Other English commentators like A.C. Swinburne, J.A. Froude and Thomas Arnold expressed similar sentiments. They promoted the belief that Irish inferiority was a permanent result of biological forces; Irish mental and physical traits were responsible for creating an inferior race.[131]

The combination of Irish inferiority and anti-Catholicism in nineteenth-century thought forms an important part of the intellectual backdrop to the Ulster revival and goes some way to explaining the British response to it. With such a negative perception of Ireland and the state of its religion, many British evangelicals were surprised to hear a revival had begun in its northern province. As outlined earlier, they had expected the revival to appear among themselves first because of Britain's natural superiority as head of the empire and the protector of true religion. Part of their surprise, however, was due to their perceptions of Ireland itself. To them, Ireland was a country of 'disloyal factious Priests, and Priest-ridden peasantry' with 'political mobs, city-riots and agrarian murders' and 'too jealous and almost dangerous Orangemen'.[132] England appeared to be 'a far more fit receptacle for Divine influence, and far more likely to experience a revival which shall preclude the latter day glory, than Ireland with its poverty and Popery, with its suffering and sin'.[133] With these images of disloyalty, factiousness and priestly domination pervading their literature, British evangelicals were astonished that a revival had broken out in a country they considered so destitute of any true religion. This fact caused some evangelicals to assume the revival was a check to their national pride and a challenge to their claims of being a religious nation. 'Is it not a bold reproof for our secularity and unbelief, that we, as a professedly Christian nation, should now be dry and parched, while showers of blessing descend upon other nations whom we have been accustomed to regard with shame and pity?'[134]

While they were waiting for a revival to visit them, British Christians took consolation in the fact that a work of revival was advancing across the channel in Ireland. This represented a strong challenge to an increasingly aggressive Catholicism. 'Notwithstanding the scoffs and scorns of infidelity, and the virulent opposition of Popery and irreligion, we are happy to believe that the good work in its soberness, and as manifested by its after fruits, is progressing.'[135] Optimistic evangelicals felt the revival was making substantial inroads into the

Catholic population. One Irish minister calculated that at least 12,000 Catholics had been converted in Ulster alone during the course of the revival.[136] Popery, it was felt, would not be able to withstand the assault.

> Its hoary and gigantic walls are beginning to crumble. The power of truth shall eviscerate it with an immortal smash; its priesthood shall be made to relinquish their blasphemous pretensions; and the Beast shall die, and heaven and earth shall shout over his expiring groan![137]

When the physical manifestations started to appear, several observers feared for the reputation of the revival. To them, such ecstatic religious behaviour looked very much like popish superstition and 'miracle mongering'. The *Belfast Daily Mercury* asked:

> Are we not in Protestant Ulster? Are we among a people who pride them-selves on their mental cultivation and their abhorrence of Popish super-stitions? Do we live in Belfast that has, we may say, inherited the proud boast of being the 'Athens of Ireland'?[138]

Such antics looked like Ulster Protestants were giving in to popery rather than battling against it. British evangelicals had pitied Ireland for its spiritual desti-tution. When the revival occurred, they were forced to contend with feelings of jealousy, disbelief and the grateful recognition of the advances the revival was making against 'popish darkness'.

Negative views of the Irish as a race were well established in British thinking. The Irish people were seen to be sentimental, sensitive to emotional impres-sions, melancholic, gregarious, excitable, undisciplined and anarchic.[139] It was the emergence of physical manifestations during the revival, and the attempt to explain them, which brought out all these latent racial stereotypes in British evangelicals. Explanations attributing the manifestations to the excitable Irish character were frequently suggested. 'The Irish mind is stronger in its emotional nature than that of the English' claimed one newspaper. 'The former is impetu-ous, either for good or evil. Perhaps, too, the religious education of the Irish tends to make strong impressions on the mind, especially among the Roman Catholics.'[140] As a result, the 'peculiar Irish character' was perceived to be particularly susceptible to such emotional phenomena.[141]

As well as being ethnically prejudiced, this analysis was incorrect. The revival was not influential among the Gaelic Irish but among the descendants of the seventeenth-century Scottish Presbyterian settlers. Some reporters seemed unconcerned about the distinction. To them, Ireland was not the 'Isle of Saints' for nothing; the natives always had a stock of religious, or at least theological fervour, stronger in its manifestations than that bestowed on the cooler-headed and less easily moved Saxons. And if in recent times the zeal of the Catholic South had declined, 'in the Protestant North the flame of religious excitement [was] burning higher than ever'.[142] British opinion was mostly aware that the

Ulster Scots were not like their Gaelic neighbours. They were described as 'a cool, shrewd, practical set, in love with argumentative preaching and quiet, intellectual religionism',[143] and as 'notoriously cool, practical, money-making, and fond of disputation'.[144] The discovery that the revival manifestations were actually occurring among the Protestants in Ireland upset racial stereotypes; as one newspaper put it, the 'Scotch Presbyterians are not usually an excitable class of people'.[145] This caused a degree of confusion about where to attribute the origins of the prostrations. The 'excitable Irish character' no longer seemed valid. Some observers, as seen above, made no distinctions between Protestant and Catholic Irish. Others made a point of distinguishing between the two ethnic groups. They wanted to refute the ethnological attempts to explain revival excitement. If such manifestations

> had made their appearance among the Irish of the South, this hypothesis might have possessed a measure of plausibility. But the Irish of the North are a distinct race. They are, strictly speaking, not Irish at all. In character, habits, and origin, they are Scotch. To impute to the cold, calculating, undemonstrative people of Belfast the impulsiveness ordinarily ascribed to the Irish character, is to confound things that differ.[146]

This conclusion created as many problems as it solved, but it opened up the way for a conveniently pious interpretation. In the north of Ireland, 'where the temperament of the people, who were partly of Scotch extraction, was much colder than that of the south,' the physical manifestations had been widespread, 'as if to disprove the assertion that the movement was of mere human origin'.[147] It seemed as if the only remaining explanation for the revival was that is was an act of God.

Ethnological arguments such as the ones quoted above were not used in any systematic fashion during the course of British debate on the revival. They were a reflection of general mid-Victorian attitudes towards Catholicism and the Irish people. British evangelicals already perceived Ireland as a backward and poor country, dominated by a tyrannical religion. That it had been blessed with revival aroused their interest and forced them to reconsider their preconceived notions of Irish inferiority. The outbreaks of physical manifestations, however, supported their original suspicions. By blaming them on the excitable Irish character, British evangelicals could explain away one of the major stumbling blocks to full acceptance of a revival in England. But what about the Ulster Presbyterians? For those who recognised the distinction between these Irish Protestants and their Catholic compatriots, the Presbyterians presented another excuse for the bodily phenomena. Since ethnic stereotypes defined Ulster Protestants as rational and level headed, they could not be to blame for such religious outbursts. A divine explanation became inevitable. The Ulster revival exposed evangelical perceptions of Ireland, Catholicism and the Irish. The evidence of religious excitement combined with racial snobbery to make British evangelicals, who had been desirous of a revival for so long, suddenly develop second thoughts.

By November 1859 British popular interest in the revival began to decline, leaving evangelicals with several unpleasant realities. They recognised that the revival was over in Ireland and that it was unlikely to spread to England or Scotland. Throughout the closing months of 1859, they had waited in eager anticipation, proposing a variety of explanations for the revival's delay. After another year had elapsed, most of them realised it was never coming. Only a remnant of evangelical opinion, centred around *The Revival*, clung to the belief that the revival had actually appeared in England and that its work was continuing as much as five years later. These optimists had extended the revival's ideological metamorphosis to its logical conclusion. Uncomfortable with the physical manifestations and doubtful about the long-term status of converts, they marginalised these characteristics of revival and substituted them with activities, such as nondenominational meetings and mission work, which were more amenable to their sense of propriety and decorum. An alteration of this nature meant that British Christians could claim the 1859 revival as a success. However, even the staunchest revival supporter had to admit that by 1865 the last vestiges of the revival had passed away. Rather than fading into history, the revival became part of the regular cycle of church growth and decline. Evangelicals incorporated it into the pantheon of past revivals used to exhort and encourage during those times when Christians were expected to wait for the Lord's blessing. In some respects it might be fair to say that British evangelicals were almost happier expecting a revival than they were with actually experiencing one. The tensions and divisions which the Ulster revival provoked certainly made some evangelicals think twice before encouraging another revival. It was easier to set it up as a standard for future behaviour; it typified the excitement to be avoided in any future religious endeavours and it represented the ideal state of the church. In the decades following 1859, the revival entered the illustrious genealogy of revivals, which acted as a constant reminder of a golden age to be recreated, if only in its most golden form.

What this chapter has sought to demonstrate is that the great Ulster revival of 1859, though rooted in the Presbyterian heartlands of County Antrim, was an event of much wider significance in the history of evangelical Protestantism in the British Isles. Those English evangelicals who had spared neither effort nor money in their passion for voluntary societies to reclaim the urban poor had reluctantly come to see by the late 1850s that 'human instrumentality' of itself was not going to roll back the tide of infidelity in the great industrial wens. Events in Ulster at once intrigued, stimulated and frightened them. As they struggled to find out what had happened in 1859 they were also forced to consider why it happened and what its implications were for the future of the evangelical message in Britain. The sources indicate that what many of them really wanted was a revival that would produce greater church attendance, the reformation of manners, higher literacy rates and an obedient and God-fearing population. All could be statistically verifiable and all could be controlled by existing ecclesiastical structures. But the reports they received from Ulster did not reflect such a tidy mixture of evangelical paternalism and self-help liberalism. Instead, they had to cope with reports of lay preaching; the pivotal role of women and children; physical prostrations and a potent cocktail of visions, prophecies, dreams, miracles and stigmata. How could such things be explained? Bibles were thumbed, anti-Irish prejudice was paraded, witnesses were sought and follow-up investigations were launched. The evidence, however, was as engagingly inconclusive for contemporaries as it has been for historians ever since. The truth of the matter, however, was that English society could not be revived on the Ulster model and that the events of 1859 did as much to produce dissent in evangelical ranks as it did to boost pan-evangelical enthusiasm throughout the British Isles. The conference of the Evangelical Alliance in Belfast in 1860, as it turned out, supplied enough ammunition for both interpretations.

What is nevertheless clear from the events of 1859–60 is that there is a story to be recounted about popular Protestantism that has not yet been told by historians with sufficient clarity or sympathy, and that is the story of the decades after 1859. American evangelists, working-class men and committed women, however much marginalised by existing denominations, continued to labour in their localities for the promise of a nationwide revival which events in Ulster had promised but ultimately failed to deliver. The following chapters are an attempt to chronicle their experiences.

PART II
PROMOTERS

'Messrs Moody and Sankey at the Agricultural Hall, Islington' from the *Illustrated London News* (1875)
(With permission of the Illustrated London News Picture Library)

CHAPTER THREE

American revivalists

IN 1875 *The Times* reflected on the recent spate of farewell meetings being held in honour of Dwight L. Moody and Ira D. Sankey, American evangelists who had been conducting a successful revival campaign in Britain and Ireland over the preceding two years. The reporter began by stating what he believed was a common perception among Victorian churches: that the religious life of the nation was 'stagnant'. 'The complaint is general,' he wrote,

> that our churches and chapels, save in exceptional instances, are not crowded, and least of all by workmen. 'Sunday tourists', 'Sunday ramblers', 'Sunday drinkers' have become the horror of religious teachers of all denominations. Many a good man and many an 'indifferent' man among those teachers has long been in despair as to the future of Christian preaching and what is called 'ministerial influence'.[1]

Confronted with this growing problem, these 'religious teachers' had set about making religious services more attractive. Shorter meetings, with more variety and livelier singing were tried. Better training for preachers and the provision of morally uplifting entertainment were tested. To *The Times* reporter, though, what all these efforts indicated was that 'men engaged in active religious work are at their wits end to discover some means to fill their respective places of worship or their lecture halls'. Of course, Moody and Sankey had been filling churches and civic halls for the past two years, and so *The Times* argued, 'religious teachers' ought to investigate this movement.

> It may sound well to say that large congregations are not the great end of preaching, as undoubtedly they are not, but a congregation of some kind is the first preliminary of preaching; you must have people to preach to, and, granted other conditions, the larger the congregation the better, we should say.[2]

In this statement the blunt, pragmatic goals of the writer coincided with those of a large number of British evangelicals. Both of them desired large congregations and were concerned by the trend towards non-attendance at church.

As *The Times* reporter so astutely realised, British evangelicals in the late nineteenth century were very concerned about what they perceived to be the rapid loss of the working classes to organised religion. Such fears were seemingly confirmed by the results of the religious census of 1851, which clearly showed that the urban working classes did not attend church regularly.[3] Evangelicals became increasingly preoccupied with the issue of 'how to save the masses' and how to prevent spiritual decline. Revivalism seemed to offer the perfect solution. It symbolised an increased interest in religion and stimulated the mobilisation of a community around a church. As a result of the numerous religious meetings, many people were converted and young, enthusiastic converts revitalised their congregations. Ultimately, a revival also promised the moral transformation of society, as large sections of the population abandoned their sinful lifestyles in favour of a respectable religiosity. Part of the attraction was that these changes took place over a short period of time. Therefore, it was not surprising that by the end of the nineteenth century revival meetings, stripped of their controversial and subversive elements, had become popular with a variety of denominations as a means of reinvigorating their religious life. *The Times* commented:

> Every sect has had its Revivals. The Roman Catholics have theirs under the name of 'Retreats' and otherwise, as a systematic part of religious life. The Ritualists have had theirs with an elaborate religious machinery never before known among Protestants in England. Lastly, the 'Evangelicals' have had theirs with the attraction of converted prize-fighters, ex-publicans, and we know not what.[4]

In theory, this sounded like the perfect methodology. The reality of using revival as a strategy for church growth was much more problematic. Reverend R.W. Dale, the eminent Birmingham Congregationalist, eulogised the benefits a revival could have on society while inadvertently pointing out its inherent dangers. In what was to be hailed as a prophetic article, he discussed the desire for revival which seemed to be gaining in popularity. When the Holy Spirit manifested its power, he wrote, as in a revival, 'the thin veil which separates us from the invisible and eternal world is rent, and the terrors and glories which it concealed are no longer the objects of faith; they are almost visibly revealed to mankind'.[5] Revivals, therefore, had the potential to reach the unsaved and to renew churches and their congregations and give them the spiritual power, under clerical leadership, to transform society. However, revivals could also unleash the potentially destructive forces of religious enthusiasm and disregard for church order.

As the nineteenth century progressed, fewer and fewer Victorian evangelicals were prepared to endorse the chaos and confusion which a revival represented. Thus, in this period there was no outbreak of an eighteenth-century style spontaneous revival on a national scale, although there were a series of small, localised revivals which often manifested the traditional revival characteristics of enthusiasm, frequent meetings and social change. For the most part, then, late nineteenth-century revivalism can be defined by its planned and organised nature. Most evangelical churches had an annual revival 'week', during which a professional evangelist would be brought in to conduct daily gospel meetings in an effort to reach the unsaved. Various preliminary work would have been undertaken, such as noon prayer meetings, house-to-house visitation and the distribution of handbills, in order to prepare the community for the impending 'revival'. Once underway, these revival 'missions' or 'special services' were generally uneventful, following the traditional pattern of hymn singing, prayer, gospel message and invitation. Depending on the church, penitents would be invited to approach the altar rail to seek forgiveness of sins, or to enter an inquiry room, where their queries would be dealt with by trained counsellors. For the most part, audiences were composed of church members and thus, the number of conversions tended to be quite small. Rather than coming from the ranks of the unsaved, these converts were more than likely to be the children of existing church members. Accounts of these services often describe the atmosphere as 'intense' or 'deeply moving', but only rarely allude to the presence of physical manifestations or verbal utterings. Technically, these services were not revivals. Instead, they were meetings which were meant to spark a revival, and as such were sometimes called 'missions' or 'special services'. However, Victorian evangelicals regularly referred to these efforts as 'revivals', thus reflecting their increasing association of 'revival' with the orderly and the respectable.

One of the most important features of this late nineteenth-century revivalism was the growing prominence of the professional evangelist. In the 1859 revival, there had been no special class of spiritual leaders. Local clergy and laity provided the leadership for the various meetings. In the years thereafter, evangelical churches in Britain and Ireland increasingly relied on full and part-time evangelists to promote revival enthusiasm among them and their communities. As the century progressed, these evangelists were more than likely to be lay people. It was not until the later nineteenth century that established denominations were prepared to set aside individual clergymen to be full-time evangelists. In 1862 the Reverend William Booth, who would go on to found the Salvation Army, left the United Methodist Free Church (UMFC) because it refused to sanction him as a full-time evangelist.[6] It was not until 1882 that the Wesleyan Methodists set aside the Reverend Thomas Cook as their first 'connexional evangelist'.[7]

Lay evangelists suffered from no such denominational obstacles. Providing they could raise the financial support they required, lay people were free to preach wherever they were invited. Depending on their background and gender, lay evangelists either preached to the full spectrum of the evangelical community or else within a particular region or denomination, or to a particular class of people. Middle-class evangelists, like Reginald Radcliffe and Henry Grattan Guinness, conducted revival services under the auspices of a number of different denominations, to a variety of different classes, in venues throughout Britain and Ireland. Lord Radstock, however, one of the few members of the gentry class who pursued a preaching career, restricted his services to Europe's aristocrats, and specialised in efforts to bring evangelical Christianity to Russia's social elite.[8] Those evangelists most likely to restrict their geographical scope were of either a working-class origin or were women. Working-class evangelists were often local preachers within the various branches of British Methodism, who had a full-time occupation but preached regularly within a particular locality. However, there was a large group of working-class evangelists who were engaged in full-time religious work, and travelled extensively throughout the country conducting revival services. This group will be discussed in more detail in Chapter 5. Women formed a significant, if numerically small, minority of lay evangelists who were active in the late nineteenth century. Although very few achieved more than local notoriety, there were, in certain areas, well-established traditions of women conducting revival services in front of mixed audiences (see Chapter 4). Another small but important group of lay evangelists present in Britain and Ireland in the late nineteenth century were Americans, the most famous of whom were D.L. Moody and I.D. Sankey. It is a discussion of their contribution to British and Irish perceptions of revivalism which is the subject of the remainder of this chapter.

Richard Carwardine has well documented the impact of Americans on the development of early nineteenth-century revivalism in Britain. Beginning with the Methodist Lorenzo Dow in the early 1800s, a steady stream of evangelists from the United States brought their own version of evangelicalism to British audiences. James Caughey and Charles Grandison Finney were the next to arrive, in the 1840s and 1850s. These two men, along with Phoebe Palmer and her husband Walter, and Edward Payson Hammond, comprised a significant group of Americans in Britain during the revival years surrounding 1859. Their popularity among British evangelicals suggests the growing prominence of the evangelist in British denominations. Unlike native evangelists like Richard Weaver or Brownlow North, who operated independently of denominational control, the Americans were essentially rooted in denominational work. James Caughey and Phoebe Palmer preached almost exclusively for the Methodists, concentrating on the Wesleyans but spending increasing amounts of time with the UMFC. E.P. Hammond was a Congregationalist, but conducted most of his services for the Free Presbyterians and Charles Finney, despite shifting allegiances several times, always conducted his meetings under the auspices of a local church. It is true that these Americans conducted united prayer meetings and committees made up of several denominations often sponsored their visits but, as Carwardine has pointed out, this sort of cooperation between the churches meant 'interdenominationalism, not extradenominationalism'. Most of this American activity was distinct from the nondenominational evangelistic efforts of, for example, William Carter and his wife, who conducted mothers' meetings and preaching services in the theatres of London.[9] Like their British and Irish counterparts, these American evangelists in general failed to attract converts from outside the established evangelical network. Unable to attract the destitute and the socially marginalised, audiences were composed primarily of 'congregational converts', an 'unregenerate but evangelically minded group of church adherents', which included the respectable working classes and a sub-stantial proportion of the middle classes.[10]

During the mid-1860s British and Irish evangelicalism was in the throes of a post-revival slump. By 1866 the last American, James Caughey, had returned home and revival activity of the native variety was at a low ebb. Interest from across the Atlantic picked up towards the end of the decade with the arrival of Philip Phillips and more significantly a young D.L. Moody. The revival efforts of the early 1870s were very different from their American and British ante-cedents. Moody's evangelistic campaign of 1873–5 was a model of middle-class respectability and religious order. The events surrounding Moody's British and Irish campaign have been widely recorded in numerous biographies, mono-graphs and theses.[11] One of the more skilful analyses is by John Kent. He argues that although the 1870s represented the high point of evangelicalism's influence on Victorian society, Moody and Sankey failed to reproduce their Scottish successes in an English context. Their goal of 'mass revivalism' and their attempts to turn regional campaigns into a 'national movement' failed for a number of reasons. Because Moody alienated certain elements within the Church of England, such as the Anglo-Catholics, and cultivated the support of prominent Nonconformist disestablishmentarians, his campaign had 'meshed with a sectional impulse, not an ecumenical one'.[12] In other words, they failed to gain the support of the Anglican church, support which Kent feels was crucial to the success of a national religious movement. Another determinant of success was the ability to reach the London poor. Kent claims that Moody failed to establish a substantial following among the working classes and cites evidence of complaints from the central organising committee about the middle-class nature of the Islington meetings and Moody's own reluctance to preach in the East End.[13] Kent's analysis of Moody and Sankey and their relationship with English evangelicals is a sophisticated one and offers numerous insights. But I do not think it represents the full complexities of Moody and Sankey's impact on Britain and Ireland as a whole. What I hope to do is to use these Americans as a way of looking at a variety of religious agendas in Victorian society. Moody and Sankey's campaign will initially be examined as part of a long-standing tradition of American revivalists in Britain, with a brief survey of their similarities and differences.

American evangelists, from Caughey to Moody, reflected the diversity of religion in their native country. They represented different denominations, had different styles and experienced different levels of success. Their British experi-ences, although separate and distinct, bound them together into a group that was to have a long-lasting effect on British revivalism. As Americans, they were shocked by British poverty, suffered from homesickness, preached temperance, and struggled with denominational restrictions. When Charles Finney worked for the UMFC in the East End of London, the plight of the inhabitants, their poverty and insufficient housing moved him deeply, although he never initiated any sort of social work among them. Moody had similar feelings when he came to Britain, speaking publicly about the terrible conditions of the urban poor and demonstrating the culture shock many of these Americans experienced when they encountered the negative results of British industrialisation. His wife Emma wrote:

> [Moody] is now preaching in a very poor district of Glasgow and among such people as you have never seen. It would make your heart ache to see the wretchedness that is here ... People in Northfield would hardly imagine such wretchedness as is to be met with here in the poor parts of the large cities.[14]

A logical outcome of this cultural encounter was the homesickness which many American evangelists frequently experienced. This was the natural result of an itinerant lifestyle which involved long periods of time spent away from home, family and friends. In the early days of Phoebe Palmer's ministry she travelled alone, without her husband or children. During her tour of England and the north of Ireland, the children were also left at home and although older (in 1859 they were aged 25, 19 and 16) it was apparent that she missed them a great deal. Because of 'our dear ones at home, and yearning for the work there' she had twice been tempted to abandon the Lord's work in Britain and return to America, only to remain because 'we could not feel quite sure it was at the Master's bidding'.[15] Moody, on the other hand, always brought his family on tour with him, although they did not travel as extensively as he did. Often Emma and their three children would stay in London, where she had relatives, or spend time in France to recover from their frequent illnesses. During these times Moody felt their absence quite strongly. In 1884 he wrote to his mother, 'Emma [his daughter] is with me and is quite well. Willie I trust is better by what my wife writes about him. Paul is also well and happy. I am in hopes I can get them with me soon. It seams [sic] a long time to have them a way from me ...'[16]

Apart from family ties, there was also the ever present tug of work which had been left at home. Finney constantly received letters from Oberlin College begging him to return, requests to which he eventually succumbed. Phoebe Palmer also missed her work. When she left New York, she had been at the centre of the American revival there and although she was experiencing success in Britain, it must have been difficult to be so far removed from that vibrant evangelical scene. Moody's home and farm in Northfield, Massachusetts were a constant theme in his correspondence. As he wrote to Willie from England, 'As Spring comes on I long to get home and to get in to the green fields and see what is goin' on.'[17] He was eager for any news from home and repeatedly asked people to write and keep him informed. He also filled his letters with advice to his brothers on the proper maintenance of the Northfield farm. A cutting from a local newspaper usually sufficed to relate any evangelistic news.[18]

For American evangelists who were married, their partners played a significant role in their public ministry. Elizabeth Finney publicly assisted in revival work and, in reference to the meetings she conducted for women, was once described as 'equally efficient with her husband'. While Finney encouraged her to pursue this ministry, there was no question about her position in relation to his work. 'Strictly confining herself to the sphere of a true lady according to the notions of woman's place', British observers saw her efforts as subordinate and respectable.[19] There were some fears that 'what has been heard in England of "woman's rights" ... on the other side of the Atlantic has created a prejudice against this particular form of usefulness here', but in general English evangelicals felt Mrs Finney's work was separate from these 'eccentric exhibitions'.[20] Such a public role may have been unusual, but because she never addressed mixed audiences, her efforts were viewed in the context of acceptable female religious behaviour. Phoebe Palmer, unlike Mrs Finney, preached to mixed audiences and was the dominant partner in her marriage. It was her husband who had given up his lucrative medical practice in order to accompany his wife to Britain. The interest surrounding Phoebe's public preaching placed Walter's address and gospel call in a merely supporting role.[21] In contrast to these partnerships, Moody's wife Emma was totally uninvolved in the public side of his evangelistic work. All accounts describe her quiet, reserved nature and her literal hatred of any remotely public role to the point that she rarely participated in the inquiry rooms. Emma's deep influence on Moody's personality, however, has been widely recognised. She was a constant support to him and he, in return, relied on her judgment and her calm, moderating influence. She was better educated than her husband and her knowledge of English society helped him gain his initial contacts there. Behind the scenes she was an active participant in Moody's work, writing letters, maintaining the finances and entertaining guests, all of which were important, if less visible, tasks.[22]

Another characteristic these American evangelists shared was their promotion of temperance. James Caughey, although not as moralistic as some American Methodists, was a firm believer in total abstinence and encouraged it among church members and penitents. In England his position was well known through the series of lectures he gave in Sheffield's Primitive Methodist chapel. Some of Caughey's Wesleyan supporters had difficulty accepting this position, believing as they did that total abstinence was unscriptural and associated with political radicalism.[23] Finney showed no interest in social or humanitarian activity and avoided the public discussion of issues such as slavery. He did, however, address the issue of temperance, mainly because the drink culture was so much more prevalent in Britain.[24] Phoebe Palmer was appalled at the difference in attitudes between British Christians and Americans on this subject. To American Christians any sort of alcoholic consumption was considered wicked and total abstinence was the norm. In Britain, however, Christians still talked about alcoholic beverages as gifts from God, and considered them acceptable as long as not taken to excess. 'I do not speak chimerically,' she once wrote, 'but really words of truth and soberness, when I tell you that it is in some religious circles regarded as a praiseworthy example to take moderately, and show thereby that the "good creature" can be taken without going to *excess*; that is, actual drunkenness.'[25] Once again, it was liberal Wesleyan supporters who balked at the extremity of her views. Knowing her position, some of the Methodists in Stroud put pressure on her to modify her beliefs. As she later recalled, 'it was not without a struggle that I held on to the shield of faith; but it was the fight of faith … and, as fighting implies *conflict* … I was more than conqueror'.[26] Phoebe felt that revival success was directly linked to total abstinence. In Windsor, although the Wesleyans were a very weak presence in the town, the relative failure of their meetings was attributed to the subsequent discovery of alcohol in the chapel basement. Victory was only achieved once the offending spirits had been removed. Similarly, when she discovered a circuit steward in Poole to be a maltster, after much soul-searching she gave one week's notice of their intended departure. The crisis this caused in the congregation forced the steward to resign and eventually to leave the church. Within a week of his departure, the Palmers claimed twenty new members had joined as a result of their meetings.[27] By the 1870s total abstinence had become much more acceptable in British and Irish evangelical circles. Moody was frequently asked about his position and in Dublin he stated clearly 'I stand on the teetotal platform fair and square', a response which elicited a hearty 'Hear, Hear' from his audience.[28] Although firm in his beliefs, temperance was not a prominent part of his early British campaign, assuming greater importance only in America, where temperance meetings were incorporated into his revival campaigns.[29]

A final similarity between these Americans, and one which illuminates much of the following discussion, was the struggle many had in relating to their host denominations. As has been pointed out earlier, these early American evangelists operated mainly within a denominational hierarchy. The response of the denominations was similar. At first they were willing to support an extra revival work, but over time they grew more hesitant. They no longer saw revival as a supplement to their denominational efforts, but as a threat to their hegemony. This point is well illustrated in the careers of Caughey, Palmer and Finney.

James Caughey visited Britain four times between 1841 and 1866, but his greatest success occurred on his first visit (1841–7), when he preached in the northern industrial towns like Leeds, Manchester and Sheffield. As a minister in the Methodist Episcopal Church (MEC) in America, Caughey arrived in Britain without an invitation and proceeded to conduct his meetings among the Wesleyan Methodists. There was a great deal of debate surrounding his activity. As Wesleyans had grown in prosperity and respectability, they increasingly rejected the noisy and chaotic methods which Caughey espoused. In 1846 the Wesleyan Conference passed a resolution requesting the MEC to recall Caughey to the United States. Two days later, in a confusing series of events, Caughey found himself the victim of a presidential decision to exclude him from all Wesleyan pulpits. In this debate the concerns about Caughey's activities centred around the issues of connectional discipline and ministerial authority, which would re-emerge in the Methodist schism of 1849–50. As Carwardine has pointed out, 'the conflict caused by Caughey and by his revivalism, then, was both prophetic of and contributory to the great upheaval in Wesleyanism'.[30] Revivals fostered an individualism in spiritual affairs which could easily get out of control. For Wesleyans, far from bringing peace and cohesion to the denomination, Caughey brought 'aggravation, divisiveness, and an unsettling passion for souls'.[31]

Similar tensions accompanied the activity of Phoebe Palmer and her husband Walter. Well known in Britain for her holiness publications and success as a revivalist, Phoebe visited Wesleyan circuits in Ireland and England between 1859 and 1863. Although Wesleyans had formally prohibited women from addressing mixed audiences in 1803, Phoebe encountered little opposition to her revival meetings. Indeed, she received so many invitations from circuits eager to benefit from her preaching that she decided to turn down offers from larger towns in order to work in smaller circuits where the work was struggling.[32] However, in 1862 the Palmers became the victims of similar concerns which had resulted in the expulsion of James Caughey over ten years before. The Wesleyan conference, concerned about its lack of control over these Americans and disturbed by the lay status of these 'extra revival efforts', passed a resolution requiring superintendents to exclude persons 'not amenable to our regular discipline' from their pulpits.[33] Writing to a friend in America Phoebe asked, 'would you think it possible that a *Wesleyan* minister could assume an attitude *against* Revivals?'[34] Her exclusion was a reflection of the ongoing difficulties English Methodists had with American revivalists. For both Phoebe Palmer and James Caughey, these denominational restrictions did not unduly hinder their work. Caughey found a willing audience in the Primitive and United Methodist churches and remained in England for a further ten months after his Wesleyan confrontation. Phoebe took a similar approach, working for another year in the UMFC and Methodist New Connexion chapels of towns like Walsall, Wolverhampton, Liverpool, Louth and Southport.

While Caughey and Palmer struggled with the restrictions their sponsoring denomination placed on their efforts, Charles Finney experienced difficulties in other ways. Although he was a Congregational minister, during his first visit to Britain in 1849–51, his co-religionists there were suspicious of his theology, as set out in his *Systematic theology* (first published in 1846–7), which argued that man was a 'free moral agent with a moral obligation to repent'.[35] Finney also discovered that English Baptists and Congregationalists were not as committed to revivalism as their American counterparts. Such a lacklustre response did not bode well for Finney's subsequent visit in 1859–60. On this second trip, he no longer had the support of some earlier advocates, several of whom were distracted by other interests. His theology also came under increasing attack. Reverend John Campbell, a previous supporter and editor of the *British Standard*, closed his pulpit to Finney and allowed those critical of Finney's views to challenge him in print. Without the support of influential Congregationalists, Finney was forced to rely on friends like James Harcourt, a Baptist minister in

London, to provide him with preaching engagements and to operate in other denominations that were more receptive to his views. Finney, therefore, conducted revival meetings for the UMFC in East London, the Evangelical Union (Morisonians) in Scotland and the Methodists (with some Congregational support) in Bolton. Not only did this changing allegiance prevent the development of a coherent campaign, but it also opened Finney up to the vagaries of denominational hostilities. When he associated himself with the Evangelical Union, he was immediately branded by other Scottish denominations as a revival enthusiast and they refused to have anything to do with him.[36]

Moody's position with regard to British evangelical denominations was different from these early Americans, although this did not mean his relationship with them was trouble free. Part of Moody's struggle to gain the acceptance of British and Irish denominations came as a result of his involvement in Christian activity which operated outside of denominational control. As a young man, Moody had had no particular allegiance to any denomination. Raised a Unitarian, he attended, after his conversion, both Baptist and Congregational churches. After moving to Chicago he associated himself with a Methodist Sunday school and eventually set up his own independent church. Alongside this disregard for denominational loyalty, Moody was active in the YMCA and the American Sunday School Movement, two organisations which operated independently of any single denomination. On his earlier visits to Britain (in 1867 and 1872) Moody met with the leaders of these two movements. George Williams, the founder of the YMCA, invited him in 1867 to give lectures on setting up noon prayer meetings and hosted a farewell meeting for him.[37] The Sunday School Union invited him to their 1867 Annual Conference to lecture on the conduct of American Sunday schools and their use of music.[38] As a skilful exploiter of evangelical networks, Moody quickly made friends with other important evangelicals such as R.C. Morgan and the Reverend William Pennefather, an Irish Anglican and founder of the London-based Mildmay Conference, which Moody addressed in 1872.[39] These preliminary visits allowed Moody to set up valuable contacts that would guarantee British support when he returned to conduct a full-scale campaign. Moody's background in extradenominational activity gave him a casual attitude towards denominationalism which, on his first extended campaign, caused unexpected problems with the British evangelical community. In general, their conservative attitudes towards revival methodology and evangelical doctrines conflicted with Moody's pragmatic and flexible approach. In this chapter two basic aspects of this clash of identities will be examined. First of all, differing perceptions of proper religious behaviour contributed to the impression that Moody was a vulgar and tasteless preacher who debased all that British evangelicals held sacred in his quest to save souls. Much of this discussion will be based on evidence taken from Moody's English campaigns. Secondly, Moody's impact will be examined from a regional perspective. Evangelicals in different parts of the country responded to Moody in different ways, depending on their own religious predilections.

Issues of clerical-lay relations, ability to reach the working classes, proselytising Catholics, denominational infighting and revival innovations bothered evangelicals in some regions more than others. John Kent has, on the basis of evidence from London, painted a tidy picture of Moody's popular success and institutional failure. Such a picture obscures the true diversity and fragmentation of the late nineteenth-century evangelical landscape.

THE CONFLICT OF TWO IDENTITIES

Much of the debate surrounding Moody's British campaign focused on his distinctive preaching style. Responses were diverse and reflected the ambivalent attitudes the British religious community had towards an individual who challenged their perceptions of proper religious behaviour, raised questions about recent developments in revival methodology and revealed their anxieties about the religious future of society. The difficulties stemmed from two very different perceptions about the nature of religion. British denominations believed that public worship ought to maintain certain standards of decorum and propriety and that conversion was a solemn event with doctrinal implications. This caused them to view Moody's efforts – with his poor grammar, American accent, sentimental stories and simplistic conception of conversion – as not only vulgar and uncouth but also in opposition to the right means of propagating the gospel. At the same time, there were those who were more pragmatic and believed the potential gains in church attendance and individual conversions which Moody's preaching promised justified the support of such a questionable style. The pragmatic were willing to accept certain deviations from acceptable religious practice as long as the renewal of individuals was the result. The traditionalists, however, imbued religious practice with such a sacred import that to alter the structure in any way – in other words, to popularise it – meant destroying the entire edifice. Moody's preaching offers the historian a way of viewing these two different identities and how they overlapped and crossed denominational boundaries in late nineteenth-century Britain.

To many British evangelicals, it seemed that Moody was willing to use any means to gain conversions and all other considerations, such as propriety, reverence and proper order simply fell by the wayside. Because Moody and Sankey were Americans and because their style of conducting meetings was bold and brash, British descriptions often compared them to a circus or popular entertainment. A poem in *Punch* referred to their meetings as 'a Revival American Circus' with 'Ira Clown in the Ring'. Such a combination of religion and entertainment, the magazine argued, would anger decent people and, as an alternative, it was suggested they should join the Hengler and Sanger circus company, saying 'If [their revival campaign] didn't conduce much to edification, it would probably pay, as a good speculation'.[40] Other critics referred to the Americans as 'gigantic Barnums', showmen who had come to England to make money from the sale of their hymnbooks at the expense of the gullible locals.[41] In many respects Moody and Sankey's meetings were very much like a travelling circus. There was the advance publicity, with posters, sandwich boards and handbills. The building in which the services were held was generally secular in function and associated with other forms of entertainment, such as the Exhibition Palace in Dublin or the Royal Opera House in London. To add to the circus metaphor, Moody had buildings constructed especially for his meetings in Liverpool and London. During his 1884 campaign in London, the central committee built two portable buildings which alternated from site to site. Venues like these could be compared to the 'big top' and were specially fitted out with appropriate revival accoutrements. Outside the hall the sale of photographs, pamphlets and song-books contributed to the atmosphere of a circus sideshow.[42] Once inside, numer-ous canvas sheets hanging from the ceiling with various Bible texts on them such as 'God is love' and 'Repent ye and believe the Gospel' immediately caught the audience's attention. The long, regimental rows of chairs drew the eye to the enormous platform which dominated one end of the interior landscape. This was the centre ring. Normally about 8 to 10 feet high, it could accommodate about 100 ministers and a 200 member choir. At the front was a smaller raised rostrum, carpeted in red baize, surrounded by a red cord and occupied by the ringmaster himself. Moody also functioned as the main act with guest evangel-ists, and Sankey and the choir occupying the roles of supporting performers. For members of the middle classes Moody's revival circus was a respectable form of 'pious entertainment'.[43]

The carnivalesque element of Moody's meetings presented a serious dilemma to British evangelicals concerned with propriety and respectability. For those without such qualms Moody and Sankey were easy targets for the satires of the music hall, pantomime and composers of street doggerel. Some of the most biting satire came from *Punch*, which struck at the heart of Moody and Sankey's entire revival strategy.

> At Islington Hall those Revivalists Yankee,
> Pious pair, D.L. Moody and Ira D. Sankey,
> Are drawing, they tell us, immense congregations,
> By eccentric devotion, and droll ministrations.
> Their manner seems strangely at odds with their matter,
> The former grotesque, and most serious the latter.
> They proclaim Gospel truths, spite of grave prepossessions,
> In colloquial slang, and commercial expressions,
> State Scriptural facts in American phrases,
> And interpolate jokes 'twixt their prayers and their praises,
> Their intent is sincere – let us trust, in all charity –
> But Religion they cloak in the garb of Vulgarity,
> And, under a visor of seeming profanity,
> As comic evangelists, preach Christianity.[44]

Even the title, 'Missionaries in motley', hinted at a perception of religion which demanded propriety of methodology. Moody and Sankey were lampooned for their efforts to peddle sacred truths by using profane methods. Although masked within the satirical form, Mr Punch posed an important question when in the second verse he inquired 'Can tomfoolery kindle true piety?' Many evangelicals were asking the same question: would Moody and Sankey's performance really translate into a revived interest in religion? Would vulgarity change the habits of the nation? Moody and Sankey obviously thought so, but the criticisms they received from British commentators indicated the latter were not convinced.

The inclination to satirise these revival meetings was made all the more tempting because of the seriousness and earnestness with which Moody and his supporters viewed his techniques. At a Dublin pantomime one evening in 1875, the clown entered the stage and delivered the line 'I feel rather Moody tonight' and the pantaloon, the traditional butt of the clown's jokes, replied 'And I feel rather Sankey-monious!' Although this was a relatively harmless play on words, according to the report, the crowd jeered and hissed at the slur, rose spontaneously to their feet and sang 'Hold the Fort', a hymn popularised by the American evangelists.[45] Other attempts to poke fun at the duo were not appreciated. Mr Punch's poem received so much criticism that he was forced to issue an apology the next week saying he 'meant to criticise only their manner and style – not to doubt their motives or sincerity'.[46] This satirical humour subverted the solemnity with which evangelicals viewed the revival proceedings.

Paradoxically, humour was a prominent element of Moody's preaching style. Numerous biographical accounts portray a man with a jovial personality and an addiction to practical jokes. After hearing Moody preach, the Earl of Shaftesbury recorded with some shock, '[Moody] abounds in illustrations, and most effective ones; in stories, anecdotes, very appropriate, oftentime bordering on the "humorous", almost to the extent of provoking a laugh!'[47] Such proceedings were seen to border on the frivolous and to detract from the serious intent of the meetings. They were also perceived as cheapening the message being presented. Moody wanted to use laughter to relate to people, to attract them to his services. The satirical press found these attempts ridiculous, while British Christians considered them to be highly disrespectful and deeply offensive. Once again, differing perceptions about the suitability of revival methods created ambivalence about the validity of Moody's efforts.

Other aspects of Moody's personality and methodology revealed this ambivalence. One newspaper, when outlining Moody's first London meeting, described him as,

> not a man of much education or culture; his manner is abrupt and blunt; his speech bristles with Americanisms; his voice is sharp, rapid, and colloquial; and he never attempts any thing like finished or elaborate composition. But he is in downright earnest. He believes what he says; he says it as if he believed it, and he expects his audience to believe it ... He is gifted with a rare sagacity, an insight into the human heart, a knowledge

of what is stirring in it, and of what is fitted to impress it ... he has a deeply
pathetic vein, which enables him to plead very earnestly at the very citadel
of the heart ... he seems to rely for effect absolutely on divine power ...
Mr Moody goes to his meetings, fully expecting the Divine Presence,
because he has asked it. He speaks with the fearlessness, the boldness, and
the directness of one delivering a message from the King of kings and Lord
of lords ... With all this, there is in Mr Moody a remarkable naturalness,
a want of all approach to affectation or sanctimoniousness, and even a play
of humour which spirts [sic] out sometimes in his most serious addresses.[48]

Immediately it is possible to detect that, although admiring Moody's intentions,
there was some criticism of his accent, style of address and lack of education.
Moody was often described as 'very American', 'full of American humour', with
a 'strange Western twang in his voice' and 'transatlantic peculiarities of manner
and accent'. This negative characterisation contributed to Moody's poor
comparison with other contemporary orators like Joseph Arch, the leader of the
Agricultural Trade Union; J.P. Gough, the American temperance orator and the
Reverend C.H. Spurgeon, the minister of the Baptist Metropolitan Tabernacle
in London. 'Hundreds of Dissenting ministers in London and in the provinces
could and do deliver very superior extempore discourses' to Moody, said one
newspaper.[49] In comparison to Henry Grattan Guinness, the Reverend J.
Denham Smith and Richard Weaver, the Dublin-based *Freeman's Journal*
deemed Moody 'a complete failure'. He was 'not eloquent, but noisy; not
attractive, but amazing; not logical or connected, but haphazard and
rhapsodical'.[50] British evangelicals were used to a more educated style of
speaking and found Moody's approach unsuitable for public meetings. Part of
the problem was his delivery. As one biographer explained, 'he is very rapid, has
little power of modulating his voice, is indiscriminate in his emphasis, careless
as to grammar and pronunciation, but apparently anxious to drive every word
home'.[51] Because of Moody's poor diction and bad grammar, British evangelicals
were surprised at his level of popular success. Reverend Elias Nason
commented, 'Without learning, without pretension, without ordination even,
these two earnest men, with an eye single to the Master's service, move the minds
of multitudes ... Such grand results, from means so simple, are surprising.'[52]
Similarly, in a letter to the Archbishop of Canterbury, the Reverend James
Moorhouse remarked, 'Mr Moody's manner is conversational, careless and very
American. I wondered at first that he sh'd exercise that power over the emotions
– he obviously does.' Convinced that it was not his oratorical technique which
made him so successful, Moorhouse went on to say '[he] produces his great effect
I believe by perfect naturalness. He never aims either at vocal or rhetorical tricks,
but talks right on as if possessed by his object, in spite of his many defects gives
one the idea of perfect sincerity.'[53] Here lies the basis for much of the evangelical
support which Moody received. Although uncertain about his professional
qualifications, ministers like Moorhouse convinced themselves that at least he

was earnest and sincere. John Lobb thought that although Moody was 'a plain speaker' with 'questionable diction', his popularity was due to his obvious earnestness, naturalness and scripturalness.[54] By attributing such success to his earnest manner, evangelicals avoided the conclusion that a badly spoken American with little education could make an enormous impression on society. Success without the traditional ministerial trappings was a challenge to traditional notions of 'good preaching' and a potential threat to the necessity of ordination. As the Earl of Shaftesbury noted, just when people were beginning to teach

> the art of preaching … here come two simple, unlettered men from the other side of the Atlantic. They have had no theological training and never read the Fathers; they refuse to belong to any denomination; they are totally without skill in delivery, and have no pretensions to the enthusiastic … Are we not right in believing – time will show – that God has chosen "the foolish things of the world to confound the wise"? Moody will do more in an hour than Canon Liddon in a century.[55]

British evangelicals often used the biblical paradox of foolishness confounding wisdom to justify unorthodox activity such as lay preaching or protracted meetings. What were the benefits of ordination, Moody's supporters argued, in the face of his obvious earnestness and simplicity? Secular opinion thought this argument was ridiculous. Moody, according to one critical report, 'evidently thought that it was the chief guarantee of his and his friend's success that they had nothing to recommend them except, indeed, their nothingness' and went on to say that 'revivalists talk as if the want of learning, and the ignorance which rather boasts of want of learning, were a positive advantage in the region of faith'.[56]

Many British commentators were pragmatic enough to recognise that whatever their personal predilection, Moody and Sankey's meetings were popular with a large section of the population who consistently filled civic halls and theatres throughout the country. So while they themselves found Moody's style distasteful, many evangelicals were willing to support him in his efforts to reach the unsaved masses. Numerous accounts record their admiration of Moody's ability to simplify difficult doctrines and make them easy to understand. One London newspaper described Moody's sermons as short, 'easily understood and characterized by that dogmatic certainty so captivating to many minds'. The process of conversion, traditionally perceived as a difficult and lengthy journey, became under Moody's teaching 'remarkably easy'.[57] The obvious intent of such simplicity was to make conversion available to the greatest number of people. When addressing a meeting of soldiers in Dublin, Moody's discourse was 'even simpler in phrase than that which we have been accustomed to hear from him … To rough, uncultivated soldiers, it is useless to speak in ornate diction. Half the meaning would escape them, and the preacher would run the risk of merely exciting their wonder without touching their hearts.'[58] Moody's lack of education and his simple style, although criticised for failing to meet Victorian standards of oratorial skill and eloquence, were tolerated because members of the British evangelical elite felt that Moody's style was ideally suited to reach the lower middle and working classes. Even though they scorned his grammatical mistakes and uncouth mannerisms, they supported Moody's efforts, recognising the appeal his approach had with this element of the population.

The content of Moody's sermons and his method of recounting biblical stories and describing biblical characters were subject to the same accusations of tastelessness. Moody tried to make the truths contained in the Bible more accessible to his audiences, although he offended religious leaders by doing so. He described individuals in modern, commercial terminology or recast events into contemporary situations. Thus, when Jesus healed the blind beggar, appropriately renamed 'Mr Bartimaeus', according to Moody, his first reaction was to run home and tell 'Mrs Bartimaeus'.[59] London audiences were amused when he explained that Satan had 'met his match' in the apostle Paul[60] and when Zacchaeus, the infamous tax collector, was described in terms of a modern-day businessman.[61] America was a frequent setting for biblical scenarios. One newspaper commented, '[i]f he wants a great city, Chicago is his exemplar; if he desires to allude to a mighty man, he parallels him to the Mayor or the Supreme Judge of the American city'.[62]

While such methods seemed to attract and entertain audiences, evangelical and Catholic opinion viewed them and their promoters as overwhelmingly vulgar and unseemly. The *Morning Advertiser* felt that audiences must look with shame on the 'illiterate preacher making little better than a travesty of all they held sacred' and the *Freeman's Journal* described his illustrations as 'quips and quirks and grotesque stories'.[63] Even the Nonconformist minister, the Reverend R.W. Dale could not conceal the fact that Moody's habit of modernising biblical stories gave him great cause for concern. In one pamphlet he confessed 'at times this gave the stories a certain air of grotesqueness, but it made the moral element in them intensely real'.[64] Once again, we see the ambivalence that these pragmatists felt. They were willing to accept Moody's grotesque stories only because they increased the possibility of more conversions.

As the defining characteristic of his style, Moody's anecdotes were subjected to similar criticisms. Taken from his own experience, these stories were overtly sentimental illustrations of doctrinal issues, such as the need for immediate repentance and the sovereignty of God. Many of his anecdotes revolved around parent-child and husband-wife relationships, areas which offered numerous opportunities to exploit feelings of guilt and duty. John Kent has deconstructed many of the themes inherent in these stories. Although Moody has been viewed as moving away from the traditional hell-fire preaching of earlier evangelists towards a more 'genial gospel', Kent has shown that Moody 'played on his hearers' residual fear of Hell, on their fear of death, and on a steadily incited fear of God', and did so in a much subtler way and without recourse to the emotionalism of previous revivalists.[65] Thus, Moody did not focus on the pains of hell so much as 'the pain of the act of God which condemned one to go there'.[66] The stories of errant sons and dying unbelievers, who forced God, by the divine justice of his nature, to condemn them to hell, were the vulgar representations of this changed perspective. One example of this emotional manipulation can be found in a sermon appropriately entitled 'Hell'. In order to impress on his audience the depravity of hell (and thus the importance of making an immediate decision for Christ), Moody told a story about being outside the inquiry rooms one evening when he saw 'a lady weeping' nearby. '"I spoke to her," he said, "but a woman grabbed her by the hand and shoved her away from me."' It was the girl's mother. Moody used this incident to state:

> It is a thousand times better for your daughter and your children to be associated with Christians than it is to have them go down to death and be associated with fiends as eternal ages go on. If a young lady going home to-night should be spoken to by some drunken man, how alarmed she would be; but did you ever think in that lost world libertines and drunkards and murderers shall be your companions? ... All workers of iniquity shall be cast into the lake of fire.[67]

Moody was playing on class fears and the importance of female propriety when he used anecdotes of this nature. If young ladies were going to mix with fiends and drunkards in hell, then salvation appeared to many middle-class individuals as the alternative, which maintained a class hierarchy and protected the reputation of respectable women. John Hopps was not the only contemporary who seized upon this particular anecdote as exceptionally distasteful. He was quick to point out the significance of describing the penitent female as 'a lady' while her mother, who was opposed to Moody's efforts, was merely 'a woman'. Hopps was not offended by the gender slur, but at the class implications of Moody granting gentility to his supporters and denying it to his opponents. When it came to gender, Hopps was a traditionalist. For Moody to suggest a lady could rub shoulders with drunkards, even in hell, was to him 'a blasphemy' and the evangelist, in his opinion, should be run out of the country, followed by the 'stern sharp words of sober British sense'. He went on to declare 'it is a burning disgrace to the British people that such brutal thoughts and brutal and essentially vulgar language should be encouraged, in the name of religion'.[68]

A similar process of simplification is evident in Moody's interpretation of other important doctrines. In typical evangelical fashion, Moody dwelt excessively on the atoning work of Christ's death on the cross. In a sermon called 'The Blood', Moody portrayed the image of Christ's blood as having the power to wash people clean from sin and make them presentable to God. In a critical pamphlet, J.M. Dixon, a Unitarian, wrote, 'Is there any sense in this talk about blood? ... [It is] suggestive of the slaughter house and utterly repugnant to good taste.'[69] Moody's reliance on 'the blood' has also been interpreted as an attempt to simplify the process of conversion. His sermons were 'organized to compel the hearers to act, not just listen; they had either to agree to do what Moody was asking them to do, or deliberately refuse to do it'.[70] Salvation was attainable only through the conscious acceptance of the atonement. Moody was able to narrow the available responses down to two: either decide for Christ or actively reject him.[71]

Looking at these criticisms from Moody's perspective, it was obvious that the restrictions of the British religious establishment and its emphasis on respectability frustrated him. In a Glasgow question and answer session with local ministers, he exclaimed 'he was tired and sick of aristocratic notions – Christianity was dying with respectability … It was not respectable for them to go out into the streets and pray. What would they say at the next dinner party?'[72] Moody had no time for social niceties and the opinions of other people. To him, it was more important 'to go and work for Christ'. This rejection of acceptable class behaviour and proper conduct was seen to be a part of his American character. Some British evangelicals supported Moody's outlook wholeheartedly, but, as has been shown, the majority were more ambivalent in their attitudes.

At this stage it is necessary to point out that much of the hostility to Moody's methods and style was a result of his middle-class nature and appeal. It was generally accepted that Moody was the visible representative of the growing influence of a middle-class ethic in society. The *Saturday Review* saw him and his friends as being full of a 'smug, self-satisfied, middle-class respectability, smirkingly confident of its own spiritual security'.[73] John Kent talks about the existence of a 'social gulf' in Moody's appeal. While he might have been popular among the middle-class shopkeepers who attended his Islington Hall meetings in London, he was rarely discussed among the Victorian intelligentsia because he was a representative of 'popular religion'. They felt his approach, in its desperation to save souls, threatened to ruin religion's reputation.[74] It also compromised doctrines which they felt were unalterable. The thousands of clerks and shop assistants who flocked to hear Moody preach had no such difficulties. He embodied their values of individualism, thrift, sobriety and self help, and presented them with commercial and homely metaphors which were easily understood. The accusations of vulgarity reflected a conflict between the increasingly confident and aggressive middle class, with its pragmatic outlook on religion, and ministers, Anglicans and other traditionalists, who were unhappy with the liberties Moody was taking with a religion they felt to be immutable. Moody and Sankey, it seemed, only exacerbated differences within Britain's religious traditions concerning the 'proper' way to promote religion.

MOODY AND SANKEY: REGIONAL IMPRESSIONS

So far, this analysis of Moody and Sankey's impact on Britain has been based on a general survey of their entire campaign from 1873 to 1875, with the primary focus being opinion in England. As such, it does not take into consideration the different responses from the various regions which they visited. Each locality was different in character, and this influenced the way people responded to the evangelists' efforts. Of all the major campaigns (defined as one month or longer) which Moody and Sankey conducted during their stay, the ones held in Glasgow, Dublin and London have been selected to represent a cross-section of British and Irish society in the urban context and to serve as a means of examining the evangelical community within a predominantly Presbyterian, Catholic or Anglican atmosphere. Local evangelicals found different aspects of Moody and Sankey's methodology troublesome, depending on their locally shaped predilections. For the Americans, each city presented a different set of problems that needed to be overcome if success was to occur. The diversity of opinion within the evangelical community hampered the spread of a revival and prevented it from becoming a national movement.

GLASGOW

Moody and Sankey experienced some of their greatest successes in Scotland and both men were very fond of the country and its people. They made close personal friends and conducted extensive tours there on both of their later campaigns. Although Edinburgh was the first major Scottish campaign, Glasgow has been chosen for this analysis because the mission there lasted for a much longer period, from 8 February to 17 May 1874, and because the revival created a great deal of discussion among ministers and lay people in the popular press. An examination of the Glasgow campaign makes an accurate impression of Scottish attitudes and responses to these American evangelists possible.

The Glasgow campaign was run essentially like all of Moody and Sankey's efforts. Initially, a group of local ministers and prominent lay people would get together and issue an invitation to the revivalists to visit their city. Upon Moody's acceptance, this group formed itself into a central committee to set dates, begin preparations and organise the advance publicity. One of the first of such preparations was the establishment of a noon prayer meeting to seek God's blessing on forthcoming events.[75] When the Americans did arrive, meetings during the day were held in the local United, Free Presbyterian and Congregational churches, while evening meetings were conducted in the City Hall, the churches being used only for overflow meetings and as locations for the inquiry rooms. Support for Moody and Sankey was general among Glasgow denominations, although the Church of Scotland remained somewhat aloof. One biographer has claimed that the campaign had the public endorsement of several eminent ministers, as well as the backing of 140 churches.[76] Once into the regular routine of evangelistic meetings, Moody branched out into his specialty meetings. He gave lectures at the Free Presbyterian College[77] and held separate meetings for women, children and young men.

Throughout the three and a half months Moody and Sankey were in Glasgow, the attendance at their meetings increased. The City Hall was full from the beginning, and by the end of their stay, to accommodate the growing size of their audiences, they were forced to hold meetings in the Kibble Crystal Palace (which had a capacity of 8,000). Such a positive response indicated that Moody and Sankey were touching a sympathetic chord among the populace and that they had the full support of the entire religious community. At the farewell meeting the crowds outside the Palace were so large that Moody was unable to reach the entrance. Ever the evangelist, he delivered his sermon from the top of his carriage to a reported 20,000 listeners.[78]

Underneath all the fanfare and bombast, however, there were deep divisions within the Scottish religious community. Moody was able to paper over the largest cracks (which might explain his success), but the fundamental differences remained unchanged.

Since the 1840s Scotland had been rocked with theological controversy. In 1843 differences over a congregation's right to choose their minister had split the Church of Scotland and led to the formation of the Free Church of Scotland, a separate denomination but with a similar Calvinistic theology. Although debates over biblical criticism were becoming commonplace in mid-Victorian England, continued adherence to the Westminster Confession of Faith kept the majority of theological innovations out of mainstream Scottish Presbyterianism. Any attempts to soften the harsher elements of Calvinism were severely dealt with through the mechanism of heresy trials, which occurred periodically throughout the 1840s.[79] Although dissent within Presbyterian circles was growing more vocal, there was still a large body of traditional Calvinists who objected to any attempts to alter theology or practice. When Moody and Sankey, with their Arminian theology and unusual methods, arrived in Glasgow the murmurings soon flared up into a public controversy. Reverend John Kennedy, a strong Free Church Calvinist from Dingwall, had received a letter from a fellow religionist, then a lawyer living in Chicago, which cast aspersions on Moody's character and business dealings. Kennedy had circulated the letter among Scottish ministers for almost two months before Moody discovered what was going on. He wrote immediately to his Chicago patron and friend J.V. Farwell, asking him to endorse his work and to get local ministers to do the same because 'the man has threatened to publish the letter if I come on to the north of Scotland and I have promised to go and shall if nothing happens'.[80] The local organising committee also wrote to Moody expressing its concern, but the letter of recommendation from Chicago soon arrived and the controversy died away. The damage to Moody's reputation could have been severe. Obviously, there were certain elements of the Presbyterian community that regarded him with suspicion.

Moody and Sankey suffered criticism on other fronts besides the personal. It was in Scotland that they were criticised for their use of music. Music was an important part of the revival culture that operated in mid nineteenth-century America. Evangelists like Moody would often employ a professional singer to accompany them on their preaching tours.[81] Ira D. Sankey was born in Pennsylvania in 1840 and had been active in the American YMCA movement as a singer, choir leader and songwriter before joining Moody as his music co-ordinator in 1871.[82] While on tour in England, the two men perfected their performance. As the crowds were filing into the hall, Sankey led the choir, composed of local church members, in a few hymns. He would then open the service with a hymn which the whole congregation would sing. After that, control of the service passed to Moody, who would call Sankey back at regular intervals to lead with a solo or a song from the choir, and eventually to conclude the meeting with a final congregational hymn.[83] By the 1870s, hymns, and organs, were largely accepted within most denominations as legitimate forms of church worship.[84] Sankey's songs, however, provoked some stiff criticism. His very simple tunes, with their rousing and repetitive choruses, were considered to be more like music hall entertainment than sacred music. His lyrics, which were deeply sentimental, were criticised for promoting a cheap emotionalism.

The acceptance of hymns in Scotland had come late in the day. This was particularly the case with the Free Church, where there was still some hostility towards the use of hymns, and more particularly, organs. Sankey was therefore concerned about his reception in Scotland, and described his first meeting in Edinburgh as 'a trying hour' because so much had been said about his 'human hymns' and his 'kist o' whistles'. By using some familiar psalms throughout the service, he seemed to avoid the worst of the criticisms.[85] Similar objections had been levelled only two years earlier against another American, Philip Phillips, who had visited Glasgow in 1872. Just prior to his 'Service of Song' charity concert, the sexton and several members of the Glasgow church in which the service was being held refused to let him use his organ. Phillips was impatient with what he felt was an irrelevant objection, and denied his organ, he refused to give the performance. A compromise was eventually reached. In later years Phillips claimed that his confrontation had prepared the way for Sankey, who, after initial criticisms, found his efforts generally well received.[86]

A much more lively debate centred around Moody's theology of conversion. For Moody, faith was the central element of the conversion process, while repentance was of only secondary importance. He emphasised the will of the individual to act for conversion, and believed the process could take place instantaneously.[87] Scottish Calvinists traditionally believed in the primacy of repentance and the necessity for sinners to be fully aware of their transgressions, and to agonise over them, in order for conversion to have any meaning. Sudden conversions were thought too easy to involve a real change of heart and were thought to produce merely flaccid converts.[88] Although Moody's preaching might stimulate the conviction of sin, local commentators felt that it did not produce true repentance. Many essentials of the conversion process were being ignored, they claimed, especially the need for time to come to a full realisation of one's sins.[89] Calvinists also pointed to the importance of election; that Christ's salvation was applicable only to a limited number of individuals, known as 'the elect'. Election denied the possibility of instant conversion, but Moody was quick to recognise that even in Scotland attitudes were changing. In a sermon he made the distinction between a 'Highland' and a 'Lowland' theology: the former claiming that a sinner could be saved in six months, while the latter, which he called 'the theology of the Bible', believing that the individual could be saved now.[90] Responses to his categorisation were very revealing. One correspondent, calling himself 'A Highlander', verified the truth of Moody's distinction. Highlanders, he observed, did believe that 'Christ died for his own – viz., those whom the Father had given him before the world was' and he felt it was deplorable that such a doctrine was being ignored.[91] Contemporaries recognised the growing shift in Scottish Presbyterian thought towards a more Arminian perception of salvation. While the traditionalists remained vocal, they were rapidly becoming a minority. Apart from Presbyterian objections, Unitarians criticised Moody and Sankey's definition of conversion because it denied rationality in its appeal to the emotions. They felt that religious meetings 'got up' in a hurry were disorderly and unnatural and not indicative of a true revival.[92] Many clergymen agreed. To 'A Clerical Spectator', instant conversions indicated that people had been pressurised into a decision, a dangerous prospect for weak minds predisposed to religious mania.[93] As an English cleric described it, true conversion was 'the lifelong turning of the whole soul to God – the gradual weaning of the heart from sin. It is not a "sensation", experienced at a certain moment, when a man begins to "feel" he is a Christian, but it is the perpetual turning of the soul to God.'[94]

Arguments against the concept of instant conversion were based on particular interpretations of doctrine and reason. For high Calvinists, the Bible and its doctrines specified a limited atonement and a firm emphasis on a prolonged repentance. When Moody preached universal access to the saving power of Christ, and the possibility of experiencing it immediately, these traditionalists were outraged. Anglicans and Unitarians felt that the doctrine was a 'mischievous theory' and promoted a 'religion of sensation' totally alien to reason, the Bible and the Church. It was a delusion that they felt could be easily dispelled through educational lectures.[95] Moody's interpretation of conversion, however, was widely received in Glasgow and elsewhere. Many liberal evangelicals found themselves in the awkward position of disagreeing with Moody's theology but supporting his efforts. R.W. Dale made clear his disagreement with the Americans' representation of Christian truth, yet stressed 'it is our duty to cooperate with them heartily and frankly'.[96]

It was, however, the position Moody and Sankey occupied with regard to the regular ministry which provoked the most heated debate. Revivals had traditionally caused fears about the future of an ordained ministry and its spiritual authority. For example, ministers in the Ulster revival of 1859 had expressed serious doubts about a movement which, by encouraging lay preaching and extra-denominational meetings, they felt would negatively impact their authority and reduce denominational allegiances. When Moody and Sankey brought their revival meetings to Glasgow, clerical anxieties surfaced once again. 'A Clergyman', writing in the *Glasgow Herald*, felt that the American evangelists had not only 'superseded the pastors of the churches in this city' but had done so with the clergy's tacit support. They had admitted the condition of their churches was one which they could not deal with 'and so they have abdicated to some extent their functions in favour of Moody and Sankey ... What will come from such confessions of weakness on the part of the ministers of the Lord?'[97] Offering invitations to travelling revivalists were obviously unbecoming to men of the cloth. Ministers found the tendency of revivals to depreciate their authority and to bypass pulpit preaching particularly distressing because they felt that true success was achieved only with the support of the settled ministry.[98] Revivals that did not translate the excitement they generated into support for existing church structures were deemed a threat to the establishment, and as such, rejected.

Suspicions about revival meetings and their threat to the regular ministry were confirmed when Moody began his special meetings for young men. Special efforts directed towards the salvation of young men were becoming more common, as evangelicals believed this group was abandoning organised religion much more quickly than women. James Obelkevich, in his local study of South Lindsey, notes that by the 1870s, Lincolnshire Anglicans had drifted towards a more effeminate service and that women formed a majority of their congregations, Sunday schools and communicants.[99] Moody and other evangelists, particularly in the late Victorian period, were at great pains to promote a masculine image of Christianity, with a muscular and robust faith that would appeal to men. Moody himself presented a strong, masculine image. Standing over six feet in height, he was heavy-set, with a barrel chest, full beard and a big, hearty laugh. His beginnings as a shop assistant in a shoe store and as a travelling salesman, enabled him to pepper his sermons with illustrations from the world of commerce and industry. His involvement with the YMCA, an organisation devoted specifically to the spiritual development of young men, gave him even more experience in making the gospel attractive to men. As a result, during his British and Irish campaigns, Moody actively cultivated male interest at his meetings and instigated a special mission designed to attract them to his services. Although Moody had conducted young men's meetings as part of his campaign before, the work in Glasgow took on a new dimension. At a planning meeting at Ewing Place Congregational Church, some students from New College, Edinburgh gave their testimonies, including a young man named Henry Drummond.[100] These young men had responded with particular enthusiasm to Moody's message, especially his call to attempt the conversion of unsaved friends and colleagues. At that meeting it was decided to set up a separate branch of the work to encourage other young men to spread their faith. As a result, a number of them began to meet nightly from 9 to 10 o'clock to help each other in the work of evangelisation, or as Drummond put it, to learn how to 'buttonhole' the man in the street.[101] Soon, Drummond and several other young converts were taking revival meetings on their own and travelling to places like Sunderland to work with the converts from Moody's recent visit.[102] These meetings eventually followed a pattern. Once the main revival services were underway, Drummond and his helpers began their meetings and held them after the main service, often in a separate venue. They usually continued their work after Moody and Sankey had left, concerning themselves with follow-up visitations.

Such activity caused problems for members of Glasgow's clerical class. 'A Clergyman' speculated 'we shall soon have a well-organised band of unordained and unauthorized preachers going round on their evangelistic crusade' without any doubts about their calling or any Presbyterian supervision. To him this was an indication of 'grave disorders' on the horizon.[103] Robert Craig expressed similar fears. Young men, he claimed, were attracted to Moody and Sankey's 'republican indifference to form' and their emphasis on instant conversion. After the experience of such meetings they would, no doubt, have a reduced reverence towards ministers.[104] Behind all of this posturing was the fear of lay preaching, of untrained individuals taking religion into their own hands and spreading bad doctrine, as well as the subversion of the clerical position as spiritual guardian to the community. Even ministers favourable to a public role were worried that lay people would use their new-found authority to form their own sects and proselytise for them. 'Why need lay preachers destroy their own usefulness, and that of others, by assuming stated local ministerial functions and setting up congregations for themselves?'[105] Such activity was clearly beyond the pale of acceptable lay behaviour. Moody and Sankey, as popular laymen, were the most visible and therefore the most threatening manifestations of what many clergy believed was a growing trend.

Scottish ministers were also concerned with the impact these American laymen would have on clerical morale. 'A Clergyman' interpreted the accolades they received in Glasgow as an admission of failure on the part of local ministers to provide adequate religious instruction for their congregations and their inability to reach the unsaved masses. Such a confession of weakness could have serious consequences. As the *Christian World* pointed out:

> Christian ministers have to prosecute their toils under difficulties suffi-
> ciently great, and disappointments sufficiently depressing, at most times;
> but if, in addition to them all, they are to have the doubt suggested whether
> their work is not altogether a grand mistake, which God has chosen to
> rebuke by this striking manifestation of His power through another agency,
> the burden will, to sensitive spirits, be all but insupportable.[106]

Some ministers would interpret Moody and Sankey's success as a deliberate rebuke from God that forced them, out of sheer discouragement, to give up the ministry altogether.

To most supporters of the revival, these objections were the responses of a class of individuals who had grown too complacent in their position and needed to have their ideas challenged. The defence of Moody and Sankey's meetings, therefore, reflected a surprisingly high degree of anti-clerical feeling, expressing local lay dissatisfaction with clerical assumptions and behaviour. Numerous letters to the *Glasgow Herald* accused the clergy of being jealous of Moody and Sankey's success, of being unable to do evangelistic work themselves and fearing for their clerical dignity more than desiring to save souls. 'A Lay Worker', for example, assumed 'A Clerical Spectator', who had written critically of instantaneous conversions, was a monotonous and boring preacher and urged him to 'descend from his clerical dignity and try and do some work, instead of being a "spectator"'.[107] Another correspondent, P.F.S., lamented the overriding clerical concern for position and desire for control. ''Tis a pity,' he wrote, 'that "the cloth is in danger" should be allowed to operate on the minds of any who themselves have found "the pearl of great price", so as to make them unwilling that others should, by any instrumentality but their own, be led to share its blessings.'[108] And 'A Working Man' no doubt expressed the cynicism felt by many when he wrote:

> All the world knows that a great many of our clericals at the present day rather desire a residence in a thinly populated part of the country, near a river with good fishing, and of course a large stipend, to taking part in the work of God among their people.[109]

Thus, the laity gave short shrift to clerical protestations concerning the possible threat of revival activity.

In some respects, ministers had every right to be afraid. Revivals did, in their desire to save souls, abandon established norms and allow informal methods to gain credibility. Revivals also challenged ordination and the barricades it placed around the public preaching of the gospel. For the vast majority of Scottish clergy ordination was a licence to interpret scriptural truth and a ticket to status within a community. Lay responses to this attitude were surprisingly anti-clerical. To 'A Free Church Layman' the recent revival meetings were a very good thing. 'Nothing that has ever happened in Scotland is so well calculated to teach our clergy the evils of a moribund Church system.' Supporting Moody and Sankey would, he felt, humble those who assumed they alone held the position of spiritual guide within the Church simply because of their ordination and without the accompanying spiritual call.[110] Seemingly, lay standards for acceptable preaching were based on evidence of a divine call, not on the possession of a title or a pulpit. Some argued the apostles, and even Christ himself, were not ordained, yet were successful preachers.[111] Lay attitudes towards saving souls also reflected a pragmatism that ministers disagreed with. As Moody once argued, if the message was true and lost souls were saved, what did it matter who the messenger was?[112] The disregard for proper form made it possible for some to argue that if only one soul was converted through this unordained ministry, then the support was worthwhile.[113] Going one step further, some commentators argued that lay status was actually an advantage when trying to do this work. Moody and Sankey were able to devote themselves fully to saving souls, while the local minister had other pastoral tasks that needed his attention. They could tell anecdotes and stories to liven up their sermons without the fear of betraying a confidence or offending a church member. And because they operated outside an official denomination, they could use unconventional methods without fear of offending tradition.[114] Their lay status eliminated barriers which ordination erected. Lay people encouraged discussions about conversion, while 'the mere appearance of a white tie seems to inspire a feeling of reticence and indifference on the part of the people'.[115]

Moody and Sankey arrived in Glasgow at a time of deep division within the Scottish religious community over the issues of doctrine and methodology. According to the historian James Findlay, Moody and Sankey's success in Scotland was a result of their ability to avoid controversy and emphasise cooperation, combined with their simple, yet essentially conservative, interpretation of the Bible. This gave people a sense of assurance which the preceding years had failed to give them.[116] But however generic Moody and Sankey tried to be in their efforts to gain the broadest base of appeal, they still created controversy. The clergy worried about the erosion of their authority within the community and the laity revealed their strong anticlericalism, which made clerical fears seem reasonable. They attracted enormous crowds to their meetings in Glasgow and had the support of prominent ministerial figures, but were still objects of disagreement.

DUBLIN

After a summer spent touring the Highlands, Moody and Sankey left Scotland for Ireland, where they conducted a successful six-week mission in Belfast (September 1874). Travelling next to Dublin, for the first time they conducted a campaign in a location where Protestants were in the minority. According to the census of 1871, the Catholic denomination was the largest in Ireland, accounting for just over 75 per cent of the population, with the Church of Ireland and Presbyterians comprising 12 and 9 per cent respectively. Methodists, Baptists and several 'other' denominations together made up the remainder, accounting for no more than 1 per cent of the population. The geographical distribution of the Protestant population was heavily concentrated in the province of Ulster, where 60 per cent of Irish Anglicans and 96 per cent of Irish Presbyterians were located. Outside Ulster, Leinster had the highest concentration of Protestants, especially in Wicklow (19 per cent) and Dublin city (21 per cent).[117] By 1874, much of the Protestant population in Dublin was affiliated with the Church of Ireland, a denomination increasingly evangelical in outlook. As a small, but affluent, minority, the Dublin Protestant community had its own sense of identity as well as maintaining links to the wider evangelical network in Britain. Dublin was part of the regular evangelistic circuit followed by many travelling evangelists. Irish preachers like Henry Grattan Guinness had been popular in English circles for many years, and in exchange the English evangelist Richard Weaver had carved out a niche for himself with Dublin audiences. Henry Bewley, the coffee house magnate, sponsored an annual series of Believer's Meetings, which were well attended by leading English evangelicals like Henry Varley, R.C. Morgan (the editor of *The Revival*), and even the Reverend C.H. Spurgeon. Many ministers active in the English evangelical scene had roots in Ireland, including the Reverend William Pennefather, who had founded the Mildmay Conference and the Reverend William Arthur, a prominent Wesleyan.[118] Moody was already familiar with the Irish evangelical network in 1872 through his connections with Bewley. Indeed, Bewley is sometimes mentioned along with Pennefather and Cuthbert Bainbridge, a Newcastle wool merchant, as offering some initial support for Moody's first extended evangelistic campaign to the British Isles.[119] Because of these existing links, it was not unexpected that Moody would travel to Ireland to conduct a revival mission there.

When Moody and Sankey began their Irish tour, it sparked off the inevitable comparisons to the Irish revival of 1859. Defenders of the American revivalists were quick to qualify the comparison, saying the revival of 1874 represented only the good aspects of 1859 and praised the 1874 revival for avoiding what had come to be seen as a negative characteristic – the excitement. When Moody and Sankey arrived in Belfast, one biographer remarked:

> [s]ince the great revival of 1859 Ireland has never been so deeply and extensively moved as during the visits of Messrs Moody and Sankey. In some respects there is a marked contrast between the two awakenings. At that time there were [sic] great physical excitement and outward signs, such as loud cries, and what were termed 'prostrations', indicating inward agony of spirit and feelings of terror. In the present revival the Spirit has been pleased to move more silently, and touch the tender chords of the heart.[120]

Reverend J. Wilson, at the Convention of Ministers which closed the Dublin campaign, said that although he had found 1859 satisfactory:

> he had learned and enjoyed more regarding the truths of the Gospel within the past five weeks than ever before ... In the past the people's feelings were wrought upon, but their minds were not trained in the great principles of the Gospel. Now, Mr Moody, with Bible in hand, gave Scripture authority for everything he said. Hence this was one of the most graciously intelligent revivals of religion that ever this part of the Christian world had been favoured with ...[121]

Paradoxically, 1874 was seen as a 'better' revival because it lacked the emotional excitement, traditionally one of a revival's defining characteristics.

The whole issue of religious excitement is crucial to any discussion of revivalism. During the eighteenth century excitement was considered an essential part of revival activity. It was a sign that the old, dead religion was being reawakened to new life, a sign that converts understood the magnitude of their decision. The growing respectability of denominations that had traditionally supported revivals made ecstatic outbursts increasingly unwelcome. As a result, the physical manifestations evident in Ulster in 1859 had severely damaged the credibility of this aspect of revivalism. In the 1870s the desire to distance revivalism from its ecstatic connotations was even stronger. Moody himself was said to despise emotionalism and had made every effort to eliminate it from his meetings.[122] At a revival meeting in London, a disturbance took place in the gallery which Moody publicly declared was an attempt by Satan to draw the audience's attention away from his sermon. '"Listen to the words," he went on to say, "they are of more importance than a woman who has fainted away in the gallery."'[123] This was a major shift from the events of 1859, where prostrations in the audience were a sign of the revival's authenticity. Evangelical supporters were relieved that Moody's meetings were free of such excitement. Professor W.G. Blaikie felt that the 1874 revival was 'much more like the ordinary operations of the Church, quickened and intensified' than it was like a revival with its connotations of 'artificial excitements, loose theology, fanatical wildness, disregard of Church order and neglect of church ordinances'. In fact, the present awakening resembled 'a revival without many of the common accompaniments of a revival'.[124] But how could a movement still be a revival if several of its fundamental defining characteristics were no longer present? Evangelicals had very little trouble altering the definition to suit their changing perceptions of what was acceptable religious behaviour. They willingly placed Moody and Sankey within the revival tradition, while believing that their work simply combined the 'ordinary forces of the ministry' with 'a new evangelistic fervour'.[125] In this manner, links to past revival glories could be maintained without offending the new respectability and its stricter definition of what revivalism really meant.

Although the 1859 revival occurred mainly within the confines of Protestant Ulster, to British evangelicals Ireland and the Irish as a whole had become synonymous with revival excitement and enthusiasm. In 1859, much of the extravagant behaviour, such as trances, clairvoyance and stigmata, were blamed on the racial characteristics of the Irish, which reflected a widespread anti-Irish racism. Such criticisms were less common in 1874, but did appear in several secondary works on the period. Robert Boyd, commenting on the response to Moody and Sankey in Dublin, remarked that 'the interest was intense, but notwithstanding the excitable character of the Irish people, the work proceeded as quietly as it had in Scotland'.[126] In this sense he was correct; the Dublin leg of Moody and Sankey's Irish tour was entirely respectable and resembled their previous campaigns.

That is not to say that the Dublin meetings were free of disruption. The campaign's steering committee had booked the Metropolitan Hall for noon prayer meetings and the Exhibition Palace for the evening services. This latter building, with its capacity of 12,000, was the biggest the Americans had yet preached in and was seen as a symbol of their growing success. However, in a hall of that size it was impossible to avoid the carnivalesque overtones of their meetings. General chaos erupted outside their first meeting on 18 October as the police and hall stewards seemed powerless to control the thousands of men, women and children trying to push their way in. 'There was some stiff crushing, and ladies who came arrayed in bright colours soon rivalled their millinery by swollen cheeks and roseate noses.'[127] As a result of the poor acoustics, attempts to gain a good seat offered the opportunity for numerous disturbances, especially in the galleries.[128] With free admission and extensive publicity, the potential to attract religious fanatics and other eccentrics was another obvious risk. The Dublin meetings were disrupted several times by a man called Abraham Dowling. Dressed in a long scarlet coat with an embroidered sash and large gilt crosses on the lapels and shoulders, he walked on to the platform and tried to engage in public prayer. After his swift ejection[129] he was arrested outside the hall for causing an obstruction, while denouncing Moody and Sankey to any passers-by.[130] These disturbances forced the introduction of stewards, which in turn sparked complaints of bullying and rude treatment.[131] Filling an enormous hall caused its own problems for Moody and Sankey, forcing them to adopt an elaborate infrastructure that reduced even further the spontaneity of their meetings.

Although there was no real change in the style or conduct of the Moody and Sankey meetings in Ireland, their Dublin campaign is noteworthy for the response of the local Protestant community, and how it viewed these two Americans from their position as a religious minority. Moody was aware of this situation and made a deliberate point of emphasising the unsectarian nature of his meetings. He avoided denominational and doctrinal issues in his sermons and rarely, if ever, referred to the religious divisions in Dublin.[132] Although Moody hoped to appeal to both Catholic and Protestant communities, it was obvious his visit had a much more significant impact on Protestants, both in Dublin and in the country as a whole. Moody and Sankey's meetings operated as a focal point of renewal and encouragement for members of the small, isolated Protestant communities in the south and west of Ireland. Groups of Protestants travelled distances of over 100 miles, from as far away as Limerick and Galway, to attend the Dublin meetings.[133] Making this 'pilgrimage' to an area of Protestant strength and attending massive meetings acted to reaffirm their Protestant identity and encouraged them to return to their local communities secure in the knowledge that they were members of a vibrant religious community.

Moody and Sankey no doubt appealed to a similar feeling among Dublin Protestants, although their numbers were much higher. Members of the central committee and ministers on the platform reflected the various denominations, including representatives from the Church of Ireland, Presbyterian and Method-ist churches. For the first time since their arrival in the British Isles, the bulk of Moody and Sankey's clerical supporters were members of the Anglican church. Besides forming the largest segment of the Dublin Protestant community, they were also overwhelmingly evangelical.[134] Anglican participation in these revival meetings was correspondingly more likely and more prominent than it had been previously. Despite the refusal of the Archbishop of Dublin to attend the closing convention, at least three other bishops made an appearance at the services.[135] Apart from a doctrinal affinity with Moody and Sankey, Dublin Anglicans were no doubt eager to maintain their denominational status in the wake of the 1869 act which disestablished the Church of Ireland, a change which they had reacted to with outrage and disbelief. Their objections – that disestablishment would undermine the Church of Ireland and remove another obstacle to the spread of Catholicism – ran against the growing tide of public opinion.[136] The arrival of Moody and Sankey in 1874, therefore, allowed Anglicans to reassert themselves as a denomination and to demonstrate their ability to adjust to the difficult changes which their new voluntary position had thrust upon them.

The boost that Moody and Sankey's visit gave to Dublin Protestants must, however, be balanced against the threat it posed to denominational hierarchies. Moody's emphasis on denominational cooperation and personal dealing with souls made him open to the criticism that his revivalism 'leads to Popery or Brethrenism ... It lacks soundness of gospel truth, that middle path so carefully selected by the Church of England for her people to walk in as they journey on to God.'[137] In Dublin, however, Moody's use of the inquiry rooms did not subject him to widespread accusations of popery. Instead, it was the nondenominational character of his meetings which prompted the charge of 'Brethrenism'. The Brethren 'movement', as it was originally formed, emerged in the 1830s in Dublin, Bristol and Plymouth, primarily among Anglicans who were interested in eschatology and desired a more scriptural adherence to the concept of Christian unity. By the 1870s differences of personality and interpretation among members of the sect had led to several schisms. Although consistently small in number, the Brethren were notorious for their custom of restricting access to communion and for their rejection of traditional denominational characteristics such as a hierarchical church structure, ordination and a fixed liturgy.[138] Moody's earliest contacts with the Dublin evangelical community had been through Brethren circles, and when he started to gain public notoriety he was accused of fostering Brethren tendencies. His disregard for ordination and denomination, it was felt, had encouraged individuals to abandon traditional denominational structures. In Glasgow, grave warnings had been issued about the possible schisms that could result from Moody's meetings. Past revivals, said one reporter, had produced the Evangelical Union, Plymouth Brethren and Adventist sects, to whom 'the ordinances of the Church are of small account, and ministries of no account at all'.[139] By implication, Moody's meetings were no different. His use of inquiry rooms, it was felt, gave the members of these 'Ishmaelite Schismatic sects' ample opportunity to proselytise unwitting penitents in an aggressive fashion.[140]

In Dublin, critics likened Moody's sermons to those of the Brethren school, which 'treat the most sacred subjects with an irreverent familiarity of expression and jocularity, which is more calculated to bring religion into contempt and scorn, rather than to promote it'.[141] In a letter to a local paper, 'Zenas' directly challenged the impression, promoted by Moody's success, that 'the highest recommendation a preacher can produce is that he belongs to no church or community of any kind'.[142] Individuals converted at these meetings, he believed, would join neither a Dissenting chapel nor the Church of Ireland, but would become part of 'the inchoate masses of religionists (the weakness of Protestant-ism in Ireland) whose highest boast is that they belong to no Church on earth but who claim individually an infallibility of opinion that is only consistent with a revelation from Heaven'.[143] Was it any wonder, he mused, that Brethrenism was increasing while Protestantism (read traditional denominations) was disinte-grating? In Ireland, dismantled denominations and unordained preachers represented a grave threat to a Protestantism already weakened by disestablish-ment. The threat which Moody's preaching posed to denominational structures in general was, in the Irish context, translated into an assault on one of the fundamental pillars of Irish Protestant strength.

Moody was aware of these concerns and sought to reduce the damage by publicly denouncing proselytism. At the Convention of Ministers he declared, to much audience approval, that the only way to maintain the cooperation his campaign had fostered among the denominations (and thus prolong the success they were all experiencing) was 'each man for his own sect. The cry is "come out from the sect". But where do they go if they do? Into another sect. (Hear, hear.) Every body of believers is a sect ... I believe proselytism is the work of Satan. (Hear, hear.)'[144] Moody's policy of unsectarian meetings and his efforts to gain the support of all denominations cut both ways. As we have already seen, it encouraged and reinvigorated a disparate Protestant population which had recently suffered the blow of disestablishment. However, his approach raised the spectre of Brethrenism and therefore the possibility that converts would reject traditional denominations in favour of a more experiential religion which dispensed with ritual and ordination.

While the Moody and Sankey campaign reveals the tensions and divisions within the Irish Protestant community, it also offers an opportunity to view this religious group in relation to its Catholic counterpart. Publicly, Irish Protestants were pleased with Moody's unsectarian approach to the Catholic community. They were proud that he did not try to stir up controversy and that he deliber-ately avoided provocative language. They felt that progress had been made in civilising relations between the two groups. There was a growing recognition that the aggressive anti-Catholicism of some Protestants, especially in Ulster, was actually doing more harm than good. As one commentator observed, 'controversial and political Protestantism is in some places the very bulwark of Romanism; while Orangeism lives Ribbonism cannot die'.[145] During Moody and Sankey's Dublin visit, Protestants felt that Catholic opinion was less hostile than it had been previously. Reverend Hamilton Magee was impressed with the extensive coverage of the revival in the *Freeman's Journal* and believed it was 'on the whole, not decidedly hostile. This itself is a matter for grateful recognition.'[146] Protestant perceptions, however, did not always mirror reality. What was the response among the Catholic population of Dublin?

Statistically, in order to fill the Exhibition Hall, a certain proportion of the audience must have been Catholics. Evangelicals were keen for this to be the case, and various stories to prove that fact were often quoted. Some Catholics were said to have received permission from their priests to attend the meetings. On one occasion, two female domestic servants were said to have recognised their priest sitting several rows in front of them.[147] If the Catholic press was any reflection of Catholic concerns, a large proportion of Catholics must have been unaware or indifferent to the evangelistic movement. Their coverage of the meetings was often scanty, or, as in the *Freeman's Journal*, quite critical. The Catholic community, therefore, never expressed more than a limited approval of Moody and Sankey's visit. *The Nation* best illustrates the basic Catholic position in an article entitled 'Fair Play!'. 'Irish Catholics,' it claimed:

> desire to see Protestants deeply imbued with religious feeling, rather than tinged with rationalism and infidelity; and as long as the religious services of our Protestant neighbours are honestly directed to quickening religious thought in their own body, without offering aggression or intentional insult to us, it is our duty to pay the homage of our respect to their conscientious convictions.[148]

Referring to the recent visit of the rationalist speakers Tyndall and Huxley to Belfast, *The Nation* felt Moody and Sankey should be applauded for preventing such developments in the Protestant community. Recognition in this instance was permitted because of the threat rationalism posed to organised religion in general. Any efforts at proselytism were firmly rejected in favour of a declaration of religious toleration. 'Here we are all children of the same land. Let each one hold firmly and fervently his religious convictions, and let each and all enjoy, as they must some day, the fullest equality of religious right and freedom.'[149] Not all Catholic opinion was so moderate. The Catholic archbishop of Dublin, Paul Cardinal Cullen, in a circular to all priests, reminded them about the forth-coming collection for a Catholic university and the festival of St Laurence O'Toole. In doing so, although he did not mention the Americans by name, he urged the clergy to pray for those Catholics who had given up the articles of their faith and become 'followers and admirers in matters of religion, of ignorant converted colliers, of roving minstrels or speculating travellers'. These men were ill prepared, Cullen argued, to be spiritual leaders and were more like the blind leading the blind.[150] While Cullen's statement was not the outright ban on attendance which some Protestant sources claimed it was, it did reveal the continued existence of animosity between the two communities. Catholics were still very sensitive to any attempts at Protestant aggression.

Evangelical hopes for the Moody and Sankey meetings were never limited to the Protestant community alone. Despite the lack of overtly proselytic methods and language, it was latent in the opinions and statements surrounding Moody and Sankey that their Protestant supporters believed the campaign would spark off a mass of conversions among the Catholics of Ireland. Although this ambition was rarely vocalised, there was a constant undertone of aggression in remarks about the revival. A few individuals bluntly expressed the opinion that Moody was not doing enough to convert 'the multitudes who are lying in the bondage and midnight darkness of Rome'.[151] More often, Protestant aspirations were expressed in much subtler terms. At a public breakfast in the Shelbourne Hotel, several hundred Protestant clergy and laity assembled to thank Moody and Sankey for the work they had been doing in Dublin. The aim of the gathering was 'the encouragement of Christian unity', which every speaker reiterated was 'especially needful at the present time, and essential to the further spread of the Gospel in this country'.[152] In an address to the central noon prayer meeting in London, Dr Macloskie, secretary of the Bible and Colportage Society of Ireland, outlined the developments within the Catholic community which made the country 'ripe for a revival of religion'. The biggest factor was the positive Catholic reception of Moody and Sankey, which he saw as an implication that many of them were ready to convert.[153] Reverend W.J. Stevenson repeated this idea at the Convention of Ministers in response to the question 'What can be done to promote the work of the Lord throughout Ireland?'. For him, although Ireland was the object of grave 'misfortunes' and was virtually 'a castaway' because of her remote geographical location, the conversions which had recently taken place showed that 'Ireland can be won for Christ. Ireland shall be won!'[154] Such a victory would have to involve the conversion of Catholics, a form of proselytism that these Protestants had no difficulty endorsing. Macloskie was quite forthright when he explained, '[w]e are very hopeful of the spread of this movement over Ireland, because of its thoroughly evangelical character, and its comparative freedom from sectarian bias'.[155] Moody and Sankey, with their generic, unconfrontational style, offered a respectable, nonsectarian front to the ongoing efforts of the Irish evangelical community to convert Catholics. Thus, there was no real shift of intention, only a growing subtlety of method. Moderate Catholics, on the other hand, welcomed Moody and Sankey as a force that would revive the *Protestant* community in the face of a mutually threatening rationalism and infidelity. Any hint of proselytism was firmly rejected as 'the wretched kind of "Protestantism" that consists in wanton insult and aggression upon the Catholic poor' and 'conducts warfare on our homes and altars'.[156] This response to Moody and Sankey reveals that the new level of civility between the two communities was merely a thin veneer covering the same old anxieties.

LONDON

In the 1870s London was a vast metropolis with over three million inhabitants from all walks of life and all religious persuasions. It was very different from any of the other urban centres Moody and Sankey had visited before and an enthusiastic reception was not guaranteed. As one newspaper predicted 'it takes a great deal to move Londoners in any such manner'.[157] S.A. Blackwood, an evangelical Anglican and evangelist, noted that it would be much harder to create the necessary support for an evangelistic campaign because of the enormous size of the city and because of the nature of the Established Church.[158] The structural limitations were obvious. It was impossible to find a building large enough to contain even a small proportion of London's entire population. Even more daunting was the likelihood of gaining a broad base of ministerial support. Moody had always insisted on the unity of local ministers. His son later claimed that he had ignored earlier invitations to go to London because ministers there lacked the 'spirit of unity' which he deemed essential for success.[159] Hostile relations between the evangelical and ritualist wings of the Church of England, and between the Church itself and Nonconformists made widespread cooperation in London an unlikely prospect. Moody himself had already experienced the danger such hostility could pose to a successful mission. Prior to his visit to Sheffield, all of the Anglican clergymen on Moody's organising committee resigned when one of their brethren expressed his discontent with the proposed scheme of house-to-house visitation. Moody had recruited Reginald Radcliffe, a popular evangelist and prominent evangelical from Liverpool, to conduct a systematic visitation of every household in the Sheffield area to distribute handbills and inform people about the revival meetings. The Anglican clergyman in question had objected to the potential violation of parochial boundaries. In response, Moody cancelled his intended visit. With the situation at a stalemate, the visitation was called off and the clergy rejoined the committee, but relations remained fraught, an indication of the conflicting interests Moody was trying to appease. Nothing so embarrassing happened in London, but differences of opinion were never far from the surface. In order to rally support and answer potential objections, Moody held an introductory meeting in the Freemason's Hall on 5 February 1875 to respond to questions from local clergy and solicit support for the approaching crusade. Addressing the clerical audience, which included a group of high church Anglicans, Moody explained his proposed strategy and defended criticisms of the inquiry rooms, his financial conduct and use of an organ. When the meeting was opened for questions, the doctrinal and controversial issues which emerged revealed the disparity of opinion among London's clerical population. Despite their reputation as respectable and uncontroversial revivalists, Moody and Sankey's efforts to convert the masses continued to bring these pre-existing tensions within the London religious community to the surface. These differences operated in three main areas: in the denominational context, in the debate over the use of inquiry rooms and in the concerns about class and respectability.

The committee which ran the Central Noon Prayer Meeting in Moorgate St formed the nucleus of the groups responsible for co-ordinating the mission. Since the Sheffield fiasco, Moody had kept the local executive committee free of clergymen. In London, this committee was chaired by a layman, while the general council represented the elite of London's evangelical network. By February 1875 the organising committees had rented both the Agricultural Hall in Islington for evening meetings and the Exeter Hall for the daily prayer meetings, while plans were in place to rent a few more locations. At the Freemason's Hall meeting, Moody had outlined his intention to divide London into four districts and spend a month in each of the north, south, east and west quadrants. This design was generally followed, although not as evenly as some had hoped. Moody began in north London and spent two months, from 9 March to 9 May, at the Agricultural Hall with its capacity of 20,000. He then moved east to the Bow Road Hall on 8 April and to the Royal Opera House in the west end about the same time, while taking Camberwell Green Hall in the south during the month of June. Both Bow Road and Camberwell held 8,000 people and were constructed specially for Moody's meetings. Both were financed by subscriptions from local supporters.

The actual day-to-day conduct of the meetings in London mirrored quite closely that of Glasgow and Dublin. As Moody travelled around the country he improved his ability to conduct revival services, although this increasing professionalism was gained at the expense of an earlier spontaneity.[160] As usual, the opening night in London was very crowded. The massive preparations which had preceded the opening services aroused a great deal of curiosity and raised expectations about their long-term impact. Sixteen thousand people pushed and shoved their way into the building which had been specially fitted out for the occasion. Moody entered the baize covered platform and without preamble started the meeting by exclaiming 'Let us praise God for what he is going to do in London' and promptly announced the first hymn.[161] Four months later, when the campaign concluded, observers estimated over 2.5 million people had attended the meetings – a substantial figure, even allowing for the prevalence of repeat attenders.

Circus overtones, noted earlier, reached their apogee in London. With such a large audience to reach, Moody employed a host of supporting performers to highlight his preaching as the main attraction. Henry Drummond continued his meetings for young men. To draw in the curiosity seekers, the Jubilee Singers, an African-American singing group, were invited to perform and spent several weeks at Bow Road Hall. Native talent like Lord Radstock, the Reverend W.H. Aitken, the Reverend Newman Hall and S.A. Blackwood lent a familiar presence to audiences and an imprimatur on Moody's respectability. Moody also recruited other American evangelists who were in the country at the time, like Major Cole and his family, and the Reverend William Taylor, a California street preacher who had conducted extensive evangelistic tours in Australia and India. This entourage either substituted for Moody in his absence or prepared an area for his eventual arrival. S.A. Blackwood had led services in the Opera House before Moody preached there and William Taylor spent several weeks at the Victoria Theatre in South London prior to Moody's arrival at Camberwell Green. By the time Moody and Sankey arrived they were guaranteed that local interest would be sufficiently stimulated to ensure large audiences. Supporting acts also allowed the Americans to conduct many more meetings than if they had worked simply on their own. All of this created an atmosphere of excitement which served to keep interest, and ultimately attendance levels, high.

Moody and Sankey actively sought the organisational support of individuals from a wide variety of denominations. On the executive committee there was Lord Cairns, the Irish Anglican, Samuel Morley, the Congregationalist MP and William McArthur, the MP and Wesleyan Methodist. Ministerial support appeared fairly wide ranging. Seven hundred invitations had been sent out to ministers across the country for the Farewell meeting on 12 July and 188 Anglicans, 154 Congregationalists, 85 Baptists, 81 Wesleyans, 39 Presbyterians and 54 from other denominations attended.[162] But such a picture of denominational cooperation and upper-class support could be deceptive. Tensions between the Established Church and Nonconformists were evident. Nonconformists had been generally supportive of Moody and Sankey's efforts from the very beginning. They were more broadly evangelical and had fewer hierarchical restrictions on such extra-denominational activity. Congregationalist and Baptist leaders lent their support to the movement through pamphleteering, as in the case of R.W. Dale or, like C.H. Spurgeon, in the offer of other forms of practical help and an empty pulpit. Some Anglican ministers, however, found cooperation with Nonconformists difficult to accept. One believed that only by avoiding chapels and holding meetings on entirely neutral ground would there be any basis for cooperation between the two parties.[163]

As for the Church of England, even though it represented the largest denominational contingent at Moody's farewell meeting, it was deeply divided over the campaign. These uncertainties were evident even among known revival supporters. Reverend Samuel Garratt, an evangelical churchman and supporter of 1859, addressing the issue of clerical participation in the proposed mission to London, wrote 'It appears to me a subject encompassed with difficulties on the right hand and on the left, through which it needs a very special measure of wisdom and grace to steer aright.'[164] Prophetic words indeed, for not even the navigational skills Moody and Sankey possessed would enable them to negotiate this road without difficulty and controversy.

The debate over Moody and Sankey's campaign reflected the growing disparity between the evangelical and ritualist wings of the Church of England. The Oxford Movement, which had emerged in the 1830s to oppose state reform of the Church of England, promoted a trend to High Churchmanship among certain Anglicans. Tractarians, Puseyites, or Anglo-Catholics, as they were also known, saw their church as a *via media* between the Catholic Church and Protestantism, stressing the Catholic dimension of the Thirty-Nine Articles and fostering a ritualistic approach to worship that relied on neo-medieval forms.[165] By 1850, concern surrounding the use of more elaborate vestments, auricular confession and veneration of the sacraments was widespread, and not exclusive to the evangelical camp. It was to continue throughout the remainder of the century.[166] Ritualists had been experimenting with methods similar to those of evangelicals in their efforts to reach the poor in the parishes of London[167] and in 1869 and again in 1874 they conducted a mission to London which greatly resembled Moody's efforts. Surprisingly, a substantial contingent attended Moody's introductory meeting at the Freemason's Hall. One, who described himself as 'a red hot ritualist', asked if Moody would discourage converts from attending a ritualist church. Avoiding a direct answer, Moody was reported as saying he was willing to receive help from churchmen of all types and would not force anyone to leave the Anglican communion.[168] Even though desirous of ritualist support, when the deputation expressed its general favourability toward the mission, albeit with some preconditions, Moody was taken aback by this 'quasi offer of help from High Churchmen'.[169] Nevertheless, their full support never materialised during the campaign. In fact, over the following months the voice of High Anglicanism, the *Church Times*, became much more hostile, labelling Moody and Sankey 'schismatics' because of their non-Anglican and unordained status. It also claimed they degraded the reputation of the church and the prayer book.[170] Their entire campaign was deemed a poor reflection on the evangelical ability to gain converts and pastor congregations; to use their words, 'none but an ill-fed flock would need food from a stranger's hand'.[171] Such attitudes were a reflection of the existing hostilities between opposing factions within Anglicanism.

Evangelical Anglicans were by no means united behind Moody and Sankey, despite ritualist accusations. In fact, it is impossible to categorise Moody's support along a strict evangelical/ritualist divide. Individuals did not always respond in anticipated ways. In a letter to the Archbishop of Canterbury, the Reverend James Moorhouse, Bishop of Melbourne, wrote critically of the revivalist habit, emulated by Moody, of calling 'small effects by great names', or turning religious feelings and a profession of Christ into a full-fledged conversion. Although this prejudiced him against the movement, he realised that if the church did not become involved then it would not benefit from the converts produced. Therefore, he concluded:

> while I refrain from going to meetings at a distance, and giving an active support and countenance to the movement by appearing in the platform, I have resolved (though not without misgivings, wh: I dare say will give way before work) to go in the platform and support them if they come into my district; that so I may give help where I can, and direct penitents to the fold where I believe they will find the best shepherding for their souls.[172]

Moorhouse recognised the importance of participation, despite his own reservations, if only to ensure that converts were directed to an Anglican church. Reverend William Cadman, on the other hand, was a prominent evangelical minister in a south London working-class parish. He also wrote to the Archbishop, and unlike Moorhouse was quite positive about the current religious movement, believing it to be nothing but the hand of God at work. There were, however, certain aspects of the work, such as the inquiry rooms and the house-to-house visitation, which he felt were dangerous both to doctrine and practice. Therefore:

> while ready to sympathize and help, and wish for and be on the look out for opportunities of spending on Satan a part in this movement I for one feel that at present I cannot commit myself to the movement without sanctioning what I disapprove as well as what I approve.[173]

Support for Moody did not correspond to any given denomination or faction, but relied more on individual conscience. In spite of the uncoordinated nature of Moody's support, enough Nonconformists, individual Anglicans and prominent nondenominational lay people united to run a campaign that dominated the religious and secular press for four months. As in the other urban centres, disagreements over Moody's approach in London manifested themselves in a series of controversies. In Glasgow, the potential threat to clerical authority concerned Calvinist Presbyterians. In Dublin, Low Church Anglicans were worried about denominational disintegration. In London, anxieties revolved around the propriety of the inquiry rooms.

In the early days of revivalism, conviction of sin during a service took place on a wide scale, disrupting the proceedings with the noise and confusion of people crying out for mercy. In most cases, the afflicted were removed to the vestry or outside the church where they could be dealt with more privately. In the Methodist tradition, this process was formalised into an 'anxious seat' or kneeling at the communion rail. The reasoning behind these measures, as Kent points out, was to separate those individuals under conviction of sin from the anonymity of the crowd by placing them in a prominent spot and bringing the collective pressure of the remaining audience to bear upon them.[174] Moody's way of dealing with converts also involved elements of intense counselling. Those desiring more information were asked to enter special 'inquiry rooms', normally separate from the main hall and staffed with Christian helpers. This procedure created difficulties for him in several ways. The separateness and the emphasis on privacy roused suspicions of undue influence and allegations that the inquiry rooms were confessionals. The restricted entry – intended to prevent unauthorized individuals from entering – only increased these suspicions. Although operating within a well-established revival tradition, Moody's inquiry rooms fell foul of the changing perceptions of acceptable revival conduct.

Inquiry rooms were set up with the intention that ministers would run them and be available to converse with troubled individuals after the regular service. When Moody and Sankey's popularity increased there was such a demand for one-to-one conversation that ministers were asked to select a few individuals from their churches who they felt would be mature and knowledgeable enough to assist in a proper manner. A ticket was then issued to each worker, who had to present it to the inquiry room manager in order to gain admittance.[175] Such procedures were common practice. In Dublin, for example, inquiry room workers had to sign a declaration agreeing to discuss only the gospel and not to proselytise. In Edinburgh, workers were expected to sit an examination to determine their theological soundness in an attempt to prevent the spread of false doctrine.[176] Inquiry rooms were meant to be quiet places, where penitents could converse reasonably with trained individuals about their souls without unnecessary distractions. The formal nature of the inquiry room procedure only heightened their 'secretive' connotations and although organisers took all the precautions they could, there were obvious risks. The potential for wrong teaching, proselytism and emotional excess was rife and on several occasions did occur. As a result, inquiry rooms were considered to be a threat to clerical control over the conversion process.

During the evangelistic meeting, those desiring to know more about the Christian life were often asked to signal their intention by standing or raising their hand or making their way towards the inquiry rooms. Many British and Irish ministers saw this as an attempt to make public distinctions in the audience between the 'saved' and 'unsaved', a process considered offensive, in bad taste and even dangerous. Reverend A.A. Rees remarked 'I do not think that public invidious and unreliable distinctions are discreet – such as calling on those who profess to be saved to lift up their hands, or rise from their seats.'[177] Reverend R. Staveley of Killiney in Co. Dublin exclaimed 'I have no admiration for the bad taste and wrong judgment that sends individuals away into a private room to be stared at as they struggle through the crowd.'[178] Moody's aggressive determination to impress his listeners with the need for conversion was increasingly out of step with the propriety expected from middle-class religion.

But to other nineteenth-century evangelicals, a little short-term embarrassment was worth the long-term gain of new converts. The acceptance of the possibility of instantaneous conversions meant decisions could be thrust on people with greater urgency. In fact, not to do so was to fail in one's Christian duty. Reverend Mr Taylor of Glasgow, inspired by the recent visit of Moody and Sankey, tried inviting penitents to stay behind in his own church and was surprised at the amount of interest there was. 'I feel certain,' he stated, 'that we ministers have in former times lost much fruit that otherwise would have followed our preaching, by not having inquiry meetings after the preaching service.'[179] Reverend J. Fletcher had been uncertain about the use of the inquiry room, but upon observation was now convinced 'it is of great importance to speak, if possible, with each anxious inquirer, while the gospel is still ringing in his ears'.[180] Arguments defending the use of inquiry rooms stressed the benefits of employing men and women from local churches. Inquirers would be more relaxed, it was felt, talking to someone from a similar background, rather than to a minister.[181] Moody thought the inquiry rooms would allow the minister to talk to his congregation and discover their needs. With his new understanding, he would be able to bridge the barriers – the 'stiffness and formality' – that existed between them and prevented people from bringing their troubles to him.[182]

Concerns about the inquiry rooms took on a new dimension when in May 1875 the Archbishop of Canterbury published his views on the current religious movement. His letter was in response to a request from Lord Cairns, the Lord Chancellor, to attend and publicly endorse the revival meetings. The letter was a cleverly worded statement which expressed the archbishop's deep interest in the mission and his belief that much good was being done, while at the same time outlining several major objections and the impossibility of an official sanction. The letter is worth quoting at some length, because it shaped much of the subsequent debate.

> I confess that the objections I originally felt, still remain in full force, now that we have had time to examine and to learn from various quarters the exact nature of the movement.
>
> That addresses urging, in whatever homely language, the great truths of the Gospel on our people's consciences should be delivered by laymen, is no innovation amongst us; and I heartily rejoice that the present movement is conducted on so great a scale and with such apparent success.
>
> It is chiefly from the 'after-meetings' for confession of sin and for guidance of the conscience, as they have been described to me, that I am apprehensive lest evil may arise. I cannot think that the delicate and difficult duty of thus ministering to anxious souls ought to be entrusted to any who have neither been set apart by the Church for this especial office, nor have given proof of such a spiritual insight as may in certain cases be held to take the place, in this particular, of the regular call to the cure of souls. I cannot but fear, from what I have heard, that the counsel given at these Meetings must often be crude and founded upon no knowledge of the real circumstances and state of mind of those to whom it is addressed; while there is danger also lest some self-constituted advisers of others may do harm to themselves, seeking to be leaders when in truth they have much need to be led.[183]

Very few people were entirely happy with the archbishop's letter. *The Record* felt that it was the first time an Anglican bishop had so openly expressed his sympathy with a lay ministry although its 'mingled courage and caution' was sure to provoke criticism.[184] It certainly did from the evangelical camp. Cairns' tone of polite regret was mild in comparison to most when he said 'I grieve much that from what is so strongly affecting, for good, large masses of the laity, and great numbers of the laity of the Church, the vast majority of the clergy, and all the heads of the Church are appearing to keep aloof.'[185] The virulent criticisms of R. W. Dale reflected the other end of the spectrum when he scathingly referred to the archbishop's 'emasculating' attempt to take both sides as 'the invertebrate or molluscous style' of writing which did not please anyone.[186]

The main point of criticism was Tait's description of the after meetings as intended for 'confession of sin and guidance of the conscience'. This was a reference to criticisms, heard in previous campaigns, that the inquiry room was nothing more than a Protestant confessional, with its Catholic and ritualist overtones. The ritualist missions of 1869 and 1874 had been accused of using after meetings to urge people to attend confession. Moody and Sankey's supporters vehemently denied all such comparisons. Reverend C.T. Astley stated:

> there is as much difference between the mode of dealing with anxious enquiries at those after meetings and the confessional of the Ritualists as there is between the New Testament and the Tridentine Decrees, or in other words, so there is between Protestantism and Popery.

The inquiry rooms, he claimed, were trying 'to deepen the impression that may have been made by public preaching to meet difficulties; to solve doubts; to take by the hand with loving sympathy; to guide to the Saviour'.[187] It was here that differences within the London religious community became apparent. Ritualists were critical of the inquiry rooms because they saw them as confessionals without the divine sanction and seal of secrecy given to them as a Church ordinance.[188] Moody and Sankey were violating Church law when they used such methods. Evangelical anti-ritualism surfaced in their frequent denials of any similarity between inquiry rooms and confessionals. To Astley, the confessional was one of the 'the foulest of abominations of the Papacy' and even 'the most inexperienced assistant at one of these after-meetings is a safer guide of the conscience than any ritualistic or Colensic clergyman'.[189] The debate over this novel form of supervising conversions exposed pre-existing tensions within the Church of England and revealed a wide range of public opinion concerning 'proper' religious practice.

Criticisms from within the London Anglican community have been interpreted as evidence of Moody and Sankey's inability to influence London society in any significant manner. John Kent, for example, is perhaps too exacting when he claims Moody's inability to bridge the differences between the various Anglican factions meant a complete failure of his entire campaign.[190] Objections to Moody did not divide neatly along party lines; he had ritualist supporters as well as evangelical opponents. Nor should failure be calculated simply on the reaction of one church alone, even if it was the national church. As R.W. Dale remarked, the official support of the Church of England meant very little to people already attending the revival meetings.[191] A survey of the newspapers of the time makes it difficult to deny the extent of Moody and Sankey's popular success. The enormous crowds who attended the meetings seemed unperturbed by the carnivalesque atmosphere and the inquiry rooms. For religious leaders, wholehearted support was a much more complicated matter. Issues of denominational influence, tradition, proper order and respectability all made it so much harder for ministers and clergymen, whether Nonconformist or Anglican, evangelical or ritualist, to endorse unconditionally a work which seemed to threaten so many of their vested interests and beliefs. Attributing failure to such a picture underestimates the diversity of opinion and conflicting tensions within the London religious community. For some, Moody and Sankey represented the epitome of respectable revivalism; they eschewed spontaneous outbursts and prolonged meetings in favour of a controlled, even orchestrated, approach. Their vulgar style and pragmatic simplification of complex doctrines, however, still made it difficult for many clergymen to embrace revivalism. In this mass of contradictory opinion Moody and Sankey lost their historical identity. They became empty symbols, used at will to reinforce pre-existing perceptions about revivalism, conversion and respectability. Depending on the opinions of the individual, Moody and Sankey could be anywhere on the spectrum from 'instruments of the Holy Spirit' to 'tools of the Devil'.

As with denominational tensions and concerns over the inquiry room, Moody and Sankey found themselves being drawn into London's class conflict. Moody was generally dismissive of class distinctions although he was aware of the importance of aristocratic influence. His ability to tap into existing networks was evident in the amount of upper-class support his London meetings received. The Bible readings which he conducted in the Opera House each afternoon were very popular with members of local society. The Duke and Duchess of Sutherland and their friends, the Princess Alexandra of Wales and the Dowager Countess of Gainsborough, who tried unsuccessfully to entice Queen Victoria along, were among the regular attenders.[192] Such patronage was an indication of the respectability which Moody's meetings had achieved. Moody, however pleased he was with this upper-class acceptance, was said to be disappointed by the lack of conversions.[193] Many regulars were part of a pre-existing London evangelical network which included prominent individuals such as Lord Cairns, the Earl of Shaftesbury and others. While representing only a minority of their class, they were influential and their public support for Moody's meetings was invaluable.[194] Support from this class was also evident in the membership of the general council. Of the eighty members, there were ten ministers, eight gentry, four MPs and four military men, with the remainder designated 'Esq.'. Men like Lord Radstock, the Earl of Cavan, the Hon. Alexander F. Kinnaird, Dr T.J. Barnardo, the Reverend William Arthur, George Moore and Samuel Morley actively used their social position to promote Moody and his meetings. Aristocratic evangelicals had their own hopes for Moody and Sankey's campaign. Despite the obvious popularity of their meetings among middle-class church attenders, Shaftesbury and others had hoped, in true evangelical fashion, that these Americans would be able to reach the working classes. At an April meeting of the organising committee Shaftesbury publicly challenged Moody's decision to extend his campaign in the Agricultural Hall and urged him to move on to Bow Road as planned. The meetings at the former, he declared, had attracted neither the very rich nor the very poor and were simply catering to the respectable church-going population. Moody was reluctant to give up his audiences of 15,000 for the much smaller sized 8,000, but criticism from this influential patron was enough to make him move sooner than he had intended.[195]

Moody was well aware of the predominantly middle-class composition of his audiences and made frequent attempts to get these repeat attenders to make room for newcomers and the unsaved. In London he lamented that 'the success of our meetings has been their failure, because we cannot get at the class of people we would like'.[196] Moody was therefore keen on reaching the working classes. The criticisms of outsiders and Moody's own complaints have given the overwhelming impression that the working classes were relatively untouched by the revival movement. This seems to have been the general trend. Special efforts, like workmen's meetings and Sunday morning services, made little headway. Sessions at Christian Conventions on 'how to reach the masses' made no significant impact. Reverend James Moorhouse declared that Moody and Sankey's meetings left the 'great mass of godless working people' untouched. 'I was at Astley's Amphitheatre', he wrote, and 'I did not see a dozen persons in the vast throng belonging to that class.'[197] Non-attendance of this nature, however, was more than simply an inability to find seats among the middle-class hordes. The occasional working-class presence at the revival meetings indicates there was also a deliberate rejection of the values, morals and style of religion which Moody and Sankey were promoting. Disturbances and the disruption of meetings lends credence to this interpretation. While some were simply the result of crowd pressure on closed doors, others had a more deliberately disruptive nature. In Dublin, meetings were often interrupted because people walked around in the galleries trying to obtain a better view or to get within hearing distance. On one occasion, 'a rough element' had to be ejected and on another several drunken men were shouting out and had to be removed.[198] At a London meeting, a drunken man tried to sing along during one of Sankey's solos. Halfway through, Moody stopped the solo and announced a hymn while five 'muscular Christians' escorted the man from the hall and into police custody.[199] People were obviously attracted to these meetings out of curiosity. They attended for the novelty value or to poke fun at such earnest religionists. On numerous occasions, young men and boys were accused of attending a meeting or entering the inquiry rooms in order to fulfil a wager. Others simply left the hall once the sermon began.[200] Working-class people, despite their curiosity, rejected this middle-class version of Christianity and continued to resist any form of organised religious instruction. Disruptions within meetings were matched by incidents of ritual humiliation. In the East End, false handbills and satirical pamphlets were distributed and sold outside Bow Road Hall, while a mob often gathered to jeer and ridicule those going inside. On one occasion fake signs were posted stating that the evening meetings had been postponed.[201] To a certain extent, the supporters of these services seemed to encourage such behaviour. Sandwich boards, with 'Moody and Sankey at Bow Road Hall tonight!' emblazoned on them, along with handbills, bell ringing and parading the streets set local organisers up for ridicule and public humiliation. Physical violence, however, was extremely rare. Only in Liverpool had Moody and Sankey's supporters ever been attacked. When a procession announcing the times of the revival meetings entered a working-class district of the city, they were set upon by an angry mob wielding brickbats and other weapons.[202]

As we have seen, Moody and Sankey's style and approach were embraced most enthusiastically by the middle-class evangelical community. Once these Americans tried to reach outside this group, either above or below, the limitations to their success became evident. The disappointing response of the working classes to the Bow Road Hall meetings was matched by the controversy which erupted when Moody announced his intention of preaching at Eton College, the most prestigious grammar school of the time. The thought of this American evangelist preaching to the future leaders of England stirred up concern for the Church of England's status, for Eton's reputation and for the mental health of the pupils. Although these fears were couched in other terms, Moody and Sankey's planned visit threatened to infiltrate a symbol of upper-class power with a tawdry display of middle-class vulgarity.

The idea to hold a meeting at Eton originated with Quintin Hogg and William Graham, both of whom had sons at Eton and were active in the London evangelical community. On 12 June 1875 they approached the provost of the college for permission to hold a meeting there. C.O. Goodford replied that although he had no authority outside the chapel, he would not oppose the meeting if the boys and tutors were in favour of it.[203] At this point he was under the impression that it was Graham and Hogg who would be speaking and when he discovered it was Moody and Sankey he tried to contact Graham to withdraw any implied sanction he may have given. However, plans for a meeting on 22 June proceeded over the following week. On 19 June Edward Knatchbull-Hugessen, an MP and High Churchman visited his son at Eton and noticed a tent, intended for the meeting, being set up in the nearby South Meadow. Discovering its intended use, he wrote indignant letters to both the provost and the headmaster demanding an explanation and the immediate cancellation of the forthcoming meeting. Replies from both men, however, reiterated their refusal to prevent the boys from attending, while at the same time stressing their refusal to sanction the gathering. Knatchbull-Hugessen was obviously not content with these responses and decided to go public with the exchange, printing the letters in *The Times* and other daily papers on 21 June and contacting Lord Lyttelton, a member of Eton's governing body. The public exposure was enough to spark a brief debate in the House of Lords that evening. The Marquis of Bath and Lord Overstone were among those concerned about the issue and urged Lyttelton to influence the governing body (which happened to be meeting the next day) to refuse its sanction. Lyttelton was evasive, as was the Earl of Morley, another board member. The Lords could have done very little. There was no time to prevent the meeting and the governing body had no authority to interfere with the headmaster anyway. With protests from the Earl of Shaftesbury concerning the legitimacy of the debate, the matter was soon closed.[204] The House of Commons had been similarly disturbed by the news and seventy-four MPs addressed a petition to the provost opposing the meeting. The 'buzz' in the lobbies was, according to *Punch*, 'quite distracting the minds of Honourable Members from [the] Committee on Merchant Shipping Bill, which, thanks to such distraction, perhaps, made some way in Committee'.[205]

In the wake of such negative publicity, Moody and Sankey had been urged to cancel the meeting. Moody refused. Eton's governing body met and declined to disallow the meeting, so it went ahead as scheduled. The preceding confusion and uncertainty had caused the location of the meeting to change several times, once from the South Meadow to the City Hall and from there to the private grounds of a local draper and prominent Nonconformist Mr Caley. The proceedings began at 4 o'clock and were quiet and uneventful. Approximately 800 people were present, 300 of whom were Eton boys. The remainder of the audience comprised respectable individuals such as the Earl of Cavan and several Eton tutors.[206] The meeting concluded with the reading of the governing body's decision and a prayer.

For such a minor affair there was an inordinate amount of interest taken in it. Newspapers remarked that such agitation had, in fact, only made the situation worse. It was a 'remarkable notion', the *Daily Telegraph* said, that the establishment was so opposed to this single meeting. Moody 'might possibly cause some little amusement, but would certainly kindle no enthusiasm'.[207] *The Spectator* was correct when it said the torrent of objections was based more on 'outraged officialdom' and 'the terror with which they [the House of Lords] hear the approach of any vulgar Middle-class influence within range of Eton'.[208]

Knatchbull-Hugessen's objections, however, centred around two issues. First of all, he feared Moody and Sankey's meeting would cast aspersions on the religious training the boys regularly received at Eton from the Church of England. Eton was traditionally seen as the training ground for future political leaders and was a known bastion of Anglicanism. By preaching there Moody and Sankey presented a symbolic threat to that religious hegemony. This explains the interest the House of Lords took in the matter. They expected Eton to train their eventual replacements properly. Knatchbull-Hugessen felt the headmaster's neutrality was a blatant criticism of the religious education the boys were receiving.[209] A similar argument was used against Moody in Glasgow when his critics argued that there was no need for extra services since the regular means of grace were functioning perfectly well without them. Such arguments were given short shrift. Emilius Bayley, another Eton parent, did not object to the occasional outside supplement to regular religious instruction. The potential for something objectionable to occur was not enough to outweigh the lasting religious impressions the boys could possibly receive.[210]

Knatchbull-Hugessen's second criticism was based on the age of the boys, arguing that because of their youth they would be extremely vulnerable to Moody and Sankey's 'semi-dramatic performances'. The 'discourses of Apocalyptic woe' could spark religious hysteria among them, disrupting regular school life. Some boys could lose their religious faith altogether and become cynics. Parents, said Knatchbull-Hugessen, had entrusted their sons to the school, unaware that they would be at the mercy of 'every itinerant religious vendor who visits Eton'.[211] Many of those involved recognised these objections as gross exaggerations. The replies of Goodford and Hornby rejected the delicacy Knatchbull-Hugessen attributed to the Eton boys' sensibilities. The headmaster said, 'considering the liberty which Eton boys enjoy, and the kind of entertainments which are open to them from time to time in this neighbourhood, I feel that it would be inconsistent, not to say hypocritical, to profess alarm and to curtail their liberty in unusual ways'.[212] Public school boys, declared *The Spectator*, were not known for being overly sensitive to religious issues and many would probably attend the meeting simply to mock and ridicule.[213] Indeed, of the boys who were present, a large number stood at the back and refused to participate.[214] According to James Findlay, the controversy emerged because Moody was seen to be 'invading one of the sacred precincts of the upper classes'. For John Kent, it was because Moody's English supporters were 'seeking to assume a religious (and inevitably social) leadership which they did not possess'.[215] Both interpretations point to the threat which Moody's middle-class vulgarity presented to members of England's social elite.

After 285 meetings in London, the Moody and Sankey campaign closed its doors. On 12 July the final Convention of Ministers was held at Mildmay Hall and on 3 August a Christian Convention was held in Liverpool prior to the departure of the evangelists for America. Crowds gathered outside their hotel and followed them to the quay to give them a boisterous farewell. The impact of these three years on Moody's personal development were enormous. As C.I. Schofield later remarked, the British and Irish campaigns saw Moody achieve maturity and 'the fullness of his great capacities'.[216] He had arrived with very little idea of how to run a successful revival campaign and with no formal plan of attack. He left the British Isles a household name, famous for his 'Yankee twang', harmonium and gospel hymns. He was now set to embark on a career which made him one of the most famous evangelists in American history. Already, he and Sankey were receiving invitations to conduct campaigns in the cities of Brooklyn, Philadelphia and New York.[217]

Moody and Sankey's popularity showed the extent to which spiritual issues could dominate the national agenda, particularly in England. The revival meetings had revealed 'the influence of mystic forces' on society and that 'Christianity, in the broadest sense of the word, seems to be popular'.[218] Moody and Sankey tapped into the middle-class ethic which saw church attendance as part of its image. Despite their aura of respectability Moody and Sankey engendered controversy wherever they went. For the most part, local evangelicals did not know what to make of them or their style. Moody's insistence on denominational unity caused him grave difficulties throughout his visit. His unordained status provoked concern for the future of the ministry. Prior to their departure Charles Spurgeon remarked '[t]hey are going away soon and perhaps it is fortunate; for if they were to stay here some of our ministers would be afraid they would take their congregations away, and they would not rally round our brethren as they do'.[219] The inquiry rooms brought up fears of wrong doctrine and the preaching of instant conversion challenged the Calvinist tradition and vulgarised what Anglicans felt to be a sacred and gradual process. A number of prominent evangelicals took contradictory positions on Moody, criticising him for his style and mannerisms, yet praising him for his ability to draw in the crowds and to gain converts. Individuals like the Earl of Shaftesbury, Reverend A.A. Rees, Reverend William Cadman and Reverend R.W. Dale all expressed doubts about the validity of Moody's efforts. In some senses Moody and Sankey's visit served to disrupt the evangelical community once again. It highlighted issues which evangelicals had always struggled with and made their unity merely a temporary occurrence.

By the time Moody and Sankey returned to England in September 1881, the religious situation had changed a great deal. Moody wrote home to his mother quite confidently saying 'My old friends seemed glad to see me and I am working a way [sic] about the same as when I was over here before.'[220] But society was very different from the 1870s. Evangelicals were much less confident about their ability to convert society. The Bishop of Rochester felt Moody and Sankey would be successful only if they could somehow 'reach that class of the population which I have reason to know they did not lay hold of in their last visit to the metropolis; and which, alas! still baffles the Church's activities'.[221] The increasing influence of biblical criticism made Moody's literal interpretation of Scripture and his emphasis on hell more anachronistic and reduced his popularity.[222] Apart from several months in Glasgow in 1882 and London in 1883, Moody and Sankey avoided extended campaigns in large urban centres. Their third visit in 1891–2 was spent on a frantic tour of the small towns of Scotland, visiting over eighty-one towns in just four and a half months.[223] Smaller campaigns reflected a growing pessimism about the likelihood of a working-class response to evangelistic endeavour. Even though the London campaign of 1883 was especially designed to reach those who did not attend church regularly, it experienced only a limited success. The organising committee built two portable halls, each with a capacity of 5,000, which could be moved to several locations specifically chosen to facilitate local attendance. Seats were reserved in the front of the hall for the working classes, and on certain evenings men only were admitted before the doors were opened to the general public.[224] In fact, working-class hostility to evangelistic efforts appears to have increased. During their tour of the south of England in 1892 'the bigotry and superstition of the uneducated masses' threatened to cause trouble on several occasions.[225]

Moody and Sankey were more successful at prompting the middle-class Christian community to begin philanthropic efforts among the unsaved both at home and abroad. They were one stimulus to the growing interest in foreign missionary work which many university students were exhibiting. Although Moody spent only a week at Cambridge, his meetings influenced several members of the famous Cambridge Seven to start what was eventually to become the Student Christian Movement.[226] Apart from the circumstantial and situational differences of the 1880s and 1890s, Moody's age and vulnerability to colds and Sankey's repeated voice failure made the novelty of the 1870s difficult to recreate.[227] British evangelicals were now less confident of revivalism's promised success.

CONCLUSION

In essence, the evangelistic campaigns of Moody and Sankey in the three king-doms between 1873 and 1875 illustrate the strengths and weaknesses of a much broader nineteenth-century encounter between the populist, but relatively classless, traditions of American popular Protestantism, and the evangelical constituency in the British Isles, which was never able to transcend the class, denominational, theological and stylistic tensions endemic in its Protestantism. For the truth of the matter is that Moody and Sankey were admired by British and Irish evangelicals more for their novelty and success in attracting large crowds than for their self-evident religious piety. These evangelicals both admired and held in contempt the brash, commercial and innovatory approach of Americans to mass evangelism, but when the dust settled they were still left with their church and chapel rivalries, their inability to interest the rougher elements of the working classes, their devotion to religion as a form of polite respectability, their undisguised contempt for Catholics and ritualists and their nervous fears about the progress of infidelity among both the educated and the great unwashed. In that sense Moody and Sankey, as with other American populists, were more instrumental in putting their fingers on the old sores of division within the religious traditions of the British Isles than they were in ushering in a new era of revivalistic success. Unlike the other forms of popular entertainment with which they had to compete, they were unable to build a tradition which could repeat and sustain itself week after week. They created noise and excitement, but they could not change historical processes or create a new religious order. The fact that they had to operate within the diverse religious traditions of the British Isles, from the metropolis to the Scottish highlands, and from Eton to the East End, shows that Moody and Sankey disturbed old fault lines without producing the religious earthquake for which they so earnestly laboured. But their enthusiasm was neither contemptible nor superficial, as many contemporaries and not a few historians have alleged, it was simply incapable of refashioning social and denominational realities in an increasingly industrial Britain and a largely Catholic Ireland.

Geraldine Hooper Dening (1841–1872), one of the most famous
female preachers of the 1860s

CHAPTER FOUR

Female preachers

O NE OF the most pervasive models for organising female experience in women's history is the concept of 'separate spheres'. It is especially prevalent for the study of middle-class women in Europe and in America and in general refers to a means of ordering gender roles, with public functions such as citizenship, work and leadership exercised by men, while issues surrounding the family and the home, defined as the private, were considered to be the responsibility of women. Relying on evangelical sermons and didactic manuals, early studies of women in the nineteenth century portrayed them as virtual prisoners in their homes. Supported by successful husbands, these women led sheltered lives free of economic responsibility. Confined within corset and crinoline, they were consigned to a constant round of social engagements and to the exercise of only the mildest forms of moral authority. According to Amanda Vickery, the model of separate spheres 'has come to constitute one of the fundamental organising categories, if not *the* organising category of modern British women's history'.[1]

Vickery, however, is no fan of the public/private dichotomy. In an article for the *Historical Journal*, she summarises and elaborates on recent criticisms concerning the validity of separate spheres. Although she admits that the language of separate spheres was important in the nineteenth century and that women did suffer numerous social disadvantages, she is at pains to point out that

> the metaphor of separate spheres fails to capture the texture of female subordination and the complex interplay of emotion and power in family life, and that the role of an ideology of separate spheres in the making of the English middle class, 1780–1850, has not been convincingly demon-strated.[2]

On the basis of her own research, Vickery would also like to reject the traditional chronology of female economic marginalisation, which sees the period 1650–1850 as one of slow decline from a golden age of feminine freedom to one of public exclusion and domestic confinement. She concludes:

> [t]he economic chronologies upon which the accounts of women's exclusion from work and their incarceration in domesticity depend are

deeply flawed. At a very general level, eighteenth and early nineteenth-century women were associated with home and children, while men controlled public institutions, but then this rough division could be applied to almost any century or any culture – a fact which robs the distinction of analytical purchase. If, *loosely speaking*, there have always been separate spheres of gender power, and perhaps there still are, then 'separate spheres' cannot be used to explain social and political developments in a particular century, least of all to account for Victorian class formation.[3]

AlthoughVickery's arguments are primarily concerned with the re-evaluation of Victorian middle-class formation and female economic marginalisation, her criticisms of the separate spheres construct have important ramifications for other aspects of women's history, aspects which also offer challenges to this interpretative model.[4] One of the loose 'spheres of gender power' thatVickery refers to, a sphere which has traditionally been associated with women, is the practice of religion. A dominant theme in the historiography of female spirituality is the idea that women are more religious than men, an idea reflected in higher levels of church attendance. In the American context, Mary Maples Dunn has argued that in seventeenth-century New England, gender roles were assigned to various goals in society in order to resolve conflict. Thus, 'to be a good woman was to be a good Christian. But to be a good man was to be a good citizen, active, competitive, self-confident.'[5] As a result, women came to dominate the membership of numerous Congregational churches. Similarly, Barbara Welter has argued that American religion underwent a process of 'feminisation' in the early nineteenth century, as feminine virtues came to dominate the content of sermons and women filled the majority of pews.[6] Hugh McLeod has confirmed high levels of female church attendance in France and Germany, suggesting that in denominations which concentrated power among an exclusively male clergy, women tended to predominate, while even in denominations with a more flexible attitude towards the sacraments and a role for the laity, male participation levels still remained slightly behind those of their female counterparts.[7] Disproportionate female attendance, in one sense, was the natural result of growing male irreligion. In a collection of essays about religion and English women, Gail Malmgreen has tentatively suggested that in the British context, churches were also predominantly female.[8] In her own analysis of domestic life in East Cheshire, Malmgreen has found that Methodist churches in rural areas were about 55 per cent female. The percentage was higher in towns like Stockport and Manchester, pointing to the influence of urbanisation as a factor in the 'feminisation' of Methodist churches.[9]

The obvious affinity between women and religion has only confirmed interpretations which portray their religious activity as a buttress to the ideology of separate spheres. Within that ideology, women were expected to be more religious than men and they were supposed to embody a higher spiritual nature. They were seen as mothers and nurturers – the perfect vessels to fulfil the

Biblical dictate to care for the sick, the hungry and the poor. 'Religious commitment and expression was, after all, an approved outlet for female assertiveness – within limits.'[10] However, such behaviour did not translate into female power. Women have been, according to one interpretation, 'excluded from formal religion, and from participating in important public rituals'. Feminists, likewise, have concluded that religion is 'a male dominated system in which women have little freedom to act', that it is 'repressive' and that it 'offer[s] little scope for challenging dominant ideologies'.[11]

A close examination of the religious dimension of women's lives in relation to the notion of separate spheres reveals a situation which is more complex than one of simple repression. Religion allowed women to make active exchanges between their public/private behaviour and between dominant/alternative ideologies. Research into the specifics of women's religious experience, be it attending church, teaching a Sunday School class, distributing tracts, visiting the sick, joining a convent or deaconess institute, paints a picture of extensive involvement in the public sphere. Indeed, the concern of this chapter – female preaching – is one of the most visible indications of women acting outside of the behaviour prescribed by the framework of separate spheres. Religious activity often acted as a liberating force for women, offering them an avenue of escape from domestic confinement, allowing them to state their own identity and develop personal skills. In this sense, religion provided the opportunity for women to challenge the separation of public and private.

As Malmgreen has stated so astutely, these two opposing interpretations of female spirituality represent 'the complex tension between religion as "opiate" and as an embodiment of ideological and institutional sexism, and religion as transcendent and liberating force'.[12] In light of this 'central paradox' it becomes apparent that a more sophisticated explanation of female religious activity is called for. Although religion was considered to be part of the domestic sphere, women often used their religious behaviour to push at the boundaries of Biblical prohibition, social expectation, church regulation and personal inhibition. In this sense they were rejecting the restrictions of the private sphere. To use Anne Digby's phrase, religious activity allowed women to move into a 'social borderland', a region between the public and the private which 'allowed "official" Victorian values to be silently transgressed'.[13] However, it is important that this behaviour be seen in its proper context. Many of these women were not consciously trying to achieve liberation from social and religious stereotypes. Nor should their behaviour be judged against the standard of political emancipation. Women's role in organised religion often challenged the boundaries of acceptable religious behaviour, even if it did not eliminate them entirely.

The rest of this chapter is concerned with an analysis of female preaching in the years after 1859. Several points should be made at the outset. Female preaching was only one element in a wide range of public female religious activity which extended from the local nexus of church and family to the international sphere of the foreign mission field.[14] The most common manifestation of such activity for women in nineteenth-century Britain and Ireland was an involvement in one of the growing number of charitable organisations, both denominational and multi-faith. Although charity and alms giving had been an important part of religion from the days of the early Christian church, it was only in the nineteenth century that this activity became so extensive and diverse. The evangelical revival of the eighteenth century, with its emphasis on personal conversion and evangelism, promoted the idea of charitable work not only as one's Christian duty but also as a means of saving souls. Of the voluntary charitable societies active in Britain in the second half of the nineteenth century, roughly three-quarters of them were evangelical in character and control.[15] Although the evidence for Ireland is less extensive, a similar trend appears to exist amongst those charities which were protestant in orientation.[16] In both countries, much of the work of these societies, and the leadership of many others, was in the hands of women. This development is not surprising, in some respects, because much of the prescriptive literature concerning women's role encouraged religious activity as part of her Christian duty. According to the literature, women were created to 'advance the comfort of man in his private relations'.[17] As wives, mothers, sisters and daughters women were expected to be the centre of the household, the model for their children and the faithful and devoted ministering angel during sickness. Their innate qualities of love, sympathy, self-sacrifice, fidelity and piety all gave women a special ability to minister to the poor and the afflicted.[18] Indeed, women were considered to be more receptive to 'Divine impressions', capable of a stronger conviction of sin and a better understanding of the atonement, all of which gave them unique powers of religious persuasion.[19] On a social level, charitable work was voluntary and allowed middle-class women to avoid the impropriety of working for wages. It also could fit around a household routine. Women were encouraged to involve themselves in charity in order to avoid idleness and frivolity, but at the same time they were warned that such activity should not cause them to neglect their home duties, still considered a woman's first mission field.[20] Women, therefore, were encouraged to become active in their parishes and localities, to serve as Sunday school teachers, Bible class leaders, Scripture readers and fund raisers for missionary societies.[21] They could also be involved in poor relief in the form of district visiting and nursing.

Women certainly did get involved in charitable work on a large scale, as any study of the nineteenth century will show. In the early stages women formed auxiliaries to well-established organisations like the British and Foreign Bible Society and the Church Missionary Society. Apart from contributing extensively to charity themselves, women worked primarily to raise funds for these organisations.[22] From there it was a small step for women to embark on the tasks of visiting, rescue work and tract distribution themselves. District visiting was the most extensive field of female charitable work and involved the division of an area (particularly poor or working-class) into districts which were then assigned to female visitors, who went from door to door offering domestic advice, access to nursing care, Bibles for sale and of course spiritual counselling. Early efforts were organised through local churches and societies and were voluntary and middle class in character.[23] Wealthy women not only had the time and money to do such work, but they were also felt to exert a moral influence over the poor and could infuse them with ideas of self-reliance and improvement.[24] Societies such as the General Society for the Promotion of District Visiting (1828) and the London City Mission (1832) were some of the earliest to use middle-class women. The use of working-class women was pioneered by Ellen Ranyard, who founded the London Bible Domestic and Female Mission in 1857, hiring 'Bible-women' to visit the various districts of London, sell Bibles, offer advice, and give basic nursing care. By 1867 she employed 234 women and over time the nursing component took priority over their evangelistic function.[25]

Visiting was, however, only the tip of the philanthropic iceberg. Women were involved in a whole range of charitable societies that sought to relieve the suffering of groups as diverse as destitute children, street arabs, pregnant women, prostitutes, the deaf and blind and the imprisoned. They were active in the campaigns for moral reform, which included temperance, animal welfare and Sunday closing.[26] By 1893, *The Englishwoman's Yearbook* estimated there were over 500,000 women engaged in some form of philanthropic work.[27] Philanthropy was one of the few outlets for female assertiveness in the nineteenth century and it acted as a major channel for their energies. Frank Prochaska has argued that charity did more than anything else, even feminism, to expand a public role for women.[28]

Female preaching, paradoxically enough, can make no such claim. Most denominations refused to sanction it and, for the most part, it occurred only on an informal basis, usually outside church walls. Because it was such a visible occupation it was not very common and the women who did preach rarely saw themselves as advocates of a general trend. Female preaching, however, by its very nature, would always be more controversial than philanthropy and may have contributed to the greater acceptance and participation in these less extremist forms of religious activity.[29] Before proceeding any further in this discussion, female preaching should be defined and placed in its historical context. Olive Anderson's ground-breaking article still contains the most succinct definition of female preaching: an activity which involves 'the deliberate undertaking by women of evangelisation, spiritual instruction or exhortation in mixed public assemblies held for that purpose, with no attempt to disguise the nature of their activities or their audience'.[30] This definition is more inclusive than Earl Kent Brown's 'modality' of 'full ministerial members of the body of Christ' which requires the proclamation or teaching of the word, the administration of the sacraments and the imposition of spiritual discipline.[31] Few women have ever fulfilled all three of these functions. When dealing with contemporary sources one needs to be careful about such a definition. In the nineteenth century there are frequent references to 'women's work', 'female ministry' and 'female evangelists' which, upon closer examination, do not indicate public speaking to mixed audiences but simply describe the standard occupations like visiting, holding women's meetings, Sunday school teaching and leading Bible study groups.[32]

Despite its fairly narrow focus, public female preaching to mixed audiences has been a periodic feature of the history of the church and is not unique to the nineteenth century. Evidence of female leadership has been a recurring theme in Judaeo-Christian culture which dates back to the early Christian church. Between the third and fifth centuries it was apparent that an office of deaconess existed, with extensive didactic, pastoral and sacramental duties among female Christians. In some areas there is even evidence that women were ordained to this function.[33] After the reformation there was little female preaching until women experienced an enlarged role with the emergence of Puritanism in the late sixteenth century, which stressed experience of an 'inner light' as the only qualification to speak publicly. During the Civil War and Interregnum women in both the radical sects and more established denominations encountered opportunities to play the parts of prophetess and preacher, even if they were never given access to positions in church government or allowed to administer religious ordinances.[34]

The rapid spread of Methodism in the eighteenth century was largely the result of female efforts. Women often formed the basis for the earliest societies, setting up prayer groups and inviting travelling preachers to conduct religious meetings in their homes. As the movement progressed women were responsible for building chapels, donating funds, serving as band leaders and speaking publicly on an informal basis. John Wesley's own thinking on the acceptability of female preaching emerged gradually from about 1755 until 1771 when he admitted the possibility of exceptions to the apostle Paul's dictum 'I do not permit a woman to teach or to have authority over a man; she must be silent'.[35] By 1787 Wesley's full conversion was evident in his letter to Sarah Mallet which gave her official authorisation to preach within the Methodist connection. Women as travelling itinerant preachers had become a recognised feature of early Methodism.[36] Support for the practice did not last much beyond Wesley's death. In 1803 opponents of female preaching passed a resolution forbidding the practice except in front of female audiences, and even then only with the express permission of a district superintendent.[37] It was left to the Primitive Methodists and the Bible Christians to continue the tradition into the nineteenth century.

Most of the research on female preaching in the nineteenth century has focused on the activities of these early Methodist women.[38] Within Primitive Methodism female itinerants were active between 1814–20, their numbers reaching a high point in 1834 after which they declined until there was only one left in 1850. In total, about 90 of these mainly young, uneducated labouring women have been identified.[39] Among the Bible Christians a similar trend is evident. About 14 women were active itinerants before the first conference in 1819 and thereafter, until 1861, 71 women travelled, with their numbers peaking between 1825–7.[40] Reasons for their decline also appear similar. The harsh conditions of an itinerant ministry with extensive travelling in often poor weather, inadequate accommodation and active persecution made illness and fatigue common excuses for early retirement. Women who married were also expected to retire. If they married another travelling preacher they lost their independent ministry and became assistants to their husbands, even if they did continue to preach. As time went on both the Primitives and Bible Christians moved from a period of expansion to one of consolidation. The novelty value of female preachers meant they had been used most extensively to open up new areas, but when it came to consolidating gains, women were excluded. The denominations were shifting their outlook from a missionary objective, where women had been successful, to chapel building and pastoral care, areas seen to be exclusive male preserves.[41] Changes within early Victorian society were also contributing to the decline of female preaching. According to Deborah Valenze, these women and the message they preached represented a response to the economic instability and political and social unrest in the early decades of the nineteenth century. Their message represented the value of familial and community interdependence in the face of an emergent liberal individualism. They affirmed the importance of family and community ties and offered a framework which allowed the life processes of birth, illness and death to be understood within a religious context. For them, mutual assistance was essential for survival. As the laissez-faire policies of early industrial England gained influence, however, the preaching of these labouring women 'provided only a passing form of expression':

> by mid-century, the increasingly prosperous Methodist sects were moving into chapels and gradually shedding many of their earlier tendencies. Female preaching occurred rarely after 1860, and virtually vanished after 1880; in the changing context of Victorian England, female piety perforce assumed a different face. Silenced by chapel hierarchy and convention, women would reappear in the pulpit only in the twentieth century, when education and professionalisation had moulded them into an acceptable form.[42]

This conclusion of inevitable decline is reinforced by Olive Anderson's analysis of middle-class 'lady evangelists' in the 1850s and 60s. She states that 'in its most undisguised and deliberate form it was not long-lived', except in the Salvation Army. The debate on female preaching declined significantly in the later 1860s, as several of the most famous preachers died or moved into other areas of service, such as foreign missions or faith healing.[43] Jocelyn Murray reaffirms this process of decline when she argues that the 1870s were 'much less favourable to the preaching ministry of women' and that 'in the remaining years of the nineteenth century there was little evidence that women preachers continued their ministry'.[44] Although these conclusions concerning the fate of female preaching have been based on extensive and valuable research, their implications cause difficulties on several fronts. First of all, the efforts of the Salvation Army should not be seen as an odd aberration in late nineteenth-century religious behaviour, but as a serious, and successful, effort to institutionalise what Catherine Booth believed were women's natural rights and abilities.[45] This trend was, secondly, reinforced by the activity of the Wesleyan Methodists and the United Methodist Free Church (UMFC), who, as early as the mid-1880s, began to sponsor and encourage middle-class female preachers. Most of these women were associated with specific circuits as local preachers, but there is some evidence that a handful operated on a much more independent level, travelling throughout the north of England and conducting special revival missions.[46] Therefore, I would like to argue that a more comprehensive interpretation of female preaching in the nineteenth century should be adopted. Rather than viewing the phenomenon from the perspective of decline, female preaching should be seen as adapting and taking on new forms in response to a changing social and religious environment. Although marginalised in the face of growing denominational institutionalisation female preaching continued to exist throughout the nineteenth century, in areas which remained favourable to popular revivalism and in a form which was acceptable to the growing respectability of many congregations. Thus, the support networks of the mid-century evangelical community encouraged the proliferation of a group of 'lady preachers'. The Salvation Army, dominated as it was by the Booth family, institutionalised a ministerial role for its female workers. Wesleyan Methodism, concerned about falling growth rates, was willing to experiment with alternative forms of evangelistic endeavour. This chapter will look at each of these movements in some detail. They will be examined separately because each movement was distinct from the other, although there are points of comparison.

Before proceeding, it would be wise to consider the position of women in Ireland. Unlike England and America, the role of Irish evangelical women is only starting to be explored.[47] Many of the theoretical models which have been developed to explain women's religious behaviour in Britain, are equally applicable to Ireland. Thus, in the eighteenth century, women were active in the spread of Methodism and in the establishment of new charitable organisations.[48] Over the course of the nineteenth century, evangelical Irish women's involvement in philanthropic endeavours increased and diversified. Irish women became Sunday school teachers, temperance advocates, district visitors and foreign missionaries. What was unique about much of this activity was its overtly sectarian nature. Irish evangelical women were often in direct and open conflict with their Catholic counterparts.[49]

What was much rarer were the instances of female preaching. Although there had been several notable female preachers within Irish Methodism, like Alice Cambridge and Anne Lutton, according to Hempton and Hill these women were only ever 'exceptional and transitional rather than officially sanctioned and accepted'.[50] Such a conclusion is reinforced by the manifestation of female leadership in the Ulster revival of 1859 (see Chapter. 1). Most women during the revival did not preach so much as exhort or lead prayer meetings. Some young girls, upon recovering from their prostrations, were certainly accorded the status, respect and attention of a spiritual leader, and those who did feel called to preach were tolerated. This sort of leadership quickly died away, and traditional norms reasserted themselves.[51] In the years after the revival, evidence of female preaching in Ireland is extremely rare. Of the accounts which do exist, they invariably tend to be of English or American women who had come to Ireland to conduct services.[52] The Salvation Army, although active in Ulster from 1880, used English women to pioneer its work, and it was several years before it began to recruit local talent. It was not until 1904 that the Presbyterian Church decided to authorise the foundation of a deaconess institution.[53] In essence, as Andrea Ebel Brozyna has shown, 'female preaching was perceived by the Ulster Protestant laity as something that occurred elsewhere'.[54] Given the scarcity of both evidence and research into the Irish context, the rest of this chapter will focus on female preaching in Britain, and in particular England.

The phenomenon of female preaching is only really comprehensible through an understanding of the Biblical and social arguments which were used to support or reject the practice. A full interpretation of the relevant Biblical evidence is a theological exercise and one that need not concern us here. However, a brief survey of the main texts and arguments would provide a useful context for the contrasting opinions about female preaching. The strongest biblical texts used against the practice of female preaching were based on the guidelines to worship given to the New Testament church by the apostle Paul. When writing to the early Christian church at Corinth he stated 'women should remain silent in the churches. They are not allowed to speak, but must be in submission, as the law says.'[55] For some ministers in the nineteenth century this passage could not be more plain; Paul 'absolutely forbids any woman to conduct worship of God in the church'.[56] Others, however, insisted that such restrictions were only a cultural ban. Paul was simply prohibiting women from arguing or debating aloud in church, like men were allowed to do. His restriction did not forbid female teaching but women publicly debating against men.[57]

The most negative statement concerning women's role was found in Paul's letter to Timothy:

> A woman should learn in quietness and full submission. I do not permit a woman to teach or to have authority over a man; she must be silent. For Adam was formed first, then Eve. And Adam was not the one deceived; it was the woman who was deceived and became a sinner.[58]

Biblical literalists claimed that because Adam was formed first, Eve was inferior. Because she was also the first to sin, she was therefore easily deceived. Her actions subsequently became a blueprint for the universal treatment of women. Eve's subordinate status meant women should not usurp authority over men. Her mistakes indicated women could not be entrusted with the responsibility of teaching Christian doctrine. The whole question of authority posed major difficulties for advocates of female preaching. Several tried to argue that women were still subject to male authority so long as they did not 'dictate' and restricted their addresses to 'edification, and exhortation and comfort'.[59] Others claimed that the Pauline restriction only prevented women from engaging in controversy and embarking on any formal theological training rather than from teaching as such. According to the Reverend John Dwyer, this was to prevent a woman from inadvertently 'usurping authority' if she ever defeated a man in an argument.[60] Active supporters of female preaching were less concerned with that eventuality taking place. Indeed, one declared '[i]s it not time somebody usurped authority over all the millions of professedly Christian men, who stand idle while the world is perishing?!'[61] Fanny Guinness, herself a female preacher, made a similar accusation, saying, 'When so many ministers of the stronger and wiser sex are useless or worse than useless in the work of soul saving, and preach for years without being instrumental in a single conversion, *is there not a cause* for woman's ministry?'[62] When men failed to fulfil their role as potential evangelists, they lost the right to object to a female ministry. Biblical restrictions became unimportant; it was simply a case of who was better at saving souls.

Biblical texts in favour of female preaching were rare. A frequently quoted passage was the prophecy of Joel concerning the 'last days' which said:

> I will pour out my Spirit on all people.
> Your sons and daughters will prophesy,
>   your young men will see visions,
>   your old men will dream dreams.
> Even on my servants, both men and women,
> I will pour out my Spirit in those days,
>   and they will prophesy.[63]

Quoted by the apostle Peter after the resurrection of Christ and the appearance of the Holy Spirit at Pentecost, this text symbolised the character of the new covenant which Christ's death had ushered in. A general disregard for gender, interpreted as female preaching, was an indication of this new covenant, a sign that the 'last days' were at hand and the Second Coming was imminent.

To determine the legitimacy of a public female ministry, apart from specific texts, other arguments focused on the role women fulfilled in the Old and New Testaments. Women like Deborah and Huldah were prophetesses, set apart to 'speak God's word on God's behalf, to be God's "mouth"'.[64] Deborah, who was also a judge, was responsible for leading the Israelites to victory over their enemies the Canaanites.[65] Huldah was consulted by a royal delegation to determine God's will after the rediscovery of the Pentateuch, the Israeli book of law.[66] Their leadership roles were unusual but undeniable. In the New Testament church women like Phoebe ('a servant of the church'), Tryphena and Priscilla ('a fellow worker') were all credited with some form of leadership role.[67] The extent of its public nature, however, remained a subject for some debate.[68]

The social arguments surrounding female preaching show an interesting spectrum of responses in relation to the concept of separate spheres. Arguments against such religious activity were obviously based on male perceptions of proper female behaviour. Angry clergymen believed female preaching would make a woman forward or masculine while others claimed it contradicted the 'shamefacedness and sobriety' that St. Paul had recommended to 'the weaker sex'.[69] Still others felt that women were especially susceptible to the spiritual pride latent in 'the public detail of self-surrender, of struggle and victory, of devotion and success unparalleled'.[70] Women placed in positions of public notoriety would be excessively vulnerable to vanity, self-admiration and ambition, characteristics deemed unsuitable for Victorian ladies. A public life for a woman was not merely unscriptural, but would contradict the ideal of a modest and retiring lady. James Gall, Jr, head of Carrubber's Close Mission in Edinburgh, expressed his concern about the implications of female preaching. Married women would have to bring their husbands along as companions, an inversion of the traditional model of female dependency. Widowed or single women might even employ male assistants who were of no relation to them at all. In Gall's opinion, the position of male travelling companion 'could never be proper'.[71] In this sense it was social propriety, rather than scriptural constraints, which motivated such objections.

Even those who were supportive of female work in other areas objected to female preaching. One editorial argued that although women should keep silent within the church and should be subject within the home, it was acceptable for them to minister to the poor, to give counsel to men and women and to tell 'the poor and dying world of Him who is the Saviour of all men'.[72] The Reverend A.A. Rees, an independent minister from Sunderland, described women speaking in church as 'disreputable and shameful; it is a breach of propriety', although he did not feel it was wrong for them to speak at women's meetings or in Sunday schools.[73] This was not a real expansion in acceptable roles for women, but merely a shift in restrictions. As women moved into the 'social borderland' of public religious activity, men responded by restating the boundaries surrounding the area of public preaching even more clearly.

Social and biblical arguments about female preaching came to prominence when the American Methodist Phoebe Palmer and her husband Walter visited Britain to conduct revival meetings. Phoebe Palmer was a popular holiness lecturer and had published several very successful books on the subject. By the 1850s she had reached the height of her popularity and a trip to Britain was a natural extension of her public preaching ministry. Between 1859–63 she travelled extensively in Ireland, Scotland and England. One of her earliest, most successful and most notorious campaigns was in Newcastle and Sunderland (September–December 1859) where she encountered widespread criticism of her preaching ministry.[74] Palmer was, however, by no means a radical. She herself was reluctant to call her work 'preaching' although she had published a sophisticated biblical treatise which argued in favour of a woman's right to public ministry. In *The promise of the father* (1859) she argued that in fact:

the word *preach*, taken in connection with its attendant paraphernalia, oratorical display, onerous titles, and pulpits of pedestal eminence, means so much more than we infer was signified by the word *preach*, when used in connection with the ministrations of Christ and his apostles, that we were disposed to withhold our unreserved assent to women's preaching in the technical sense. But our desire is to stand up fairly with truth on this point, and, fearful that we may be misunderstood, we wish to state unequivocally, that in a scriptural sense we believe all Christ's disciples, whether male or female, should covet to be endued with the gift of prophecy; then will they proclaim, or, in other words, *preach* Christ crucified, as far as in them lies, under all possible circumstances.[75]

Although this appeared to be a radical defence of female ministry, Palmer's contradictory thinking concerning women's proper role is evident. Consequently, she never argued for ordination nor did she feel women should hold ecclesiastical office. She deliberately distanced herself from 'the question of "Women's Rights"'.[76] In fact, much of Palmer's argument promotes the importance of women remaining within the domestic sphere for by doing so they were more likely to exhibit the 'true piety' necessary to testify for Christ.[77] This attitude was reflected in the writings of other advocates of female preaching, such as Fanny Grattan Guinness and Miss I.T. Armstrong. Despite a clear statement of the right of women to preach the gospel, Armstrong later qualified it by saying that 'generally speaking, home is woman's peculiar sphere'.[78]

Regardless of this essentially conservative basis for female preaching, Phoebe Palmer's public activities elicited a vociferous response from several opponents of the practice. Most notable was the Reverend A.A. Rees, an independent minister from Sunderland, who argued that female preaching was both unnatural and unscriptural, combining both social and biblical objections.[79] The Reverend P.J. Jarbo based his criticisms on the standard Pauline texts and rejected the argument that the 'last days' had come.[80] Palmer was not without her defenders. The Reverend Robert Young, the Wesleyan Methodist who had originally invited the Palmers to Newcastle, reworked the standard Biblical arguments to support female preaching, but relied on a female stereotype to defend her actions socially. Palmer, he argued, was 'peculiarly fitted to address mixed assemblies. She does not take the pulpit, or preach according to the popular acceptation of the term, but with great modesty and simplicity she speaks to edification and exhortation and comfort.'[81] Catherine Booth, the co-founder of the Salvation Army, also published in Phoebe Palmer's defence. The ideas in her pamphlet, intended as a response to Rees, were the most advanced outline of her thinking on female preaching, a process which had begun in 1850 when she heard a Congregational minister demean women and wrote a letter to him on the subject.[82] Booth's pamphlet argued that female preaching was not unnatural, as Rees claimed, nor was it unscriptural. Taking his arguments one at a time she set out to refute him systematically through an extensive discussion of the Pauline texts, Joel's prophecy and the examples of women in the Bible. In her conclusion she stated

> we have endeavoured in the foregoing pages to establish, what we sincerely believe, that woman has a *right* to teach. Here the whole question hinges. If she has the *right*, she has it independently of any man-made restrictions, ... she is at liberty to exercise it without any further pretensions to inspiration than those put forth by the male sex.[83]

Some of Booth's best arguments were those which refuted Rees' social objections,[84] but even outspoken advocates in favour of a public evangelistic role for women allowed the idea of separate spheres to infiltrate their arguments. In a later, substantially edited version of her pamphlet, Booth declared that by nature a woman was more suited to preach because of her refined manners, clear voice and spiritual demeanour. Rather than debase her character, preaching would actually protect her from the coarser elements of society and would 'exalt and refine all the tenderest and most womanly instincts of her nature'.[85] Fanny Guinness made a similar defence when she discussed the story of Eve and original sin. Opponents of female preaching claimed that because Eve had persuaded Adam to sin, women could not be trusted to preach the gospel. Guinness turned this argument on its head and argued that if women had such strong powers of persuasion, they would certainly make good evangelists.[86] A woman's nature, therefore, made her a superior candidate for public ministry. In their efforts to justify female preaching, these women ended up reinforcing the stereotype public female behaviour challenged.

Other arguments in favour of female preaching indicate a growing disregard for the public/private dichotomy. The evangelical concern to reach the masses made all other considerations irrelevant. In a typically pragmatic fashion, George Railton, secretary to William Booth, denounced the contradiction between perceptions of public occupations such as the theatre and female preaching. In an appeal to Christian women he stated:

> Oh, yes, by all means, go on to the stage. Dance there half-dressed, if you like. Take part unblushingly in the representation of the vilest iniquity before a dense crowd of the highest and most learned in the land ... But to stand upon that very same stage to lead men to heaven! To speak, or sing, or pray there! Oh, horrible! Abomination! Degradation of your sex! ... you must be demented – lost to every sense of propriety, utterly without respect for yourself, to dream of anything of the sort! Surely, you will not make such an exhibition of yourself, and disgrace family and friends for ever! ... Woman of God, make thy choice! There is the stage – there is the open-air stand.[87]

In similar pragmatic fashion, other evangelicals came to believe that the failure to use women in religious work was a waste of their potential usefulness. Henry Chapman, head of the Lady Lane Mission in Leeds, argued that there was a surplus of women who were educated and had no domestic responsibilities. These women were not being used to their full potential, even though they would make ideal evangelists, simply because of the social status an idle female conferred on her family. The demands of society, he lamented, only reinforced a concern for ecclesiastical propriety which made 'the preservation of church etiquette and denominational custom' more important than the 'salvation of souls'.[88] Miss C. Wilson, herself an active female preacher, enquired of her fellow Methodist women, 'Can we not, as stewardesses of our Lord's property lay it out to better advantage than in fancy work and evening parties, and the many other things over which women are frittering away their lives?'[89] In the great quest to save souls, social boundaries and ecclesiastical restrictions on female activity were becoming increasingly irrelevant, even for men.

The debate surrounding female preaching was largely *about* women and not a reflection of their opinions on the subject. So how did women themselves feel about their preaching? And what were their motives? The most important element for all female preachers was the necessity of having a Divine or extra-ordinary call. This was a woman's conviction, brought about by the influence of the Holy Spirit, that she was meant to preach publicly. Proof of the truth of this call was in the results. If God was calling her to preach he would 'own her labours' with crowded meetings and numerous conversions. This explains why the Reverend P.J. Jarbo was convinced that Phoebe Palmer's meetings had not been sanctioned by God nor had she been the means of even a single conversion.[90] Advocates of female preaching argued that the Divine call was supported by scripture, for how could the Bible prohibit what the Holy Spirit was promoting? If the call was legitimate, the only logical conclusion was to accept the fact that 'God does call and qualify women to preach … His Word, rightly understood, cannot forbid what His Spirit enjoins.'[91] Taking the argument one step further, defenders of a Divine call argued that to receive a call, but to refuse to pursue it, was 'quenching the Holy Spirit' and was an act of disobedience. Such disobedience was sinful, but part of the blame should be ascribed to those who had created an environment where sinning was preferable to offending religious propriety.

While a call was essential for a public ministry, the exact nature of that call often took different forms. At revival services in Bolton, a woman explained how she had come to the point of speaking publicly. After her conversion God tested her 'by a call to witness with the mouth, and she said, "I have done nothing yet that cost me anything, and if I lose the good opinion of everybody, I will obey."'[92] Most women had a similar experience; their Divine call to preach gave them the strength and courage to attempt a public ministry that must have seemed daunting in the extreme. For the woman mentioned above, it was her experience of entire sanctification that really led her to preach. The holiness concept of full surrender to the will of God made the acceptance of socially alienating tasks a privilege to be exercised. In some cases the call could be of a more dramatic nature. Elizabeth Baxter was from a wealthy middle-class Anglican family who disapproved of her conversion and her subsequent rejection of their affluent lifestyle. She was in the habit of making a weekly visit to the local workhouse, holding a Bible-meeting with the inmates. One week it was quite foggy and she had lost her voice so her mother did not want her to make the trip. Elizabeth felt God was telling her to go anyway and upon her arrival she found that her voice was miraculously restored. She conducted the meeting and by the time she arrived back home her voice was gone again. 'This incident,' she said, 'greatly strengthened my faith in God and helped to carry me through difficulties in my own home'.[93] Geraldine Hooper, another Anglican 'lady' preacher, had discovered her gift for preaching quite by accident. In 1862, she had established a small meeting in a poor area of Bath, when she unexpectedly gave a short address. After several months the meetings became very popular. About this time she had what she termed a 'God-sent dream'. She was standing on the edge of a cliff when she heard voices, so turned to look and saw a crowd of people heading for the edge. She tried to stop them by calling out to them, but only a few heard her and turned back. The rest hurtled over the cliff unheeding and were lost forever. Although contrived, to Geraldine this dream symbolised a Divine justification of her public activity and an endorsement of the attempts she was making to save souls. It seems that a supernatural event, such as a dream or miracle, could encourage women to take the huge risk involved in starting a public ministry. They needed the security of God's approval if they were going to offend family and friends and challenge social norms. Similar motives lay behind the women who were involved in the Salvation Army. When Jane Hockey, an evangelist stationed in Northwich was asked how she could stand so boldly before an audience she replied, 'It is not my strength ... it is God's. I know he will go with me, and so I am not afraid to go anywhere.'[94] Female preachers needed to feel that God not only called them to a public ministry, but that he would sustain them in it.

The preceding discussion about the debate over female preaching and the motivation behind it has hopefully created a context in which the actual evidence of female preaching can be understood. In late nineteenth-century Britain, female preaching existed in three different forms: first, in the emergence of 'lady' preachers of respectable Anglican backgrounds in the 1850s and 60s; second, in the institutional acceptance of female preaching within the Salvation Army; and third, in the re-emergence within Wesleyan Methodism of female evangelists in the closing decades of the century. Each of these traditions will be examined in turn. It should become apparent that despite the obvious differences of background, class and audience that the women involved were surprisingly similar in their attitudes towards their public activity. Be they Anglican or Methodist, working class or middle class, all suffered from the isolation, family disapproval and sense of personal inadequacy which their move into the borderland of female preaching had created.

One of the most interesting developments in mid nineteenth-century evangelicalism was the emergence of a new breed of middle-class female evangelist. The careers of these women have been admirably examined in the work of Olive Anderson.[95] During the 1860s and early 1870s a group of mainly middle-class women from Anglican backgrounds caught the attention of the evangelical subculture which centred on the London-based Mildmay conference and the periodical *The Revival*. Most of these women were young and unmarried, like Miss I.T. Armstrong, Miss S.A. Robinson and Miss Graham. Unlike the female itinerants of early Methodism many of these women continued to preach even after marriage. Geraldine Hooper married Henry Dening in 1868 but maintained her public ministry until her death in 1872.[96] A substantial minority were already married when they started their preaching careers. Mrs Colonel William Bell's husband was 'in rather delicate health', but often accompanied his wife giving her 'every encouragement ... to go and preach in every direction'.[97] Matilda Bishop Bass married in 1856 but did not begin formal preaching until 1867.[98]

Such a career choice was not easy and these women encountered numerous difficulties and entrenched opposition in the course of their labour. One significant hurdle was their own sense of personal inadequacy. One woman who worked among a group of coprolite diggers was moved to say:

> Oh, few know the deep exercise of soul many women have to endure in going forward to the hedges and byways to proclaim that 'yet there is room'. Let me tell my sisters how I have had to hold by a gate to stay the beating of the heart, and get breath, while the silent cry went up for strength to go forth and minister unto these perishing ones, remembering it was not them, but souls for the diadem of our Saviour.[99]

Women also had to overcome social stereotypes about the suitability of their public activity. One female evangelist from Gloucestershire believed many women shrank 'from the responsibility [of public preaching], and are very well pleased with any excuse for silent nonentity, while others seem to have an idea that it is a proof of superior humility and modesty to turn with horror from anything so public'.[100] Such hostility could even translate into active prejudice. The church in Scotland which Jessie McFarlane attended threatened to revoke her membership and the leaders of the Bible Women's Mission, where Mrs Thomson was a superintendent, asked her to resign her position.[101] Swansea magistrates arrested Mrs Bell and her assistant Mr Sutherland for 'limiting a full and free use of a public thoroughfare'. More a symbolic gesture than anything else, the pair were released upon payment of a 20s fine.[102] Most opposition, however, was said to melt away when these women were actually heard preaching. The first time Matilda Bass heard Geraldine Hooper Dening was in 1867. She:

> sat wondering what the service would be like, but feeling little sympathy with the preacher. When Mrs D. appeared and gave out the hymn, 'Tell

me the old, old story', and led it with her own sweet voice, all Mrs Bass's prejudice vanished, and she was carried along by the intense earnestness and enthusiasm of the speaker.[103]

Earnestness, along with the qualities of simplicity and tenderness were common adjectives used to describe the content of female preaching. Mrs Thomson, said one report, dealt 'with the truth of God in a very calm, cool, regular manner, but very solemnly'.[104] Mrs Bell spoke with 'great earnestness and womanly tenderness, urging her message on the hundreds of prodigal sons and daughters before her'.[105] Women were not expected to preach theology nor were they considered good at it. According to one opinion, Jessie McFarlane's '*forte* lies in the picturesque and illustrative rather than in powerful reasoning and logical sequence'.[106]

The venues in which these women preached varied. At the start of their careers, women tended to preach in 'cottages', 'schoolrooms' or other small meeting places.[107] From this base they moved into larger music halls, town halls, assembly rooms and theatres which had been hired for the purpose of an evangelistic campaign. The most famous meetings were those held in the London Polytechnic Institute on Regent Street. Over a series of Sunday evenings in 1866, female preachers like Mrs Thistlethwayte, the ex-courtesan and intimate friend of William Gladstone, conducted religious services.[108] Preaching in chapels, mainly Baptist or Primitive Methodist, also took place, although it was more controversial. Women were careful to avoid the worst criticism by refraining from entering the pulpit. Gospel halls and independent 'iron rooms' were safer and more frequent alternatives.

As for the audiences, Anderson argues that they were not drawn from the ranks of the poor but 'were always respectable, and ranged from the most prosperous members of the "working orders" and lower middle classes ... to the "better classes" ... and the "fashionable and thoughtful"'.[109] While this is no doubt an accurate assessment, it is important to remember that many women got their start preaching to audiences from a lower social class than themselves. Elizabeth Baxter started her career by addressing meetings at her local workhouse and conducting prayer meetings in a poor cottage. Indeed, the public preaching of women was often justified if it was restricted to the poor, even poor men. The ministry of Catherine Marsh, the daughter of an Anglican vicar, was aimed entirely at the conversion of navvies working on the construction of the Metropolitan railway.[110] Mrs Daniell was well known across the country for her mission halls for soldiers which she visited regularly and at which she frequently preached.[111] Women may not have been 'missioning among the poor and outcast',[112] but they were reaching an audience of a lower class than themselves.

Apart from understanding the character of this female preaching it is important to come to an accurate explanation for it. Why did these women emerge and why at this time? Once again, Olive Anderson has some insightful suggestions. She is right to point out the irrelevance of a secular woman's movement and the desire to alleviate the 'spinster problem'. Her analysis also offers a suitable word of caution about the importance of the 1859 revival. Although female preaching is often the result of popular revivalist enthusiasm, there is more behind the female preaching of the 1860s than that. Certainly, these women benefited from the growing indifference to clerical status among the evangelical community which was promoting the existence of professional, full time lay evangelists like Brownlow North, Hay McDowall Grant, Henry Grattan Guinness and Reginald Radcliffe. The sensationalism of a woman evangelist, and the crowds she could attract, were no doubt factors behind the initial support for such evangelistic activity. Such pragmatic motives alone do not explain the persistence of female preaching. The influence of revivalism found an equal partner in the movement for personal holiness which was gaining ground in this period. The holiness emphasis on total surrender to God's will (what Phoebe Palmer called 'laying it all on the altar') provided an apt incentive for women struggling with obedience to their inner leadings.[113]

Other explanations of female preaching can be seen from a closer examination of the lives and motives of the women themselves. Anderson does not consider in great detail the process whereby these women began to preach. Such an inquiry reveals that philanthropy and local evangelistic work were often important starting points for more public activity. Most women were already active in Bible classes, district visiting and other forms of charity. While this in itself could be a test of nerves, it did not involve any sort of public activity beyond knocking on doors and reading scripture to a mainly female audience. Over time, as women gained confidence and assurance, their ministry shifted from an exclusively female audience to an increasingly mixed one, and from relatively small, informal gatherings to often large, formal and very public meetings. This was the experience of Geraldine Hooper Dening, who began her association with Trinity Church, Bath by leading a weekly Bible class for women. Eventually these women asked her to speak to their husbands. When she agreed the services became so popular that they had to be held in the local Temperance Hall. Soon she was assisting the vicar, the Reverend William Haslam, in his open-air meetings, conducting a rescue work for prostitutes and giving her first public address. Within a year she was holding her own open-air services and by the time of her death ten years later had travelled extensively and preached countless sermons to crowds numbering in the thousands.[114] A similar scenario describes the early years of Elizabeth Baxter's career. With the confidence gained from her workhouse meetings (described earlier), she moved on to lead the fledgling Association of Women Workers, an early deaconess institute run by the Pennefather's in London. Only after her marriage to Michael, himself a popular preacher and prophecy lecturer, did she really begin her public ministry.[115]

Local beginnings may have provided women with the experience but it was the people they associated with who encouraged them to preach. The mid-nineteenth century saw the emergence of an extensive but close-knit evangelical community that centred around the Anglican clergymen William Haslam, Robert

Aitken and William Pennefather. Each of these men had extensive networks of friends and acquaintances, no doubt assisted by the proliferation of annual conferences at Keswick, Barnet and later Mildmay. Each one of them had close connections to one or more of the female preachers active in this period. Haslam encouraged Geraldine Dening, as well as his wife, to begin a public ministry.[116] Robert Aitken was a close friend of Elizabeth Baxter's, performing her marriage to Michael in 1868. William Pennefather was well known for his work at Mild-may and with the deaconess institute. These men of authority and respect created a community which supported female preaching and encouraged women to fulfil their public potential. Female preachers themselves acted as important inspirations to other women considering the same decision. It was Geraldine Hooper Dening's visit to Olney which convinced Matilda Bass to adopt a public ministry.[117] Women also established important support networks amongst themselves. Fanny Guinness met Geraldine Dening in Bath and for the next six years they cooperated in several gospel missions. Even after Guinness moved away, the two women remained close friends, comforting each other during illness and rejoicing together over marriage and childbirth.[118] When Dening died it was Guinness who wrote her obituary.[119] Despite the vitality and enthusiasm within this group of lady preachers, it is apparent that their version of female preaching had virtually ceased by the mid-1870s. Anderson's opinions concerning the decline and significance of these women do not need to be repeated here (see pp. 107–8).

Although the Salvation Army represented a form of female preaching very different in tone from the work of these middle-class women, there is evidence to suggest that female preaching, rather than declining, simply adapted to a new environment. Anderson hints at such an interpretation when she points out Catherine Booth's connection to both the respectable preaching of the 1860s and her influence on the Salvation Army, which incorporated public roles for women as a rule of the organisation.[120]

Founded in 1865, the Salvation Army (or the East London Christian Revival Union as it was then known)[121] was undoubtedly the most significant organisa-tion to incorporate and foster the use of female preaching. This was in large part due to the influence of Catherine Booth, whose advanced ideas about public roles for women have been outlined already. By the age of 26 Catherine had already come to the conclusion that women, as human beings, were equal to men. Any inferiority of intellect was the result of poor training, which from babyhood:

> even in this highly favoured land, has hitherto been such as to cramp and paralise [sic] rather than develope [sic] and strengthen her energies, and calculated to crush and wither her aspirations after mental greatness ... [it] has been more calculated to render her a serf, a toy, a plaything, than a self-dependent reflecting intellectual being.[122]

William Booth's opinions were not quite so advanced. As to a woman's ability to achieve intellectual equality with men, he once wrote, '*that* is contradicted by experience in the world and [by] my honest conviction'.[123] It was only when Catherine was preparing her defence of Phoebe Palmer's public ministry that he became convinced of its acceptability.[124] A year later, in William's Methodist New Connexion (MNC) chapel in Gateshead, Catherine felt 'the Spirit come upon her' so she approached the platform and said 'I want to say a word'. William introduced her and sat down while she gave her testimony. Thus began a thirty year preaching ministry.[125]

In 1861 William broke with the MNC, moved to London and began an open-air ministry in the east end. When the work expanded into the East London Mission Booth had no firm ideas about the part women were to play. Being a practical man, he was willing to use any means as long as they would promote the salvation of souls. 'I am for the world's *Salvation*,' he once said, 'I will quarrel with no means that promises help.'[126] When Eliza Collingridge 'gave herself up to do and bear anything for Christ' at a holiness meeting in Bethnal Green, Booth assisted her in organising 12 local women into a group called the 'Christian Female Pioneers' or more commonly 'The Female Band'. These women travelled around London conducting services and sharing their testimonies. Caroline Reynolds, one of the original members recalled, 'We caused a great sensation in London. It was a great cross to us and a great curiosity to the people.'[127] The initiative Collingridge had shown, along with the apparent success of these women, impressed the leaders of the Mission. Persuaded that she should continue her activities, they began to pay her a modest wage so she could afford to work full time for the Mission.[128]

The expansion of the Christian Mission in the early 1870s created a huge demand for workers and thus, 'without any deliberate plan, or even very serious consideration', women were encouraged to address open-airs and conduct meetings so that 'by degrees, and without any preconceived arrangement, ... woman took for herself a place in the Mission.'[129] It was a slow process. In 1875 there was only one female station leader, but by 1878, out of a total of 36 stations, women led 9 of them, while 355 more women spoke at their own local stations.[130] My own preliminary calculations from the *Christian Mission Magazine* indicate that between 1876 and 1879, 144 women were mentioned in the capacity of 'evangelist'. Of that 144, 84 held the position of 'No. 1', while 45 actually opened stations themselves. This rapid growth of female evangelists continued into the 1880s, expanding even more when the Mission branched out overseas.

With numbers as large as these, it was obvious women were responding to the opportunities the Christian Mission offered them. The women who got involved were usually drawn from the ranks of the respectable working class. Eliza Collingridge was a candle factory worker, Rose Clapham a staymaker, Sister McMinnies, a former barmaid, Pamela Shepherd was a rag sorter and her daughter Kate was a domestic servant, as was Kate Watts. They often began their evangelistic careers at an early age. Louisa Lock was converted at 14, became an officer at 16 and by the time of her death at age 21 had been assigned to 9 stations. Kate Shepherd was only 12 when her mother was assigned to open the station at Aberdare. By the time she was 17 she was married and had been to 12 stations. Rose Clapham began Mission work at 16, Kate Watts was 21 and Hannah Clarke was 19. On average, women became officers at 19.[131] The earliest evangelists were not always so young. Pamela Shepherd had five children when she began work with the Mission. Eliza Collingridge, Annie Davis and Caroline Reynolds were also older.

Most of these women began their work relatively free of domestic constraints. Pamela Shepherd's husband had deserted her on numerous occasions, and she was virtually on her own when it came to family management. Marriage was strongly discouraged as a substantial deterrent to women's ministry. Elizabeth Agnes Pollett and Ellen Hall abandoned their public ministry after their marriages, even though Booth had urged them not to give up the work.[132] Successful evangelists like Annie Davis, however, were praised for 'hold[ing] their position' against what George Railton referred to as 'this most terrible form of attack'.[133] Even after marriage a large number of women continued to pursue active public careers within the Christian Mission. Women like Caroline Reynolds had husbands who seemed to have no difficulty with their wives' public role. Mr Reynolds may have accompanied his wife on her travels, but he was never actively involved in the Mission himself. Marriages within the Christian Mission allowed many women to continue their public work as wives of station evangelists. They continued to receive separate billing on advertisements and were always named as co-authors on station reports.[134]

No doubt because of their youth, these women became famous for their aggressive and enthusiastic preaching style. Sarah Dexter and Jane Hockey were quite young when they began a work in Northwich in the fall of 1878. They overcame some initial difficulties and soon were preaching to huge audiences, unaware, however, that they were leading the singing far too fast and 'utterly disregarding the fact that their hearers had not been used to such a pace'.[135] 'Happy' Eliza Haynes became famous for driving through the streets of Nottingham on top of a carriage while playing the fiddle and throwing tracts to the people. A local satirical magazine commented that 'ranting, shouting, waving of umbrellas and backward marching are not the time honoured means of carrying the citadel of the New Jerusalem'.[136] These women, some of them little more than girls, stood on street corners and conducted open-air services. They led processions through working-class neighbourhoods, rang bells, beat drums and shouted the times for upcoming gospel meetings.

Although the Booths' attitude towards female preaching provided the opportunities for a female ministry to flourish, the practice of using women became established in the Christian Mission only when Booth experimented with women as station leaders in 1875. By the end of the year Annie Davis had in Barking a 'good society and congregation, free from debt and fear', and was able to set aside funds for the arrival of her subsequent replacement.[137] Davis was the first 'of a new order of feminine leaders who developed capacity to get together and to manage a congregation and society, as well as preach to it', and 'to prove amid every possibility of difficulty their equality to their brethren'.[138] The success of the experiment was not realised until 1878 when 'a cloud of women officers were suddenly sent flying all over the country, with full power to attack and take possession of towns, just as the men had done'.[139] Women were now entrusted with the charge of more distant fields of labour such as Coventry, Felling, Bolton, Gateshead, Merthyr Tydfil, Sheffield and Belfast, all of which were opened by women.

This endorsement of female leadership was not entirely the result of enlightened attitudes. Local committees, composed entirely of men, were often hostile to female leaders and made it almost impossible for women to exercise any sort of leadership role within the station, regardless of the liberal attitude taken by Booth himself.[140] Opposition was not restricted to the rank and file members but also to a number of Mission workers themselves. According to Bramwell Booth, 'some of the men who had been raised from the very gutters – as soon as they found themselves in office and with certain influence in their own societies, demurred when women were placed beside them in similar positions'.[141] Part of this male antagonism may have been a jealous reaction to the often superior abilities of these women to gather a crowd and control it. Rose Clapham, along with Jenny Smith, was assigned the task of beginning a Mission work in Barnsley. On Monday they started with an open-air meeting, 'and when [the inhabitants] saw us two little things stand there, hundreds of colliers came round us at once'.[142] They went on to have a very enthusiastic meeting and at the time of reporting had a congregation free of debt with about 140 members. The implication was obvious. Because they were women, Clapham and Smith had a drawing power among these rough colliers that a male worker simply would not have. Women seemed to attract bigger audiences and were better able to control their more unruly elements. In some respects women had an unfair advantage over men when it came to the difficulties of evangelistic work, such as attracting and controlling crowds. Women benefited from the deference men automatically gave to the female gender. Kate Watts and Harriet Parkins experienced this when they went to preach in Merthyr Tydfil in 1878. 'It's really laughable when we go out,' they reported. 'The women make curtsies, and the men almost fall on their face.'[143] When George Clegg, a Wesleyan Methodist and Halifax businessman, visited his first Christian Mission meeting, he was impressed by the superior control these female officers had over the rough working class men in the audience.[144]

When the Christian Mission began using women extensively, William Booth and other leaders discovered that not only did women have a superior drawing power and a calming influence, but they actually fulfilled the role of station administrator better than men. According to some reports, women were better disciplinarians, better managers of people, more popular with audiences and less easily discouraged by the task before them.[145] It was felt that women 'could often win the sympathy of those to whom they spoke more easily than could the men',[146] and because of their working-class origins were able to reach a class of people 'that even Messrs Sankey and Moody failed to reach'.[147]

If it was deference which gave women their powers of crowd control, it was the novelty of their performance which brought the people into the hall. In the 1860s 'unusual' was defined as a middle-class woman standing behind a communion rail, or on the platform of a music hall. Miss Graham of Edinburgh, with her 'distinctive utterance', 'effective gestures', and a 'clear, well-formed, though, somewhat monotonous voice', attracted huge audiences of the curious in Peterhead.[148] When it came to sensationalism, however, it was the Christian Mission which excelled. Their extravagant forms of advertising, the noisy public processions and the employment of women in the open air earned them the approbation of all but the most fanatical of evangelicals. An especially controversial technique was the 'Female Band' or 'Hallelujah Lasses', a moniker used to describe the group of female evangelists employed by the Christian Mission to assist in the opening of new stations. There were six of them between the ages of 20 and 30 and they all dressed in severe black with white neck ties and black bonnets.[149] The performance these women gave – complete with poignant testimonies, sentimental solos and heart-wrenching appeals for salvation – may have been vulgar display to some, but it was an innovation which caught the interest of a large number of the working classes who formed the bulk of the audiences. Curiosity was often the only reason some people attended Mission meetings. One convert from Aberdare recalled how, when his wife invited him to hear Pamela Shepherd preach, he went only because it was a 'new thing'.[150] When Honor Burrell started an open-air meeting outside the police station in Rotherham, a crowd of about 300 gathered within minutes because of the novelty of a woman taking to the open-air stand.[151] Whatever the attraction – whether it was a result of their superior management skill, the deference accorded them as women, or simply as a circus side-show – William Booth felt he could claim in the opening months of 1878 that 'the prosperity of the work in every respect just appears most preciously at the very time when female preachers are being allowed the fullest opportunity'.[152]

Despite the confidence William Booth displayed, it was not always easy for women to do the work of an evangelist. In their reports to the *Christian Mission Magazine* they reveal a little of what it was like to struggle with personal doubts, hostile audiences and the numerous administrative responsibilities that confronted a female evangelist each day. When these early women of the Christian Mission agreed to take up leadership positions, their initial response was almost always one of fear and anxiety. Several women remarked on the difficulties they had leaving family and friends to take up the work of the Christian Mission. Hannah Scaif of Sunderland cried when she left home to begin work in Southwick but after a few months she could look back on that time and say, 'I feel all right now, it will do me good, and do my parents good, they will feel if we cannot meet here on earth, we will meet in heaven ... If I had been in the world, I could never have left home and parents, but I can do anything for Jesus.'[153] Rachel Agar was from London and at first refused to go to the North of England because she would have to leave her family. But like Hannah, her reliance on the love of Jesus gave her the strength to continue.[154] Over and over women insisted that personal ambition to become a female evangelist would not have enabled them to overcome their attachment to a secure domestic environment. It was often after the decision to leave had been made that women suddenly began to doubt the wisdom of it. Only when Kate Watts was actually on the train to Merthyr Tydfil did she realise how far it really was from London. Describing the journey years later she said, 'my heart sank within me and I felt I only had God to fall back on'.[155] For women, leaving family and friends was hard enough. What made it worse was the growing realisation that they were not equal to the task. As Annie Davis recalled, 'My first thought on entering upon my new sphere of labour when I beheld the teeming masses around me on every hand, was, "Who is sufficient for these things?"'[156] Obviously, it could only be God. Feelings of inadequacy ran so deep that some women consistently denied their evangelistic role. When William Booth asked Pamela Shepherd to go to Aberdare, she was horrified at the proposal. 'Me go to Aberdare!' she said, 'I'm no good. I can't preach.'[157] When Sarah Sayers was brought before the courts in Salisbury, she rejected the term 'preacher' as a description of herself and used expressions like 'female minister' and 'exhorter' instead.[158] These new positions of authority, with their concomitant responsibilities, brought women face to face with their feelings of anxiety and inadequacy.

Besides personal obstacles to embarking on a career with the Christian Mission, there were a wealth of practical difficulties awaiting a woman upon her arrival to her new field of labour. The first report of Caroline Reynolds and Honor Burrell from Coventry provides an excellent illustration.

> Upon our arrival in the town we wandered about for hours seeking lodgings and finding none. At length a woman took pity on us, and let us occupy a room all night. There was a broken window and we all caught cold.
>
> The next day we found a room which we had to put up with for the next fortnight. But it was several days before we could satisfactorily settle for the place we wanted for Sunday services. And then we had no place for week nights ...
>
> Our first Sunday seemed to us gloomy enough. A few hundred people came to the theatre, including some lads who got into the top gallery and gave us trouble. The offerings were small – very small – and we got no souls at all. We had been moved on from our open air stand just as we had got a grand crowd, and we went home sad indeed.[159]

For most Mission workers the most pressing problem was finding personal accommodation. Reynolds and Burrell had difficulties finding any vacancies, but other women suffered direct discrimination because they were known to be the new female preachers. When Rose Clapham arrived at her prearranged lodgings, the landlady asked her, 'Are you the woman that's coming to preach without Christ?' Rose replied, 'No, ... I am going to speak for him.' But the woman refused to let her stay and she was forced to look elsewhere.[160] Even though Rose tried to downplay her role as 'preacher', the landlady was not convinced. Once living arrangements had been settled, other problems surfaced, like finding a proper meeting place. Popular hostility, in the form of ritual humiliation and disruptions were another difficulty. Women were not exempt from verbal abuse, rotten tomatoes and even arrest. Rose Clapham, Jane Smith, Louisa Lock and Eva Booth (William's daughter) were all arrested at one point in their careers for obstructing public roads and footpaths or creating a disturbance. Charges were normally dropped and women were often given preferential treatment; only Louisa Lock had to serve any gaol time.[161] Although the arrests were largely symbolic attempts by local authorities to maintain control, they illustrate the level of hostility the Mission created among certain elements of the local populace.

Female preaching and other idiosyncrasies of the Christian Mission did not always cause such a violent response but they were unusual methods and could provoke hostility and suspicion. Kate Watts, who went on to become an officer in the Salvation Army, recalled her reaction to the first Mission meeting she ever attended.

> They were kneeling, and in their tremendous earnestness thumping the forms with their hands. When the meeting was over and my brother asked how I had liked them, I replied: 'They ought to be chained up and not let loose.' I had often heard of ranters, but never seen any.[162]

Rose Clapham recalled similar suspicions. Although she was impressed with Annie Davis' shoes – they were slippers, and not boots, the sign of a real lady – she was offended by the impropriety of a woman preaching.[163] In a more humorous vein, Brother Davey of Bolton testified that when he was first invited to hear Mrs Booth preach, he replied, 'I don't want to hear any women's preaching, I have enough of that at home'.[164] If the testimonies of these eventual converts to the Salvation Army are any indication, while audiences may have been willing to attend meetings, they were still reluctant to accept female preaching and the excitement which seemed to accompany it. Certainly their behaviour revealed a certain reluctance to embrace fully Mission practices such as the all night prayer meeting or the after meeting. Women evangelists noted with dismay that despite their best efforts, audiences refused to stay after the evening service to the prayer meeting, and instead 'flocked out like bees'.[165] The converts at Poplar were frightened by Annie Davis' zeal and ran out of the all night prayer meeting she had planned.[166] Once within the community of the Salvation Army, such enthusiastic behaviour became part of the normal routine. For new converts, however, it was still unusual and alienating.

To their credit, these women were not distracted by personal and practical difficulties for long. Although they expressed their fear and trepidation about the future, at other times they appeared enthusiastic, exhilarated and determined to continue their work for the Salvation Army. E. Jane Malthouse, from Stroud declared, 'People tell me I have no business to open my mouth to speak for Jesus, but I mean to speak to every poor sinner I can get at.'[167] When Brother Bennett went to Attercliffe to preach he left Honor Burrell behind to lead the service on her own for the first time. Her account hints at the excitement she must have felt. 'I led a large procession of men singing through the streets; but praise God, I felt quite bold.'[168] These women obviously found their careers exhilarating, and in one sense liberating. Despite their fears, they found that through God's strength, they could persevere and actually experience the sweet taste of success.

This reliance on God was a constant theme running through the reports and testimonies of these early Salvation Army women. They could cope with the fear, prejudice, hostility and administrative difficulties, as long as they had a realisation of the presence of God. Thus, women often described Him as a person with arms to surround and comfort or with hands to hold. Mary Goddard felt that 'underneath and round about me were the everlasting arms, and that was such a complete comfort to me'[169] and Jane Wright asserted when she was sent to Leeds, 'I laid myself entirely in the hands of my Father and bless God He is always with us'.[170] Even if a woman lacked the confidence to commence a public work for God, it was possible to leave those fears with Him, and to experience His comfort and approval. The difficulties and anxieties of the external world were no match for the internal comfort and Divine presence these women claimed to experience.

Apart from the notion of a Divine call, there are several explanations behind female involvement in the Salvation Army. In general, the idea of a self-determining community appealed to men and women alike. Belonging to a distinct group conferred a sense of separateness and acted as a foundation for self-identity.[171] The Salvation Army offered the opportunity for status and improvement. It offered a clearly delineated hierarchy that was available to all and based on ability. Women had the chance to occupy leadership positions that were simply unavailable to the vast bulk of working women. Rose Clapham began her working life as a staymaker, earning 16s a week. By the end of her Army career she had been a missionary to South Africa and the administrator of the Female Training Home.[172] Along with the concepts of community and improvement was the idea of a last resort. Pamela Shepherd had been abandoned by her husband, lost her job and attempted suicide. For her, the Salvation Army gave her the employment, security and friendship she so desperately needed to put her life back together. For her, the risk of social ostracism was worth taking. In the Salvation Army, the practical needs of a growing organisation gave women the opportunity to fulfil their spiritual ambitions.

According to nineteenth-century standards, the Salvation Army was virtually unique in the role it assigned to women. No other group gave them such open and equal opportunities to fill leadership positions. Those in favour of female preaching, looking in at the movement, felt that '[t]he extravagances of the Salvation Army should be avoided, but certainly the Army has shown what women can do in winning souls'.[173] This creative use of women had sparked an interest within mainline denominations. From the mid-nineteenth century institutional opportunities for women had been expanding as first the Anglican church and then later the Wesleyan Methodists re-established the ancient orders of sisterhoods and deaconesses.[174] A growing openness towards improved public roles for women was evident in Wesleyan Methodism, where the restriction of 1803 was still the official position on female preaching. Between 1803 and 1870, despite the ban, 31 women are known to have commenced a preaching ministry.[175] Although Primitive Methodists and the UMFC still allowed female preaching in theory, it seems to have been very rare and it may have only existed at a local level. In the 1880s and 1890s both Wesleyans and the UMFC began to experiment with various forms of institutionalised roles for women. Most is known about the Wesleyan Deaconess Order, especially because of its role as the supposed source of twentieth-century calls for female ordination.[176] However, recent research by John Lenton has found that there were at least 47 women functioning as Wesleyan local preachers in the late nineteenth century.[177] Perhaps of greater significance in promoting such formal recognition of female preaching was the informal and unofficial 'Female Evangelist Homes' run by two Wesleyans, one a minister and one a layman, and the surprising evidence of a large number of seemingly independent female itinerant evangelists. Between 1885 and 1907 there were at least 275 women mentioned in the pages of the Wesleyan weekly newspaper *Joyful News* as performing some sort of public preaching role. At the outset it should be stated that apart from names, locations of meetings and brief comments, no other details are known about these women and any sort of in-depth analysis is thus rendered extremely problematic. The situation is complicated still further by the fact that some of the women designated 'female evangelists', upon closer inspection, did nothing more than glorified visiting. Caveats aside, the discovery of these women acts as a welcome corrective to traditional interpretations which emphasise the decline of middle-class female preaching in the late nineteenth century.

Among Wesleyan Methodists, the move towards an institutional role for women was initiated by the Reverend Thomas Champness, a minister with a long history of evangelistic activity. His ministerial career began in 1857 at the age of 25, when he went out as a missionary to Sierra Leone. Returning to England in 1858 to recover from a bout of fever, he married his first wife Mary and the two of them returned to Nigeria. Within two years she was dead but Champness stayed on until 1863 when exhaustion forced him to abandon his labours. In 1865 he married his second wife Eliza and for the next twenty years held positions in a number of different circuits and participated in a variety of evangelistic activities, such as touring Ireland with Ira Sankey and conducting connectional revival meetings. In 1882 he was appointed to Bolton as a District Missionary and within three years had started up a revival newspaper. The idea for such a work had originated with the President of the Wesleyan Conference, but lack of financing seriously jeopardised the venture. The discovery of an inexpensive local printer and the donation of Eliza's small legacy provided the capital necessary to begin. Although Champness had full editorial control, the daily work of editing fell to Eliza and in her capable hands circulation of what was eventually named *Joyful News* soon reached 30,000.[178] By 1889, Champness' efforts to reach the villages with suitably trained lay agents had become institutionalised as the Joyful News Mission and had moved to Castleton Hall, a large house on the outskirts of Rochdale. Within seven years (1892) *Joyful News* had grown from Champness' pet project into a recognised mission work within the Wesleyan denomination.[179]

Champness was quickly overwhelmed by requests from various circuits for trained lay agents. As early as March 1885, the Reverend William Tindall had written a letter to *Joyful News* expressing his approval of Champness' work with lay men and offering a solution to the problem. Referring to the shortage of men available in relation to the demand, Tindall suggested women would be particularly suited to village work. In fact, they might even do better than men. Women had recently been preaching at City Road Chapel in London to mixed audiences, so 'why not use the gifts bestowed on these or others, in quickening spiritual life and reviving drooping societies in the villages?' In an editor's note, Champness expressed his willingness to 'put forth a helping hand' to female evangelists and to act as a bridge between them and any interested circuit superintendents.[180] His progressive attitudes towards a role for a lay agency also surfaced during the 1885 Wesleyan conference debate over a woman's right to preach.[181] According to Champness, most people were willing to listen to anybody preach as long as God had blessed them with the grace and talent to do so. Since women were called to promote the Gospel, like men, there should be nothing wrong with the practice as long as they operated under the authority of a local Superintendent.[182]

In the winter of 1887–88 Mr George Clegg, a Wesleyan businessman from Halifax, approached Champness with a request for permission to advertise for female evangelists in his paper. Apparently, Clegg had already started a work with female evangelists, having been inspired by the successful employment of women in the Salvation Army, many of whom had once been Methodists.[183] By November 1887 he had taken a house and employed seven women. As their appointments were listed in the pages of *Joyful News*, Champness must have been aware of this work, but it was not until March 1888 that formal links between the Joyful News Mission and Clegg's Female Evangelists' Home were established. In the official announcement, Champness stated that Clegg was the financial head of the organisation and Miss Susannah Cook was the Superintendent of the Home, which from now on was referred to as the '"Joyful News" Female Evangelists' Home'.[184] Money was not solicited nor would the women receive wages, but room and board would be provided, along with an allowance for clothes and minor expenses.[185] At the time of affiliation, there were nine women involved in the work. By the end of the following year, 25 women had passed through the doors on Gladstone Road, although only 16 remained active.

After November 1896, the continued existence of the Home becomes somewhat uncertain.[186] As of 1899 52 women had been employed in the work at one time or another.[187] These were by no means large numbers, but did represent an institutionalised form of what appeared to be a fairly extensive practice within the Wesleyan Methodism of the late nineteenth century.

By 1892 Champness was becoming convinced that there were numerous openings for 'godly women' in the foreign mission field and stated his intention of opening up a home similar to Clegg's.[188] In September of the same year he had made some progress, training four women in various circuits with the primary intention of sending them overseas. When his daughter Mary officially opened a separate Joyful News Female Evangelists' Home in Rugby in April 1893 it was obvious that Champness had decided to use women as domestic workers. Over the next twenty years 86 women were associated with the home in Rugby.[189] On average there were 19 women active at any one time; the most was in 1899 when 31 women were working. In 1900 the Home moved 'to a red brick house facing the Wrekin' in the town of Wellington, in Shropshire. According to Mary Champness, Rugby had had its fair share of the work and as there was an opportunity to start a new work in Wellington, they decided to move.[190] When Thomas Champness retired from active duty the work of Joyful News was transferred to Wesleyan control. Male evangelists were transferred to Cliff College, a Methodist lay training institution in Derbyshire.[191] Female evangelists either retired, continued on an independent basis or became Wesleyan deaconesses.[192]

In addition to these two institutional manifestations of a re-emerging public preaching role for women, there is also ample evidence from within the pages of *Joyful News* and elsewhere that there were many women who worked as independent evangelists. Their activities resembled that of the professional revivalist much more than the work conducted by the women of the Halifax or Rugby Homes, but very little is known about them. Fifty-nine have been traced in the pages of *Joyful News*. Two of the most prominent were Hilda Tindall and Miss C. Wilson. Hilda Tindall was from Southport, the daughter of the Reverend W.H. Tindall and an occasional contributor to Champness' newspaper. In 1885 she held three mission campaigns where, assisted by the local Methodist clergyman, she sang and delivered addresses to substantial audiences.[193] Miss C. Wilson[194] was from Carlisle, in Cumbria and was perhaps the most active of all of these Methodist women. Once described as 'a lady gifted as an Evangelist and an untiring worker in the Master's service',[195] Wilson's private life, however, remains hidden. Details concerning her public preaching career are also scanty, apart from the fact that she travelled regularly conducting mission services from at least 1885 (maybe earlier) until 1903. No other woman preached for such an extensive and continuous period. She first came to public notice with a report of her seven week mission at Black Hill and Shotley Bridge with the assistance of Miss Watson, who was to be her regular companion for the next few years. Like many of her subsequent meetings, these were quite successful, with 550 adults and 700 children 'saved' at Black Hill, and 150 adults and 200 children 'saved' at Shotley.[196] While Tindall, Wilson and the other independent women operated outside of the Joyful News organisation, they were familiar with it and were publicised by it.

Although the original inspiration for the Female Evangelists' Home came from the Salvation Army, its manifestation in a Wesleyan mould differed in a number of respects. For a start, unlike the Army, Clegg's and Champness' original idea was to establish a work for middle-class Methodist women. When soliciting support in late 1887 Clegg made it clear he wanted women who could 'give of their services, as our funds will not allow us to pay them'.[197] And in order to volunteer one's services, women had to be from homes wealthy enough to survive without the wages of one of its members. The Reverend H.T. Chapman commented on the quality of the women he met after taking a tour of the Evangelists' Home in 1890. He asserted that contrary to some rumours, these were not women 'who had failed in other departments, [nor] those who were seeking better wages'. Instead, they were 'intelligent, well brought up, capable, godly young women', some of whom had sacrificed waged employment to get involved.[198]

Lack of evidence makes any generalisations impressionistic but it seems that not only were these female evangelists predominantly middle-class, but they were also older. Salvation Army women were, as we have seen, little more than youths when they undertook their positions. Ages are only available for four of the Joyful News (Halifax) women, and except for one, the other three were all in their middle twenties.[199] Marriage also appeared to be more of a hindrance. The overwhelming majority of these institutional evangelists were single. When Mary Jane Smith got married in 1896 her public evangelistic activity with Champness' home ceased. Presumably, she gave up her career once the responsibilities of creating her own home were thrust upon her. For the independent women listed in *Joyful News*, marital status appears less of an issue. Thirty-six were single, eleven appear to have been widows while twelve travelled with their husbands.[200]

H.T. Chapman's tour of the Female Evangelists' Home in Halifax indicated that in fact a large proportion of the Halifax (and by extension Rugby) women rarely conducted preaching services in front of a mixed audience. Once a woman entered a Home, she could be guaranteed a life characterised by a fairly regimented daily schedule. Breakfast was at 7:45, there was visiting from 10:00 until 12:30 when the women returned for dinner, after which they would visit in the afternoon for another two hours. In the evenings a variety of evangelistic services were held, either in the open air, the nearby school chapel, or mission centre. Female class meetings were conducted and on occasion, Sunday evening services were taken as well. Biblical studies, which culminated in exams administered by the local minister, topped off a day of ceaseless activity. Most women did not live at the Home, but in the various circuits which employed them where their routine was probably less regimented but no less busy. After her initial training period in Rochdale, Mary Jane Smith was assigned to the Devon and Dorset Mission, where, her diary reveals, she spent the bulk of her time visiting the sick, holding class and prayer meetings and teaching Sunday School. She did hold the occasional open air meeting where she sang and accompanied herself on the portable harmonium. Besides these regular duties, she conducted at least three revival missions in the Wiltshire and Devon region: one in Collingborne, one in Branscombe and another in Chard. At all of them she addressed mixed audiences. The results of her efforts were disappointingly small. Over a three week period there were only two converts at Collingborne, although things improved at Chard, where within a week 13 had indicated conversion.[201] In such small villages, better results may have been excessively optimistic. To Mary Jane, however, these figures were something to praise God for. One evening, when the chapel at Branscombe was full (it seated about 200) Smith noted 'I had much liberty in speaking. Mr Peart took the after meeting and Praise God for 2 converts.'[202] Such optimism masked the struggle Wesleyan Methodism and other denominations were experiencing in their efforts to make progress of any sort among the villages, let alone stimulate a revivalistic atmosphere. If Mary Jane's predicament was at all typical, the demands of propriety and the apathy of their audiences acted as the biggest hurdles to success for these middle-class female evangelists.

Because of a lack of detailed sources, it is extremely difficult to answer the interesting questions such as, how did people respond to these women? and how did the women themselves view their preaching? With regards to the former, promoters of a female agency within the Wesleyan connection were quick to point out that once people saw God was blessing the work their prejudices melted away and they became 'our best friends'.[203] However true that may have been is debatable, but the popularity of some of these female evangelists was undeniable. In 1887 the Methodists of Dunstan-on-Tyne had been expecting Miss Wilson's arrival for nearly two years. Joint prayer meetings between the Wesleyans and the UMFC were held and her services were crowded with men and women who were not regular church attenders. Unfortunately her voice gave out, forcing her to leave sooner than expected. Nevertheless, widespread gratitude for even this brief visit was expressed.[204] On Sunday, 15 May 1887, Miss Kate Russell from Hereford conducted an open air meeting in Moulton as part of a week's mission. Fifty-two men from the local ironworks were converted and it was remarked that 'Miss Russell not only preaches but sings the gospel with great power'.[205] Notwithstanding the connectional ban on female preaching, it seems apparent that a substantial group within the Wesleyan connection actually favoured and promoted the activity of women both within the institutional framework of the Joyful News Mission and on a more independent basis.

The UMFC effort to begin a work similar to Joyful News provides further evidence for the existence of a subgroup within Methodism which supported female preaching. The cause was really taken up by H.T. Chapman and Alfred Jones, the UMFC connectional evangelist and frequent contributor to the *Free Methodist*. Articles appeared regularly throughout 1890 detailing the slow process of establishing a Female Evangelists' Home. In March the idea was presented in a series of articles on sisterhoods.[206] In June Chapman visited the Joyful News

Home in Halifax, reported on its work and issued a call for UMFC candidates. This appeal was repeated in August and in December Jones reported he had gone ahead and hired a woman to work in his circuit under his direct supervision. Miss Garnett had six weeks training at the Joyful News home and was now at Stapenhill, near Burton, for three weeks holding various services and prayer meetings. Although Jones and Chapman were enthusiastic, they did admit they received little support from the connection itself with regards to this matter.[207] As with the Wesleyans, the widespread use of female evangelists was never promoted by more than a small group of UMFC clergy and laity.

In many ways, the attitudes of these middle-class female evangelists was remarkably similar to that of the Salvation Army women. The personal difficulties facing Mary Jane Smith when she decided to join the Joyful News Home reflect the same attachment to home and concern about familial disapproval that so many Salvation Army women record. Before actually taking up her post as a female evangelist, Mary Jane encountered severe familial disapproval of her decision. As she recorded in her diary:

> [b]ut the thought that souls were perishing without a hope beyond the grave gave me no rest. God clearly revealed to me His will and through much opposition I left home for the work. It was hard to leave home without my parents wish but I felt I was only doing right and following the guiding hand of God. Therefore he gave me grace to do and bear.[208]

Mary Jane also struggled with her own preaching ability. During the Collingborne mission she wrote 'the Service tonight was well attended but not much power. The fault was in me. Forgive me, Lord.'[209] Just like the Salvation Army women, she had to confront the barriers of parental objection and feelings of personal inadequacy once she had embarked on her career. And like those working-class women, Mary Jane persevered because of a deep reliance on God and a belief in his approval of her work. Speaking in anticipation of her first revival mission she was prompted to say 'I believe that God will use me in the conversion of many souls and make me a blessing to others'.[210] In some respects, however, Mary Jane's lot was quite an easy one. She and the other Joyful News women never had to worry about money, or finding proper accommodation for their meetings because they were operating within a pre-existing denominational structure. Nor did they have to worry about hostile audiences because for the most part they were preaching to church attenders and their children, people already predisposed to view their message in a favourable light.

Although the numbers of women involved in this Methodist movement remained small, their influence on the denomination, and on society as a whole, was significant. Within the Wesleyans, their existence pointed to an ongoing support for female evangelistic activity directed towards mixed audiences. The impact of the Joyful News Home on the UMFC influenced the latter denomination to consider similar measures, even if never adopted. Despite these rumblings, female preaching never got beyond its fundamentally 'fringe' status among most late nineteenth-century Methodists. Most of the women preached in rural locations where acceptance of their roles may still have had links to the female preachers from the early part of the century and where, in a smaller context, their chances of success were better. That female preaching still existed is testimony to the internal desires of these middle-class ladies to take up some form of evangelistic activity. Certainly they experienced the restrictions of Victorian standards of propriety more deeply than their counterparts in the Salvation Army. As such, the routine and regulations of a Female Evangelists' Home could be as restrictive as they were empowering. Despite the potential radicalism of such behaviour, the women themselves were unwilling to go all the way to demand equality in the social sense. These middle-class women were much more controlled – by their environment, by ideas of propriety, and by their daily routines – than the teenagers working for the Salvation Army. It seems that the barriers to the full participation of middle-class women in religious life were simply too high to be totally overcome.

It is obvious that there was a substantial amount of female religious activity in the late nineteenth century that was not philanthropically oriented. These women, or evangelists, were relatively unconcerned with social issues facing the poor and focused the bulk of their attention on the state of people's souls. Female preaching as such was a diverse phenomenon in the latter part of the century. There were middle-class women from Anglican backgrounds, working-class women from the east end of London and rural middle-class Methodists. It was also a controversial phenomenon, and as such much more popular than its numbers might reflect. Even William Gladstone went to hear a woman preach.[211] Like all sensational events, reactions were wide-ranging. Clerical male opinion ranged from outright hostility to regulated approval and female opinion could be equally negative. But for the women themselves, it must have been an empowering experience, at least on a personal level, because it offered many women an opportunity to exercise skills such as leadership, organisation and public speaking.

Female preachers, be they spontaneous and informal, as in the 1859 revival, or institutionalised within a denominational structure, challenged the double restrictions of religious and social divisions between public and private. In order to pursue such activity social notions of the female role were rejected and biblical prohibitions were ignored. Women in the nineteenth century pushed the boundaries of their religious 'sphere of power' to its logical extreme. Paradoxically, the women who embarked on this public evangelistic activity never directly translated their power over crowds into a political context, an indication, perhaps, of the continued strength of Victorian ideals of womanhood. For these women, political emancipation was simply not part of their agenda. Historiographically, there is tension between the interpretation of female evangelistic activity as a political process of emancipation and as a quest to fulfil internal religious ambitions. If the first was not achieved, then the second certainly was, and for that reason alone female preachers achieved what they set out to accomplish.

MR. ALBERT SHAKESBY, AS HE NOW APPEARS IN THE PULPIT,
THROUGH THE GRACE OF GOD.

MR. ALBERT SHAKESBY,
As he appeared on the stage and in pleasure fairs.

Albert Shakesby the evangelist, before and after his conversion

CHAPTER FIVE

Working–class evangelists

THE PURPOSE of this chapter is to bring to life a vigorous tradition of working-class evangelistic preaching within popular Protestantism in the second half of the nineteenth century. The current state of research and the dispersed nature of the sources make it impossible to attempt a nationwide survey of working-class lay preachers to parallel Professor Brown's comprehensive social history of the Nonconformist ministry in England and Wales.[1] That such a survey needs to be undertaken is becoming clear from recent work on the north of England, which suggests that Methodist and other traditions of lay preaching and evangelism were more ubiquitous in Victorian Britain than the most ardent exponents of secularisation theories have been prepared to admit. For example, Mark Smith has shown that the lay-inspired evangelistic enthusiasm of Wesleyan and Primitive Methodists survived into the mid-Victorian period and continued to throw up working-class preachers of conspicuous enthusiasm. Smith writes that 'the majority of local preachers, like their congregations, probably came from working-class occupational groups, but clear occupational data are available on only four nineteenth-century local preachers – two weavers, a miner, and a plasterer's labourer – and it would be unwise to draw firm conclusions from such inadequate data'.[2] That the author of such an intensely local study should find it impossible to arrive at conclusions about the occupational status and social role of local preachers is an indication of how difficult this subject is and of how much remains to be done. By contrast, my ambitions are strictly limited.

This chapter represents an analysis of a self-selecting group of some eighty-eight working-class preachers who exercised a public ministry in the second half of the nineteenth century. That this is a relatively small sample of the total number of lay preachers who serviced the various Methodist and popular dissenting denominations is not in doubt, but my concern has been less with those tied into particular religious denominations than with those sturdy individuals who sat loose to denominational discipline and other social controls. The main sources consulted include a range of religious periodicals, especially those, like *The Revival*, which regularly listed the evangelistic activities of popular preachers, and the published biographies and autobiographies of the evangelists themselves. Most of the biographies were written by sympathetic ministers, friends or relatives and most of the autobiographies were edited by colleagues and friends with greater literary pretensions than the subjects themselves. This study is therefore restricted to those evangelists who, for whatever reason, were deemed worthy enough to attract a biography or a mention in the religious press. This information requires careful handling. The almost uncanny similarity of the childhood experiences, conversion narratives and religious enthusiasm indicate that many of these accounts were written for a particular audience and according to a particular model. Religious lives of working-class evangelists are as much a literary genre as the lives of other religious groups, from nuns to city missionaries, in Victorian Britain. In short, we are dealing with the sturdiest and most influential representatives of a much wider tradition. The respective sizes of the tip and the body of the iceberg will become clearer only with the publication of more local studies of later Victorian religion.

For the sake of clarity, this chapter has been divided into three sections. The first deals with shared themes in the lives of working-class evangelists, including the importance of childhood experiences, the relevance of denominational connections and their links with the female preaching surveyed in the previous chapter. The second examines the various strategies and colourful devices these evangelists used to spread their religious message. The third section discusses the complex relationships between working-class evangelists and the wider evangelical community, which they at once enlivened and embarrassed. In particular, middle-class attitudes and popular hostility against working-class preachers will be examined in the light of the content and style of their discourse. Above all, the aim has been, as much as possible, to re-create the vulgar zeal and tender pieties of those who were regarded as dangerous eccentrics by established interests, but whose unmitigated enthusiasm and 'common touch' made them serviceable religious instruments within the eclectic world of popular evangelicalism.

CHARACTERISTICS

Tom Holland was born on 5 November 1870 in the townland of Old Lenton, near Nottingham. His father moved the family to a colliery village in Co. Durham two years later, where he found work in the mines. But 'Mussel Bob', so nicknamed because he sold mussels in local public houses, struggled to support his family as well as a substantial drink habit. Tom's mother took in some sewing, but she and her four children were often on the brink of starvation. In 1878, Tom was asked to join the local Primitive Methodist church choir. Although the other boys ostracised him because of his poverty, he discovered he had a talent for singing and persevered. Several years later the Salvation Army came to town, with its noisy processions, late night meetings and enthusiastic preaching. One of the most unexpected outcomes was the conversion of 'Mussel Bob'. As the living standard of the Holland family started to increase, now that

Robert had signed the pledge, Tom himself remained unconverted. He had started work in the local colliery and had become quite famous for his singing. He formed a choir which sang throughout the county, raising money for charity events such as the soup kitchens which operated during the Durham miners' strike. After a number of years, Holland went into business for himself and was extremely successful, opening a number of musical instrument and confectionery shops in South Moor and Stanley, villages just south of Newcastle. Business success, however, contributed to his moral downfall. He started playing cards and gambling, and although he attended church regularly, he was by no means religious. These habits worsened until they affected his family life, his singing and even his business. Only when gambling threatened the closure of his shops did Holland realise the error of his ways and begin to desire something better for his life. One night in 1904 he had been engaged to sing at Ousten Primitive Methodist Chapel along with two other local preachers. The conversation he had with them, along with the solo he sang, combined to give him a vivid impression of his parents praying for him. That very same night, he recalled:

> I sought mercy and found it in a sense of forgiveness and the possession of an inexplicable joy and peace which the world had never given me, and I am certain so long as I trust the hand that healed me and to which I committed myself that night, there can come no power that will separate me from the Love of Christ nor take away that peace and joy.[3]

He then asked God for forgiveness and mercy and found peace. For Holland, his conversion represented the start of a completely new life. He joined the local Primitive Methodist minister, Reverend W.J. Willis, in his full-time evangelistic work for the next six years, singing at missions throughout Durham, Cumbria and North Staffordshire. After that, he branched out on his own, preaching and singing across the country with his three daughters.

In many ways, this brief sketch of Tom Holland's life represents common themes in the biographies and autobiographies of a majority of working-class preachers. All the evangelists gave their childhood and early development a prominent place in their accounts, many of which reflected the troubled and transitory nature of working-class domestic life throughout the nineteenth century. Like Tom Holland, several other evangelists had fathers who were alcoholics and thus had thrust the responsibility of supporting the family on to the mother. Virtually all working-class biographies place a greater emphasis on the mother figure.[4] For the evangelists examined here, the mother was eulogised as the source of their earliest Christian influences, even if ignored or resisted for many years. William Willis' mother taught him his prayers and sent to him to Sunday school, which was probably the extent of her own personal spirituality.[5] Gipsy Smith, a nationally known evangelist, was born a Romany gypsy. His mother died when he was quite young and his account of her spiritual influence over him pushed the limits of Victorian sentimentality to new heights.[6] Tom

Holland felt so strongly about his mother that he was moved to exclaim, 'there is an urgent need to-day for godly mothers to restore the neglected altars of our homes so that once more the fires of holy religious passion may be lighted. I am becoming more and more convinced that we have underestimated the far-reaching influence of Christian motherhood.'[7]

While the loss of a mother could be a traumatic experience, several evangelists lost both parents to an early death. William Foster, an early Salvation Army officer, lost his father when he was only 8 years old, leaving his mother to cope with five children. She herself died three years later, leaving relatives to adopt Foster and his siblings.[8] Albert Mahomet, an evangelist born in the east end of London, was virtually orphaned when his alcoholic mother and stepfather were arrested for drunken and disorderly behaviour. Despite his strenuous objections, he and his three siblings were taken to Limehouse Workhouse, where after three years they were removed by a kindly uncle from Norfolk.[9] For many working-class evangelists, childhood was associated with violence, hardship, death and economic uncertainty. That such an existence could be idealised indicates how far these men had moved away from such a lifestyle.

It should be noted that the majority of evangelists studied here did not come from the ranks of the lowest classes. Many of their fathers could be more accurately described as 'comfortable', working as farmers, butchers, whitesmiths, handloom weavers, innkeepers and blast furnacemen. What often made the difference between a comfortable existence and poverty was the presence of alcohol. Tom Holland made a direct correlation between his father's drinking habit and the family's poverty when he recounted the practical result of Mussel Bob's conversion experience. 'Father worked and handed his pay to mother instead of to the publican. We soon had plenty of good, substantial food.'[10] He himself received a new suit of clothes, giving him the respectability he longed for so he could hold his head up in the choir.

The years of young adulthood were also fraught with traps and pitfalls. Many young men renounced the religion of their mothers in favour of a vigorous and aggressive working-class culture which placed value on physical prowess and mental agility. Prominent among these pastimes were boxing, wrestling, cock-fighting and dog-racing, along with gaming, pigeon-flying and of course, copious amounts of drinking. Working-class evangelists had often been the leaders of the rough culture within their local community. Richard Weaver is only one example. Nicknamed 'Undaunted Dick' after winning a bar fight which lasted 32 rounds, Weaver was infamous in the area around his native Shrewsbury for his feats of strength, practical jokes and narrow escapes from the law.[11] Henry Moorhouse was known as 'a prince among card players' and was financed by the owner of a gambling den in Manchester against all opponents.[12] Even in their unconverted state, Weaver and Moorhouse exhibited the leadership that would eventually see their names become household words within the evangelical community.

Tom Holland's autobiography also reveals the importance of work in the working-class evangelist's life. Holland started his working life in the coal mines of Hetton-le-Hole when he was seven years old. After his marriage he moved to South Moor, where he was employed in the local colliery. After about six months he quit in order to sing professionally and open his own businesses.[13] Of the 57 evangelists whose occupations are known, by far the largest proportion came from the ranks of skilled craftsmen, or Class C in Table 1. Within this group the most common occupation was in the mining industry, where 10 evangelists had been employed. Men like Richard Weaver, Peter Mackenzie, Cheyne Brady, James Flanagan and Moses Welsby had all started their working lives as coal miners. Other skilled occupations included a calico weaver, one joiner, an engine driver, a navvy and a stone quarryman. A significant number of evangelists had some connection to the world of popular culture, as pugilists, conjurors or professional singers and have been included in the ranks of Class C. The second largest group was Class F, the labourers, servants and paupers. Within this group the most prominent occupation was that of agricultural labourer (4), followed by cab drivers (2), mason's labourer (1), canal labourer (1), thief (1) and two gypsies. Among Class B, working-class evangelists emerged out of the self-employed service sector as butchers (2), and one grocer, a printer and a local shopkeeper. Most evangelists, therefore, while distinctly 'working class', were not from the lowest ranks of society. Many had a skill and some were relatively

Table 1: *Working-class evangelists, by occupation*

Class	Occupation			Number
A	gentry and professions			0
B	merchants, manufacturers, retailers			6
C	skilled craftsmen			
		textiles	4	
		wood	1	
		metal	4	
		building	4	
		mining	10	
		other*	5	28
D	agriculture (excluding labourers)			0
E	maritime, naval and military			2
F	labourers, servants, paupers			11
G*	sport and entertainment			10
U*	unknown			31
			Known Total:	57
			Overall Total:	88

This classification is based on Clive Field, 'The social composition of English Methodism to 1830: a membership analysis' in *Bulletin of the John Rylands Library*, 76 (1994), pp. 153–78. Categories with an * have been added to the original classification. Since a number of these evangelists had several different occupations, they were assigned to the catergory which represented their most significant occupation.

prosperous. This point should not be overstated. A childhood spent thieving and peddling trinkets was by no means 'comfortable' or secure.[14] Life remained precarious well into adulthood, as the frequency of the preachers moving in search of work will attest. Several working-class preachers went through a succession of different occupations, an indication of their ongoing economic instability. Recourse to poor relief was not uncommon. Mary Poole was forced to apply to the local workhouse to bury two of her children because Joshua, her husband, drank their entire income away. When he was finally arrested for physically abusing her, she supported herself and her remaining children on parish relief payments of 2s 6d per week.[15]

In the evangelical press, discussions about recently converted working men exhibited a tension between those who had 'honourable' occupations, which could be kept after conversion, and those involved in 'wicked' occupations, which had to be renounced. With regards to the latter, middle-class evangelicals were fond of saying that 'almost every class and every type of wicked occupation has been converted' and that the farther down one descended the 'scale of respectability', the more lay preachers were to be found.[16] Although evangelical propriety demanded the renunciation of these dishonourable occupations, the exotic pasts of these former reprobates represented a dangerous but exciting working-class subculture, which many middle-class evangelicals found scintillating and at the same time repellent. Working-class evangelists who had been former conjurors, acrobats, or pugilists or prize fighters were expected to abandon what were now wicked and sinful occupations. The hint of the forbidden, however, added a dash of the exotic to ordinarily mundane mid-week preaching services or anniversary teas. Because these individuals now rejected their old lifestyle, it was 'safe' for discussion and made the individual an object of congratulation. When Albert Shakesby was converted, he proclaimed his intention, before he left the chapel, of closing his athletic school and gymnasium the next day.[17]

For some working-class evangelists, it was while they were working for religious employers that they were converted. Charles Richardson was an agricultural labourer and had worked for several farmers in and around Tetford, before being hired by William Riggall. Riggall was a Wesleyan Methodist whose home was the centre of society activity and it was not unexpected that Richardson, already a serious, hard-working young man, was converted under his influence.[18] Richardson did not give up his secular occupation; instead he adopted a career which gave him the opportunity to be more flexible with his time. As a woolwinder, Richardson could use his visits to the surrounding farms as opportunities to spread the gospel, because if the farmer was religious, he would often get a congregation together for Richardson's visit.[19] In other cases, working-class evangelists, by keeping their jobs, were seen as exerting a good influence on their employers. William Hickingbotham was an agricultural labourer in Derby and worked for an irreligious employer. After Hickingbotham's conversion, he reproved his employer for excessive swearing, prompting the man to threaten him with dismissal. Of course, this threat was never implemented and Hickingbotham worked for him for over thirty years. He eventually became his employer's spiritual advisor, leading the family devotions. The employer called for Hickingbotham during a dangerous illness and the latter was able to gain his conversion.[20] Again, middle-class observers of working-class evangelists idealised the honest fulfilment of secular employment as a simpler, purer expression of faith. A humble occupation could actually enhance the status of a working-class evangelist – be it a coal miner or conjuror.

Biographies stress the importance of conversion as a watershed experience. Working-class evangelists saw it as the single most important event in their lives and a large number of them could identify the specific date, place and means of change. Albert Shakesby, a music hall strongman and prize fighter, knew the time of his conversion down to the exact minute when he recalled 'God's hand laid hold of me while in Gt. Thornton St, and on January 13th, 1904, at 9:25 pm, at the penitent form in the Gt. Thornton St Primitive Methodist Chapel, I realised, through faith in Christ, all my sins were washed away.'[21] While the actual conversion may have been sudden, it was one of many which was preceded by a series of coincidences and religious struggles, sometimes lasting for several years but all designed to point the individual towards Christ. Robert Annan had attended the revival services in Dundee throughout 1860–1, until one night, after fifteen hours of mental anguish and lonely torment, he found salvation.[22] Part of the trauma and melodrama surrounding conversion can undoubtedly be attributed to the relatively young age at which it was experienced. Of the working-class evangelists examined in this study, age at conversion is known for twenty-six of them. Only 5 were converted between the ages of 10 and 20; 16 between ages of 21 and 30; 4 between 31 and 40 and 1 over the age of 60. Tentative as these figures are, they do indicate a tendency for conversion to occur during the mid-twenties. Young men were involved in the rough culture around them and it was often only under duress that they even considered attending church, let alone contemplated conversion. The influence of a godly wife or relative, the death of a close friend, a desire to settle down or a mystical vision were just some of the reasons these men embraced a religious life.

When conversion occurred, associations with their former lives ceased. The rough culture was shunned, old habits were broken and friends from the old life were avoided. These working-class evangelists believed such visible and sudden behaviour was a reflection of the reality of their conversion. When Albert Shakesby was converted, he gave his boxing regalia to the minister to have it thrown on the fire.[23] When W.J. Willis was converted, he drowned and buried his champion racing dog, rather than sell it to anyone else.[24] Now that their religious sensitivities were awakened, these young men were at great pains to distance themselves from their former lives, although the process was often more difficult than it first appeared. At first no one in Biddulph took Richard Weaver's protestations of conversion seriously, until they saw him testifying at the local lovefeast and preaching to his fellow colliers. One night, when some men were harassing his fiancée, he beat them up. His apparent spiritual failure shamed him so much that he renounced religion, broke with his girlfriend and left the town.[25]

The next logical step after conversion was to join a church. Looking at the sample of working-class evangelists studied, the breakdown of denominations can be seen in Table 2.

Table 2: *Working-class evangelists, by denomination*

Denomination	Number
Primitive Methodist	17
Wesleyan Methodist	15
Nondenominational	13
Baptist	3
Bible Christian	2
Presbyterian	2
Welsh Methodist	2
Plymouth Brethren	5
Free Church	1
Jewish (converted)	1
unknown	27
Total:	88

Adherence to any one denomination was not considered permanent for most working-class evangelists. Many of them participated in two, or sometimes even three, during the course of their careers. Movement was almost always from the more liturgical and ministerially dominated to the more spontaneous and lay inclusive. Henry Varley, a self-employed butcher, had been brought up a Baptist and was a member of Bayswater Baptist Church in London. In the late 1850s, the Reverend John Stoughton of Kensington Congregational Church invited him to start a Sunday school among the pig feeders living in the Notting Hill area. After several months of attracting large congregations, Varley instituted a communion service and began acting as the resident minister. This nondenominational, and highly irregular, work cost him his membership at Bayswater Baptist. Built in 1860, Varley's 'Free Tabernacle', as it was called, remained an nondenominational church with a lay minister, despite pressure from established denominations to join them. Varley believed denominationalism was unscriptural and that it restricted spiritual freedom, ideas which prompted the Reverend C.H. Spurgeon's remark that Varley was 'a bad Baptist and a half-bred Plymouth Brother'.[26]

Spurgeon's remarks were probably not too wide of the mark. Varley and many other working-class evangelists had connections, some stronger than others, with the religious group known as Plymouth Brethren. The doctrines which this group espoused and the characteristics which it exhibited tended to promote an active interest in lay evangelism. In the early days of the movement, those associated with the Brethren were keen to stress the concept of 'Christian unity', that the growth of denominations within Protestantism was wrong and had created numerous obstacles to what they perceived to be the simple New Testament directive of Christian fellowship. Thus, as long as individuals could testify to their conversion and Christian life, the Brethren were prepared to 'meet' with them, that is, to have communion with them and to hold services together. George Brealey, an evangelist in the Blackdown Hills area of England, was fond of saying 'My parish is the world. Anywhere for Jesus I would go, and anywhere I would preach, provided I be allowed to take the Truth, the whole Truth, and nothing but the Truth.'[27] This flexible and pragmatic attitude meant that the Brethren attracted like-minded individuals from a range of denominations and backgrounds, whose primary desire was to supersede denominational barriers and preach the gospel. Henry Varley was just one example; Richard Weaver was another.

The Brethren insistence on Christian unity manifested itself most clearly in the character of the movement. There were no ordained clergy and each 'assembly', as their churches were called, was independent unto itself. Both of these features contributed to the prominence of working-class preachers within the group. Without a clerical class, the Brethren were totally reliant on lay men from within the assemblies to conduct all religious services. In the nineteenth century, Brethren assemblies were generally composed of the lower echelons of society, and this would have given enterprising working men frequent opportunities to preach.[28] Without a formal structure to link the various assemblies together, the Brethren were forced to develop a series of informal networks of communication and mutual support. Centres of Brethren teaching soon sprang up in large cities and acted as a focal point for meetings and conferences. A good example of this is Merrion Hall in Dublin, which was built in 1863 as 'an evangelising centre for the whole country'.[29] Here, evangelists and preachers from all over the British Isles came to speak and to participate in religious services. The Dublin Believer's Meetings, which had been founded by Henry Bewley, were held there and attracted some of the leading lights of British and American evangelicalism. These meetings were designed to teach and encourage the numerous evangelists and other Christian workers who functioned as the essential infrastructure of a movement which lacked any sort of centralised government.

Another reason why working-class preachers feature so prominently within Plymouth Brethrenism lies in the fact that, as a group, they remained committed to an interpretation of conversion which many other evangelical denominations were beginning to eschew. Thus, in the late nineteenth century, many evangelicals began to shift their focus away from exclusively 'gospel' preaching and move towards a more social interpretation of their spiritual role. Methodist efforts to reach the unsaved, for example, increasingly involved elements of philanthropy and popular culture, as can be seen in the development of their large central missions.[30] The Brethren, however, resisted such innovations and continued to hold revival services as they had done for years. Thus, working-class evangelists with a commitment to saving souls, and a desire to avoid denominational constraints, found in the Brethren assemblies an environment which accepted their lay status, encouraged their speaking talents and left them free to pursue their ministry without excessive interference.

Lay evangelists within the Church of England, by contrast, are noticeable by their absence. Some of the evangelists in this survey had been brought up as Anglicans, but after their conversion had left to join denominations perceived to be more spontaneous and lively. Jonathan Ireland, a preacher from Manchester, became concerned about the way he was leading his life, so he began to attend the local parish church. He also held informal meetings with several other people who felt the same way and together they recited prayers out of the prayer book. Ireland, however, was not satisfied with this form of religious expression and began to pray in an extempore fashion. He experienced feelings of guilt because he knew the clergyman disapproved of such behaviour. When a workmate was converted to Wesleyanism, he urged Ireland to leave the Church of England. Unhappy, yet reluctant to abandon what he still considered the 'true' church, Ireland finally reached the conclusion that:

> the ordinances were good only so far as they led us to Christ, and enabled us to grow in grace and in the knowledge of the Lord. And as I found the Wesleyans were to me more productive of good, and their discipline afforded greater usefulness to men like myself, I exchanged the Church for the chapel, and the Book of Common Prayer for the prayer which sprang up at the moment from the heart to the mouth. No one was more surprised at this change than myself.[31]

Active and devout men like Jonathan Ireland found nothing to hold them to Anglicanism. Its renunciation of any active role for the laity and its general contempt for any sort of rustic spirituality was its downfall in the mid-nineteenth century.[32]

What is striking about these biographical accounts is the almost total lack of concern with two subjects which occupied the minds of a large proportion of Britain's population throughout the nineteenth century – philanthropy and politics. Very few of the working-class evangelists examined here were involved in philanthropic work in any systematic manner, with the important exception of temperance. Most evangelists had signed the pledge, and some considered it to be a personal watershed along the lines of their spiritual conversion. Roger Haydock from Blackburn had always enjoyed the occasional drink until one night he was persuaded to attend a temperance meeting and he signed the pledge, recalling the exact date as if it was a conversion experience. From then on he was active in local temperance meetings organised by the Rechabite Order and the United Kingdom Alliance.[33] For Haydock, temperance reform was the first step towards spiritual conversion. For others, it was a required badge of religious seriousness. The Joshua brothers, who ran a nondenominational mission hall in Neath, made membership contingent upon a personal commitment to total abstinence.[34]

Apart from a few exceptions, working-class evangelists did not participate in any sort of political activity, although several had fathers who had been active in various radical movements like Chartism or machine breaking. John Ashworth, an evangelist and founder of the Chapel for the Destitute in Manchester, was an exception. Asked to chair a meeting of moderate Chartists in 1843, the proceedings turned into a riot when more radical activists arrived.[35] Also exceptional was John Wright, a Primitive Methodist local preacher who had served in the local branch of the Agricultural Labourers' and Small Holders' Union as their treasurer.[36] Apart from these few examples, political activity simply did not enter into the life of the average evangelist. His concerns were focused on the salvation of souls. Politics was seen as a dangerous distraction from the 'business of heaven'.

A surprising outcome of this study has been the significant number (twelve) of working-class evangelists who had some sort of connection to female preaching. Several evangelists mention female local preachers as being instrumental in effecting their conversions. It was probably not that surprising for Abraham Bastard, a prize fighter and notorious reprobate, to give Betsy Reed, a Bible Christian, the credit for his conversion sometime during 1817.[37] Similarly, Roger Haydock was taken by a friend to hear Mrs Susannah Pickle at Branch Road Chapel in Blackburn. Labouring under a sense of conviction, he longed for someone to show him the way of salvation. '[And] when I heard this lady preach, she was so plain and earnest, that I kept saying "This is the place for me, this is the place for me."'[38] Later on in the century, working-class evangelists often worked in conjunction with female preachers. Thomas Langton preached the opening sermon at Shiney Row, Pelton Fell to help Miss C. Wilson, of Carlisle, start a series of special services. Langton's biographer stated 'Miss Wilson is a lady of much power and grace. She is a good speaker, and a very successful evangelist and Mr Langton considered it an honour to be a co-worker with her.'[39] Tom Holland seemingly employed his three daughters to assist him in his evangelistic labours, but whether or not they actually preached remains unclear. Mrs Daniell and Sarah Robinson, both of whom established mission halls for soldiers, employed John Hambleton and Lancelot Middleton, respectively, as evangelists.[40] Daniell and Robinson, as middle-class women, hired working-class men who could not only be responsible for the daily management of a mission hall, but who could also relate to the intended clientele.

Some working-class evangelists worked in partnership with their wives, who also preached. Joshua Poole and his wife were well known in the pages of *The Revival* for their shared preaching duties. In the early 1870s, the couple conducted a mission in Glasgow for the Dovehill Mission. William Quarrier, the organiser of the visit, remarked that 'Mrs Poole accompanied her husband and was a most acceptable speaker at his meetings.'[41] Gipsy Smith's second wife accompanied him on his mission tours as his soloist, but 'on at least one occasion took services for him when he was ill'.[42] Individuals like Poole and Smith operated outside the restrictions of later nineteenth-century denominations and were not bound by the rules of proper conduct. Engaged in full-time evangelism they would have been receptive to the argument that if God blessed the work of a woman, then it must be acceptable to Him and therefore worthy of support. Working-class evangelists, to some extent, also operated outside the boundaries of acceptable religious behaviour and their attitudes to evangelism were consistently unconcerned about propriety. For them, the important question to ask about a potential female preacher was not 'is she acceptable?' but 'is she effective?'.

STRATEGIES

The role of working-class evangelists within the British evangelical community was hotly contested. Much of the tension emanated from the often controversial methods and strategies these evangelists adopted in order to inform people of their need to achieve conversion. These strategies were imaginative, multifarious, aggressive and individualistic. They rejected denominational control and flouted clerical advice about propriety in the pulpit. At the same time, however, working-class evangelists and their work were subject to countervailing pressures. Missions and Bible carriages needed the financial support of wealthy patrons if they were to be effective. This created a tendency for independent efforts to become institutionalised or brought within the boundaries of denominational control, a process which was not always unwelcome. Working-class men acquired status and prestige from their involvement in a well-established mission; working within a denomination offered them a modicum of financial stability. The number of evangelists who moved back and forth between the positions of lay/ordained, settled/itinerant, and independent/denominational, indicates a casual attitude to institutional discipline and social control.

Working-class preachers adopted certain methods of evangelism because of a pragmatic assessment of what would work. Based on their own personal experiences, these methods reflected their popular imagination, their love of the unusual and their willingness to stop at virtually nothing to get their message across. One such technique was the use of children as revival leaders. Many evangelicals believed that children possessed an 'instinctive religious sense' and as a result were especially gifted at gaining conversions. The idea of a 'child-leader' is a powerful concept within revivalist ideology.[43] The belief in the special ability of children was encouraged on a working-class level, and reflected itself in the emergence of travelling 'bands' of Christian youths who would conduct special revival services for adults. The most prominent of these all-male groups was the Woolwich Boys. During an address to the Woolwich Boys Christian Association in 1857, Captain Orr, of the Royal Arsenal, himself a popular evangelist, effected the conversion of one boy. Soon seven boys were praying together in a 'band', eventually forming the basis of a regular and well-attended tea meeting. By 1861, the boys were conducting public meetings in the local temperance hall three or four times a week.[44] Representatives of the group were then asked to participate in meetings around London, as well as in more distant locations like Dublin.[45] As their popularity grew and word about their methods spread, imitation groups, like the Shoreditch Boys' Christian Association, were formed.[46] Part of their popularity was no doubt linked to the sentimental attitudes many Victorians had towards children.

Working-class preachers reflected the popular belief among many Victorian evangelicals that the text of the Bible alone was enough to ensure conversion. As a result, a great deal of evangelistic activity focused on the printing, sale and distribution of Bibles and a wealth of religious tracts, books, pamphlets and magazines. John Vine's approach to evangelism was simply to parade through the streets reading the Bible aloud and issuing the occasional appeal.[47] Robert Annan used chalk to inscribe Bible verses on the pavement in an attempt to attract the attention of passers-by.[48] More common was the use of a Bible stall, a standard practice in every evangelist's repertoire. Edward Usher and John Hambleton had a portable book table which could be transported to strategic locations such as town markets, fairs and races. Upon arrival, they would erect a pole with a Scripture verse on it as a means of drawing attention to themselves. The two men would then set up their table, selling gospel literature and conducting open-air meetings in the evenings. Profits from the sale of the literature went towards their salaries. When Usher and Hambleton were at Hyde market in Derbyshire they met Richard Weaver, at that time still a young convert. He soon joined them at their open airs and eventually took over the stand when they moved on.[49] Bible stalls of this sort relied on minimum capital and maximum initiative. They were seen as a good starting point for the aspiring evangelist; they often gave him his earliest opportunities to preach with the security of a reasonable wage.

By the middle of the nineteenth century, the bulk of evangelical opinion believed that greater evangelistic activity outside of the churches was essential 'in order to meet the spiritual condition of a large class of persons who scarcely ever attend a church or chapel'.[50] Upper-class men like Lord Shaftesbury and Lord Congleton were at the centre of the London theatre preaching movement, which based its work on the presumption that while the working classes would not go to church, they would listen to an evangelistic message in a civic hall or theatre.[51] The impulse towards outdoor meetings was also a reflection of this attitude. Street preaching was the most common form of outdoor evangelism. It involved no expense, requiring only the courage to speak in public, and it required no props (although they were often used), apart from an open patch of ground. Street preaching was something which anyone could do, and although it could be organised in conjunction with a local church or mission hall, it was frequently conducted on an independent and informal basis. David Davis preached mainly to the 'quay-side roughs' of Newcastle-on-Tyne, using the large crane which loaded ships as his regular stand. Like many other street preachers, he experienced the physical abuse which often accompanied such public work. When it came to his preaching style, locals thought Davis often spoke 'a good deal of nonsense, so that some people are pleased to say he is mad'. Despite the dubious state of his mental health, his work was looked upon favourably by the local evangelical community because he preached 'the glorious gospel of the grace of God with much sweetness, simplicity and power'.[52] William Barter was another such street preacher. During the summer months, he maintained a regular stand in Brighouse, outside the mill where he worked. Every Sunday evening, he conducted an open-air meeting and distributed tracts.[53] Neither of these men were connected to any sort of organisation, nor is there evidence that they were accountable to any denomination. What is more significant about their work is its invasion of public space. The importance of informing people about the gospel meant evangelists developed methods which made them mobile. Transportable Bible stalls were one technique. A variation was the Bible carriage. William Carter, the converted chimney sweep, founded the Institution for Reading Aloud the Word of God in the Open Air and Sale of Scriptures at Cost Price in 1861. His intention was to fit and supply 100 carriages, assign each one to an evangelist and then blanket the city of London with cheap Bibles and tracts. The carriages themselves resembled glass topped boxes on wheels and stood about four feet high. The base of the box contained a supply of religious literature, which was available for sale. The top of the box contained an open Bible under the glass, so people walking past could read for themselves. Carter's primary concern was to be comprehensive; every district of London had to be reached. Putting the Bible on wheels made that objective all the more possible. Street preaching and Bible stalls represented an invasion into the public sphere which created curiosity, but also hostility among the very people they were designed to reach.

In their opening stages, the strategies which working-class evangelists adopted to preach the gospel were often independent in nature, like individual street preaching, or else were spontaneous responses to revival enthusiasm. While such activity represented evangelical strategies at their most imaginative, they were prone to disintegrate once the initial excitement had passed. A good example of this trend is the 'Hallelujah Bands' which arose out of the Black Country revivals in 1863–4. The original group was composed of eight working-class men who had been converted through the revival preaching of James Caughey, Phoebe Palmer and Richard Weaver. Prior to their conversions, they had been some of the most notorious reprobates in the area. Among the company was Jim Cleaver, 'the Birmingham Rough', and William Mee, who had committed the great silk robberies on the Midland Railway in 1862. Others, known only by their initials, included a former jockey and horse trainer, a publican and prize fighter, a thief and a pugilist. Once saved, they had banded together to form a travelling group of popular revivalists who would conduct local church services. A designated leader would select various members of the band to address the audience with short, five-minute sermons, interspersing them with lively hymns, solos and prayers. According to William Booth, who witnessed a meeting in Walsall, they 'were not troubled with any scruples about vulgarity', taking off their coats, collars and neckties to preach, repeating hymns over and over until some members of the audience '[fell] like bullocks under the power of God'.[54] These meetings, along with the revival services which the Methodist Reverend Thomas Whitehouse conducted, contributed to the general excitement in the area and resulted in a great many conversions. Ten years later, Whitehouse claimed nine churches had been established to accommodate all the people who had been converted.[55] While denominational Methodism may have benefited, the Hallelujah Band's original success collapsed once revival excitement had died down. Some of the members had been offered positions with a church which left the group without leadership. A shortage of funds, combined with a lack of discipline, made the emergence of 'infidelities' almost inevitable.[56] Because the Hallelujah Band operated outside of a denominational context, when the popular enthusiasm which had sustained the meetings declined, there was no infrastructure to support it. The spontaneity which had made it so popular proved to be its ultimate downfall.

This was not the end of the story. William Booth, as an evangelist in London, had been impressed with the flexibility of the services under these rough converts. With a sensitive leader, he believed, the various components of the service – sermon, hymn, solo and prayer – could be ordered in such a way as to create a unified message on a theme which best suited the given audience. People liked the variety, the lively nature of the meetings and the opportunity for them to participate in the prayer meeting at the end. Booth took these ideas, along with several band members, back to London to help him in his work in the East End, where they formed the basis of his approach to open-air preaching. When Booth took over this spontaneous expression of working-class spirituality, he ensured that it was no longer subject to the whims of individual members or the approval of the populace. Although guaranteeing its survival as an evangelistic 'technique', Booth had brought a working-class initiative under institutional control.

The tendency towards institutionalisation is an important dimension of working-class evangelistic activity. Independent initiatives were quickly taken over by well meaning middle-class institutions and organisations. On a non-denominational level, the growth of lay evangelists in the middle years of the nineteenth century prompted some concerned 'Christian gentlemen' to develop the idea of a 'Registry of Evangelists', a directory of lay evangelists, which included where they lived and the type of preaching they did. This directory was available so that churches, particularly in rural areas, could apply and hire a suitable evangelist. The Evangelization Society emerged out of the need to administer this system. In 1867, it was remodelled and based on two central tenets: first, that all evangelists be screened to determine their suitability for the client church; and second, that evangelists avoid all controversy and church doctrine in their preaching and hold meetings only in civic buildings.[57] Similar rules applied to the Irish branch of the society, which had formed in Dublin in 1874. With such a nonsectarian policy, the Irish Evangelization Society (IES) claimed that it was willing to work with all denominations and cooperate with

Christians in any locality. Given Ireland's denominational make-up, this claim was more controversial than it at first appeared. In the IES's first report, their desire to convert Catholics was clearly apparent. David Rea, after a meeting of the IES in Keady, Co. Armagh, reported with obvious pleasure that

> The Roman Catholics came out in numbers, men, women, and children, and stood apart, but perfectly quiet and respectful. The Evangelist, deeming the opportunity suitable, stood up upon a car and preached the Gospel to them for about a quarter of an hour, and was heard with the most still attention.[58]

Although the organisers of both societies were upper and middle-class men, they employed working-class evangelists for their novelty value and their ability to reach other members of their class. Letters from the ministers who had hosted William Taylor, a converted navvy who worked for the society, often conveyed this sentiment. After Taylor's successful meetings in Barnet in 1884, Reverend H.J. Browne wrote:

> One had got the idea that the Salvation Army alone had attractions now-a-days for the lower stratum of society, but these meetings were thronged by this class of people. I had not indeed expected that such thoroughly satisfactory results could be arrived at. Your evangelist abounds in, if I may make use of such an expression, 'the eloquence of the cottage'.[59]

Efforts to incorporate working-class evangelistic efforts into institutional structures took place, not only in nondenominational organisations, but also in established denominations. As the nineteenth century progressed there was a growing sense of the need for serious efforts to evangelise the mass of the population. Early attempts among the Methodists involved the creation of connexional evangelists, ordained ministers who were relieved of pastoral duties in order to conduct evangelistic missions throughout the connexion. Methodism had always stressed the idea that each minister should be an evangelist as well as a pastor and expositor, and thus there was a certain amount of resistance to this development. Although the annual Conference of the Methodist New Connexion had given William Booth freedom from his pastoral responsibilities to conduct revival missions, it was not a popular move. A majority of ministers at the next Conference felt it was a dangerous precedent and Booth's privilege was revoked.

Even among the Wesleyans there were signs of change. In 1882 the Reverend Thomas Cook was appointed to the Home Missionary Committee to conduct special missions.[60] Reverend Thomas Waugh was appointed in 1883.[61] These ministers were not members of the working-class but opportunities for laymen existed in other areas of the Methodist hierarchy. Methodists had traditionally encouraged lay participation in church life through the honorary positions of exhorter, class leader, society steward and more importantly, local preacher. In most rural congregations local preachers were the most influential members of the church because they conducted services in the absence of the minister.[62] James Obelkevich has discovered that in rural South Lindsay local preachers in Primitive Methodist chapels conducted more than four-fifths of all Sunday services held during a given quarter.[63] This seeming independence was tempered by the restrictions of a denominational framework. Among the Wesleyans, if a local preacher desired to preach outside his circuit, he needed the permission of the District Superintendent or at least an invitation from the local minister.

Wesleyan Methodism, in the closing years of the nineteenth century, initiated efforts to provide these men with better training. The original initiative came from the Reverend Thomas Champness, who wanted to revive the spiritually neglected villages of England. As a district missionary in Bolton, he had started taking young local preachers into his home and training them in basic sermon and evangelistic techniques before sending them off to a rural circuit. The Joyful News Training Home, as it came to be called, was eventually based in Rochdale and operated virtually independently of denominational control. Champness actively sought men who were willing to embark on such a rural ministry and provided them with room, board, clothes and basic biblical training.[64] In 1883 Champness had already sponsored four evangelists and was in the process of training five more. Over the next five years, this figure would more than triple. By 1889, he was responsible for eighty-nine evangelists, twenty of whom were in training and sixteen of whom were posted as overseas missionaries.[65] By 1903, Champness' work had been taken over by the Wesleyan connexion and formalised into a lay training institution based at Cliff College, Calver.[66] Although the connections remain unclear, it seems both the Primitives and the UMFC copied Champness and established training homes of their own. The former based its home in Liverpool, and it was run by the Reverend Joseph Odell.[67] Methodists were taking a greater interest in the training of their lay preachers and institutionalising the practice through training institutes.

In some respects the middle-class takeover of working-class evangelistic activity was essential. Without the financial backing of wealthy patrons, independent efforts could easily fold. William Carter's efforts to fund his Bible carriages quickly foundered on the rock of insufficient funds. With £15 worth of books and a £3 a week salary for the evangelist, Carter estimated that it would cost £2,000 to build the 100 carriages he envisioned for London. After nine months, when the required funds were not forthcoming, Carter was forced to abandon his idea.[68] When funding was available, evangelistic work could be very successful. Carter's efforts to evangelise the poor of South London during the winter of 1863–64 consisted of a series of twenty-five tea meetings. With an average attendance of 400 or more, each meeting cost £10, all of which had been met by subscription. From these favourable beginnings, Carter went on to hold more meetings, and organised them on the basis of occupation. Over the following years, he sponsored meetings specifically for costermongers, sweeps, thieves, woodchoppers, gasmen, lamplighters and dustmen.[69] To do work on this scale required the support of wealthy evangelicals, who could supply the necessary finance as well as valuable organisational skills. While it was Carter who made the decisions, he was answerable to his sponsorship committee, which included men like Lord Shaftesbury and T. Shuldham Henry.[70] If working-class efforts were to be successful on a wider scale, they needed the support of the evangelical community as a whole.

The shift from a spontaneous, individualistic, working-class evangelism to one which was financed and controlled by middle-class patrons was not always a negative process. Many working-class evangelists welcomed the security of a settled ministry and a regular income. At the beginning of their careers, working-class evangelists were more likely to be involved in a travelling or itinerant ministry. Unusual success in a certain area presented the possibility of a permanent ministry. Members of the community, impressed with the evangelist's obvious success, often invited him to stay in the area and begin a mission work, usually among the working classes. The temptation to settle down and build on that success was difficult to resist, and on a number of occasions working-class evangelists gave up their itinerant lifestyle in favour of a more secure ministry. By the middle of the 1870s, Richard Weaver's success as an itinerant evangelist was well established throughout the country. In 1876 he met Mr Edwin Stansfield, a businessman from Hollinwood in Lancashire. Stansfield invited Weaver to come to Hollinwood, work among the people of the area and conduct meetings in the Workmen's Hall on Sundays. Weaver agreed, and he quickly became involved in a number of other activities, including Bible distribution and street preaching. He conducted a series of evangelistic meetings in the local Working Men's Institute, and many working men were converted at them. The success of his work prompted Weaver's employers to construct a new mission hall at a cost of £3,000. Weaver remained in Hollinwood for five years, but eventually left to fulfill the numerous invitations he was receiving to conduct evangelistic meetings elsewhere.[71] A similar situation occurred in the life of Gipsy Smith. He had been working for the Salvation Army in Hanley in 1881, and from a small number of 50, his Sunday services grew in attendance to 7,000–8,000 by June of the following year. When it came time to be transferred, the members of a committee representing all the denominations in Hanley presented Smith with a gold watch as a token of their esteem. William Booth did not allow such gifts to be accepted, and a nasty exchange of letters led to Smith's eventual dismissal. All the publicity brought in numerous requests for his services, but with congregations in Hanley averaging 12,000 on a Sunday, Smith agreed to continue his work there for one more month. Four years later he was still there, having conducted meetings every night for the first two years, and receiving a salary of £300 per year.[72] In 1891, he accepted an offer to conduct a revival mission in a Congregational church in London. As he later recalled, '[i]t opened my eyes to my true gifts and capacities, and showed me clearly that I was called to the work of a general evangelist'.[73] A few months later he resigned his post at Hanley and began itinerating again. Smith was glad to leave Hanley because he felt he was returning to his true calling. 'I perceived clearly', he once said, 'that my voice and words were for the multitude, that I had their ear, and that they listened to me gladly.'[74] Although Weaver also felt he had made the right decision, he regretted the security he had lost now that he no longer had a steady income.[75] For a full-time working-class evangelist this was an important consideration.

While it was apparent that some evangelists chafed under the restrictions of a settled ministry (even if only a nondenominational one), it was equally true that others enjoyed the life it presented to them. James Flanagan was working in a coal mine when he was converted in the region of Ilkeston, near Nottingham, in 1881. His independent efforts at public preaching caught the attention of the local Primitive Methodists, and he was taken on as a local preacher and hired out by various circuits to conduct six or twelve-month mission efforts. Thus, his work actually resembled that of a connexional evangelist more than a local preacher. His biographer records that from 1881–5 he went 'wherever God called him in the Primitive Methodist connexion'.[76] His success led the connexion to invite him to take over a church in South London and start a 'forward movement' there.[77] After ten years as a lay evangelist, Flanagan was ordained, a step considered necessary in order for him to accept the leadership of the South East London Mission.[78] A similar situation confronted John Bayliffe, a trained lay evangelist with the Primitive Methodists. He had worked for Star Hall in Manchester for seventeen years, when he felt that it was God's will he be ordained and start the life of a circuit minister.[79] Why did these working-class evangelists seek ordination? For Flanagan, it seemed a mere formality, necessary for his position as head of a connexional organisation. For Bayliffe, he seemed tired of the work at Star Hall and perhaps wanted to explore new fields of ministry. Whether or not these men were status conscious, ordination was a visible indication of how far the individual had come from his humble beginnings. It represented his acceptance into the clerical class and into the world of respectability.

The process of institutionalisation was not simple or fixed. Some working-class evangelists remained outside any denominational or organisational control throughout their careers. Others were willingly coopted into the leadership positions of established missions. Even within the confines of a denomination, the boundaries between strictly denominational activity and independent evangelism remained fairly fluid. As we have seen, some working-class evangelists began their preaching careers independently of any organisation or denomination. Influential members of the church they attended would notice this activity and suggest their appointment as a local preacher. Thomas Langton of Malton was converted in 1857 and became an exhorter in the Wesleyan Methodist chapel. He eventually gave up his job to become a full-time evangelist, conducting services all over North Yorkshire. After sixteen years without a holiday, his health completely broke down. Two years later he was back, this time as a hired local preacher in Malton. After several years, he started accepting invitations to conduct protracted services in a variety of circuits. Although

Langton never left the Wesleyan denomination, the scope of his evangelistic activities reveals a local flexibility concerning denominational restrictions that was not apparent on a national level. And although the connexion was very important to some evangelists, the variety of their activities and their casual attitude towards the constraints of denomination bear witness to their independence and resistance to denominational control.

PERCEPTIONS AND ATTITUDES

So far, we have examined some of the general characteristics and strategies of working-class evangelists. In order to understand the full implications of their activity, it is important that working-class preaching be seen in relation to its surrounding culture, and in particular to the evangelical community in which it operated. Working-class evangelists were for the most part poorly educated, and their lack of knowledge was reflected in the context of their sermons. Most combined a lack of cultivated theology with an enthusiastic preaching style. Together, these characteristics illustrate the gap between middle-class perceptions of what constituted a proper sermon and appropriate pulpit behaviour, and actual working-class practice.

Education, for most working-class evangelists, was an erratic and periodic experience. The little schooling they did receive was often interrupted by family migrations in search of work, lack of funds or the necessity of earning an income. It was the latter which seemed most prevalent, and many of the evangelists examined here had to start work at a very early age. Roger Haydock was seven when he began work as a weaver's assistant, as was Richard Weaver when he first went down the mines. James Flanagan was nine when he was taken out of school to help in his father's pipe-making business, and Henry Varley was eleven when he arrived in London looking for work. These men often did not learn to read or write until they were adults, usually propelled by their new-found desire to read the Bible. Even then, it was a laborious process. As John Wright confessed, 'I read my Bible as best I could, not being a good scholar, and I often had to inquire the meaning of words and how to pronounce them.'[80] This lack of formal education was reflected in their preaching style. Referring to Isaac Marsden, a Wesleyan local preacher from Doncaster, William Carter declared that for the first eight or nine years after his conversion:

> he had scarcely any idea of the grammatical laws of speech, and none whatever of the graces of utterance. ... He poured out heaps of metaphor in wild disorder, often bewildering instead of instructive to his auditors. As may be supposed, he showed scarcely any method or order in his pulpit deliverances.[81]

This ignorance of oratorical technique was matched when it came to sermon content. Working-class evangelists generally restricted their orations to the simple gospel message, embellished with illustrations from real life or extracts from their own experiences. A lecture based on their conversion story was a stock-in-trade for many working-class evangelists, and constituted one of their primary selling points. In a week of special services, one or two nights would be devoted to telling the tale and making a gospel call at the end.[82] According to *The Revival*, because many evangelists were young and inexperienced 'there is doubtless little beyond the simple gospel' in their addresses, 'and it is found with some that ignorance exists, so soon as teaching or sermonising is tried'.[83] The conclusions these and other observers made about the educational qualifications of these evangelists were harsh, but in some respects very true. Working-class evangelists were notorious, not for their ability to elucidate Scripture, but for their eccentric behaviour and native wit. They were tolerated by an often disapproving clergy because of their skill at preaching the gospel and saving souls.

Although not openly disrespectful, working-class evangelists did not attach the same importance to the pulpit that many middle-class evangelicals did. Nor, as we have seen, were they concerned with oratorical niceties or proper grammar. Several working-class evangelists would take their jackets off to preach, a characteristic their biographers felt indicated their enthusiasm and religious fervour.[84] Thomas Dinsdale earned his nickname 'the Singing Preacher' because of his habit of breaking into song in the middle of a sermon.[85] If unexpected, such a technique could startle the audience and enable the preacher to maintain their attention. Wild hand movements were another common sight in the pulpit. When John Wright preached his trial sermon, he remembered 'putting one hand into my pocket, as I thought the Minister would not like to see it swinging about; but when I got warm, I forgot all about it'.[86] If the style of a trained clergyman was the standard of pulpit behaviour, it was no wonder these flamboyant individuals were considered so eccentric.

In the nineteenth century, sermons were normally based around a text from the Bible. Working-class evangelists followed this model for a great deal of their preaching, although the actual content often had only the vaguest resemblance to the stated topic. Their sermons were intended to portray the gospel message in a lively fashion. In doing so, preachers paraphrased biblical stories into not only the dialect of their listeners, but also into a social context which would reflect their own experience. Biographers were fond of quoting the sermons for which their subjects were famous, and sometimes had them written out in dialect, as they would have been spoken. A good example is John Shaw's sermon on Mark 5:1–13, in which Jesus cures a demon-possessed man and causes the evil spirits to enter a herd of pigs nearby. According to Shaw's description:

> Yo sud ha seen hah t'devils scampered off to ther new lodgin's. They didn't stop on t'way. They were glad enought to get aght o't seet o' Jesus. An' yo sud ha' seen hah flaid t'men, women, and t'childer wor. An t'keepers at swine wor o'most as mad as if t'devils had entered into them.[87]

This was by no means advanced exegesis, but it was an entertaining rendition of an unusual story. Other evangelists would take a text and twist it to suit the purpose of their message. One local preacher named Treverthen was preaching in West Cornwall on the subject of Peter's denial of Jesus. 'Ah! Peter! No wunder ye danied the Lawrd', he exclaimed. 'He went down to the ketchen, me friends, after the sarvant maids, a coortin' ov 'em; and hem a marred man!' And from that conclusion, the preacher went on to emphasise the necessity of strict marital fidelity, because if Peter could sin, then no man could safely play with temptation.[88]

When the sermon was over and the prayer meeting started, other eccentricities surfaced as it came time to save souls. Working-class evangelists were not discreet or polite in their appeals. Because local preachers were familiar with their congregations, they often made direct references to certain individuals from the pulpit, detailing their personal habits and their reasons for attending the service, and then pressing on them an appeal to convert. Within a small community, where everyone knew one another, the pressure this exerted on individuals could be enormous and they more often than not ended up at the penitent form. Evangelists working in an urban context took this rural, community-based method and adapted it to suit the large, anonymous city audiences where people did not know each other and the evangelist was largely ignorant of their spiritual condition. Richard Weaver was an expert at creating guilt among his listeners. As a typical example of his approach, Weaver once preached:

> There's a thief somewhere here tonight, that's come to pick pockets. I can't point thee out but God knows thee; there thou art, and thy name is Thief. Thou has been in gaol, and unless thou repent, thou wilt lie for ever in the dark damned cell of everlasting death. But, glory to God, my Jesus is a thief-Saviour, and his blood can wash thee; and if thou wilt commit thyself to Him, his Holy Spirit will cleanse thee, and make thee an honest man, and an heir of his eternal glory. And then thou shalt not want to steal; for as sure as God gives thee life in thy soul, He'll give thee a jacket to thy back.[89]

Weaver was undoubtedly making an educated guess. If there was no thief present, he had nothing to lose; in fact, others in the congregation might worry that he would detail their secrets in public next. If there was a thief in the audience and he came forward, Weaver would appear to possess amazing powers of perception, increasing his credibility and therefore the likelihood of gaining souls.

To the twentieth-century mind such techniques seem forthright and even rude. To the average nineteenth-century evangelist they were a standard part of every sermon. The quest for conversions was nothing to be ashamed of. Indeed, for these men it was a constant feature of daily life. Biographers noted with pride that their evangelist had never passed up an opportunity to enquire of anyone they happened to meet, 'Brother, are you saved?'[90] Samuel Jeffcock, a former engine driver, was fortunate enough to have divine assistance in this process. Prior to his evangelistic services '[s]ometimes the Lord assures me before-hand that souls will be saved, and He has even given me to see who they would be'. The night before a service at the Old Park Ironworks in Wednesbury, Jeffcock dreamt that two women, who he described as 'owdashus characters' and 'stout women', would be saved. As the people arrived, he was able to point them out and make them an object of special prayers.[91] Conversions were not always so easy to come by. If appeals from the pulpit did not work and divine inspiration was not forthcoming, it was not unusual for the evangelist to descend the pulpit steps and go up and down the aisles looking for individuals who might be under conviction of sin. In prayer meetings, Isaac Marsden:

> would go from pew to pew, and from side to side and end to end of the chapel, observing the tokens of emotion among the people; then, accosting them with words of warning or of encouragement, would invite and urge them, individually and generally, to go up to the penitent form, or the communion rails, for the benefit of such prayers as might suit their individual cases.[92]

Such individual and close attention only heightened the pressure on an individual. No longer one of an anonymous crowd, people were forced to examine their souls and answer the inquisitive promptings of the preacher. A trip to the penitent form was almost inevitable. Methods like these were normally sufficient to bring a few lost sheep into the fold, but if the church was 'cold' or 'formal' then more drastic measures would have to be taken. John Bayliffe, getting no response to his call for converts from the audience in Haydon Bridge, ran out of the pulpit and out of the sanctuary, locking the doors of the church, bringing the key with him, and claiming no one would be allowed to leave until someone got converted.[93]

Such aggressive tactics reflected the strength of will and self-confidence these working-class evangelists possessed. Henry Varley was said to be very strong willed, determined and confident of his own judgement. When he was a travelling evangelist, he did not have a congregation or mission committee to which he was accountable and his opinions went virtually unchallenged. Regardless of what other people thought, he followed what he felt was the leading of the divine will.[94] When his close friend John Kensit, that 'stalwart champion of aggressive Protestantism', died in an anti-Catholic riot in Liverpool, Varley felt it was his duty to continue his work. He therefore gave a great deal of 'time, thought and energy to a strenuous Protestant propaganda' and wrote many articles and pamphlets denouncing the evils of Roman Catholicism.[95] Charles Bayliss, an early Primitive Methodist evangelist, was described as being very 'opinionative' and stubborn to the point of stupidity, especially when it came to breaking the sabbath, or making any innovations in church policy.[96] Certainly such forthright attitudes could have gained these evangelists some notoriety, but over time, what was previously considered 'confident' was now seen as 'stubborn'.

The preaching life of a working-class evangelist was not all harsh words and pointed inquiries. Many of them had a sense of humour and liked the occasional practical joke, but it is apparent that their amusing anecdotes served a more serious purpose. Preaching in the open air to apathetic or hostile audiences required a catchy message and a spunky delivery which would attract a sympathetic hearing. Using a witty retort to upstage hecklers and sceptics was essential to establish the reputation of the speaker and the credibility of his message. Moses Welsby, a former coalminer, recalled one such situation:

> Some of the people I meet seem to think they are witty, and know a great deal when drink is in, and they always think if they can turn a laugh on you from their mates they have done something wonderful. So one of these poor, deluded, wise men shouted one evening in the market-place: 'Hollo, 'Owd Mo,' tha says a lot about that Bible thou art offering for sale. Now, does tha believe all it says?' Of course, I said, 'Yes!' 'Well, look here; does tha mean to tell me that donkey we read about spoke to Balaam?' So, looking at my man, I was bound to answer, for the clothes that he was wearing was not worth twopennyworth of salt. So I said, 'Look here, brother; I have read a little about animals, and I have kept a good few myself, and I find out that donkeys has a great deal more sense than men like thee has, because donkeys gets a new coat every year.' ... So when the laugh turned, the poor fellow went off, I hope a wiser man.[97]

Evangelists like Welsby needed to have their wits about them in situations like this. The challenge of drink-inspired bravado gave them an opportunity to show the superiority of the gospel. Laughter was important as a means to silence opponents and a healthy dose of 'native wit' was necessary for one's protection and credibility as a preacher. These working-class evangelists preached what was an eccentric, but self-confident and even aggressive message as a call to those around them to turn from their worldly habits to a Christian life. Humorous attempts to win over the working classes revealed continued links with the rough culture of their youth, which valued a witty reply and the ability to answer all critics.

For obvious reasons, the propriety of this working-class style of preaching was a matter of some concern among ordained ministers. Scotland was notorious for its conservatism in this regard. The Established Church Presbytery of Aberdeen passed an injunction against one of its ministers, Reverend John Campbell, to prevent laymen, such as Reginald Radcliffe and Brownlow North from entering his pulpit. An appeal was made to the synod and the meetings continued unabated. Reporting this controversy in the *Revival Advocate*, the editors were moved to comment, 'Our northern brethren must be prepared, if they wish to keep pace with the enlightened teaching of the age, to greatly relax their rules respecting lay preaching in their churches.'[98] This controversy was caused only by middle-class preachers. When William Carter first came to public notice, *The Revival* described him as a 'chimney sweep' who was now conducting theatre services. Apparently, his dubious social status created some discussions about his right to preach publicly. *The Revival* was forced to publish a correction, saying Carter was actually 'a highly respectable master sweep'.[99]

These objections reflect the concerns ministers had with lay preaching on a social rather than a spiritual level. Middle-class evangelicals and ministers claimed that working-class evangelists were in bad taste – that they were unlearned, ignorant, vulgar and spoke bad English.[100] Others claimed they were 'Plymouthists', members of the Plymouth Brethren who had done away with an ordained ministry altogether.[101] And still others were convinced it was a novelty, a sensation, or a fad which Satan was using to distract people from giving the respect due to an ordained ministry.[102] Supporters of a working-class ministry did not deny any of these objections. To a certain extent, they probably agreed with them. It was just that they did not think they were important. In defence of Joshua Poole, a Baptist minister stated his belief that Poole should not be criticised for his unusual methods because he was preaching the gospel. God had often chosen to use the weak things of this world to confound the wise, he argued. 'If to thank God for such as Joshua Poole be vulgar, then I will be vulgar still, and am by no means ashamed of my vulgarity.'[103]

Supporters of working-class evangelism agreed that the men were unlettered and ignorant, but they also believed the preachers were talented enough to win converts. Referring to the Woolwich Boys, *The Revival* stated, 'there is no worldly wisdom or talent in the addresses of these boys, it is the power of the Spirit accompanying their simple entreaty, "Come to Jesus, just now."'[104] Charles Bayliss' biographer admitted he was rough and illiterate, but added that his preaching contained a 'native talent'.[105] Education was not a requirement in order to be influential in the working-class community. A great deal of respect was based on the possession of qualities like native wisdom, common sense and remaining true to one's spiritual commitment. In fact, some middle-class commentators argued that ignorance was often a condition of success. George Hooper, a UMFC connexional evangelist, had been so successful at his evangelistic efforts in Todmorden because the people felt an affinity with his manner of preaching. 'Christ was everything in his sermons. His plain English suited them. He spoke the language of the market, the home, and workshop. His deep and broad sympathy with the working class, ... were frequently spoken of by them.'[106] William Booth, in his *How to reach the masses with the gospel*, stated his belief that because the Christian Mission employed blacksmiths and sailors they could:

> speak to the working man as belonging to the same class, illustrating their exhortations with their own experience. They know the life of a working man; they understand the temptations which specially beset his downward

path ... They can fall back in all their appeals to the crowd on their OWN EXPERIENCE .... . This *always tells*, and is *unanswerable*.[107]

In one way, this indicated a practical attitude towards saving souls. If the working classes would respond only to someone from their own class, then it was important to encourage working–class evangelists. Middle-class evangelicals recognised the class difficulties their denominations were encountering. The aforementioned Baptist minister believed that Joshua Poole had accomplished a great deal among the lowest classes, 'for which, of course, his rough style is peculiarly adapted'. Besides, he argued, who else would do this work? 'I confess my utter incapacity for anything of the sort,' he concluded, 'and therefore welcome with all my heart the man who does what I can't do.'[108] Wealthy businessmen often hired working-class evangelists to work in mission halls set up to reach the working people of their town. Other working-class evangelists were invited to work as paid travelling preachers within a certain area. A gentle-man from Tunbridge Wells hired John Hambleton, the converted comedian and stage player, to address the working classes in the town hall.[109] Some middle-class evangelists recruited working-class partners in an attempt to broaden their own appeal. Reginald Radcliffe and Richard Weaver were probably the most popular example of this sort of partnership. Weaver would usually speak first, telling the story of his conversion as a lead in to Radcliffe's sermon and altar call. Sympa-thetic ministers would invite a working-class evangelist to come and hold a mission in their church. Reverend M. Baxter asked Albert Mahomet to conduct a three-month mission at his church in Littleborough.[110]

Despite the patronage which these working-class evangelists received, their style was frequently disparaged by both the middle-class evangelicals who employed them and the working classes who they were meant to save. The working-class response to evangelistic efforts was typically hostile. Riots and other forms of mob violence were a constant companion to outdoor evangelical activity in the late nineteenth century. It seemed that the more aggressive evangelical attempts to convert the masses were, the more resistant the audience became. Open-air meetings were often disrupted by violent mobs hurling both verbal abuse and material objects at the speakers. Preachers were assaulted with lime, flour, eggs, potatoes, beer, treacle, clods of dirt, stones and dead fish. They were also attacked personally. Charles Bayliss was beaten with sticks when he went to start the Primitive Methodist work in Wildmoor, and Richard Weaver was dragged through the streets of Wolverhampton.[111] Summonses and arrests for obstructing the thoroughfare, or causing disturbances were frequent, and evangelists were often brought before the magistrate and sentenced with a fine or imprisonment. Many chose the latter option, as much for the publicity it would create, as for their inability to pay. The reasons for such violence are not difficult to locate.[112] On one level, there was hostility to the erosion of popular entertainments. A great deal of outdoor preaching took place in centres of local amusement such as the fairground, the market or the local races. The success evangelicals had in closing such venues created tension among those who looked forward to such events as one of the few outings their working lives permitted. When a group of evangelicals purchased the Gladstone Music Hall in Leicester, they promptly changed it into a gospel hall, complete with religious services, Bible classes, temperance meetings and a Band of Hope, despite the opposition of the working people who lived in the area.[113]

Violence resulting from outdoor evangelical meetings was also a reflection of hostility to what the working classes perceived to be an invasion of their privacy. Such evangelistic meetings were very self-confident, aggressive and visible. The custom of "processioning the streets" increased local hostility to evangelistic efforts. Before a service began, a group of supporters and the preacher would gather at the church, and with a mission band or with drums and tambourines would march through the streets, stopping occasionally to conduct short gatherings and shout for the local people to come and attend the meeting. More people would join the procession until it reached the location of the open-air meeting. The meeting would then be held, and the group would return to the church for a prayer meeting and the penitent form. Such processions could be very noisy affairs, and often took place quite early in the morning. William Corbridge and his Hallelujah Band regularly led a Sunday morning procession of 200 through the streets as early as 6am. Although the residents of Leicester remained hostile to these efforts, the evangelicals involved considered it a small price to pay for the few individuals they reached. Corbridge himself admitted that:

> we find, by this means, we wake people up; some of them no doubt are ready to give us a pail of water ... We know that people are sleeping on their way to the bottomless pit, and if we can sing them up at an early hour, and bring them to our meeting, we think it is quite right, and we have had three or four saved before breakfast.[114]

Evangelicals often appeared unreasonable in their demand for a right to preach outside and for police protection if the crowd got out of control. William Foster was involved in some serious riots in Salisbury, which could have been avoided if he and the other Salvation Army workers had stayed off the streets and let community tensions return to normal levels. Not wanting to give the impression that he had backed down in the face of oppression, his constant battles with local people resulted in several arrests and jail sentences being imposed on both sides of the conflict.[115]

Those members of the communities who felt economically threatened by this working-class preaching also stirred up hostility. Publicans feared that if a revival took place then they would lose their business. In Wildmoor, the publicans persuaded a number of 'rough and half-besotted men' to insult Charles Bayliss, steal his money and drive him from the village.[116] Clergymen no doubt had similar fears. Outdoor preaching challenged everything the Church of England represented, such as an ordained clergy, a proper liturgy, set prayers and sacred buildings. If it caught on, it presented the threat of defection, as recent converts looked to other denominations more willing to incorporate them into church activities. Outdoor preaching was also a challenge to the spiritual leadership exercised by the clergyman within the community. Speaking about the violent mobs James Flanagan encountered in Newark, his biographer somewhat smugly remarked, 'Sometimes an ungodly parson, jealous of a preacher who obtained a larger hearing than himself, headed the opposition in person.' [117] Other clergymen, it was claimed, rang the church bells when an open-air meeting was being conducted, or even hired a band of local ruffians to disrupt meetings. [118]

The need to stem a growing flood of irreligion, scepticism, apathy and vice pervaded the thinking of many working-class evangelists. This made them aggressive and powerful voices in the towns, villages and cities of Britain and Ireland, crying out for repentance. A strong belief in the absolute truth of their message, and the necessity of telling the world, enabled these men to endure the disdain of the 'respectable' middle classes and the violence of working people. Despite changing attitudes towards the nature of revivalism, and the conduct of evangelistic meetings, these men remained committed to the old traditions, convinced that the hostility their behaviour created was worthwhile. The salvation of souls more than compensated for the hostility engendered; to be allowed to suffer for Christ's sake was considered a blessing and a privilege. Developments in the wider religious environment had left the spiritual world of the working-class evangelist relatively untouched. Such men still wanted to change the world but were slow to realise that audiences were finding their message increasingly old fashioned.

Despite all their confidence and bravado, working-class evangelists often expressed the opposite sentiment, as if they almost believed the middle-class assumptions made about them, frequently declaring their inability to preach and apologising for their pulpit style in advance. After one year as a Primitive Methodist lay evangelist, John Bayliffe still thought someone more successful should be in his place. He wrote in his diary, 'I never felt the burden of souls nor appreciated the power of the Holy Spirit as I do now. Still I never felt more unfit for this great work. If Thy grace deem fit to use me, the meanest of Thy creatures, prepare me.' [119] W.J. Willis had no inkling that he was to preach one night until the minister called him into the pulpit, then asked him to pray, and then asked him to preach. After the last request Willis recalled:

> Well, I nearly fell on the floor, I hadn't got a speech. "Oh no, Mr Gelly, I cannot speak before a crowd like this. Had there only been a few, like a class meeting, I could have told them my experiences. But I cannot talk to all these." "Oh," he said, "you will manage all right." "Well, but," I said, "I am not going to try. You speak yourself." "Oh," he said, "you will manage to talk to them all right." I said, "Had there only been a few I would have tried, but the place is crowded." [120]

After these negotiations, Willis discovered the people were actually there to hear him, and not wanting to disobey the call of God, got up and preached on the only text he could remember, 'Follow me'. His hesitancy and embarrassment were obvious. Other preachers were aware of their pulpit style and its offensive nature. John Wright, as mentioned earlier, was worried about waving his arms around too much during his trial sermon, simply because the minister was in the audience. These working-class evangelists knew what the acceptable notions of pulpit preaching were, and they were aware how much they deviated from them.

This seeming deference masked a sometimes powerful anticlericalism. Working-class preachers expressed quite negative views about the need for education and ordination in order to preach. Isaac Marsden felt that if a man was educated, but did not have the gift of the Holy Spirit, then he was still not worthy to be a minister.[121] Abraham Bastard, a former wrestler from Cornwall, made negative references to the clergy in his sermons, especially if one was in the audience.[122] Moses Welsby felt they spent too much time in their studies. If evangelists converted those who never attended church, then the ministers would be forced to 'lead their regiments, and stand at the head of the battle'.[123] Working-class evangelists were aware of their own shortcomings, but at the same time maintained their independence and right to criticise what they often saw as the inefficient evangelistic tools of the clergy.

Many of these evangelists lived remarkably long and active lives, travelling to meetings right up until their deaths and rarely taking holidays. Sometimes the excessive work brought about a breakdown in health. Thomas Langton was only 41 when he became seriously ill for two years and John Wright only 43 when he had a nervous breakdown and entered a convalescent home.[124] When Moses Welsby gave up his mission van due to ill health, he worried that he would be unsuited for any other type of religious work. As he later remarked, 'when I could not do the van work I was depressed, and afraid I might be like a broken oar in the boat'.[125] This devotion and deep affection for their work was a common theme in the lives of working-class evangelists. To quote 'Owd Roger', '[b]it Bible-selling wur a grand thing for me. Yo see I used to get among the' people an' preach to them religion an' teetotalism. If I had my days to come over again, I'd sooner sell Bibles than owt else.'[126]

CONCLUSION

When Robert Flockhart preached in the streets of Edinburgh in the 1840s and 50s, he gained a reputation for his hellfire message and vivid biblical imagery. Sinners, he once preached, were 'vipers on the very hand o' God' and if they did not repent God would 'shake the vipers off his hand into the fire, the devouring fire, the unquenchable fire, and yet he'll feel no harm!'[127] These expressions were recorded by the Reverend James Robinson, a friend of

Flockhart's, as evidence of his zeal in soul saving and were recorded with approval. By the beginning of the next century, attitudes had shifted rather dramatically. Gipsy Smith, his biographer noted proudly, never preached about hell, unlike some other evangelists he could mention.[128] The implication was that to do so was considered unfashionable. Tom Holland, in his meetings, apparently made no undue appeal to the emotions and did not badger people in their pews,[129] a favourite tactic of evangelists like Isaac Marsden and William Thompson, who had preached in previous decades.

Throughout the later part of the nineteenth century, working-class evangelists continued, to play an important part in popular evangelicalism. They conducted a vast number of religious services, evangelistic meetings, special services and outdoor gatherings. They both flourished and wilted in the many crevices they exploited. Their unorthodox methods and crude populism both excited and alarmed their middle-class evangelical sponsors. Their repudiation of old habits and appropriation of new religious disciplines made them exotic creatures among the working classes they sought to convert. They flirted with organisational structures, but were not easily controlled by them. They took on new evangelical methods, but refused to give up their inherited familiarities with working-class life. They preached sermons, but obeyed less the conventional laws of structure and trusted more to homely metaphors and rough intuition. They were an unsettled and unsettling social group with their own stars at the top and their own feckless behaviour at the bottom. They were vulgar, populist, street-wise and immensely colourful. The success of their attempts to stem the tide of working-class religious infidelity in late Victorian Britain should not be exaggerated, but neither should they be written out of history before their time.

PART III
INTERPRETATIONS

Sketches of the first meeting of the Torrey-Alexander Mission, 1905
from the *Illustrated London News* (1905)
(With permission of the Illustrated London News Picture Library)

CHAPTER SIX

The idea of 'revival' in late nineteenth-century Britain and Ireland

I N MANY ways, 'revival' is an empty word. It is a term which can be manipulated to suit vastly diverging goals. It has a variety of meanings, and in the course of its existence has had numerous definitions forced upon it. The negative connotations of such changeability are obvious. Meaning becomes blurred and significance is threatened. 'Revival' is reduced to a catch-all phrase which means everything and nothing. There are, however, positive aspects of such flexibility. The concept reveals its adaptability to different situations and its continued importance to a variety of individuals in a variety of times and places. In late nineteenth-century Britain and Ireland revival and revivalism, both as events and as linguistic forms, were complex phenomena and subject to a number of interpretations and perceptions which revealed a wealth of contradictory opinion and divergent viewpoints. The twin themes of 'continuity' and 'change' are ones that apply here. A full understanding of the concept of revival involves more than an appreciation of these two rather rough categorisations. Revivalism represented a plethora of ideas, attitudes, perceptions, opinions, stereotypes and criticisms, all of which, like the strands of a tapestry, crossed and knotted with each other. It represents one of nineteenth-century religion's most colourful manifestations.

With so many tangled threads, a clear and accurate assessment of late nineteenth-century revivalism is very difficult. As recent research using church-going statistics has indicated, an explanation of simple religious decline will no longer suffice.[1] There is no doubt that revivalism encountered substantial change in this period. In technical terms, the definition of revival remained surprisingly constant. What altered was the way in which the expression was interpreted by individuals, the churches and the nation. By the 1890s there was a widespread feeling of despair among the British evangelical community. They felt that evil, in the form of social amusements and a growing disregard for religious ordinances, was taking over society. A small group of them came to regard a revival, an idealised version of the events in 1859, as a potential solution. Evangelicals turned to this prospect as a panacea, confidently expecting it to revolutionise society and reorder it according to spiritual guidelines. This renewed interest manifested itself in a number of different ways, from theoretical and inspirational articles to annual conferences, and culminating in the revival activity surrounding the years 1903–5. The Torrey-Alexander Mission of 1903–5 and the outbreak of the Welsh revival in 1904 embody many of the contradictory attitudes towards revivalism in this period. The former, with its links to the respectable, middle-class and planned tradition of D.L. Moody, was worlds away from the spontaneous, enthusiastic, almost mystical quality of the latter, with its distinct Welsh and working-class character. Despite superficial appearances, the re-emergence of revivals at the turn of the century did not represent a return to the old evangelical self-confidence. Rather, it was a series of events that occurred at the margins of British religion and society. Torrey and Alexander's meetings, along with the events in Wales, did enough to sustain the enthusiasm for revival among a section of the evangelical community, but no longer had the religious or social foundations to effect a major change in British culture.

At this point several caveats should be made. This chapter is an attempt to analyse ideas rather than events, to examine the evolution of revivalism and responses to it over a broad time frame and a wide geographical area. There are numerous possible pitfalls with this approach. With a survey of this nature it is easy to obliterate difference and to compare 'like' with 'unlike'. Variations in region, class, culture, gender, time and denomination all affect the nature of revivalism – how it is received, its character and its chances of success. These components should be recognised as vital factors in understanding the mechanism of revivalism, as many historians have done. Taking this into consideration, I would like to step back and view revivalism in a general way, to examine trends and perceptions amongst evangelicals as a group. Because of this approach, the contributions of the Torrey-Alexander mission and the Welsh revival are not treated in any great detail. Wales presents its own problems because of the language barrier. My analysis rests on the standard sources available in English.[2] Torrey and Alexander, despite their claims to the contrary, were simply not as successful or as controversial as their American predecessors, Moody and Sankey. My primary concern in both cases has been with British perceptions and responses. An in-depth analysis of Torrey and Alexander's internal mechanisms would be tangential to my argument, and has been adequately covered elsewhere.[3]

THE EVOLUTION OF 'REVIVAL'

The discussion of definitions is one of the enduring characteristics of any revival writing, be it contemporary or modern.[4] John Kent has argued that the traditional definition of a revival, emerging out of the eighteenth-century evangelical awakening, was of a spontaneous and unexpected supernatural intervention in the life of the Church. By the early part of the nineteenth century, however, this meaning had given way, under the influence of revivalist preachers like Calvin

Colton, to a new definition of revival as a 'historical event' which could be planned and executed by men.[5] The character of revivals in the latter part of the nineteenth century in Britain make the reality of this change indisputable. I would, however, differ with Kent as to its extent and would like to argue for the continued existence of revival defined as a spontaneous outpouring of the Holy Spirit. Although the event itself occurred with increasing rarity, the definition continued to serve the function of an ideal, to which a large number of evangelicals aspired.

In the late nineteenth century, definitions of revival abandoned the structural aspects which Calvin Colton had outlined (spontaneous or planned) and instead focused on the spiritual elements of revival. Some definitions claimed revival was 'simply the appearance of new vigour and life in a Church, whatever may have been its previous condition'[6] or 'the recovery of lost spiritual vigour, and the regaining of power to extend the kingdom of God among men'.[7] Such definitions highlighted the 'renewal' aspect of revival, its ability to restore life and vitality to individuals and institutions that had become cold and ritualised. Other definitions emphasised the conversion element considered so essential to any revival. Therefore, the efforts of Moody and Sankey were described as an attempt 'to bring the Gospel to those who are apparently beyond the reach of the ordinary efforts of the ministers of the churches, and to preach the Gospel so simply and effectively that the result may be to draw sinners to the Saviour'.[8] The most common occurrence was to conflate both aspects of revival into one definition. In 1903, Theodore Cuyler, a prominent American evangelical minister, said a revival 'describes a state of things in a church or in a community when Christians become more spiritually-minded and active in good works, and the conversions of impenitent souls are more than ordinarily numerous'.[9]

These theoretical musings accompanied the practical application of revival definitions. As John Kent has pointed out, revivals were traditionally seen to be national movements. The Ulster revival of 1859 was widely believed to have been the last example of this phenomenon which saw:

> such a manifestation of the converting power of God, as shall mark a new epoch in the moral and religious history of mankind; ... a pervasive, national quickening, reaching into every parish, going into the centre of society, ... and carrying forward the cause of vital religion.[10]

As the years went by there was no repeat of this movement and revivalism took on a more institutionalised role. It was incorporated into church calendars and peddled by itinerant evangelists. Alterations in the definition soon followed the shift in practice, expanding the territory of the term 'revival' to include operations of the Holy Spirit in the local context, within a parish, circuit or even congregation.[11] With this development, revival abandoned its origins as a diffuse, in some ways indefinable, movement to become the concrete set of 'consecutive meetings' held 'day after day and night after night' which characterised R.A.

Torrey's perception of his urban missions.[12] The concept of revivalism had come to represent not only the idealised spontaneity of an earlier generation, but also the spiritual dynamics of conversion and renewal and the physical presence of the meetings themselves.

Such a multiplicity of meanings undoubtedly created confusion. In order to counteract this trend evangelicals started to use terms such as 'special services' or 'missions' to describe the planned, evangelistic meetings of a local church or a famous evangelist. Special services, organised by individuals like the Earl of Shaftesbury, were held in theatres to evangelise the working classes of London. Ten-day missions, organised by the Church Parochial Mission Society, were a regular feature in many evangelical Anglican churches in the 1880s. Every winter similar events conducted by connexional or district evangelists took place in Methodist chapels across the country. Needless to say, the term 'revival' fell into disuse and for many became obsolete and old fashioned. However, perceptions of revival which relied on its spontaneous nature died hard. During the forty-five years between the 1859 revival and the outbreak of its Welsh counterpart, this interpretation was never completely eradicated. In 1873, Reverend Samuel Garratt declared 'a Mission is no more like a Revival than a hot-house plant is like a tropical forest', despite the similarities between them. Revivals, he explained, did not emerge out of special plans, nor could their beginnings and ends be predicted.[13] When the Welsh revival broke out, supporters were unanimous in their opinion that this phenomenon was not a mission. Dr J.C. Jones declared, 'it is independent of all human organizations – straight from heaven. Missions are not *revivals*. Men can organize the former, not the latter, and it is a pity the distinction should be so often overlooked.'[14] Jones need not have worried. Other commentators were quick to apply the criterion which he used to distinguish the events in Wales from the efforts of Torrey and Alexander. 'Mission' was the term which was consistently applied to the urban, middle-class, civic hall-based meetings of these respectable Americans. Their work was considered to be only one aspect of the general preparations for the 'revival' which took place in Wales and included other events such as a general increase in prayer, conventions at Llandrindod and the efforts of local evangelists and ministers.[15] The decline of 'revival' as a concept was a direct consequence of its continued significance as an unplanned religious movement. Because of their divine origin, cyclical nature and often spectacular results, revivals became idealised as the most effective way to convert the masses and the best form of church growth. In his efforts to forge agreement between liberal objectives ('the regeneration of the individual') and evangelical concerns (the conversion of souls), W.T. Stead, editor of the *Pall Mall Gazette*, observed that religious revival 'often succeeds in achieving the result which we all desire more rapidly, more decisively, and in a greater number of cases, than any other agency known to mankind'.[16] Once again, the spiritual justification for revival was based on a solid foundation of evangelical pragmatism.

With their ideal in place, evangelicals were keen to protect it from potential impostors. They wanted to control how a revival was perceived and the factors which determined it. A hint of this manipulation is evident in the distinction evangelicals made between a revival and a mission. By applying the criterion of 'methods used', any unplanned, spontaneous religious activity was termed a 'revival' while human organisation and prearrangement signified a 'mission'. Taking it one step further, evangelicals placed a value judgment on this distinction to enable them to determine which kinds of revival were acceptable. 'True' revivals, therefore, were those which most closely resembled the ideal of a divine origin and therefore were impromptu in their nature. Influential evangelicals, through magazines like *The Christian*, argued that God alone was the source of true revivals, that it was impossible to have a revival without him and that he willed them to happen. W. Monro Collings, an evangelist, claimed 'the beginning, the middle and the end of all true revival is in God. And every tide of grace which overflows in blessing to a lost world is an incoming of God.'[17] Such an indefinable requirement meant it was possible to manipulate the actual meaning of revival to suit the required ends. Most commentators felt 'false' or 'spurious' revivals were those which did not meet the ideal of divine origin, relying on human methods to initiate them. It was openly admitted that missions relied on such human instrumentality, and as such, missions never received the disapprobation reserved for religious services attempting to masquerade as a spontaneous revival. Evangelicals never outlined in specific terms the difference between a legitimate mission and a false revival. The idea of 'false' revivals guaranteed that Christians constantly tried to fulfil the requirements of a 'true' one. Reverend William Unsworth agreed that although it was possible 'to galvanize a dead Church', to do so would involve employing false methods to achieve only temporary results, in the long run causing more harm than good. F.B. Meyer, the prominent Baptist minister, was critical of American Christians because of their reliance on revivalist preachers and advertising to 'get up a revival, the reaction from which has been disastrous'.[18] The true/false dichotomy was a useful way to control the perceptions of legitimate revivalism. Revivals that offended respectable, middle-class sensibilities could easily be written off as efforts by deluded individuals to construct a poor imitation of a divine model. The threat of false revivals was greater than any specific accusation. Evangelicals had a formula which they could use to determine the legitimacy of a revival and to distinguish it from a mission, and a model to flaunt to average churchgoers as the standard they should be pursuing.

Evangelical literature was obsessed with the importance of 'true' revivals and squirmed under the restrictions placed on their activity by this definition. Evangelicals were torn between the requirement to wait on God for a revival and their desire to gain converts and experience religious vitality. Despite these constraints, evangelicals were not deterred from talking about revival or discussing the proper ways to bring it about. Henry R. Cripps, in a letter to *The Christian*, remarked on the recent interest in revivals and the desire it had awakened among many for a return to spiritual vigour. 'There is a danger,' he warned, 'that a revival may be "worked up" instead of being "brought down" – that it may be merely enthusiasm and excitement instead of the working of the Holy Spirit.' But in almost the same breath, he asked, 'how can we prepare for this revival?'[19] Cripps' answer to this question encapsulated the evangelical perception of revival and what were considered legitimate means to promote one. Restricting preparations to the spiritual realm, Cripps urged individual Christians to expect a revival. Believers were then exhorted to pray, preach the gospel and 'abide in Christ'.[20] Evangelicals were once again making distinctions. According to their ideal, spiritual efforts to promote a revival were acceptable, while concrete and visible plans were not.

One of the most powerful continuities about evangelical perceptions of revival was the predominance of prayer as the only true way to bring one about. English Christians in 1859 who desired to see the spread of revival from Ulster to their shores were exhorted to 'use effort, all legitimate effort, to bring about the happy results you are seeking' or in others words, to be consistent in prayer.[21] In 1892, E.G.F. explained 'the means or the way to obtain a revival is prayer, real earnest, believing prayer, and this is within the reach of all. We can all pray, "O Lord revive Thy work." ... What need there is that we should pray this prayer now, both often and earnestly.'[22] Although it was the spirit of the prayer – believing and sincere – which was seen to guarantee success, evangelicals also invoked history to support their assertions. They saw prayer as a return to 'the primitive ways of seeking a revival', as had been done during Pentecost.[23] Past revivals, such as the Reformation, Kirk of Shotts and the American revival of 1857 had all started as a result of prayer and, by implication, people could expect the same in the present. This perception of prayer remained fundamentally unchanged throughout the nineteenth century and it was thought that 'it is possible to have revivals without preaching, without churches, and without ministers; ... without prayer a genuine revival is impossible'.[24] The result of this emphasis was the institutionalisation of prayer as a formula for revival that could be invoked at any time. Such a process was implicit in the writings of many evangelicals. Referring to prayer, the Holy Spirit and preaching, Reverend W. Percy Hicks concluded that 'there never will be revivals of any great value to the Church of Christ without relying upon these conditions, which seem to be indispensable'.[25] It was a short step to convert an internal process into a mechanical prerequisite. Such a step was taken decisively by R.A. Torrey. He was a fervent believer in prayer as the source of all true revivals and looked to the history of American revivalism as proof of the fact. He believed that 'one of the great secrets of the unsatisfactoryness and superficiality and unreality of many of our modern so-called revivals, is that more dependence is put on man's machinery than upon God's power, sought and obtained by earnest, persistent believing prayer'.[26] Torrey, however, appeared to fall victim to his own criticisms when, in his thirteen-step outline of 'how to organize and conduct a revival meeting', he formalised the spiritual process of prayer into public united prayer meetings, which he said should be organised once the support of all church members had been solicited.[27]

Torrey even went so far as to equate the quantity of prayer with the quality of a revival. Because his engagements for 1903 were made all at the same time, Belfast, being visited last, had the longest time in which to pray for successful meetings. As a consequence, he felt it was the most rewarding of all his English and Irish campaigns to date.[28] Prayer was trumpeted as the spiritual ideal and the only way to bring about a truly spontaneous revival. Torrey avoided the restrictions this placed on the legitimate means which people could employ to promote a revival by turning prayer into a means in itself.

Throughout the nineteenth century, the object of all this prayer was to exhort God to send the Holy Spirit, believed to be the second condition of any true revival. The continuity of this perception was remarkable, right down to the illustrations. In 1859, English evangelicals prayed that the Holy Spirit would come and breathe life into the 'dry bones' of London's spiritual condition, a reference to the prophet Ezekiel's vision in the Old Testament. In 1892, E.G.F. visualised the state of contemporary churches in the same way.[29] To the evangelical mind, the Holy Spirit was the guiding force in any true revival. It was he who inspired people to pray for revival in the first place. He directed all the preparations and gave power to sermons and testimonies, so that they convicted people of sin. The Holy Spirit was the only means by which individuals could be converted, and the only way to get him to work was through prayer. This was a crucial point, and one which was reiterated over and over. If a revival was truly desired then there was 'the absolute necessity of the putting forth of the living energy of the Holy Spirit, in order to [promote] the conversion of men and the maturing of their spiritual affections'.[30] Reverend R.W. Dale recognised that most of the work of conversion could be accomplished without God's help. Homes could be visited, meetings could be held in an attractive church, with an inspirational sermon and a professional choir. 'All of this may be done without God', said Dale, 'but if men are to be moved to real penitence and to be inspired with real faith, the light and power of the Holy Spirit must reach individual hearts.'[31] Evangelicals set up an idealised revival which would originate with God, involve only the prayers of believing individuals and result in an outpouring of the Holy Spirit's power. Although this process was supposed to be forbidden to human agency, evangelicals, by the end of the nineteenth century, had formalised these familiar requirements into a canon of methods which rivalled those ostensibly reserved for mission services.

THE EVANGELICAL RESPONSE TO EVIL

Evangelicals believed that all their hard work in prayer and supplication to the Holy Spirit made a revival practically inevitable. In 1859, when news of the Irish revival became known, British evangelicals were confident that a revival would spread from Ireland to their churches (see Chapter 2). Such optimism was at the root of Reverend J. Idrisyn Jones' article entitled 'Is a revival at hand?'[32] In it he listed five reasons he felt a revival was within a 'measurable distance'. Firstly, if the condition of religion could decline, then based on what he called 'the law of reaction', it could also increase and thus bring about a revival. Secondly, the evidence of numerous local revivals was a premonition of a still greater movement. Prayer was a third and prominent feature of his analysis. Many people were praying for a revival and according to the Bible, if petitions were made in sincerity God was obligated to fulfil them.[33] Jones' fourth explanation was based on the cyclical nature of revivals. It was well known that revivals were periodic and intermittent. The time that had elapsed since the last major revival in 1859 was the longest in recent memory, so it was safe to assume that the next revival must be imminent. Finally, there were signs in the world of a universal crisis, which could be met only by a universal revival. In response to such indicators, Jones urged believers to work harder for the conversion of souls, to be encouraged and to 'assume an attitude of expectation'.

For Jones and other evangelicals like him, it was obvious that revival was still a relevant construction. Why did evangelicals continue to desire a revival? What purpose did it serve for them? And why did the concept of revivalism continue to fulfil those functions? In late nineteenth-century Britain many evangelicals began to look at the world around them, and what met their gaze horrified them. They saw a decline in church attendance, a loss of the working classes to organised religion, the encroachment of theological liberalism on traditional evangelical beliefs and the general growth of what they called social 'evils', such as gambling, intemperance and the breaking of the Sabbath. For them, the only way to halt this seemingly inevitable decline was through the apostolic fervour and spiritual vigour that came out of a time of revival. A revival would halt the drink traffic and improve Sunday morning sermons, close music halls and abolish the opium trade. Not content only to wish for a revival, evangelicals confidently expected one. The history of revivals was clear on this point – they always followed a time of wickedness or formalism, which to many evangelicals were features of their present society. As evangelicals harked back to the glory days of 1859 and the reform of society which resulted, the anticipation of revival became more important to them.

Most historians are in agreement that new ideas about science and theology had an enormous impact on many members of the traditional evangelical camp. Most Congregational and a substantial proportion of Baptist ministers had abandoned conservative evangelical views well before the end of the nineteenth century.[34] A substantial proportion, however, did not embrace these new ideas, agreeing with the Reverend C.H. Spurgeon in the Down-Grade controversy of 1887–8, that the trend to theological vapidity was a dangerous one.[35] Like Spurgeon, who left the Baptist Union in protest against this trend, other conservative evangelicals felt spiritually isolated and under assault. Many would no doubt have agreed with the *Daily News*' remarks on the *British Weekly*'s survey of church attendance in 1886, when it claimed that the census showed 'an immense and startling alienation of the London public from the regular organisation of religious worship' and that the churches were 'failing in the primary purpose of gathering the people to public religious institutions and religious worship'.[36] Similar responses arose out of the *News'* own census in 1902–3, when Canon H. Scott Holland 'gloomily scan[ned] the Census returns' to see 'the dreary trickle of worshippers, so scanty and meagre, disappearing into the vast unworshipping crowd'.[37] There certainly were no shortage of objects to blame. Evangelicals were quick to point out the weaknesses in the churches themselves, and many called attention to unpopular styles of preaching, long services, easy tolerance of minor sins and a lack of pastoral concern. This 'low type of Christianity' had robbed missions of their ability to make an impact on the masses of humanity suffering from a condition of 'spiritual death'.[38] Rather than lay blame, however, evangelicals were urged to examine their own lives and work to change the situation from within. The structural weaknesses within evangelical nonconformity were perceived to be a result of the watering down of essential theological truths, such as eternal punishment and the necessity of conversion. R.W. Dale made, in a sermon published as *The old evangelicalism and the new* (1889), a distinction between the theology of the eighteenth century and its contemporary counterpart. He stressed its nondenominational temper, its lack of intellectual concerns and its passion for souls. Unlike the evangelicals of today, Dale argued, the old evangelicals did not see 'the love of truth for its own sake, but the love of truth as a necessary instrument for converting men to God, and placing them permanently in a right relation to Him'. Modern evangelicals, however, had begun to view theology and the Bible, not as weapons in the battle for souls, but as a disinterested pursuit of truth. While Dale was firmly in favour of this trend, he did wonder: 'If we have lost something of the passion for men which characterized the Revival, is there adequate compensation in the results of the passion for truth?'[39] When William Booth was interviewed by the *Westminster Gazette* in 1894, he was asked whether the world had improved 'since you were what you called saved'. Booth replied:

> There you are. You've just hit it. Your expression 'what you call saved' just indicates the change. Fifty years ago people weren't afraid of talking about being saved. Nowadays it is bad taste, and you worldly people think it foolish even to use the expression. No; the world has not grown better.[40]

Conservative evangelicals blamed the forces of modernism for the erosion of traditional doctrines like conversion. They also felt modernism was weakening the ability of the churches to prevent the growth in social evils.

The influence of theological liberalism reduced the urgency of doctrines like conversion, and was combined with a growing tendency among middle-class evangelicals to view revivalism's overt conversionism as vulgar and old fashioned. Church attendance now symbolised a respectable standard of belief. Religious practices that encouraged the fervour and zeal of the evangelical awakening were increasingly rejected. This obviously had negative implications for revivals, which had always suffered from criticisms of unorthodoxy and emotionalism. Harold Murray, in his biography of Gipsy Smith, one of the most popular evangelists of the late nineteenth century, wrote:

> Many reasons are given for the delaying of revival. The most obvious one is that we do not really want it. We are too comfortable, we do not want to be disturbed. We do not want to be shamed. We want to sit in a comfortable pew and be comforted ... We should feel uncomfortable if we were suddenly asked, as members of a Christian Church, to leave our pews and put our arms around kneeling penitents and lead them into the way of life. We have never done it, and we are too shy, and reserved, and too uncertain about our own qualifications, ever to do it. The whole thing is too open, too public.[41]

The component of this respectable religion which concerned Murray was its increasingly private nature. Revivalism was no longer countenanced because it made public demands and involved communitarian efforts to save souls, which these middle-class evangelicals were unwilling to fulfil. Such behaviour offended the growing trend towards an individualistic perception of evangelism. Conversion was no longer a public statement in front of a community of witnesses, but an individual and internal contract with God. Inquiry rooms and decision cards were both innovations which heightened the private character of what had been previously a public and communal decision.

This privatisation of religious behaviour, along with the influence of modern ideas, gave evangelicals reason to believe that the spiritual state of the nation was very unhealthy. These perceptions combined with their willingness to observe a corresponding moral declension in society, as tirades against the drink traffic and the opium trade proliferated. Reverend Elder Cumming lamented the fact that 'bookmaking, as it is called, on the open street for lads, shop-boys, and messengers, has become in some quarters a public nuisance which has called for the interference of the law'.[42] Reverend Thomas Champness conducted an often isolated, but nevertheless vigorous and persistent campaign against the drink traffic. Between 1897 and 1903, he unsuccessfully presented a resolution to the Wesleyan Methodist Conference asking it to prevent those individuals directly engaged in the liquor trade from holding office in the connexion. At the conference of 1904 he presented a petition with 12,000 names and 100 circuit memorials in support of his resolution. This was only enough to get it adopted as a recommendation.[43] Although Champness was positive about his achievement, many others who urged such social purity felt they were becoming voices in the wilderness.

With such a negative picture of the social and spiritual aspects of British society, it was still possible for evangelicals to look to the future with a modicum of hope. In their *Weltanschauung*, all of this doom and gloom meant a revival was just around the corner, a revival which promised to reinvigorate churches and to reorder society along scriptural lines. In 1904, Reverend Thomas Phillips also mourned the power of the drink traffic. He claimed that it was capturing the wealth of the country, controlling its women and labourers and gaining the support of legislators. In response to this evil he urged the church 'to regain its spiritual might and splendour, to recover that apostolic fervour and force that destroyed evil' by forming temperance societies to promote revival.[44] The confident expectation that the present wickedness was merely temporary was an outgrowth of the cyclical perception of history which many evangelicals held. As individuals, Christians went through various stages in their spiritual life, from decline to conviction to empowerment. The same was true for the Church; it also experienced cycles in its spiritual condition. Thus, the present reaction against religion could be explained as a phase in the cycle.[45] As one observer has noted, a declension of this sort actually 'points ahead to a renewal by appealing for the purer past as a reachable standard ... Without a declension, revival is both conceptually and programatically impossible.'[46] While disheartened, evangelicals were assured that a time was coming when a revival would change everything, reversing recent theological innovations, restoring God to his position of authority, re-establishing doctrinal certainty and returning churches to a salvation-oriented preaching style.[47] 'The preaching of declension and the preaching of revival are the alternating currents of revivalistic culture.'[48]

To buttress these ideas, in the absence of any contemporary manifestations of revival, evangelicals turned to revival genealogy for proof and reassurance that times of spiritual awakening had invariably followed a period of declension. The 1890s witnessed a burst of interest in past revivals, much of which was influenced by romantic and nostalgic perceptions of the last manifestation of revival in Ireland. From his vantage point of thirty-five years later, Reverend Samuel Garratt could say that 'that time of Revival in the retrospect looks to me like a bright defined period of grace unlike anything before or after it'.[49] In 1894 R.C. Morgan planned a thanksgiving meeting to commemorate the 1859 revival, partially motivated by his memory of a previous meeting held in 1861. At the time, he had called the meeting 'interesting and happy' but 'now we look back upon it as inaugurating a period of spiritual blessing'.[50] Perhaps he thought the 1894 meeting would produce similar results. What really happened in the years after 1859 was that, despite the growth of church work and evangelistic effort, another revival did not take place. By the 1890s, therefore, much of the debate and discussion about the nature of revival and how to promote one began to take on a historical tone. Articles in *The Christian* which appeared to be current revival news turned out to be contributions from veteran evangelists reminiscing about events in 1859, or reprints from newspapers of the time. Evangelistic work in Ireland, regardless of its actual character, was portrayed as a 'revival', perhaps in the hope of achieving truth by association.[51] All of this attention promoted 'the invention of tradition', or the idealisation of the 1859 revival.

Eric Hobsbawm has defined 'invented tradition' as 'a set of practices, normally governed by overtly or tacitly accepted rules and of a ritual or symbolic

nature, which seek to inculcate certain values and norms of behaviour by repetition, which automatically implies continuity with the past'.[52] This continuity,
however, is largely factitious and is created as an attempt to keep some elements
of a changing society invariant or familiar.[53] This theoretical model applies very
well to the use of a revival tradition in late nineteenth-century Britain. As we
saw earlier, evangelical definitions of revival were manipulated to promote
acceptable forms of religious behaviour. When late nineteenth-century evangelicals called for a remembrance of 1859, the memories they invoked were largely
self-constructed and bore little resemblance to the actual event. No mention was
made of the physical manifestations and how controversial they were. No
mention was made of the jealousy British Christians experienced when similar
revival fervour was not forthcoming in their churches. Ministerial concerns
about the expansion of lay leadership and the control of religious services were
glossed over entirely when 1859 was invoked as an ideal. Bessie Howieson, a
witness of the revival, inadvertently challenged the manipulation of tradition
which was taking place when she urged Christians to deeper sincerity in their
quest for revival. In a letter to *The Christian* she referred to an earlier writer who
wanted people to pray 'so that a similar manifestation of the Holy Spirit might
be given to us'. She stated:

> I think, however, that very few of your English readers have the faintest
> conception of what form the manifestation took.
>
> It was not simply an expression of sorrow for sin or of enthusiasm in
> loving service, but a tempest of the Holy Ghost shaking souls to their
> foundations, like the rushing mighty wind on the day of Pentecost. Tongues
> of fire were not visible, but bodily prostration, caused by a sense of the
> wrath of God, and the unveiling of the terrors of the invisible world to the
> unrepentant, were everywhere present … Are England's professing
> Christians really and whole-heartedly desiring the abiding presence of the
> messenger of rest?[54]

Howieson was right. The calls to revivalism she had been reading about did not
have the proceedings she remembered as their goal. Evangelicals had invented
a completely different perception of the same event. Their distance, both in time
and place, from the actual location of the revival made the translation that much
easier. Martin Hope Sutton remarked:

> those who witnessed the awful manifestations of the Spirit of God 35 and
> 36 years ago will scarcely presume to pray for a repetition almost of the
> same outward visitations, but we must all rejoice and praise God for the
> 'fruits of the Spirit' we are now witnessing in the works I have alluded to,
> and prayer should continually be made in churches, chapels, halls, and in
> families, for a mighty outpouring of God's Holy Spirit on all these institu-
> tions and on those carrying them on.[55]

Sutton here gives his tacit support to the transformation of the 1859 revival, assuming that those who desired a revival now were obviously not praying for a return of the controversial physical manifestations, but for the continued success and prosperity of the evangelistic societies which emerged in the revival's wake. Physical manifestations, one of the classic defining features of a revival, were jettisoned in favour of an 'invented' definition, which portrayed a much more acceptable version of events in 1859.

By the 1890s, then, the revival of 1859 had been re-created in the evangelical mind as a golden era. It was a time when Christians were reinvigorated, sinners were saved, society was transformed and evangelicals felt they had come close to their goal of the Christian nation. Evangelicals sought to commemorate those times with a series of conferences and meetings. Much of the interest grew out of the continued influence of important evangelicals who were favourably disposed towards revivalism. R.C. Morgan, Reginald Radcliffe, Robert Paton, Arthur Kinnaird, George Williams and James Mathieson had all been prominent in arranging revival meetings of one sort or another. All had participated in Moody and Sankey's meetings; Robert Paton chaired the London organisational committee, and several others could trace their involvement back to the 1859 revival itself. These men continued to sponsor activities which involved revival elements. In 1892 Paton planned a one day conference to discuss the best way to promote a revival and held Bible study meetings for that purpose at the Aldersgate St YMCA throughout the year. Two years later he was involved with R.C. Morgan in setting up an annual Thanksgiving meeting 'to thank and praise our God for all the wonderful things he has done, not only for the East End of London, but for the whole world' since 1859. The third annual Dundee Conference in 1894 chose as its theme 'revival in relation to the individual, the family, the church and the nation'.[56] Of the numerous speakers at these meetings, all of whom were male,[57] several were accorded special status because of their connection with the 1859 revival. The presence of individuals like J.G. McVicker, the Irish Presbyterian turned Baptist minister who went on to join the Plymouth Brethren, gave the services the authentic flavour of the past they were commemorating. Other eyewitnesses, like Lord Radstock, Captain Hawes and Reginald Radcliffe, acted as visible examples of the power revival could exert over individuals and of its ability to engender long-term commitment to an evangelistic life. These men and their reputations as 'veteran evangelists' gave their opinions an added credibility and guaranteed the audience a firsthand, if somewhat laudatory, perception of the revival. When *The Christian* interviewed Archibald Bell, a lay preacher from Belfast who was actively involved in the revival, he confidently assured them that it had begun on the same day as the revival in America. Although such an assertion was historically dubious, it increased the spiritual significance of the revival substantially in the eyes of many of its supporters. Memory was changing the past to suit the perceptions of the present.

Such reminiscences, and the whole phenomenon of revival commemoration, were used deliberately to pass on perceptions of revival to younger generations of believers who had never experienced such a spiritual movement. G.E. Morgan, the son of R.C. Morgan, chaired the Thanksgiving meeting in 1895. He stated that the object of the evening gathering was 'to awaken in the hearts of the younger generation a determination to assume the burdens of Christian work which their elders were perforce laying down'.[58] The stalwarts of mid–century revivalism like Morgan, Radcliffe and Weaver, were either dead or growing too old to maintain a prominent role in the evangelistic field. Young evangelists had to be imbued with a sense of the revival's significance. Remembering past glories, therefore, kept those old values alive. 'Memories of the past', it was thought, 'are great incentives to faith and expectation for a renewal of such Divine working in the souls of men.'[59] If 1859 lost its significance, then evangelicals would lose an effective and emotive paradigm for a religious life.

On the whole, evangelical efforts to maintain interest in revival and to promote a sanitised view of 1859 were successful, at least within a subculture which was showing resistance to change in other areas of its religious practice. The perception of 1859 – as a source of power to renew individuals and revive churches, as a time when evangelicals controlled society's agenda, as a time when religious institutions flourished, when preaching was effective and audiences attentive – came to determine perceptions of revival until well into the twentieth century. Such a golden era, stripped of all the dissension, stress and controversy of its historical origins, guaranteed the continued existence of an evangelical desire for a repeat performance. When a revival did eventually break out in Wales, evangelicals from across Britain could whole-heartedly agree with the Dean of Westminster when he said:

> They who saw around them in England many marks of a new interest in religion, of a spirit of inquiry, were naturally concerned to ask whether the revival would reach themselves, and, if so, what form it could take that would be in harmony with their religious instincts. Was there room in the Church's ordered life for any such manifestations of exceptional emotion? They could not organize a revival if they would, for this was not a mission for the delivery of God's message; it was a Divine movement, quickening the seed which had long been sown, as the spring quickened the corn. They might pray for it, and he thought they should do so, trusting that it should take the form God willed. They might be sure that it would be appropriate to their instincts and training, that it would stand in some true relation to their past ... That there was need in their Church of a revival of spiritual life none would deny. Organization was more thorough than it had ever been; they had better approached churches, more frequent services, a larger number of communicants, a better instructed, more diligent, more devout clergy, and yet they were not given such a witness for the living God as compelled men to fall down in penitence and confess that God was in them. Of a truth something was needed, something of an inspiration.

What they wanted was not a new order or a new method, not a fresh form of worshipping God, but life racing through the limbs of the duly ordered body, life lifting their worship to the spiritual level to which its ancient form bore witness.[60]

THE SURVIVAL OF AN ANACHRONISM?

Over the course of the late nineteenth century, the basic concept of revival remained a valid and useful one for many evangelicals, although what it involved had, of course, altered in several ways. Revival had come to encompass several different layers of meaning, and evangelicals used this versatility to control the standards that determined 'proper' religious behaviour. A revival, therefore, could be whatever they wanted it to be. While maintaining the essential components of prayer, the work of the Holy Spirit and the importance of expectancy, the evangelical mentality, over the course of the nineteenth century, altered the function they thought a revival would fulfil. Evangelicals turned to revival as the answer in a society which seemed to be growing more corrupt, trusting it to transform what had resisted their most persistent efforts. For them, the sinfulness of the times heralded a fresh outpouring of spiritual power. Such a perception was based largely, if not entirely, on hypothetical situations. In theory, evangelicals knew how a revival should come about and how to distinguish a false one from the real thing. But many of them had never actually experienced one. Between 1903 and 1905, two religious movements took place which allowed evangelicals to test their beliefs and to show how relevant their version of revivalism was in 'modern' society. The Torrey and Alexander mission and the Welsh revival were two quite distinct events, although they did overlap when the Americans' Cardiff meetings in October 1904 coincided with early reports of a spiritual awakening in Cardiganshire. Together, the two movements represent the diverse nature of British evangelicalism and the oftentimes ambivalent role of revivalism within it. In the early twentieth century evangelicals manifested elements of both continuity and change within their attitude towards revivalism; both trends will be discussed in turn.

Historically, one of the most frequent controversies surrounding revivalism involved the role of emotion, a subject which was consistently the object of divergent opinions. Those who believed in revivals felt emotion was an essential element of the conversion process. It indicated that the presence of the Holy Spirit was working to convict the soul of sin and that the conversion was genuine. In 1859, the excessive and sometimes spurious nature of the physical accompaniments to this process prejudiced many middle-class Christians against any sort of visible proof of conversion. This, along with the growing respectability of congregations, combined to promote a general move towards quieter meetings. By the 1870s D.L. Moody was praised for the 'promptitude, tact, and practical wisdom with which he presides over meetings, so as to prevent mere physical excitement, and so to let the Word of the Lord have free course without the obstructions and perversions of nervous feeling or prostration'.[61] The services of Torrey and Alexander followed exactly in this tradition. Torrey was the epitome of the respectable, earnest and austere evangelical and was known for his unemotional sermons. 'He cannot weep with men, as other great preachers have done, as he pleads with them to come to Christ, for he is not built on that plan, and his appeal is more to the intelligence, the common-sense, and the conscience than to the heart.'[62] Even his physical style of preaching was restrained; he eschewed all gestures.

However, this controlled form of urban revivalism was just one of the many ways revivalism manifested itself in the late nineteenth century. Other traditions were much more willing to embrace emotionalism and continued to do so. For example, during the late 1860s the 'Hallelujah Bands' which toured the Black Country were immensely popular. The lay-led meetings, with their fast-paced and upbeat style reflected the prolonged willingness of the working classes to embrace emotional religious behaviour.[63] Drawing on another tradition, there was the ongoing existence of rural enthusiasm, especially among non-Wesleyan Methodists. In 1885, Reverend George Warner, a Primitive Methodist, conducted a two-week series of meetings with Durham miners, which exhibited all the characteristics of a revival service. One strong man was convicted of sin and 'presenting himself at the penitent form, he did roar for mercy in great earnestness'. At another meeting, when the chairman was praying, 'the Holy Spirit so fell upon him, and revealed Christ to him, that he literally leaped and danced like David before the ark'.[64] When the Salvation Army sent Pamela Shepherd to set up a mission in the Rhondda valley in 1879, her work quickly took on revival overtones when physical manifestations, chaotic meetings and improvements in social habits occurred. In a fit of spiritual reform, men broke their pipes and threw away watch chains, while women removed their hat feathers and de-flounced dresses.[65] The tradition of emotionalism which these revivals represented did continue, but only for an increasingly narrow section of the evangelical community, concentrated in small denominations and rural areas.

The emotionalism which accompanied the Welsh revival was part of a long-standing tradition. At the time, the national press recorded familiar descriptions of crowded meetings lasting sometimes for as long as eight hours. Conducted entirely in Welsh, these meetings followed a spontaneous format of singing, testimonies and prayer, with only minimal leadership from ministers or evangelists.[66] With remarkable similarity to the events of 1859, there were claims of the Holy Spirit inspiring unlettered farm servants and plough boys to pray in classic Welsh.[67] The most fantastical stories, however, circulated around the person of Evan Roberts. This 26-year-old collier turned Bible college student had felt led, in a series of early morning 'conversations' with God, to return to his home village of Loughor and conduct revival services. They were immensely successful and soon he began travelling throughout the country presiding over ecstatic and hymn-based meetings. His style was deemed unusual from the start.

He actually said very little during his services and often spoke only to make predictions about individuals in the audience or to chastise them for wrongdoings, which he claimed were 'quenching the Spirit'. Visions in the pulpit were a common occurrence and normally took quite violent forms; during one meeting Roberts fell forward in the pulpit, wracked with sobs and groaning in agony, and ended up prostrate on the floor. When he recovered he claimed the Holy Spirit had allowed him to experience the sufferings of Christ. This activity culminated in his 'week of silence', a self-imposed verbal exile, which he claimed was an imperative from God if his forthcoming meetings in Liverpool were to be successful.[68] The press response was surprisingly neutral. The notion that God had deliberately selected not the 'chosen vessels of gold and silver' but the 'common pottery of earth'[69] was one which had been expressed in the context of lay preaching in 1859, and in D.L. Moody's work. Evan Roberts was described as 'a man without the remotest claim to the title of orator', who came to prominence to allow 'the weak things of the world ... confound the things that are mighty'.[70] Ethnological arguments, so often used to categorise the Irish during 1859, were another familiar sight. W.T. Stead, in explaining the excitement, said '[t]he Welsh are an emotional race, and they are apt to demonstrate their feelings more effusively than phlegmatic Saxons'.[71] *The Times* described the 'Welsh Celt' as 'warm-hearted and wayward, intelligent and superstitious, impulsive and obstinate, anarchic and easily led', an individual who had 'always shown a certain instability of character, a tendency to exaggeration, and a greater love for music and oratory than for veracity and purity'.[72] Such categorisations indicate that popular perceptions of revival emotionalism had changed very little since the mid-nineteenth century.

A second continuity with earlier forms of revivalism was the ongoing concern among clergy with the link between revival and regular church life, which included ministerial authority. In 1859, the proliferation of prayer meetings and open-air services had forced ministers to endorse lay leadership, although they were never entirely happy with these arrangements. Enormous steps had been taken to expand the lay role in church life since then, but the position of 'evangelist' was still a subject of debate. In Wesleyan Methodist circuits the minister was supposed to fill evangelistic requirements along with his pastoral duties. It was not until 1882 that the denomination recognised the special evangelistic gifts of some of its ministers and released them from circuit responsibility to become full-time 'connexional evangelists'. This was a way of encouraging evangelism, while at the same time avoiding any irregularities which might arise from the employment of non-Methodist evangelists who would be outside denominational control.[73] During the Welsh revival, however, there was no real ministerial leadership. Most ministers who opened their churches for revival services seemed willing to allow Evan Roberts into the pulpit and to let the meeting find its own path. But there were hints at their concern. At a Tylorstown meeting someone discovered an atheist in the audience. Roberts singled him out and asked him to state his beliefs publicly. Reluctantly, the man did so and upon hearing a denial of God's existence the audience began to shout, demanding the man's forcible eviction. Roberts was able to control the crowd and said 'No, let us pray for him.'" One of the ministers present later recalled, 'when these oppositions began to pour in a number of us ministers were trembling, but seeing them disposed of in such a masterly way we "praised God, from whom all blessings flow'.[74] At a meeting in Abertillery, the local minister, 'evidently an earnest soul-winner', interrupted the proceedings to urge the people to come to Christ in the traditional fashion. According to one visitor, he seemed not to understand 'the way of the Spirit ... standing aside until [He] should need them'. The meeting quickly 'fell flat' and people began to leave until the minister stepped down from the pulpit.[75] Ministers did not act to stop the revival, but evidence of their anxiety, as they hovered on the fringes of this movement, is a poignant testimony to their continued concerns about propriety and convention.

Surprisingly enough, it was the Torrey-Alexander Mission which engendered the loudest ministerial criticisms. In February 1905 a letter to *The Times* from 'An Evangelical Churchman' challenged the authority under which the Americans had come to London. He claimed the London Evangelistic Council, a group with no authority, had invited them to the city. They had not been 'sent' and were clearly violating the apostolic rule which safeguarded the Church from 'irresponsible and unauthorized teachers'.[76] A Dublin Anglican felt that the efforts of these 'itinerant and irresponsible preachers' simply interfered with the steady work of the churches and had no lasting benefits.[77] In their defence, other Anglican ministers pointed out that all spiritual movements – from Christ through to Luther, Wycliffe, Wesley and Whitefield – had been formed apart from the Church leadership, which recognised them only when it was too late. They argued that such efforts to limit evangelistic activity to clergymen, 'who, apparently need not necessarily be "converted" or have a vestige of preaching power', would drive the laity away from the church.[78] Ministers, even those calling themselves 'evangelical', were still trying to control, limit and determine the parameters of what they felt to be appropriate revival behaviour.

Opposition and criticism is a third continuity in late nineteenth-century revivalism. It was not exclusively ministerial. In Wales, the criticisms invariably focused on physical manifestations and emotionalism. The most public attack was from Reverend Peter Price, a minister from Dowlais who claimed the meetings which Roberts had started were 'a sham ... a mockery, a blasphemous travesty of the real thing' and dismissed the ecstatic phenomena as sheer exhibitionism.[79] Other individuals were also concerned about the negative effects of such emotional and protracted meetings, claiming the revival had actually increased drunkenness and contributed to a large number of illegitimate births.[80] One man, a Welsh innkeeper, told a *Times* reporter:

There's too much of it, Sir; there's no sense in it. I baint agin religion, but this [the revival] goes too far. It's out of all reason. Me and my missus were only saying last night as how our takings has fallen by the half this last fortnight. What's to become of the people if this goes on? The men must have a drop of drink if they are to do their work proper. Why, only last night I see'd scores of our best customers pass our door with their heads down, and looking that miserable as if they were going to the asylum, and I tell you what it is [he said in a voice husky with emotion], that's where a lot of 'em will be if they don't drop it soon.[81]

The emotionalism, the lack of proper authority and the criticisms which revivals engendered were issues which continued to preoccupy evangelicals and British society.

Despite the inevitable changes in audience perceptions, issues and arguments surrounding revivalism were remarkably long lasting. Why? No doubt a partial explanation emerges from the ideas discussed earlier, such as the existence of an evangelical subculture which ensured revivals continued to be perceived as important and valid. The continuity of an evangelical leadership kept the idea of revival alive through the print media as well as in commemorative meetings. The nature of revival itself no doubt assisted this process. Because it had so many different meanings, people could invoke it to describe almost any form of evangelistic activity they liked. Revival, in the late nineteenth century, had the reputation that it could improve society and transform individuals. This appealed to evangelicals, who wanted to maintain their church attendances. As will become apparent, it also appealed to a strand within modern thought which saw revivalism as a successful and direct way to bring about progress.

THE INROADS OF 'MODERNISM'

On 22 January 1890 the *Christian World* remarked on how the term 'modern thought' was being bandied about so frequently that it was on the verge of becoming a cliché. Some individuals, they admitted, were not so enthusiastic about its growing popularity. 'The revivalist, mourning the Laodicean temper of his church, and urgently demanding more fire and brimstone in appeals to the unconverted, is told by his brethren that such methods are wholly unsuited to modern thought.'[82] While the term was overused, the realism and scepticism which 'modern thought' had brought to intellectual life made it an important concept. This, however, did not say much for the poor revivalist. Although we have seen examples of revivalism's continued relevance to certain members of Victorian society, there is evidence which suggests that for a growing number of people revivals were considered at best only socially useful and at worst old fashioned and obsolete. Such criticism did not advocate throwing the baby out with the bath water. Most commentators, usually liberal clergymen and ministers, wanted to alter the nature of revivalism to fit in with their changing belief systems. Alterations to the concept of revival took place on a number of different fronts. New definitions were constructed. Traditional objectives, such as the conversion of souls, were jettisoned in favour of more 'modern' goals such as individual improvement, social concern and political harmony. The increasingly formalised and predictable methodology of missions was criticised. Evangelicals were forced to admit that their efforts to convert the nation were failing. Perhaps in response to these failures, the revivals that were 'planned' took on the overtones of holiness meetings by fulfilling their literal meaning and reviving those already within the scope of the churches.

As we have already seen, a flexible definition of revival meant the concept could be manipulated to reflect the ideas of the party using it. In January 1890, Congregationalists were confident that the year to come would witness 'a glorious outburst of religious life' and felt a revival of religion was at hand. Such a revival, trumpeted their unofficial newspaper, promised 'not to be any outbreak of sanctified selfishness, or lapse into sensational obscurantism, or triumph of narrow pietism, but an uprising of human nature on all its sides to realize … that social ideal of the Kingdom of God which was for ever revealed in and through the person of our Lord Jesus Christ'.[83] This was not the conversion of souls or the quickening of believers, but an improvement in human nature which would promote a liberal theology and commitment to the social institutions of the denomination. Revival was still felt to be important, but it was essential that it should be reviving the right things. 'What the churches should aim at' argued one liberal minister, 'is not the rehabilitation of mediæval dogmas, but such a realization of the spiritual meaning of life and the universe as we now know them, as will constitute a new birth of religion.'[84] Revivals could no longer promise to save souls from the everlasting punishment of hell or to transport them, on death, to heaven to enjoy personal fellowship with Christ. Instead, they could appeal to men and women 'to turn from more sordid thoughts and feelings to a higher conception of life'.[85]

Traditionally, the main objective of a revival was to convert people from a sinful life to one which was pleasing to God. One popular technique used to achieve this was fire and brimstone preaching. In the early nineteenth century revival preachers described the eternal punishment which hell represented in graphic detail in an effort to frighten their listeners into belief. In a similar fashion R.A. Torrey described hell in 1904 as:

> a place of memory and remorse. Hell was the madhouse of the universe, where men and women remembered … It was a place of ever-increasing moral degradation and ruin … The New Testament did not hold out one ray of hope for any man or woman that died without Christ. 'For ever and ever' was the never-ceasing wail of that restless sea of fire. Such was hell – a place of physical anguish, a place of agony of conscience, a place of insatiable torment and desire, a place of ever-increasing ruin and infamy, a place of evil companionship, a place of shame, a place without hope.[86]

Torrey was aware of the criticisms such preaching would provoke, but believed it was his duty to preach what he felt the Bible taught. He and other evangelists felt the preaching of eternal punishment was essential to the success of a mission. One of them declared, 'it is kind to tell people they are in danger. There is wrath to come!'[87]

Over the course of the nineteenth century the perception of hell as eternal punishment had become increasingly old fashioned; a decreasing number of individuals believed in it. Hell-fire sermons were now considered speculative and morally offensive as the nature of hell was modified to suit changing ideas. Part of the shift occurred because of changing views about the nature of secular punishment. Under the influence of Jeremy Bentham and the utilitarians, punishment no longer served a retributive function but operated to deter criminal behaviour or to reform it. They argued that, as a punishment, hell was not a deterrent, and that it did not take the intentions of offenders or the severity of their crimes into account.[88] This sociological challenge combined with growing theological concern to reduce the effectiveness of eternal punishments as a motive for conversion. The influence of free inquiry and private judgement made fixed doctrines seem outmoded. The importance of progress and rationalism made the severity of hell appear vulgar and cruel.[89] Unitarians, who early on in the nineteenth century had rejected a traditional idea of hell, were the strongest critics. John Page Hopps judged D.L. Moody's sermons on hell 'brutal' and 'indecent', and offensive to the concepts of justice, reason and common sense.[90] Responses to R.A. Torrey's views were similar. One critic said, 'we are bound by all the laws of self-respect to dissent from such teaching, and to protest against such ideas of God and man as the wildest mythology of antiquity may be challenged to equal in monstrous absurdity, and flights of superstition'.[91] These objections to traditional eschatology became widely accepted, even within certain sections of the evangelical community. The evangelical Anglicans Samuel Garratt and Hay Aitken both abandoned their belief in eternal punishment and adopted, in the case of the latter, conditionalist views.[92] Some evangelicals, however, were unwilling to discontinue preaching hell. Torrey felt 'the cruellest man on earth was the man who believed that there was a hell, but did not say so right out, lest he be unpopular'.[93] Such opinions were becoming increasingly marginalised. The inroads of biblical criticism and 'modern thought' made this element of revivalism untenable and contributed to the erosion of its traditional definition.

Among a growing number of individuals, revivals now served to improve human nature, rather than transform souls. The growing unpopularity of eternal punishment was a reflection of intellectual developments in late nineteenth-century Britain such as 'meliorism', the belief that 'if only skills were exerted, the human race would make rapid progress'.[94] For some people, it seemed, revivalism and meliorism had come to represent the same thing, the former losing its conversionist objective and the latter gaining a spiritual dimension. Revivalism was now a way to improve people, to lift them out of the ignorance and depravity of their daily lives and give them the hope of better things. One of the most vocal proponents of this idea was William T. Stead. He was converted in 1859 when a revival swept his boarding school at Silcoates, and ever since then believed revivals to be 'realities to those who come under their influence, permanently affecting their whole future lives'.[95] Such a traditional conversion experience was only one of his eclectic mix of religious influences. As he freely admitted, he had come to believe that through Christ's death the entire human race had been saved, except those who actively rejected him.[96] In an effort to prove the extent of juvenile prostitution and the white slave trade, Stead had gone undercover to procure a girl, and serialised the story as 'The Maiden Tribute of Modern Babylon'. His behaviour caused an enormous sensation and led to his arrest for abduction.[97] He was a friend of William Booth's, helping him edit the Salvation Army's scheme for social reform *In darkest England and the way out* (1890). He was also an active spiritualist and wrote several books via the spirit of an American woman named 'Julia'.[98] On top of all of this he supported the Welsh revival – visiting the scenes of revival and writing articles for several newspapers on the subject.[99] The main reason Stead supported the revival was that it did directly what most social reformers could do only indirectly and that was to effect 'the regeneration of the individual'. The object of a revival, therefore, was to lift people to a higher level of morality. 'What I want', he once argued:

> is a plan that will take hold of such lower types as myself, which will give 'such spasms of desire and accessions of joy' as will lift us semi-humanised, sensual men to a higher moral level, a plan which will make the drunkard forswear his cups, and make the wife-beater a loving husband. I admit that the Revival does not by any means reach everybody, but I do without hesitation assert that it reaches thousands of us poor, legitimate descendants of the anthropoids, and makes new men of us.[100]

Despite his traditional description of Welsh revival meetings, on closer examination it is apparent that Stead had quite a different definition in mind. Revivalism was important not because it spiritually transformed people, but because it gave them the opportunity to improve themselves.

The natural outcome of Stead's perspective was the evolution of revival into a type of social reform, albeit fast and efficient social reform. This had always been a latent tendency in revivals. The Ulster revival of 1859 had been often justified, in the face of offensive emotionalism, by its moral results and the changes it effected in people's habits. Stead and others, however, turned this into the goal of revivalism and not simply a positive side effect. A growing awareness of poor social conditions promoted a shift in emphasis from evangelism to social concern in some evangelical circles. The London Congregational Union declared 'The condition of the people [of London] suggests a much wider ministry than that of the Word ... The starving must be fed. The outcast must be succoured. The slaves of misfortune and vice must be reclaimed. Otherwise the Gospel itself, with all its superhuman graces will fail to reach them.'[101] Preaching the gospel was not enough. Spiritual conversion was insufficient to improve human- ity; there had to be social activity as well. Revivals were no longer necessary to fulfil the requirements of an obsolete theology but to give people 'an impulse to better things',[102] promoting philanthropy and thereby improving social conditions.

For W.T. Stead, such progress also involved a political dimension. He and other liberal commentators saw the potential that revival had to reform society and renewed the idea often expressed earlier in the century that political institutions could benefit from this moral transformation of society. Such con- nections were frequent in Wales, where the links between Calvinistic Methodism and radical politics had always been close. Mr Thomas Richards, a Labour MP speaking at a revival meeting, felt that the revival had convicted many people who were opposed to trade unions and strengthened the labour movement in Wales.[103] A meeting of the West Wales Miners' Association (the first *not* to be held on licensed premises) was opened with a prayer that 'the revival influence which had already taken hold of the workmen would also lay hold of the employers, and that the result would be the carrying on of the coal industry of the district with greater harmony'.[104] David Lloyd-George, the Liberal MP, speaking at a meeting at Deganwy, said:

> The revival movement was certainly the most remarkable movement which he had seen in his life, and was, he hoped, destined to leave a very perma- nent impression on the Welsh people ... It was ennobling and elevating the aims of the individual life in Wales, and he should also like to see it have some effect upon the national expression of that life. That was one reason why he trusted that at the next election Wales would declare with no uncertain sound against the corruption in high places which handed over the destiny of the people to the horrible brewing interest, which had clutched the nation by the throat. There was no party that desired reform that would not thrive upon such great manifestation as had been witnessed in Wales recently.[105]

Politicians recognised the power revival had as a symbol within Welsh society. They liked the fact that it improved morality and industrial relations and encouraged it as a way to win votes and to promote their policies.

As was noted earlier in this chapter, the evangelical ideal of a revival was one which could not be planned or organised. Despite these assertions, evangelicals essentially had been planning revivals ever since Charles Finney published his *Lectures on revivals of religion* in 1835. They embraced a growing repertoire of methods and institutions designed to win souls. Reinforcement of these develop- ments emerged in the evangelical press. In 1859 the *Revival Advocate* told its readers 'God works by means: he employs human agency; the church, therefore, has a great deal to do in promoting a revival of religion.'[106] Calls like this became more frequent as the century wore on. By 1900 a revival was considered 'a magnificent spiritual miracle' that was 'the simple result of the use of means'. Christians were told, 'we are not justified in idly waiting till some overwhelming influence comes upon us, and almost against our will bears us onward in God's work'.[107] As part of the trend, more and more evangelistic workers were using a growing variety of methods with an increasing frequency. By the late nineteenth century, these had become formalised into a well-established group of tech-niques and practices which were widely used and often aggressive in tone. As methods of saving souls, however, they came under increasing criticism, from both supporters and opponents of revivalism, and undoubtedly contributed to the general decline in revival as a whole.

Elements of revival which had caused so much controversy in 1859 were rapidly becoming institutionalised by the end of the century. Lay preaching, for instance, was receiving denominational approval among Wesleyan Methodists in the form of training institutions, like Reverend Thomas Champness' Joyful News Training Home, which offered young men the qualification of 'lay evangelist'.[108] The formalisation of the evangelistic procedure also took over the preparations for mission services. Churches and evangelists were both encouraging the impor-tance of advance preparations, the former because it got church members active in local Christian work, and the latter because it prevented any embarrassingly empty meetings. This process was becoming more elaborate as the century wore on. To prepare for a mission in Leeds, local Methodists suspended huge banners across the main street two months prior to the meetings, posted notices throughout the city, visited homes and left invitations, as well as distributing handbills in the streets before each service.[109] In Wiltshire a Town mission was set up; a united meeting, with Baptists, Congregationalists and Methodists in attendance, was organised, and several open-air services were held before the actual revival meetings had even commenced.[110]

Once revival services were underway, it was apparent to late nineteenth-century observers that the actual conduct of the meetings were changing. The traditional sermon-based revival meeting was still the most common, but various incidentals were being added. D.L. Moody had started the trend with the introduction of a choir and the gospel solo. Other evangelists used 'magic lanterns' to give illustrative lectures. The most controversial innovation was the use of decision cards, and this revealed the reductionist tendency of mission services first seen with D.L. Moody. R.A. Torrey distributed cards to potential converts that reduced the salvation message to seven statements of essential doctrine. Salvation became a verbal assent to a standardised statement of 'I have taken Jesus as my Saviour, my Lord and my King'.[111] Despite his claims that prayer was the only source of a true revival, Torrey, more than anyone else, reduced revival to a collection of methods which anyone could reproduce. His books, *How to work for Christ* (1893) and *How to promote and conduct a successful revival* (1901) were literally step-by-step accounts of revival methods and requirements. Every contingency – parlour meetings, tent work, gospel wagons, worker training, types of inquirers, follow-up work and sermon preparation –

was outlined and justified. Planning for success was becoming so prevalent that even the Holy Spirit found himself becoming marginalised as just one method among many.

Some of these methods had a long history in evangelical circles. Prayer and fellowship meetings were often the prelude to revival activity in eighteenth-century Scotland, as well as in Ulster, America and elsewhere.[112] In the late nineteenth century, however, there was a trend towards the more aggressive application of these traditional methods. Revival preachers were notorious for their pointed sermons, often singling out an individual and speaking directly to them. Evan Roberts was fond of this method, berating those in the audience who he claimed were spoiling the meeting with their selfish intentions.[113] Evangelicals were also growing more aggressive in their evangelistic efforts outside of revival services. 'Button-holding', as it was called, was the practice of 'direct, personal, individual, face-to-face pleading with others who are unsaved'[114] and grew out of the belief that everyone had the ability and duty to save souls. It appealed to the Victorian sense of efficiency and the necessity of making good use of one's time. Approaching a stranger in the street or standing on a train platform were only two of many opportunities allowing the aggressive evangelist to confront people with the gospel.[115] During revival meetings at Portgordon, such activity was so prevalent that as one 'backslider' put it 'the ungodly were forced to hide themselves, and I among the rest, for if you went out some young soldier of the cross was sure to attack you about your soul'.[116]

Such methods, however effective they might have appeared to believing evangelicals, were becoming the objects of increasing criticism. Reverend Samuel Garratt, a staunch supporter of revivals, said, in reference to 1859:

> I sometimes think, but perhaps I may be wrong, that the perpetual efforts at producing by human methods something of the same kind without the characteristics I have mentioned, are a hindrance to its coming. But God is able to grant it whatever mistakes we may make.[117]

Such misgivings were the basis for a number of objections surrounding the Torrey-Alexander mission. Liberal nonconformists rejected Torrey's method-ology as 'more material than spiritual'[118] and felt his efforts at conversion 'contrived to take the soul at a disadvantage'. Critics felt he harassed individual souls until they capitulated out of intellectual exhaustion, no longer able to resist. One Presbyterian minister grumbled:

> Their teaching is eloquent of abstract methods of closing with Christ, dispensing salvation as they would write out a prescription, propounding redemption as if 'what must I do to be saved' were a problem in Euclid which one man here, and another there could work out, and which the rest only needed to follow. To me it savours too much of the press gang. If human nature were made in one unvarying mould there might be some show of reason for issuing this spiritual timetable and way-bill, but

inasmuch as man's nature is multiform the imposition of such a standard is tyrannous in the extreme.[119]

Torrey's sermons, which denounced card-playing, theatre-going, dancing and gambling also met with substantial criticism.[120] These obvious drawbacks to Torrey's system made the spontaneity of the Welsh revival appear as a rebuke from God for this 'over-organisation'.[121]

The general reliance on methods did not hide the fact that in the late nineteenth century revivals were no longer as successful as they once had been. Audiences, for the most part, were small and largely composed of church members. Conversions were normally confined to a mere handful. R.A. Torrey blamed the very methods which his entire career had promoted when he predicted the coming revival could be 'a spurious revival gotten up by the arts and devices of man'.[122] Whatever the reason, it was obvious that revivalism was experiencing setbacks. When George Hooper, the United Methodist Free Church connexional evangelist, held a mission at Prudhoe-on-Tyne, there were no conversions and it failed to reach the non-churchgoing proportion of the population. The local minister blamed a theatre recently erected across from the chapel and said to be a popular attraction among many of the village youth.[123] Even well-known evangelists were suffering. W.H.M.H. Aiken was a prominent Anglican clergyman who had been relieved of his parish duties to conduct mission work throughout the country. In the 1880s the places he visited were getting more difficult to awaken and the results of his work were not as sensational or effective as had been the case several years earlier. The 'ever-increasing indifference of the masses to the "mission" form of appeal' was cited as one obstacle. Aiken, with a painful honesty, also blamed himself. In a letter to his wife he said 'it is humbling that many of us who can preach as well as Moody, and with many more natural advantages, should yet fail with our hundreds, where he succeeds in bringing in his thousands'.[124] During a North American tour he wrote:

> if it please God to give me power to win my way to the hearts of the Canadians, it will be a comfort to get work on a somewhat larger scale than these poor meagre missions, which seem now the rule wherever I go. I sometimes think, however, that I must have fallen off greatly in my preaching, or there never could be so great a falling off in the attendances.[125]

Gipsy Smith, who was preaching to audiences of 7,000 on Sunday mornings in the 1880s, found himself the object of heckling and catcalling at a Sheffield meeting of working men in 1922. The shouts of 'What is your remedy?' and 'What practical solution have you?' indicated an audience more concerned with social issues than with the salvation of souls. The disruption preceded the general disintegration of order until the meeting had to be abandoned.[126] Smith's biographer was only partially successful in his attempt to show that the evangelist, even in the final years of his career, 'went his way, conducting his meetings pretty much as he did a century ago, and getting the same results'.[127]

It was obvious to most others that despite their best intentions and best methods, mission work was not reaching its intended audience and that revival blessing was not forthcoming.

Critics of revivalism, however, felt this decline was a positive development. Frederick Davenport claimed that people were revolting against the psychological absurdity of the conviction of sin, that they had undergone 'a marked mental evolution under the stress of a complex experience and a rapidly differentiating social environment' which had made them more self-controlled, more rational and less vulnerable to suggestion. As a result, they found revivals less relevant and, as he predicted, 'if we remain a sanely progressive people, moving steadily and rationally forward in the path of social evolution, primitive religious habits will be sloughed off, and popular religious movements will assume new forms in harmony with modern development and enlightenment'.[128]

A final development in late nineteenth-century revivalism was its connection to the holiness movement. Holiness was a view of the religious life which believed that Christians should have a second decisive experience after conversion, promoting them to a higher level of spirituality and giving them victory over sin. Achieved by faith and personal sacrifice, this experience had a variety of influences, including the Methodist concept of 'perfection' and Quaker spirituality. The beginnings of the movement can be traced back to the revival circles of the mid-nineteenth century. Revivalists of the 1860s promoted ideas and used language which would eventually become the specific terminology holiness adherents adopted.[129] The line of influence, however, went in both directions. Revivals not only influenced the holiness movement but revival theory came to advocate the importance of quickening believers before a revival could take place. This brought accusations that holiness had shifted the focus away from sinners and on to the sanctification of believers. In justification, advocates felt 'personal holiness is a state of preparation which feeds and replenishes revival power'.[130] What hindered the conversion of sinners was the spiritual weakness of existing Christians. I.E. Page declared, 'we need a revival: and the need for revival *is in the Church*, giving a higher life to the people of God'.[131] Once that had been completed, churches could look outwards to the world around them. Revival had once again, chameleon-like, shifted meaning. Revival, in this context, meant entire sanctification for church members. Meetings with the intention of promoting holiness often bore a strong resemblance to traditional revival proceedings. The spontaneity, testimonies and emotionalism of holiness meetings made it difficult to tell the difference.[132]

CONCLUSION

The old notion of revivalism as a dramatic outpouring of God's spirit on a sinful people was coming under strain at the turn of the century. Denominational respectability, conservative evangelical caution, the decline of the concept of hell, persistent working-class infidelity in the cities, new cults of theological sensibility, holiness movements and the social gospel were all sapping the social foundations of revival enthusiasm. For a hard core of evangelistic evangelicals, revivals nevertheless remained the ideal method of changing individuals and communities. Confronted with a society that was apparently abandoning religious standards, these evangelicals turned to the notion of revival as their ultimate hope and persuaded themselves that they were living in the lull of apathy which must precede the storms of blessing. The continuation of the transatlantic tradition in the shape of Torrey and Alexander, along with the remarkable events in Wales, persuaded them that evangelical planning and divine initiative could still generate the necessary spiritual power. But the reality was that neither American evangelists, nor explosions of religious zeal in Wales and Ulster could threaten to halt the social processes that were undermining the old evangelical self-confidence. Efforts to convert the masses were becoming increasingly difficult, and ministers of all denominations were becoming increasingly reluctant to endorse unconditionally religious movements that threatened their control and offended their sensibility. Unrestrained emotionalism and public conversions made traditional revivalism appear vulgar and old fashioned.

Evangelical attempts to crank up the old pragmatism by resorting to soloists, choirs and decision cards stirred up opposition on all sides – for abandoning divinely ordered procedures and reducing the process of conversion to a repetition of set phrases, on the one hand, and for failing to take account of 'modernizing' trends in theology and society on the other. Revivalism and its proponents could not avoid the monicker 'old fashioned' or 'obsolete' for very much longer. The Welsh revival and the Torrey-Alexander mission revitalised interest and rallied supporters for a while, but interest began to fade soon enough. By the beginning of the twentieth century revival had come to mean the revival *of* something – be it art or architecture, literature or religion. It is important, however, not to overestimate the extent of decline. The idea of revival could still warm the hearts of British and Irish evangelicals, but their enthusiasm not only entailed an edited version of history (with the messiness of raw revivalism left out), but a selective and limited understanding of the society they were trying to revive. The concept remained, but its emotional power, even in the minds of its supporters, was in decline.

Conclusion

T HIS BOOK has been concerned with reinterpreting the role of revivalism in late nineteenth-century Britain and Ireland. From Ulster in 1859 to Moody and Sankey in 1874 to Wales in 1905, the appearance, conduct and theology of revivals was surrounded by controversy and disagreement. This is not the picture which subsequent evangelicals were keen to portray. For many of them, a revival represented a time when religion exercised a pervasive influence over society, when conversions were frequent and moral improvements widespread. In historical terms, however, revivals caused tension and division among the evangelical community on a number of different levels. Apparently spontaneous varieties, like the events in Ulster in 1859, were supported by the laity, while the clergy expressed their concerns about the potential for excess among the revived. Planned revivals were considered to be an acceptable alternative, but they too were criticised for their manipulative tactics and simplistic theology. Conversion was the ultimate goal for all, but some had more scruples about methodology than others. Such contradictory attitudes towards revivalism emerged from differing perceptions about the essential role of religion in society. Evangelicals had always adopted a pragmatic approach to conversion, church attendance and the improvement of social morality. For them, the end result was the most important consideration and justified the use of a variety of different methods, ranging from the vulgar to the sensational. By the late nineteenth century, however, there were a growing number of people who viewed religion in a more reverent and respectable light. They argued that certain standards of religious behaviour had to be maintained in order for processes such as conversion to have any real meaning or significance. As the Reverend R.W. Dale put it, evangelicals were traditionally concerned with 'truth' because it was 'a necessary instrument for converting men to God'. Modern religionists, however, were concerned with 'truth' simply for its own sake.[1] The differences between these two positions reflect the contradiction in evangelical thought, outlined by W.R. Ward, between the sufficiency of grace and a denominational machinery committed to works. The spiritual ideal, in the context of revivalism, was a spontaneous outpouring of the Holy Spirit's divine power, which could not be planned or organised. In reality, many evangelicals and their churches devoted a great deal of effort to promoting a revival. Although the evangelical tradition treated works-righteousness as filthy rags, it nevertheless worked furiously to promote its own brand of that righteousness.

The close examination of late nineteenth-century revivals in this book has hopefully revealed their complex and multi-dimensional nature. Revivalism was not an isolated phenomenon. It evolved under the influence of a changing society and operated within a religious context. Study of its development has, therefore, thrown new light on other aspects of nineteenth-century evangelicalism. The interest which the Ulster revival of 1859 sparked among British evangelicals has shown the extent of evangelicals' information network. Three months after the revival was first reported, a national magazine devoting itself to revival news started publishing in London. Annual conferences, such as those in Dublin, Mildmay and Keswick, brought evangelicals of different denominations together, providing a forum for exchanging ideas and building relationships. Town and village mission committees promoted opportunities for evangelical cooperation through their nondenominational gospel meetings. Lay evangelists, both middle and working class, who travelled throughout Britain and Ireland, enjoyed a wide reputation as the visible symbols of this subculture. Thus, it was possible for an evangelist like Richard Weaver, originally a collier born in Shropshire, to be well known among the evangelical communities of London, Dublin and Glasgow, and to count wealthy merchants and gentry among his close acquaintances. It is important to remember that Ireland, Scotland and to a lesser extent Wales, functioned as equal partners in this London-based subculture. Dublin, Belfast, Glasgow, Edinburgh and Cardiff were all important centres of evangelical influence and were regularly included in the revival tours of well-known English and American evangelists.

No doubt the extent of this network was due in part to the common middle-class background of many of the participants. This is certainly the case for those activists whose lives are recounted in the numerous available biographies. The connections between prominent members of the evangelical community were often based on personal acquaintance or mutual friends. Although evangelical-ism was often equated with the Victorian middle class, the preceding chapters have shown that the evangelical community embraced a broad cross-section of the population, from aristocrats to prize fighters. The individuals who supported revivalism in the nineteenth century reflected the broad, eclectic mix of indi-viduals who gave evangelicalism its diverse character.

This breadth of support makes consideration of religious motivation essential to any true understanding of nineteenth-century evangelicalism. As this study has shown, the individuals who supported and participated in religious revivals did so often for deeply personal reasons. Female preachers, for example, were aware of the restrictions, both theological and social, on the public exercise of their religious talents, but many of them were unable to resist what they felt to be the divine sanction of the Holy Spirit on their actions. Similar motives drove the numerous working-class evangelists to challenge clerical misgivings about the propriety of lay leadership. The participation of these individuals in evangelistic activity makes it difficult to explain revival simply as the result of external, social factors or as the victim of religious decline.

The developments in late Victorian religion have been interpreted as having a negative impact on revivalism. The decline in spontaneous outbursts of religious fervour has often been used as evidence that the modernisation of society was incompatible with such pre-modern forms of religious behaviour. The argument presented here is that evangelical perceptions of revival were more complex than this rather simplistic analysis makes out. Revivals were still considered to be an effective form of church growth and many evangelicals continued to desire them and to work for them. Planned revivals, in the form of gospel meetings, evangelistic services and mission hall gatherings, testify to the ongoing concern to reach the irreligious masses. Localised revivals, especially in rural areas, still had the potential to imitate the excitement of earlier days, even if they occurred on a smaller canvas. But as revivals became increasingly marginalised, Victorian evangelicals forgot the tensions which previous manifestations had caused and began to idealise them as high points on the spiritual calendar. Paradoxically, as the chances of another 1859 became more remote, evangelicals began to desire its repetition with more urgency. Under the influence of modernity, however, they had adapted the definition and meaning of revival to suit their changing perceptions of proper religious practice. At the beginning of the twentieth century, the evangelical desire for revival remained, but outside a number of restricted pockets of religious enthusiasm, evangelicals were relying more on distorted memories than on clear-sighted aspirations for the future.

Unlike previous studies of religious revivalism in the second half of the nineteenth century, the aim here has been to try to bring to life those who sought to produce revival, as well as those who criticised it. By including Scotland, Wales and Ireland and focusing on American evangelists, female preachers and working-class enthusiasts, I have tried to penetrate further into the vexed question of religious motivation than some others have done. One unexpected benefit from this approach is the way in which it has highlighted the tensions and ambiguities within popular evangelicalism itself. The apparently simple business of saving souls in fact stirred up any number of disputes over means, proprieties, personnel and results. Not only was the biblical template upon which their approach was based more ambiguous than many evangelicals could accept, the social processes of revivalism, once unleashed, had an uncomfortable tendency to shock Victorian evangelical sensibilities. Physical prostrations and raw enthusiasm offended middle-class respectability; those who promoted revivals disturbed accepted notions of gender, class and nationality; new techniques and methods apparently produced results but they also offended taste; and evangelical claims to depend on the sufficiency of grace sat uneasily with the remorseless commitment to works in the propagation of revival. The resultant tensions, embracing ultimately the nature of historical reality itself, not only illuminate the many paradoxes of the evangelical tradition, but also reveal much about the society they tried so hard to change.

Notes

INTRODUCTION

1 E.R. Wickham, *Church and people in an industrial city* (London, 1957).
2 K.S. Inglis, *Churches and the working classes in Victorian England* (London, 1963) and Hugh McLeod, *Class and religion in the late Victorian city* (London, 1974).
3 Wickham, *Church and people*, p. 11.
4 James Obelkevich, *Religion and rural society: South Lindsey, 1825–75* (Oxford, 1976); Alan Gilbert, *Religion and society in industrial England: church, chapel and social change, 1740–1914* (London and New York, 1976); Stephen Yeo, *Religion and voluntary organisations in crisis* (London, 1976).
5 Gilbert, *Religion and Society*, p. 205.
6 Jeffrey Cox, *English churches in a secular society: Lambeth, 1870–1930* (Oxford, 1982) and Callum Brown, *The social history of religion in Scotland since 1730* (London and New York, 1987). For a more provocative explanation of Brown's ideas see his article, 'Did urbanization secularize Britain?' in *Urban History Yearbook* (1988), pp. 1–14.
7 See Alan Gilbert, *The making of post-Christian Britain* (London, 1980); Steve Bruce (ed.), *Religion and modernization: sociologists and historians debate the secularization thesis* (Oxford, 1992); Hugh McLeod, *Religion and irreligion in Victorian England* (Bangor, 1993); Robin Gill, *The myth of the empty church* (London, 1993); John Wolffe, 'Religion and "secularization"' in Paul Johnson (ed.), *Twentieth-century Britain: economic, social and cultural change* (London and New York, 1994), pp. 427–41 and Alan Gilbert, 'Secularization and the future' in Sheridan Gilley and W.J. Shiels (eds), *The history of religion in Britain* (Oxford, 1994), pp. 503–21.
8 S.J. Connolly, *Religion and society in nineteenth-century Ireland* (Dundalk, 1985), pp. 3–4.
9 See J.D. Walsh, 'Origins of the evangelical revival' in G.V. Bennett and J.D. Walsh (eds), *Essays in modern English church history. In memory of Norman Sykes* (London, 1966), pp. 132–62; W.R. Ward, 'The relations of enlightenment and religious revival in central Europe and in the English-speaking world' in *Reform and Reformation: England and the Continent c. 1500–1750: Studies in Church History. Subsidia 2* (Oxford, 1979), pp. 281–305; W.R. Ward, 'Power and piety: the origins of religious revival in the early eighteenth century' in *Bulletin of the John Rylands University Library of Manchester*, 63 (1980), pp. 231–52.
10 David Bebbington, *Evangelicalism in modern Britain: a history from the 1730s to the 1980s* (London, 1988), p. ix. Other studies devoted to evangelicalism include Ian Bradley, *The call to seriousness: the evangelical impact on the Victorians* (London, 1976); Kenneth Hylson-Smith, *Evangelicals in the Church of England, 1734–1984* (Edinburgh, 1988); and Keith Robbins (ed.), *Protestant evangelicalism: Britain, Ireland, Germany and America, c. 1750–1950: Studies in Church History. Subsidia 7* (Oxford, 1991).
11 For the social impact of the evangelicals, see Kathleen Heasman, *Evangelicals in action* (London, 1962); and Donald Lewis, *Lighten their darkness: the evangelical mission to*

working-class London, 1828–60 (Westport, CN, 1986). The political manifestations of evangelicalism are discussed in David Thompson, *Nonconformity in the nineteenth century* (London, 1972); D.W. Bebbington, *The nonconformist conscience* (London, 1982); and R.J. Helmstadter, 'The nonconformist conscience' in Gerald Parsons (ed.), *Religion in Victorian Britain* (4 vols., Manchester, 1988), iv, pp. 61–95.

12 David Hempton and Myrtle Hill, *Evangelical protestantism in Ulster society, 1740–1890* (London, 1992), p. xi.

13 Gerald Parsons, 'Emotion and piety: revivalism and ritualism in Victorian Christianity' in Gerald Parsons (ed.), *Religion in Victorian Britain* (4 vols., Manchester, 1988), i, pp. 223–9.

14 G.M. Ditchfield, *The evangelical revival* (London, 1998), pp. 13–17; W.R. Ward, *The protestant evangelical awakening* (Cambridge, 1992), Chapters 1, 2.

15 Ward, *Protestant evangelical*, pp. 67–72.

16 John Walsh, 'Origins', pp. 132–62.

17 David Hempton, 'Evangelicalism in English and Irish society, 1780–1840' in Mark Noll, David W. Bebbington and George A. Rawlyk (eds), *Evangelicalism: comparative studies of popular protestantism in North America, the British Isles and beyond, 1700–1990* (Oxford, 1994), pp. 157–62.

18 Ditchfield, p. 50.

19 Leigh Eric Schmidt, *Holy fairs: Scottish communions and American revivals in the early modern period* (Princeton, 1989), pp. 41–50.

20 David Hempton, 'Noisy Methodists and pious protestants: evangelical revival and religious minorities in eighteenth-century Ireland' in George Rawlyk and Mark Noll (eds), *Amazing grace: evangelicalism in Australia, Britain, Canada and the United States* (Montreal and Kingston, 1994), p. 63.

21 Peter Brooke, *Ulster Presbyterianism: the historical perspective 1610–1970* (Belfast, 1994), pp. 88–9, 125, 145–8; Hempton, 'Noisy Methodists', p. 71.

22 David Hempton, *Religion of the people: Methodism and popular religion c. 1750–1900* (London, 1996), pp. 35–40.

23 Hempton, 'Noisy Methodists', p. 71.

24 Richard Carwardine, 'The Welsh evangelical community and "Finney's revival"' in *Journal of Ecclesiastical History*, 29 (Oct. 1978), p. 463.

25 J.E. Orr, *The second evangelical awakening in Britain* (London and Edinburgh, 1949), p. 8.

26 The most controversial interpretation was E.P. Thompson's oscillation theory, argued and later defended in *The making of the English working class* (Penguin edn, with post-script, 1980, of orig. edn, London, 1963), pp. 385–440, 917–22. See also R.B. Walker, 'The growth of Wesleyan Methodism in Victorian England and Wales' in *Journal of Ecclesiastical History*, 24 (1973), pp. 267–84; John Baxter, 'The great Yorkshire revival 1792–6: a study of mass revival among the Methodists' in Michael Hill (ed.), *A sociological yearbook of religion in Britain*, 7 (1974), pp. 46–76; and David Miller, 'Presbyterianism and "modernization" in Ulster' in *Past and Present*, 80 (1978), pp. 66–90, for discussions of the external factors causing revival.

27 See Carwardine, 'The Welsh evangelical community', pp. 463–80; Christopher Turner, 'Religious revivalism and Welsh industrial society: Aberdare in 1859' in *Llafur*, 4 (1984), pp. 4–13; David Luker, 'Revivalism in theory and practice: the case of Cornish Methodism' in *Journal of Ecclesiastical History*, 37 (1986), pp. 603–19; and Christopher Turner, 'Revivalism and Welsh society in the nineteenth century' in Jim Obelkevich, Lyndal Roper and Raphael Samuel (eds), *Disciplines of faith: studies in religion, politics and patriarchy* (London, 1987), pp. 311–23.

28 Thompson, *Making*, p. 919.

29 Richard Carwardine, *Transatlantic revivalism: popular evangelicalism in Britain and America, 1790–1865* (Westport, CN, 1978), pp. 172, 199–200.

30 See Hempton and Hill, *Evangelical protestantism*, Chapter 8. Other discussions of the revival in its Irish context are Myrtle Hill, 'Ulster awakened: the '59 revival reconsidered' in *Journal of Ecclesiastical History*, 41 (1990), pp. 443–62; and Janice Holmes, 'Lifting the curtain on popular religion: women, laity and language in the Ulster revival of 1859' (unpublished MA dissertation, Queen's University at Kingston, 1991).
31 Hempton and Hill, *Evangelical protestantism*, p. 151.
32 John Kent, *Holding the fort: studies in Victorian revivalism* (London, 1978), pp. 356–7.
33 *Ibid.*, p. 31.
34 Passing references are made in R.B. Walker, 'Growth of Wesleyan Methodism' and Louis Billington, 'Revivalism and popular religion' in Eric Sigsworth (ed.), *In search of Victorian values: aspects of nineteenth century thought and society* (Manchester, 1987), pp. 157–61.
35 P.B. Morgan, 'A study of the work of American revivalists in Britain from 1870–1914, and of the effect upon organized Christianity of their work there' (unpub. B.Litt. diss., Oxford, 1961); Mark Toone, 'Evangelicalism in transition: a comparative analysis of the work and theology of D.L. Moody and his protégés, Henry Drummond and R.A. Torrey' (unpub. PhD diss., St. Andrew's, 1988).
36 Again, recent analysis of the Welsh revival is restricted to an unpublished thesis. See Christopher Turner, 'Revivals and popular religion in Victorian and Edwardian Wales' (unpub. PhD diss., University of Aberystwyth, 1979). Also see Eifion Evans, *The Welsh revival of 1904* (Port Talbot, Glamorgan, 1969) for a rather laudatory appraisal. Torrey and Alexander's activities have been examined in Toone's thesis, but he has concentrated on Torrey's theology, not on his evangelistic methods. See Toone, 'Evangelicalism' PhD, pp. 217–84.
37 Kathryn Teresa Long, *The revival of 1857–8: interpreting an American religious awakening* (New York, 1998).
38 Kent, *Holding*, pp. 361–2.
39 Inglis, *Churches*, p. 333; McLeod, *Class and religion*, pp. 30–1; Cox, *English churches*, pp. 25–7; Hempton and Hill, *Evangelical protestantism*, p. 129; Hugh McLeod, 'Female piety and male irreligion? Religion and gender in the nineteenth century', English typescript, pp. 1–2 of 'Weibliche foömmigkeit, männlicher unglanbe?' in Ute Frevert (ed.), *Bürgerinnen und Jürger* (Göttingen, 1988), pp. 134–56. For a nineteenth-century opinion see the account of Reverend R. Dunlop, Newbliss, Co. Monaghan in William Gibson, *The year of grace: a history of the Ulster revival of 1859* (Edinburgh, 1860), p. 297.
40 Martha Vicinus, *Independent women: work and community for single women, 1850–1920* (Chicago, 1985), Chapter 2; Deborah Valenze, *Prophetic sons and daughters: female preaching and popular religion in industrial England* (Princeton, 1985); Gail Malmgreen (ed.), *Religion in the lives of English women, 1760–1930* (London, 1986); Brian Heeney, *The women's movement in the Church of England, 1850–1930* (Oxford, 1988); Alex Owen, *The darkened room: women, power and spiritualism in late Victorian England* (London, 1989); Hempton and Hill, *Evangelical protestantism*, Chapter 7; Anne Hogan and Andrew Bradstock (eds), *Women of faith in Victorian culture: reassessing the angel in the house* (London, 1998); Andrea Ebel Brozyna, *Labour, love and prayer: female piety in Ulster religious literature 1850–1914* (Belfast and Kingston/Montreal, 1999).
41 This decline most commonly refers to the popular female ranters of early Methodism. See Louis Billington, 'Female labourers in the church: women preachers in the north-eastern United States, 1790–1840' in *Journal of American Studies*, 19 (1985), pp. 390–4; Billington, 'Revivalism', p. 154; and Wesley Swift, 'The women itinerant preachers of early Methodism', part 2 in *Proceedings of the Wesley Historical Society*, 29 (1953), p. 76. Others allude to the transformation of this preaching into a middle-class phenomenon, but conclude that even this latter form of preaching declines. See Olive Anderson, 'Women preachers in mid-Victorian Britain: some reflexions on feminism, popular

religion and social change' in *Historical Journal*, 12 (1969), pp. 467–84; and Jocelyn Murray, 'Gender attitudes and the contribution of women to evangelism and ministry in the nineteenth century' in John Wolffe (ed.), *Evangelical faith and public zeal: evangelicals and society in Britain 1780–1980* (London, 1995), pp. 97–116.

42 W.R. Ward, 'The evangelical revival in eighteenth-century Britain' in Sheridan Gilley and W.J. Shiels (eds), *A history of religion in Britain* (Oxford, 1994), pp. 271–2.

43 One useful attempt at defining revivalism is Russell Richey, 'Revivalism: in search of a definition' in *Wesleyan Theological Journal*, 28, Nos 1 and 2 (Spring and Fall 1993), pp. 165–75.

44 Hempton and Hill, *Evangelical protestantism*, p. 146.

45 See Lambeth Palace Library, Tait Papers, Vols. 94, 209.

46 Jeffrey Cox uses a large number of early twentieth century 'crisis of faith' biographies in *English churches*. Hugh McLeod, James Obelkevich and Deborah Valenze all use biographies, but they pertain only to one specific locality.

47 See, for example, Ian Murray, 'Explaining evangelical history' in *Banner of Truth* (July 1994), pp. 8–14.

CHAPTER ONE

1 Testimony of Reverend R. Dunlop, "Newbliss" in Reverend William Gibson, *The year of grace: a history of the Ulster revival of 1859* (2nd edn, Edinburgh, 1860), p. 298. See also J.T. Carson, *God's river in spate: the story of the religious awakening in Ulster in 1859* (Belfast, 1958), p. 81.

2 David Bebbington, *Evangelicalism in modern Britain: a history from the 1730s to the 1980s* (London, 1989), p. 3.

3 J. Edwin Orr, *The second evangelical awakening in Britain* (London and Edinburgh, 1949), pp. 5, 6. For similar opinions, see Gibson, *Year of grace*; Carson, *God's river*; and Ian Paisley, *The 'fifty-nine' revival: an authentic history of the great awakening in Ulster in 1859* (Belfast, 1958).

4 See Peter Gibbon, *The origins of Ulster unionism* (Manchester, 1975) and David Miller, 'Presbyterianism and "modernization" in Ulster' in *Past and Present*, 80 (1978), pp. 66–90.

5 R.F.G. Holmes, *Our Irish Presbyterian heritage* (Belfast, 1985); Peter Brooke, *Ulster Presbyterianism: the historical perspective, 1610–1970* (Dublin, 1987); and W.J.H. McKee, 'The Ulster revival of 1859 and the development of Presbyterianism' in R.F.G. Holmes and R. Buick Knox (eds), *The General Assembly of the Presbyterian Church in Ireland, 1840–1990: a celebration of Irish Presbyterian witness during a century and a half* (Coleraine, 1990), pp. 39–55.

6 Richard Carwardine, *Transatlantic revivalism: popular evangelicalism in Britain and America, 1790–1865* (Westport, CN, 1978).

7 John Kent, *Holding the fort: studies in Victorian revivalism* (London, 1978).

8 Myrtle Hill, 'Ulster awakened: the "59 revival reconsidered"' in *Journal of Ecclesiastical History*, 41 (1990), pp. 443–62; and David Hempton and Myrtle Hill, *Evangelical protestantism in Ulster society, 1740–1890* (London, 1992), Chapter 8.

9 Hempton and Hill, *Evangelical protestantism*, p. 146.

10 Paisley, *The 'fifty-nine'*, pp. 11–12.

11 A.R. Scott, 'The Ulster revival of 1859' (unpub. PhD diss., Trinity College Dublin, 1962), pp. 65–77; and Hempton and Hill, *Evangelical protestantism*, p. 148.

12 Articles entitled 'Do we need a revival?' and 'Are we to have a revival?' appeared regularly in the Presbyterian press during the 1850s. These are both taken from the *Irish Presbyterian*, 1 (1853) and 6 (1858) respectively.

13 Gibson, *Year of grace*, p. 18.

14 'Extraordinary religious excitement at Ahoghill' in *Ballymena Observer*, 26 March 1859, p. 1.

15 Hempton and Hill, *Evangelical protestantism*, p. 157.

16 Reverend John Edgar remarked, 'There are, it is true, most encouraging cases of conversion among the lowest outcasts – ... but these are only exceptions, establishing the great general fact, ... that the overwhelming proportion of those believed to have been savingly awakened in this revival, are those who had received a religious education, – Sabbath-school teachers and scholars, the children of religious parents, persons previously under the influence ... of religious precept and example.' Quoted in Reverend William Reid (ed.), *Authentic records of revival, now in progress in the United Kingdom* (London,   1860), pp. 215–16.

17 For a description of a typical revival meeting, see Gibson, *Year of grace*, pp. 41–2. An open-air meeting at Kilconriola well illustrates the potential for confusion and the abandonment of normal procedure. See 'Religious revivals in the north of Ireland' in *Coleraine Chronicle*, 28 May 1859, p. 6.

18 Hill, 'Ulster awakened', pp. 460–1.

19 Reverend David Adams, *The revival at Ahoghill* (Belfast, 1859), p. 15.

20 Charles Foy in *Northern Standard*, 20 Aug. 1859, quoted in Lindsay Brown, 'The Presbyterians of County Monaghan', part 1 in *Journal of the Clogher Historical Society*, 13 (1990), p. 40.

21 Reverend Francis King, *Revivals in religion, with some cautions concerning them, being a lecture, delivered in the scriptural schools, Newry* (Newry, 1859), p. 7.

22 Letter from 'An Observer' in *Londonderry Standard*, 30 June 1859, p. 1.

23 Adams, *Revival at Ahoghill*, p. 24.

24 Reverend John Baillie, *The revival: or what I saw in Ireland; with thoughts suggested by the same. The result of two personal visits* (London, 1860), p. 54.

25 Reverend William McIlwaine insisted lay preachers had told their audiences that salvation depended on 'their receiving the Revival and being "struck"'. See Reverend William McIlwaine, *Revivalism reviewed* (Belfast, 1859), p. 10.

26 Reverend Charles Seaver, *Religious revivals: two sermons, preached in St. John's Church, on Sunday, 10th July* (Belfast, 1859), pp. 22–3.

27 For similar conclusions, see Hempton and Hill, *Evangelical protestantism*, p. 154.

28 Letter of Reverend J. Kennedy in *Londonderry Standard*, 18 August 1859, p. 1.

29 *Ibid.*

30 'The religious revivals in Belfast' in *Belfast News-Letter*, 8 June 1859, p. 2.

31 Reverend John Weir, *The Ulster awakening: its origin, progress and fruit. With notes of a tour of personal observation and inquiry* (London, 1860), pp. 11–12.

32 A variety of people make these suggestions. See Reverend Isaac Nelson, *The year of delusion: a review of 'The year of grace'* (Belfast, 1860), pp. 174–5; [Isabella Bird], 'Religious revivals' in *Quarterly Review*, 107 (Jan. 1860), p. 162; and Reverend Samuel Moore, *The history and prominent characteristics of the present revival in Ballymena and its neighbourhood* (Belfast, 1859), p. 34.

33 Reverend R.T. Simpson, *Recollections of and reflections on the revival of 1859* (Dungannon, 1909), pp. 22–3.

34 These comments were made as a result of two meetings held on subsequent days in Downpatrick. The first meeting was addressed by laymen and was very crowded, while the following meeting, led by Reverend Mr White, was not so well attended. See 'Present religious movement in the north' in *Armagh Guardian*, 24 June 1859, p. 2

35 Letter from 'Looker On' in *Belfast News-Letter*, 15 June 1859, p. 3. These sentiments were widely held among the British evangelical community throughout the nineteenth century and provided the justification for numerous working-class lay preachers such as Richard Weaver and those employed by the Salvation Army. See William Booth, *How*

to reach the masses with the gospel (London, 1872).

36 There are numerous examples of clerical opposition to lay preaching. See the sermon of Reverend William Craig in *Belfast News-Letter*, 13 July 1859, p. 2; Reverend George Salmon, *Evidence[s] of the work of the Holy Spirit. A sermon preached in St Stephen's Church, Dublin on Sunday, July 3, 1859. With an appendix on the revival movement in the north of Ireland* (Dublin, 1859), p. 49; Gibson, *Year of grace*, pp. 116–17; J.B. Armour to John Megaw, Ballyboyland, 8 May 1860 (Public Records Office of Northern Ireland, Armour Papers, D1792/A2/3).

37 'The religious revival' in *Coleraine Chronicle*, 30 July 1859, p. 4.

38 'Religious revivals' in *Belfast Daily Mercury*, 3 June 1859, p. 2. Morrison's displeasure at this disruption was evident in his report. He said, 'I have doubts about the propriety of presenting such young persons before such a large and enlightened audience, assembled under such solemn circumstances.'

39 For a more detailed analysis of the relationship between women and cottage forms of religion, see Deborah Valenze, *Prophetic sons and daughters: female preaching and popular religion in industrial England* (Princeton, 1985).

40 Reverend William Hamilton, *An inquiry into the scriptural character of the revival of 1859* (Belfast, 1866), p. 143.

41 Testimony of Reverend William Magill in Gibson, *Year of grace*, pp. 133–4.

42 *Ibid.*

43 'Religious revivals in the north of Ireland' in *Coleraine Chronicle*, 28 May 1859, p. 6.

44 Testimony of Reverend Adam Magill in Reid (ed.), *Authentic records*, p. 28.

45 Reverend James Morgan, *Thoughts on the revival of 1859* (Belfast, 1859), p. 7.

46 The most famous explanation of this argument was Reverend E.A. Stopford's work *The work and the counterwork; or, the religious revival in Belfast* (Dublin, 1859). He argued that Satan was promoting the acceptance of the physical manifestations as a sign of Divine favour. In actuality, they were a bodily disease and were eroding the true work of the Holy Spirit in the revival.

47 'The physical phenomena of revivals' in *The Lancet*, 23 July 1859, p. 94. For other discussions of hysteria as a cause of the phenomena, see A. Cuthbert, 'On the prominent features of the Ulster revival' in *Medical Times and Gazette*, 5 November 1859, pp. 451–2; the review of *The work and the counterwork* and other relevant pamphlets in *Quarterly Review*, 107 (January 1860), pp. 148–68.

48 For a discussion of the insanity controversy, see James Donat, 'Medicine and religion: on the physical and mental disorders that accompanied the Ulster Revival of 1859' in W.F. Bynum, Roy Porter and Michael Shepherd (eds), *The anatomy of madness: essays in the history of psychiatry* (3 vols., London, 1985–8), iii (*The asylum and its psychiatry*), pp. 125–50. See also 'Insanity and the revivals' in *The Lancet*, 1 October 1859, p. 344; 'Ireland – Lunacy' in *The Times*, 26 September 1859, p. 4.

49 'A new phase of revivalism' in *Daily News*, 16 September 1859, p. 3, quoting the *Northern Whig*.

50 *Ibid.* For Breakey's own account, see 'The revival movement. The marking imposture' in *Belfast Daily Mercury*, 17 September 1859, p. 3. Other criticisms can be found in Nelson, *Year of delusion*, pp. 171–2 and *Coleraine Chronicle*, 17 September 1859, pp. 4–5.

51 This is the implication of comments made by Reverend J. Simpson and H.M. Waddell in Gibson, *Year of grace*, pp. 96 and 295.

52 *Belfast Daily Mercury*, 29 September 1859, p. 2.

53 'The revival in Portadown' in *Portadown Weekly News*, 23 July 1859, p. 2.

54 Reverend Nathanael Brown, Newtonlimavady in Reid (ed.), *Authentic records*, pp. 344–6. For other examples, see accounts in *Coleraine Chronicle*, 4 June 1859, p. 5 and *Portadown Weekly News*, 11 June 1859, p. 4.

55 Brown in Reid (ed.), *Authentic records*, p. 52.

56 References to clothing were common images in many female visions. See Reverend

George Hughes, Newtownards in Reid (ed.), *Authentic records*, p. 295; Reverend F. Buick, Ahoghill in Reid (ed.), *Authentic records*, p. 170; Gibson, *Year of grace*, pp. 170–1.

57 'Ballymena' in *Coleraine Chronicle*, 16 July 1859, p. 3.
58 'Religious revivals in the north of Ireland' in *Ibid.*, 28 May 1859, p. 6. For another similar case, see Salmon, *Evidence[s]*, pp. 57–60.
59 For examples of prayer meetings and Sunday schools set up, see Reverend Thomas Witherow, Maghera in Gibson, *Year of grace*, p. 232; Reverend J. Morgan, Fisherwick Presbyterian Church, Belfast in Reid (ed.), *Authentic records*, p. 14. Such meetings were also set up by women for themselves and their female neighbours. See 'Belfast' in *Coleraine Chronicle*, 11 June 1859, p. 5.
60 Moore, *History and prominent characteristics*, pp. 17–19; Reverend G.H. Shanks, Boardmills in Reid (ed.), *Authentic records*, p. 41; and Reverend William Richey, *Connor and Coleraine; or, scenes and sketches of the last Ulster awakening* (2 vols., Belfast, 1870), i, p. 172.
61 David Bebbington points to the influence of the 1832 cholera epidemic on Methodist growth rates in *Evangelicalism in modern Britain: a history from the 1730s to the 1980s* (London, 1989), p. 115. Christopher Turner claims the constant threat of a pit disaster among Welsh mining communities kept revival interest high. See 'Religious revivalism and Welsh industrial society: Aberdare in 1859' in *Llafur*, 4 (1984), pp. 4–13.
62 *Ballymena Observer*, 25 June 1859, p. 1.
63 Diary of the minister of Kilwarlin Moravian Church, Kilwarlin, Co. Down, 11 September 1859 (Public Record Office of Northern Ireland, MIC 1F/2A).
64 *Ballymena Observer*, 13 August 1859, p. 1.
65 Letter of Reverend D'Arcy Sinnamon, rector of Portadown in *Portadown Weekly News*, 24 September 1859, p. 2.
66 'The revival in Portadown' in *Portadown Weekly News*, 23 July 1859, p. 2.
67 *Ballymena Observer*, 3 September 1859, p. 1.

CHAPTER TWO

1 Louis Billington, 'Revivalism and popular religion' in Eric Sigsworth (ed.), *In search of Victorian values: aspects of nineteenth-century thought and society* (Manchester, 1988), pp. 148–50.
2 Richard Carwardine, *Transatlantic revivalism: popular evangelicalism in Britain and America, 1790–1865* (Westport, CN, 1978), pp. 103–7.
3 *Ibid.*, pp. 151–4.
4 David Bebbington, *Evangelicalism in modern Britain: a history from the 1730s to the 1980s* (London, 1989), p. 116.
5 *Ibid.*, pp. 169–70. A good example of this in the Irish context is the formation of the Belfast Parochial Mission in 1856. These Anglican ministers were concerned to extend church provision in poor areas and in the summer of 1857, several of the members embarked on a controversial series of open-air sermons. See Reverend Abraham Dawson, 'The annals of Christ Church, Belfast' (1858) (Public Record Office of Northern Ireland, T. 2159) and Janice Holmes, 'The role of open-air preaching in the Belfast riots of 1857', *Transactions of the Royal Irish Academy* (forthcoming).
6 Richard Carwardine, 'The religious revival of 1857–8 in the United States' in *Religious Motivation: Studies in Church History*, 15 (Oxford, 1978), pp. 393–406. See also Kathryn Teresa Long, *The revival of 1857–58: interpreting an American religious awakening* (Oxford, 1998), Chapter 1.
7 Reverend John Angell James, *Revival of religion: its principles, necessity, effects* (London, 1859), p. 15.
8 *Ibid.*, p. 20.

9 Reverend John G. Lorimer, *The recent great awakening in America and the lessons which it suggests* (Glasgow and London, 1859), pp. 173–5.

10 *Ibid.*, p. 178.

11 Reverend Robinson Scott, *The American revival: its facts and lessons. A lecture, delivered in the Centenary Chapel, Dublin* (Dublin, 1860), p. 51.

12 Reverend J.A. James, 'The bearing of the American revival on the duties and hopes of British Christians,' in Charles Reed and J.A. James, *On religious revivals. Two papers read by request at the annual meeting of the Congregational Union* (London, 1858), p. 41.

13 'Religious revivalism: its signs and significance' in *Wesleyan Times*, 27 June 1859, p. 416.

14 'Ireland for sixty years' in *British Standard*, 11 November 1859, p. 356.

15 Reverend John Graham was an Independent minister based at Craven Chapel, London. Reverend William Arthur was a Wesleyan Methodist, born in Kells, Co. Antrim who lived most of his adult life in England. Reverend John Weir was minister at the English Presbyterian Church in Islington, London. The other two ministers were Reverend Mr White, also a Presbyterian, with a congregation in Liverpool composed mainly of Ulster immigrants. Reverend John Peters had been brought up in Ballymena and was the minister of the UMFC church in Liverpool.

16 See the account of Professor Hoppus, University College, London in Benjamin Scott, *The revival in Ulster: its moral and social results* (London, 1859), p. 105.

17 The *Baptist Magazine* constantly urged its English readership to go to Ireland to assist in the work there, and even to start up new churches. Cf. Reverend C.J. Middleditch, 'The religious revival in Ireland' in *Baptist Magazine* (October 1859), pp. 657–9.

18 Scott, *Revival in Ulster*, p. 108.

19 'The Irish religious revivals' in *The Times*, 16 September 1859, p. 7.

20 Scott, *Revival in Ulster*, p. 5.

21 Reverend John Weir, *The Ulster awakening: its origin, progress and fruit. With notes of a tour of personal observation and inquiry* (London, 1860), p. 128.

22 'The religious revivals' in *The Record*, 28 October 1859, p. 4, quoting his letter to the editor of the *Daily News*.

23 'The Reverend F.A. West on the revival in Ireland' in *British Standard*, 22 July 1859, p. 230.

24 'A daily united prayer meeting for London' in *Ibid.*, 18 November 1859, p. 364.

25 'London' in *The Revival*, 6 August 1859, p. 13.

26 'Free Synod of Glasgow and Ayr' in *Scottish Guardian*, 14 October 1859, p. 2.

27 Reverend John Weir, 'London' in Reverend William Reid (ed.), *Authentic records of revival, now in progress in the United Kingdom* (London, 1860), pp. 420–1.

28 'The religious revival in Ireland' in *Scottish Guardian*, 29 July 1859, p. 6.

29 William Arthur, *The conversion of all England* (Revival Tract No. 2, London, 1859) p. 13.

30 Weir in Reid (ed.), *Authentic records*, p. 420. Reverend J. Canning, a Presbyterian minister from Coleraine, believed the revival would spread to Scotland because the people in his local united prayer meeting had been regularly praying for it. 'The revival in Ireland' in *Scottish Guardian*, 12 August 1859, p. 3.

31 'The London clergy and the revivals' in *The Record*, 28 December 1859, p. 3.

32 Weir, *Ulster awakening*, p. 4.

33 *Ibid.*, p. 7

34 'Revival in Newcastle-upon-Tyne' in *British Standard*, 23 September 1859, p. 300.

35 William Arthur, *May we hope for a great revival?* (Revival Tract No. 1, London, 1859), p. 9.

36 'Revival prayer meetings in Manchester' in *Manchester Guardian*, 8 September 1859, p. 3.

37 An unusual figure, Robert Baxter had been involved with the Irvingite movement (Catholic Apostolic) before rejoining the Anglican church and adopting evangelical views. He subsequently made two unsuccessful attempts to achieve parliamentary office,

founded the Evangelization Society with Lord Radstock and was the father of Michael Baxter, the itinerant preacher and famous prophecy lecturer. Cf. Nathaniel Wiseman, *Michael Paget Baxter* (London, 1923), pp. 58–98. For an account of Robert Baxter's revival address, see 'The revivals, prayer-meetings, and special services' in *The Record*, 21 December 1859, p. 3.

38 'The religious revivals in Ireland' in *The Times*, 7 September 1859, p. 10.
39 'Irish "revival"' in the *Daily Telegraph*, 8 September 1859, p. 5. Mr Hibbs was from Edmonton.
40 'The religious revivals in Belfast and Coleraine' in *Morning Chronicle*, 10 September 1859, p. 5.
41 'Revival prayer meetings in Manchester' in *Manchester Guardian*, 8 September 1859, p. 3.
42 'Penkhall, Stoke-on-Trent' in *The Revival*, 19 November 1859, p. 134.
43 'Prayer in connexion with revival' in *Ibid.*, 3 September 1859, p. 41.
44 Carwardine, *Transatlantic*, pp. 171–2.
45 Relying primarily on this source, J. Edwin Orr makes a similar misjudgement in *The second evangelical awakening in Britain* (London and Edinburgh, 1949), pp. 263–5.
46 'Penley – Ellsmere' in *The Revival*, 5 November 1859, p. 116.
47 'Bedford' in *Ibid.*, 3 December 1859, p. 149.
48 Reverend William Gibson, *The year of grace: a history of the Ulster revival of 1859* (2nd edn, Edinburgh, 1860), pp. 20–4; John T. Carson, *God's river in spate: the story of the religious awakening in Ulster in 1859* (Belfast, 1958), pp. 5–8; Ian Paisley, *The 'fifty-nine': an authentic history of the great Ulster awakening of 1859* (Belfast, 1958), pp. 14–17; Albert R. Scott, 'The Ulster Revival of 1859' (unpub. PhD diss., Trinity College, Dublin, 1962), pp. 99–103.
49 'Meeting at Birmingham' in *Morning Advertiser*, 3 October 1859, p. 2, quoting the *Birmingham Herald*.
50 'Free Synod of Glasgow and Ayr' in *Scottish Guardian*, 14 October 1859, p. 2. See *British Messenger* (October 1859), pp. 265–6.
51 Theo Hoppen, *Ireland since 1800: conflict and conformity* (London, 1989), pp. 72–4 and S.J. Connolly, 'Mass politics and sectarian conflict' in W.E. Vaughan (ed.), *A new history of Ireland* (11 vols., Oxford, 1982–95), v (*Ireland under the union, 1800–1870*), pp. 73–80.
52 'The religious revival' in *Ballymena Observer*, 27 August 1859, p. 1.
53 'Torrington, Devon' in *The Revival*, 3 December 1859, p. 149, quoting the *North Devon News*.
54 'North Lancashire' in *Ibid.*, 3 March 1860, p. 68.
55 'The revival in Ireland – public meeting in the City Hall' in *Scottish Guardian*, 12 August 1859, p. 3. See also Reverend John Bruce, *The revivals and the church* (Edinburgh, 1859), p. 3.
56 'The revival in Ulster' in *The Record*, 18 January 1860, p. 3.
57 These letters appear throughout January 1860.
58 Evangelical Alliance, *The Evangelical Alliance, its aims and operations* (London, 1861), p. 1.
59 Conference for Promoting Christian Union, *A brief statement of the proceedings of the Conference in Liverpool for promoting Christian union, and of the object of the proposed Evangelical Alliance* (London, 1845), pp. 3–4.
60 *Ibid.*, p. 6.
61 Evangelical Alliance, *Transactions of the 13th annual conference, held at Belfast, Sept. 20–24, 1859* (London, 1860), p. 27.
62 Reverend Edward Steane (ed.), *The Ulster revival, in its features and physiological accidents. Papers read to the Evangelical Alliance in Belfast, September 22, 1859* (London, 1860), p. iii.

63 Evangelical Alliance, *Report presented to the 13th annual conference, held in Belfast, September 1859. With a list of subscribers* (London, 1860), p. xvii.

64 The revival papers were presented by Reverend Charles Seaver, Belfast (C of I); Reverend J.A. Canning, Coleraine (Presb.); Reverend Robert Knox, Bishop of Down, Connor and Dromore (C of I); and Dr J.C.L. Carson, Coleraine. They were subsequently published in pamphlet form. See Steane (ed.), *Ulster revival*. At the 1860 conference in Nottingham, three of the four papers focused on the revival and detailed its progress in Ireland, Wales and Scotland. See Reverend William Gibson, 'Present aspects of the Irish revival'; Reverend John Venn, 'The revival in Wales'; and Reverend Hamilton Magill, 'On the present revival of religion in Scotland' in Anon (ed.), *Present aspects of the Irish revival, being papers read at the conference of the Evangelical Alliance, held at Nottingham, October, 1860* (London, 1861).

65 Evangelical Alliance, *Report presented to the 14th annual conference, held in Nottingham, October 1860. With a list of subscribers* (London, 1861), p. 7.

66 'Belfast Conference' in *Evangelical Christendom* (September 1859), p. 293.

67 'The Evangelical Alliance' in *Belfast Daily Mercury*, 23 September 1859, p. 4.

68 'The Ulster revival' in *Daily News*, 26 September 1859, p. 3.

69 'The Meeting in the Free Trade Hall' in *The Watchman*, 17 August 1859, p. 264.

70 *Ibid.*, p. 266.

71 'The Wesleyan Conference – Manchester' in *Wesleyan Methodist Magazine* (September 1859), p. 819.

72 'Means to promote a genuine revival in our connexion' in *Methodist New Connexion Magazine* (February 1860), pp. 103–5.

73 'Irish revivals' in *Congregational Yearbook of 1860* (London, 1861), p. 47.

74 Reverend John Bruce, *Revivals*, pp. 3–4; 'The General Assembly of the Free Church of Scotland' in *The Revival*, 17 September 1859, p. 60.

75 'The religious revivals' in *The Record*, 21 October 1859, p. 4.

76 Eifion Evans, *When he is come: an account of the 1858–60 revival in Wales* (Bala, 1959), pp. 28–31.

77 Richard Carwardine, 'The Welsh evangelical community and "Finney's revival"' in *Journal of Ecclesiastical History*, 29 (1978), pp. 463–80.

78 Reverend Owen Thomas, 'The recent revival in the principality of Wales, and its results' in *Testimony to the Lord's reviving work in Wales, Scotland, Ireland and Syria, being addresses delivered in Freemason's Hall in the first week of January, 1865* (London, 1865), p. 4; Carwardine, *Transatlantic*, p. 174; and Reverend J.J. Morgan, *The '59 revival in Wales. Some incidents in the life and work of David Morgan, Ysbytty* (Mold, 1909).

79 Orr, *Second evangelical*, p. 93.

80 Christopher Turner, 'Revivalism and Welsh society in the nineteenth century' in James Obelkevich, Lyndal Roper and Raphael Samuel (eds), *Disciplines of faith: studies in religion, politics and patriarchy* (London, 1987), pp. 319–21.

81 Reverend Thomas Phillips, *The Welsh revival: its origin and development* (London, 1860), pp. 78, 95, 104. See also the Reverend John Venn, *The revival in Wales. A paper read at the conference of the Evangelical Alliance, held at Nottingham, Oct. 1860; with subsequent additions* (London, 1860), p. 6; and the Reverend Evan Davies (ed.), *Revivals in Wales: facts and correspondence supplied by pastors of the Welsh churches* (London, 1860), preface.

82 Carwardine, *Transatlantic*, p. 174; and Orr, *Second evangelical*, pp. 78, 93.

83 'Welsh ministers visiting Ireland' in *The Record*, 21 November 1859, p. 3.

84 *The Revival* began circulation on 30 July 1859 in response to the growing amount of revival news being generated. See *The Revival*, 30 July 1859, p. 1. It was published by R.C. Morgan, a young evangelical with no fixed denominational attachment, who was soon to become one of the central figures in late nineteenth-century evangelicalism. Because the Ulster revival was such an epoch-making event, 'the need for a Press organ, which should serve as a record, an advocate, and a stimulus, became increasingly

obvious'. George E. Morgan, *R.C. Morgan: his life and times* (London, 1909), p. 97.
85 'Revival movements in the United Kingdom' in *The Record*, 20 June 1859, p. 4; and 'England' in *The Revival*, 13 August 1859, p. 23.
86 'Revival in Newcastle' in *Daily News*, 12 September 1859, p. 3, quoting the *Newcastle Guardian*.
87 'A religious "revival" at Newcastle-on-Tyne' in *The Record*, 21 September 1859, p. 2, quoting *The Times*.
88 'Diffusion – the Newcastle revival' in *British Standard*, 21 October 1859, p. 300.
89 'Newcastle' in *The Revival*, 22 October 1859, p. 102, quoting Reverend Robert Young.
90 'The climax – Newcastle-on-Tyne revival' in *British Standard*, 18 November 1859, p. 366.
91 'Revival movements' in *Ibid.*, 9 December 1859, p. 390.
92 John Kent, *Holding the fort: studies in Victorian revivalism* (London, 1978), p. 171.
93 Carwardine, *Transatlantic*, p. 159 and Bebbington, *Evangelicalism*, p. 117.
94 'Bicester, Oxon.' in *The Revival*, 10 December 1859, pp. 156–7.
95 *The Revival*, 22 July 1859, pp. 230–1.
96 Janice Holmes, 'Lifting the curtain on popular religion: women, laity and language in the Ulster revival of 1859' (unpublished M.A. diss., Queen's University, Kingston, 1991), pp. 56–7.
97 Reverend William McIlwaine, *Revivalism reviewed* (Belfast, 1859), pp. 5–6.
98 'The "religious revival"' in *Coleraine Chronicle*, 6 August 1859, p. 8.
99 Reverend Charles Seaver, 'The Ulster revival: a paper read before the conference of the Evangelical Alliance at Belfast' in Steane (ed.), *The Ulster revival*, p. 11.
100 *Ibid.* For similar conclusions, see Reverend John Baillie, *The revival: or, what I saw in Ireland; with thoughts suggested by the same. The result of two personal visits* (London, 1860), p. 54; Weir, *Ulster awakening*, p. 171.
101 *The Times*, 17 September 1859, p. 6.
102 Baillie, *The revival*, p. 90.
103 *Ibid.*
104 For a full account of this aspect of the 1859 revival, see James G. Donat, 'Medicine and religion: on the physical and mental disorders that accompanied the Ulster revival of 1859' in W.F. Bynum, Roy Porter and Michael Shepherd (eds), *The anatomy of madness* (3 vols., London, 1988), iii (*The asylum and its psychiatry*), pp. 125–50.
105 In the nineteenth century, hysteria was the term given to psychological disorders.
106 'The physical phenomena of revivals' in *The Lancet*, 23 July 1859, p. 94.
107 'The Irish revival fever' in *The Spectator*, 1 October 1859, p. 1003.
108 'Ireland – Lunacy' in *The Times*, 26 September 1859, p. 4. Such statistics are refuted in Weir, *Ulster awakening*, p. 149. He says none of the lunacy cases can be traced conclusively to the revival.
109 *Daily Telegraph*, 15 October 1859, p. 4.
110 *Ibid.*, 11 October 1859, p. 4.
111 'Revivalism' in *The Buteman*, 6 August 1859, p. 1, quoting the *Aberdeen Herald*.
112 *Daily Telegraph*, 15 October 1859, p. 4.
113 *Ibid.*, 11 October 1859, p. 4.
114 *Morning Advertiser*, 3 October 1859, p. 2, quoting the *Birmingham Herald*.
115 'Testimonies to the reality of the revival' in *The Revival*, 5 November 1859, p. 118.
116 An example of this analogy being used to defend lay preaching can be found in *Londonderry Guardian*, 14 June 1859, p. 2.
117 'Great meeting at Canterbury' in *The Revival*, 15 October 1859, p. 93.
118 'Religious awakening in Ireland' in *Daily News*, 15 October 1859, p. 2.
119 Quoted in 'England' in *The Record*, 21 November 1859, p. 3.
120 'Ireland' in *The Times*, 29 September 1859, p. 7.
121 'The revival and its opponents' in *The Record*, 25 April 1860, p. 3, quoting a letter from

Reverend Charles Seaver. Cf. 'Irish revivals' in *The Times*, 26 October 1859, p. 9.

122 Reverend Charles Seaver in *Ibid.*

123 'The press and the revival' in *The Revival,* 1 October 1859, p. 78.

124 Reverend Robert Knox, Bishop of Down, Connor and Dromore, 'The fruits of the revival' in Steane (ed.), *Ulster revival*, p. 62. See also Seaver in *The Record*, 25 April 1860, p. 3; Weir, *Ulster awakening*, p. 148; and *The Revival*, 21 April 1860, p. 125.

125 'The slanders of "the Northern Whig", quoted by "The Times"' in *The Revival,* 21 April 1860, p. 125.

126 'The clerical meeting at Islington' in *The Record*, 16 January 1860, p. 4.

127 'The fruits of the revival' in *The Revival*, 23 November 1861, p. 161.

128 *Ibid.*, 14 August 1862, p. 65; 19 January 1865, p. 37.

129 Bebbington, *Evangelicalism*, pp. 101–2.

130 Frederic Faverty, *Matthew Arnold, the ethnologist* (New York, 1968), p. 118.

131 L.P. Curtis, *Apes and angels, the Irishman in Victorian caricature* (Newton Abbot, 1971), p. 96.

132 J. W., 'The English press on the Irish revivals' in *Wesleyan Methodist Magazine* (January 1860), p. 23.

133 Reverend Thomas Cartwright, 'The great revival' in *Methodist New Connexion Magazine* (October 1859), p. 597.

134 *Ibid.*, p. 598.

135 'The religious revivals' in *The Record*, 21 September 1859, p. 1.

136 Reverend Daniel Mooney of Ballymena in *The Revival*, 11 February 1860, p. 47.

137 'Irish revivals' in *British Standard*, 8 July 1859, p. 213.

138 *Belfast Daily Mercury*, 3 October 1859, p. 2.

139 Faverty, *Matthew Arnold*, pp. 129–44.

140 'The revival in Ireland' in *Revival Advocate* (August 1859), p. 627.

141 For numerous other references to this perceived character weakness, see *The Times*, 1 October 1859, p. 9; *Daily News*, 15 September 1859, p. 2; *Wesleyan Times*, 27 June 1859, p. 419.

142 'The Irish religious revivals' in *The Times*, 16 September 1859, p. 7.

143 'The press and the revival' in *The Revival,* 17 September 1859, p. 58.

144 *The Times*, 16 September 1859, p. 7. Other descriptions of the Ulster Scot can be found in *The Record*, 21 December 1859, p. 3; Reverend William Arthur, *Beginnings of a great revival* (Revival Tract No. 4, London, 1859), pp. 2–4.

145 'Revival of religion in the north of Ireland' in *The Record*, 15 June 1859, p. 4.

146 'Recent publications on religious revivals' in *Baptist Magazine* (August 1859), pp. 502–3. Other references to this include *The Record*, 9 November 1859, p. 4; *Morning Advertiser*, 3 October 1859, p. 2.

147 Quoting Reverend A.R.C. Dallas in 'The clerical meeting at Islington' in *The Record*, 16 January 1860, p. 4.

CHAPTER THREE

1 'The American revivalists' in *The Times*, 16 July 1875, p. 4.

2 *Ibid.*

3 Gerald Parsons, 'A question of meaning: religion and working-class life' in Gerald Parsons (ed.), *Religion in Victorian Britain 2 (Controversies)* (Manchester, 1988), pp. 64–5.

4 *Ibid.*

5 Reverend R.W. Dale, 'Religious revivals' in *The Congregationalist* (January 1873), p. 5.

6 W.T. Stead, *General Booth: a biographical sketch* (London, 1891), pp. 49–50.

7 Henry T. Smart, *Thomas Cook's early ministry* (London, 1892), pp. 69–80.

8 Nickolai Leskov, *Schism in high society: Lord Radstock and his followers* (Nottingham, 1995 reprint of St Petersburg, 1877 orig. edn).
9 For more details of his work see William Carter, *The power of grace. Results of theatre preaching, extraordinary tea meetings, and mothers' meetings, in the south of London* (London, 1863); Idem., *The power of truth: or, results of theatre preaching and extraordinary tea meetings in South London* (London, 1865).
10 The preceding discussion has been drawn from Richard Carwardine, *Transatlantic revivalism: popular evangelicalism in Britain and America, 1790–1865* (Westport, CN, 1978), pp. 186–97.
11 The basic details of Moody's life can be found in any of the numerous biographies which have been written about him. Traditionally, William R. Moody's *The life of Dwight L. Moody* (Chicago, 1900) has been considered the most reliable. But while it provides a detailed chronology of Moody's activities there are several inaccuracies. Thus, it should be supplemented with James Findlay's excellent *Dwight L. Moody: American evangelist, 1837–1899* (Chicago, 1969), John Kent's chapters in *Holding the fort: studies in Victorian revivalism* (London, 1978), J.C. Pollock, *Moody without Sankey* (London, 1963) and, for a local approach, Mark J. Toone, 'Evangelicalism in transition: a comparative analysis of the work and theology of D.L. Moody and his proteges, Henry Drummond and R.A. Torrey' (unpub. PhD diss., St Andrews, 1988). Most of the standard facts in the following discussion can be found in these main sources.
12 Kent, *Holding*, p. 142.
13 *Ibid.*, pp. 156–8.
14 Emma R. Moody to Edward Moody, 19 May 1882 (Moody Bible Institute (hereafter MBI) Archives, Chicago, IL, filing cabinet #22).
15 Reverend Richard Wheatley, *The life and letters of Mrs Phoebe Palmer* (New York, 1916), p. 391.
16 D.L. Moody to his mother, 12 March 1884 (MBI Archives, 13 uncatalogued volumes of Moody's letters, Vol. 2: 1879–86).
17 D.L. Moody to his son William, 10 May 1884 (MBI Archives, 13 uncatalogued volumes of Moody's letters, Vol. 2: 1879–86).
18 D.L. Moody to his brother George, 22 June 1882; 18 February 1882 (MBI Archives, 13 uncatalogued volumes of Moody's letters, Vol. 2: 1879–86).
19 *Revival Advocate* (November 1859), p. 719.
20 'Bolton' in *The Revival*, 7 March 1860, p. 83.
21 Harold Raser, *Phoebe Palmer: her life and thought* (Lewiston, NY, 1987), p. 68.
22 Reverend J.H. Batt, *Dwight L. Moody: the life work of a modern evangelist* (London, 1900), p. 78; W.R. Moody, *Life* (1900), pp. 75–6; Paul Moody, *My father: an intimate portrait of Dwight Moody* (London, 1937), pp. 62, 78–9.
23 Carwardine, *Transatlantic*, pp. 119–20.
24 *Ibid.*, p. 145.
25 Phoebe Palmer, *Four years in the old world* (New York, 1866), pp. 691–2.
26 *Ibid.*, p. 339.
27 *Ibid.*, pp. 325–8.
28 'Messrs Moody and Sankey' in *Irish Times*, 25 November 1874, p. 6.
29 Findlay, *Dwight L. Moody*, pp. 282–3.
30 The bulk of this discussion has been from Carwardine, *Transatlantic*, pp. 126–33.
31 *Ibid.*, p. 133.
32 *Ibid.*, p. 183.
33 Raser, *Phoebe Palmer*, pp. 136–7.
34 Wheatley, *Life and letters*, p. 369.
35 Carwardine, *Transatlantic*, p. 138.
36 *Ibid.*, pp. 177–190. For an account of Finney's time in England, see also Keith J. Hardman, *Charles Grandison Finney 1792–1875: revivalist and reformer* (Grand Rapids,

1987) and Garth M. Rosell and Richard A.G. Dupuis (eds), *The memoirs of Charles G. Finney: the complete restored text* (Grand Rapids, 1989).

37 *The Revival*, 25 April 1867, p. 236 and 23 May 1867, p. 289.

38 In the mythology surrounding D.L. Moody's first public appearance in Britain, a story has emerged which claims he was asked to move a vote of thanks to the Earl of Shaftesbury and was introduced as 'our American cousin, the Reverend Mr Moody'. In reply, he is supposed to have said, 'The chairman has made two mistakes. To begin with, I'm not the "Reverend" Mr Moody at all. And I'm not your American cousin – I'm your brother ... And now about this vote of thanks to the noble Earl for being our chairman this evening. I don't see why we should thank him, any more than he should thank us.' W.R. Moody, *Life* (1900), p. 132. I have found no evidence to support this vignette. According to the *Union Magazine for Sunday School Teachers*, the Earl of Shaftesbury had been in the Chair, but had given it up to Mr Charles Reed because he had to leave. Moody was not asked to move a vote of thanks to the Earl. He was asked to second a resolution thanking God for the Sunday School Union and those who worked for it. His remarks about making 'two mistakes' are in essence correct, but there is absolutely no basis for the remarks made about Shaftesbury. For a full account of this meeting see *UMSST* (June 1867), pp. 296–318.

39 Reverend J. Wilbur Chapman, *The life and work of Dwight Lyman Moody* (London, 1900), p. 128; Reverend W.H. Daniels, *D.L. Moody and his work* (London, 1875), p. 238; John Lobb, *Arrows and anecdotes by Dwight L. Moody; with a sketch of his early life, and the story of the great revival* (London, 1876), p. 17.

40 'Missionaries in motley' in *Punch*, 20 March 1875, p. 123.

41 A London Physician, *Emotional goodness; or, Moody and Sankey reviewed. The people go mad through religious revivals* (London, 1875), pp. 8–9.

42 'The American revivalists' in *The Times*, 16 July 1875, p. 4.

43 There was a strong critique of this categorisation in 'The evangelistic services' in *Dublin Evening Mail*, 23 October 1874, p. 4. If a comparison of Moody and Sankey's services was to be made with Catholic forms of worship, the letter writer asked rhetorically, which of the two services 'partake more of the theatrical element'?

44 'Missionaries in motley' in *Punch*, 20 March 1875, p. 123.

45 'The pantomime and revivals' in *The Christian*, 25 February 1875, p. 14.

46 'An explanation' in *Punch*, 27 March 1875, p. 139.

47 Edwin Hodder, *The life and work of the seventh Earl of Shaftesbury, K.G.* (3 vols., London, 1886), iii, p. 358.

48 Quoted in Rufus W. Clark, *The work of God in Great Britain: under Messrs Moody and Sankey, 1873 to 1875. With biographical sketches* (New York, 1875), pp. 41–3.

49 'Moody and Sankey in London' in *Daily Telegraph*, 10 March 1875, p. 5.

50 'The new evangel' in *Freeman's Journal*, 19 October 1874, p. 6.

51 Anon., *Moody and Sankey, the new evangelists, their lives and labours; together with a history of the present great religious movement* (London, 1875), p. 3.

52 Reverend Elias Nason, *The American evangelists, Dwight L. Moody and Ira D. Sankey, with an account of their work in England and America; with a sketch of the lives of P.P. Bliss and Dr Eben Tourjée* (Boston, 1877), p. 3.

53 Reverend James Moorhouse, Bishop of Melbourne to Archibald Campbell Tait, Archbishop of Canterbury, 25 March 1875 (Lambeth Palace Library, London, Correspondence of A.C. Tait (hereafter Tait Papers), Vol. 94, ff. 175–8).

54 Lobb, *Arrows and anecdotes*, pp. 35–6.

55 Hodder, *Shaftesbury*, iii, p. 358.

56 'Messrs Moody and Sankey in London' in *The Spectator*, 13 March 1875, p. 334.

57 'The American revivalists' in *The Times*, 16 July 1875, p. 4.

58 'Messrs Moody and Sankey' in *Irish Times*, 17 November 1874, p. 5.

59 Reverend R.W. Dale, *Mr Moody and Mr Sankey* (London, 1875), p. 21.

60 'Messrs Moody and Sankey' in *Daily Telegraph*, 2 April 1875, p. 3.
61 Batt, *Dwight L. Moody*, pp. 101–4.
62 'The new evangel' in *Freeman's Journal*, 22 October 1874, p. 3.
63 *Ibid.*; Pollock, *Moody without*, p. 138.
64 Dale, *Mr Moody and Mr Sankey*, p. 22.
65 Kent, *Holding*, pp. 201–2.
66 *Ibid.*, pp. 186–7.
67 'A sermon about Hell' in D.L. Moody, *The London discourses of Mr D.L. Moody, as delivered in the Agricultural Hall and Her Majesty's Opera House* (London, 1875), pp. 112–13.
68 John Page Hopps, *Mr Moody's late sermon on hell. A lecture* (Glasgow, 1874), pp. 3, 4.
69 James M. Dixon, *Messrs Moody and Sankey: a peep behind the curtain* (n.p., 1878), p. 4.
70 Kent, *Holding*, p. 171.
71 *Ibid.*, p. 173.
72 Anon, *The new evangelists*, p. 20.
73 'Religious sensationalism' in *Saturday Review*, 20 March 1875, p. 374.
74 Kent, *Holding*, pp. 143, 176–8.
75 Peter Morgan, '… And some evangelists' (London, 1956), p. 335.
76 Nason, *The American evangelists*, p. 108.
77 'Messrs Moody and Sankey's evangelistic operations' in *Glasgow Herald*, 21 February 1874, p. 4.
78 Clark, *Work of God*, p. 155.
79 Toone, 'Evangelicalism' PhD, pp. 60–1, 71; Gerald Parsons, 'Victorian Britain's other establishment: the transformations of Scottish Presbyterianism' in Gerald Parsons (ed.), *Religion in Victorian Britain 1 (Traditions)* (Manchester, 1988), pp. 118–25.
80 D.L. Moody to J.V. Farwell, 7 May 1874 (MBI Archives, 13 uncatalogued volumes of Moody's letters, Vol. 1: 1854–79).
81 See the biography of P.P. Bliss and Philip Phillips' autobiography. Major D.W. Whittle and Reverend W. Guest (eds), *P.P. Bliss: his life and life work* (London, [1877]) and Philip Phillips, *Song pilgrimage around and throughout the world* (London, [1877]).
82 Ira D. Sankey, *My life and sacred songs* (2nd edn, London, 1906), pp. 3–8.
83 A good description of this order of events can be found in the description of the Aberdeen meetings in 1874. See *The Christian*, 25 June 1874, p. 5.
84 John Wolffe, '"Praise to the holiest in the height": hymns and church music' in John Wolffe (ed.), *Religion in Victorian Britain 5 (Culture and Empire)* (Manchester, 1997), pp. 61–5.
85 Sankey, *My Life*, p. 22.
86 Phillips, *Song pilgrimage*, pp. 184–6.
87 Toone, 'Evangelicalism' PhD, p. 123.
88 *Ibid.*, pp. 129–30.
89 Letter from 'A clerical spectator' in *Glasgow Herald*, 13 March 1874, p. 6.
90 'Messrs Moody and Sankey's Meetings' in *Glasgow Herald*, 2 March 1874, p. 4.
91 Letter from 'A highlander' in *Ibid.*, 5 March 1874, p. 4.
92 Letter from John Page Hopps, 'The revival movement – hysterical revivals' in *Ibid.*, 9 March 1874, p. 4.
93 Letter from 'A clerical spectator' in *Ibid.*, 11 March 1874, p. 7.
94 A Priest of the Church of England, *The London mission of 1874. A protest against a theory of 'conversion', as preached by some 'missioners'* (London, 1874), p. 9.
95 *Glasgow Herald*, 12 March 1874, p. 7. Letter from 'Anti-revivalist' in which he describes instantaneous conversion as a fallacy.
96 Dale, *Mr Moody and Mr Sankey*, pp. 28–9.
97 Letter from 'A clergyman' in *Glasgow Herald*, 27 February 1874, p. 4.
98 'The revival movement' in *Ibid.*, 5 March 1874, p. 7.

99　James Obelkevich, *Religion and rural society: South Lindsey 1825–1875* (Oxford, 1976), pp. 150, 179–80.

100　George Adam Smith, *The life of Henry Drummond* (11th edn, London, 1902), p. 64.

101　Clark, *Work of God*, pp. 121–2.

102　Smith, *Henry Drummond*, pp. 66–7. Drummond became one of the most important figures in late nineteenth-century religious circles. As a lecturer at the Free Church College in Glasgow, he published *Natural law in the spiritual world* (1883), a controversial work in the growing debate over science and its impact on biblical literalism. After moving to Edinburgh, he began an evangelistic work among the students at the university and published *The ascent of man* (1894). He remained a close friend of Moody's, although his ideas became increasingly liberal as time went on. For a brief summary of his life see Toone, 'Evangelicalism' PhD, pp. 146–216.

103　Letter from 'A clergyman' in *Glasgow Herald*, 27 February 1874, p. 4.

104　Letter from Robert Craig in *Ibid.*, 28 February 1874, p. 3.

105　Letter from 'Vigilanticus the younger' in *Dublin Evening Mail*, 28 October 1874, p. 4.

106　'The revivalists and the ministry' in *The Congregationalist* (April 1875), p. 193.

107　Letter from 'A lay worker' in *Glasgow Herald*, 13 March 1874, p. 6.

108　Letter from 'P.F.S.' in *Ibid.*, 12 March 1874, p. 7.

109　Letter from 'A working man' in *Ibid.*, 17 March 1874, p. 3.

110　Letter from 'A Free Church layman' in *Glasgow Herald*, 28 February 1874, p. 3.

111　Letter from 'P.F.S.' in *Ibid.*, 12 March 1874, p. 7.

112　This was at a meeting in Dublin. See 'Messrs Moody and Sankey' in *Daily Express*, 9 November 1874, p. 3.

113　Letter from Alexander Callendar in *Glasgow Herald*, 13 March 1874, p. 6.

114　'Religious revival: Newcastle-upon-Tyne' in *The Congregationalist* (January 1874), p. 26.

115　Letter from 'Watchman' in *Glasgow Herald*, 3 March 1874, p. 7.

116　Findlay, *Dwight L. Moody*, pp. 159–62. Kent expresses a similar view in *Holding*, p. 137.

117　W.E. Vaughan, 'Ireland c. 1870' in W.E. Vaughan (ed.), *A new history of Ireland* (11 vols., Oxford, 1982–95), v (*Ireland under the union, 1800–1870*), pp. 738–9.

118　Richard Braithwaite, *The life and letters of William Pennefather* (London, 1878), pp. 2, 259, 283, 328; Norman Taggart, *William Arthur: first among Methodists* (London, 1993).

119　W.R. Moody, *Life* (1900), p. 154; Pollock, *Moody without*, p. 96.

120　Clark, *Work of God*, p. 201.

121　'Messrs Moody and Sankey' in *Irish Times*, 25 November 1874, p. 6.

122　Gamaliel Bradford, *D.L. Moody: a worker in souls* (New York, 1927), pp. 70–2.

123　'Messrs Moody and Sankey' in *Daily Telegraph*, 19 March 1875, p. 3.

124　W.G. Blaikie, 'The revival in Scotland – I' in *The Christian*, 23 July 1874, p. 4, originally published in the *British and Foreign Evangelical Review*.

125　*Ibid.*

126　Reverend Robert Boyd, *The wonderful career of Moody and Sankey, in Great Britain and America* (New York, 1875), p. 386. For similar remarks see also John Hall and George H. Stuart, *The American evangelists, D.L. Moody and Ira D. Sankey, in Great Britain and Ireland* (New York, 1875), p. 385; and 'Messrs Moody and Sankey' in *The Times*, 27 March 1875, p. 5.

127　'The new evangel' in *Freeman's Journal*, 19 October 1874, p. 6.

128　'Messrs Moody and Sankey' in *Daily Express*, 20 October 1874, p. 3.

129　*Flag of Ireland*, 7 November 1874, p. 1.

130　'Preaching in the streets' in *Irishman*, 14 November 1874, p. 307.

131　'Messrs Moody and Sankey' in *Dublin Evening Mail*, 24 October 1874, p. 4.

132　Findlay, *Dwight L. Moody*, p. 165.

133　Clark, *Work of God*, p. 221; Hall and Stuart, *American evangelists*, pp. 264–5, 266; Boyd, *Wonderful career*, p. 385.

134　David Hempton and Myrtle Hill, *Evangelical protestantism in Ulster society, 1740–1890*

(London, 1992), pp. 65–9. See also Donald H. Akenson, *The Church of Ireland: ecclesiastical reform and revolution, 1800–85* (New Haven, NY, 1971), p. 207.

135 Boyd, *Wonderful career*, p. 387; Daniels, *D.L. Moody*, p. 326.
136 Hempton and Hill, *Evangelical protestantism*, pp. 162–3.
137 'Revivals and missions' in *The Christian*, 14 August 1873, p. 7, quoting *The Record*.
138 F. Roy Coad, *A history of the brethren movement* (Exeter, 1968), Chapters 1–3.
139 Letter from 'A clergyman' in *Glasgow Herald*, 27 February 1874, p. 4.
140 William J. Irons to A.C. Tait, 31 May 1875 (Lambeth Palace Library, Tait Papers, Vol. 209, ff. 27–32).
141 *Flag of Ireland*, 24 October 1874, p. 1.
142 Letter from 'Zenas' in *Dublin Evening Mail*, 22 October 1874, p. 4.
143 *Ibid.*, 17 November 1874, p. 4.
144 'Messrs Moody and Sankey' in *Irish Times*, 25 November 1874, p. 6.
145 *Dublin Evening Mail*, 19 October 1874, p. 4, quoting *The Christian*.
146 Reverend Hamilton Magee, 'Messrs Moody and Sankey in Dublin' in *The Christian*, 29 October 1874, p. 8.
147 R. Grant Barnwell, *Life of Moody and Sankey, the American evangelists. Together with scenes and incidents of the revival in Great Britain* (Philadelphia, 1875), p. 25.
148 'Fair play!' in *The Nation*, 7 November 1874, p. 4.
149 *Ibid.*
150 'The Cardinal Archbishop' in *Freeman's Journal*, 7 November 1874, p. 2. In the biographical literature, this oblique reference has been transformed into an outright ban which specifically names Moody and Sankey and forbids Catholics from attending their meetings. See 'The American revivalists' in *Church Times*, 12 March 1875, p. 134; Anon., *The new evangelists*, p. 56; Daniels, *D.L. Moody*, pp. 316–18; and Chapman, *Life and work*, pp. 148–9.
151 Letter from 'Evangelicus' in *Dublin Evening Mail*, 19 October 1874, p. 4.
152 'Messrs Moody and Sankey' in *Irish Times*, 7 November 1874, p. 2.
153 'The central noon meeting' in *The Christian*, 12 November 1874, p. 13.
154 'Convention of ministers of the gospel' in *Daily Express*, 25 November 1874, p. 3.
155 'The central noon meeting' in *The Christian*, 12 November 1874, p. 13.
156 'Fair play!' in *The Nation*, 7 November 1874, p. 9.
157 Hall and Stuart, *American evangelists*, p. 376, quoting the *Daily Telegraph*.
158 'The American evangelists' in *Dublin Evening Mail*, 9 November 1874, p. 4, quoting *The Record*.
159 W.R. Moody, *Life* (1900), p. 223.
160 Findlay, *Dwight L. Moody*, p. 171.
161 'Moody and Sankey in London' in *Daily Telegraph*, 10 March 1875, p. 5.
162 This was about an 85 per cent response rate. See 'Messrs Moody and Sankey's farewell meeting' in *The Christian*, 22 July 1875, p. 8.
163 Reverend A.C. Smith, 'Messrs Moody and Sankey and church cooperation' in *Church Times*, 2 April 1875, p. 167.
164 Letter of Reverend Samuel Garratt in *The Christian*, 14 August 1873, p. 8.
165 Sheridan Gilley, 'The Church of England in the nineteenth century' in Sheridan Gilley and W.J. Sheils (eds), *A history of religion in Britain* (Oxford, 1994), pp. 297–9.
166 Kenneth Hylson-Smith, *Evangelicals in the Church of England, 1734–1984* (Edinburgh, 1988), pp. 126–7.
167 David B. McIlhiney comes to the conclusion that ritualists, broad churchmen and evangelicals all used very similar methods in their efforts to reach the London poor. See *A Gentleman in every slum: Church of England missions in east London, 1837–1914* (Allison Park, PN, [1988]), pp. 99–104.
168 Reverend A.C. Smith, 'Messrs Moody and Sankey's approaching visit to London' in *Church Times*, 12 March 1875, p. 128.

169 'Messrs Moody and Sankey' in *Church Times*, 12 February 1875, p. 82.
170 Letter from 'V.X.' in *Ibid.*, 9 April 1875, p. 180; Reverend A.C. Smith, 'Messrs Moody and Sankey and church cooperation' in *Ibid.*, 2 April 1875, p. 167.
171 Reverend A.C. Smith in *Ibid.*
172 Reverend James Moorhouse to A.C. Tait, 25 March 1875 (Lambeth Palace Library, Tait Papers, Vol. 94, ff. 175–8).
173 Reverend William Cadman to A.C. Tait, 25 March 1875 (*Ibid.*, ff. 179–80).
174 Kent, *Holding*, p. 162.
175 'Messrs Moody and Sankey in Dublin' in *Irish Evangelist*, 1 November 1874, p. 126.
176 *Ibid.*; Daniels, *D.L. Moody*, p. 271.
177 Reverend A.A. Rees, 'After-meetings' in *The Christian*, 2 October 1873, p. 3.
178 Anon., *The new evangelists*, p. 31.
179 D.L. Moody, 'The inquiry meeting' in *The Christian*, 18 June 1874, p. 4.
180 'Messrs Moody and Sankey in Dublin' in *The Christian*, 12 November 1874, p. 9.
181 Reverend R.W. Dale, *The day of salvation: a reply to the letter of the Archbishop of Canterbury, on Mr Moody and Mr Sankey* (London and Birmingham, 1875), p. 7.
182 D.L. Moody, 'The inquiry meeting' in *The Christian*, 18 June 1874, p. 3.
183 'The archbishop of Canterbury on Mr Moody's missionary movement' in *The Record*, 24 May 1875, p. 2. Tait's response to Cairns was originally a private one, which the archbishop later allowed to be published.
184 *The Record*, 28 May 1875, p. 2.
185 Lord Cairns to A.C. Tait, 21 May 1875 (Lambeth Palace Library, Tait Papers, Vol. 94, ff. 208–13).
186 Dale, *Day of salvation*, p. 6.
187 Reverend C.T. Astley to A.C. Tait, 29 May 1875 (Lambeth Palace Library, Tait Papers, Vol. 209, ff. 375–80). See also the letter from Reverend F.S.C. Chalmers, 31 May 1875 (*Ibid.*, ff. 382–5).
188 'The American revivalists' in *Church Times*, 12 March 1875, p. 134.
189 'Messrs Moody and Sankey in Dublin' in *The Christian*, 12 November, 1874, p. 9.
190 Kent, *Holding*, p. 141.
191 Dale, *Day of salvation*, pp. 8–9.
192 Pollock, *Moody without*, pp. 143–5.
193 'Afternoon meetings, Haymarket' in *The Christian*, 29 April 1875, p. 13.
194 Kent, *Holding*, pp. 147–8. Kent dismisses these individuals, saying they were on the 'fringes of institutionalized religion, not its centre', without, I feel, adequately accounting for their social influence.
195 Pollock, *Moody without*, p. 142; Kent, *Holding*, pp. 157–9.
196 'Messrs Moody and Sankey's movements' in *The Christian*, 11 February 1875, p. 8.
197 Moorhouse to Tait, 25 March 1875 (Lambeth Palace Library, Tait Papers, Vol. 94, ff. 175–8). For similar sentiments see 'A clerical spectator' in *Glasgow Herald*, 11 March 1874, p. 7; and Will Skerry, 'The Lord's work at Newcastle-on-Tyne' in *The Christian*, 6 November 1873, p. 7.
198 'Messrs Moody and Sankey' in *Daily Express*, 20 October 1874, p. 3; 'Messrs Moody and Sankey in Dublin' in *Dublin Evening Mail*, 6 November 1874, p. 4; 9 November 1874, p. 4.
199 'Moody and Sankey in London' in *Daily Telegraph*, 10 March 1875, p. 5.
200 'Sunday's meeting, Bow Road Hall' in *The Christian*, 15 April 1875, p. 15; 'Bow Road Hall' in *Ibid.*, 22 April 1875, p. 15; 'The work in the east end' in *Ibid.*, 29 April 1875, pp. 15–16.
201 For these various instances see W.R. Moody, *Life* (1900), p. 230; 'Moody and Sankey's services' in *Daily Telegraph*, 25 March 1875, p. 3; and 'The work in east London' in *The Christian*, 6 May 1875, p. 9.
202 'Revivalists in Liverpool' in *The Times*, 31 March 1875, p. 10.

203 'Revivalism at Eton' in *The Times*, 21 June 1875, p. 9.
204 Hansard 3, iv (21 June 1875), pp. 226–30.
205 'Punch's essence of parliament' in *Punch*, 3 July 1875, p. 281.
206 'Moody and Sankey at Eton' in *Daily Telegraph*, 23 June 1875, p. 3.
207 *Daily Telegraph*, 21 June 1875, p. 5.
208 'Parliament and the Eton boys' in *The Spectator*, 26 June 1875, pp. 811–12.
209 'Parliamentary intelligence' in *The Times*, 22 June 1875, p. 6.
210 'Revivalism at Eton' in *Ibid.*, p. 8.
211 *Ibid.*
212 *Ibid.*
213 'Parliament and the Eton boys' in *The Spectator*, 26 June 1875, p. 811.
214 'Messrs Moody and Sankey at Windsor' in *The Christian*, 1 July 1875, p. 14.
215 Findlay, *Dwight L. Moody*, p. 179; Kent, *Holding*, p. 167.
216 A.P. Fitt and W.R. Moody, *Life of D.L. Moody* (London, 1900), p. 85.
217 Findlay, *Dwight L. Moody*, pp. 190–1.
218 'The American revivalists' in *The Times*, 19 July 1875, p. 4.
219 George J. Stevenson, *Pastor Charles H. Spurgeon, his life and work to his fiftieth birthday* (London, 1885), quoted in W.D. Smith, *An annotated bibliography of D.L. Moody* (Chicago, 1948), p. 47.
220 D.L. Moody to his mother, 22 October 1881 (MBI Archives, 13 uncatalogued volumes of Moody's letters, Vol. 2: 1879–86).
221 'The Bishop of Rochester and Messrs Moody and Sankey' in *The Times*, 2 November 1883, p. 5.
222 Findlay, *Dwight L. Moody*, p. 186; P. Moody, *My father*, p. 192.
223 William Ross, *D.L. Moody: the prince of evangelists* (London, 1926), pp. 39–41.
224 Advertisements in *The Times*, 8 October 1892, p. 8; Morgan, '... *And some evangelists*', p. 212.
225 W.R. Moody, *Life* (1900), p. 397.
226 John Wesley White, 'The influence of North American evangelism in Great Britain between 1830 and 1914 on the origin and development of the ecumenical movement' (unpub. D.Phil thesis, Mansfield College, Oxford, 1963), pp. 64–70.
227 W.R. Moody, *Life* (1900), p. 397.

CHAPTER FOUR

1 Amanda Vickery, 'Golden age to separate spheres? A review of the categories and chronology of English women's history' in *Historical Journal*, 36, (1993), p. 389. A more recent survey which reaches similar conclusions is Robert B. Shoemaker, *Gender in English society 1650–1850: the emergence of separate spheres?* (London, 1998).
2 Vickery, p. 401.
3 *Ibid.*, p. 413.
4 For a discussion of the impact of a domestic ideology on working-class women, see Elizabeth Roberts, *Working women 1840–1940* (Basingstoke, 1988), pp. 14–17.
5 Mary Maples Dunn, 'Saints and sisters: Congregational and Quaker women in the early colonial period' in Janet James (ed.), *Women in American religion* (Philadelphia, 1980), pp. 35, 37, 39.
6 Barbara Welter, 'The feminization of American religion: 1800–1860' in Mary Hartman and Lois Banner (eds), *Clio's consciousness raised* (New York, 1974), pp. 137–57.
7 Hugh McLeod, 'Female piety and male irreligion? Religion and gender in the nineteenth century', English typescript, 30 pp. of 'Weibliche foömmigkeit, männlicher unglanbe?' in Ute Frevert (ed.), *Bürgerinnen und jürger* (Göttingen, 1988), pp. 134–56.
8 Gail Malmgreen, 'Introduction' in Gail Malmgreen (ed.), *Religion in the lives of English*

women, 1760–1930 (London, 1986), p. 2. David Bebbington reaches similar conclusions in *Evangelicalism in modern Britain: a history from the 1730s to the 1980s* (London, 1989), p. 128.

9 Gail Malmgreen, 'Domestic discords: women and the family in East Cheshire Method-ism, 1750–1830' in Jim Obelkevich, Lyndal Roper and Raphael Samuel (eds), *Disciplines of faith: studies in religion, politics and patriarchy* (London, 1987), p. 60. For a slight modification of Malmgreen's conclusions concerning Methodists, see Clive Field, 'The social composition of English Methodism to 1830: a membership analysis' in *Bulletin of the John Rylands University Library of Manchester*, 24 (1994), pp. 155–8. Field concludes, from a survey of 108 membership lists between 1745–1830, that on average women formed 50.2 to 60.8 per cent of members and that this figure was surprisingly stable over time.

10 Malmgreen, 'Introduction', p. 5.
11 Pat Holden, 'Introduction' in Pat Holden (ed.), *Women's religious experience* (London, 1983), p. 2.
12 Malmgreen, 'Introduction', pp. 6–7.
13 Anne Digby, 'Victorian values and women in public and private' in T.C. Smout (ed.), *Victorian values: proceedings of the British Academy*, 78 (Oxford, 1992), p. 198.
14 Frances Knight implicitly considers women as regular churchgoers in her book *The nineteenth-century Church and English society* (Cambridge, 1995). Linda Wilson does the same for Nonconformist women in '"Constrained by zeal": women in mid-nineteenth-century Nonconformist churches' in *Journal of Religious History*, 23 (June 1999), pp. 185–202.
15 Kathleen Heasman, *Evangelicals in action* (London, 1962), p. 14.
16 Maria Luddy, *Women and philanthropy in nineteenth-century Ireland* (Cambridge, 1995).
17 William Antliff, *Woman: her position and mission. A lecture delivered in various places* (3rd edn, London, 1864), p. 31.
18 Reverend John Dwyer, *Christian work for gentle hands: thoughts on female agency in the church of God* (London, 1873), pp. 22–9.
19 *Ibid.*, p. 22.
20 *Ibid.*, pp. 38–61.
21 W.R. Collett, *Women's work in the church* (Norwich, 1863), pp. 13–19.
22 F.K. Prochaska, *Women and philanthropy in nineteenth-century England* (Oxford, 1980), pp. 21–46.
23 For a survey of the main visiting agencies in the early nineteenth century, see H.D. Rack, 'Domestic visitation: a chapter in early nineteenth-century evangelism' in *Journal of Ecclesiastical History*, 24 (1994), pp. 357–76.
24 Donald Lewis, '"Lights in dark places": women evangelists in early Victorian Britain, 1838–1857' in *Women in the Church: Studies in Church History*, 27 (Oxford, 1990), p. 421.
25 F.K. Prochaska, 'Body and soul: Bible nurses and the poor in Victorian London' in *Historical Research*, 60 (1987), pp. 336–48.
26 Brian Harrison, 'Religion and recreation in nineteenth-century England' in *Past and Present*, 38 (1967), pp. 98–125.
27 Prochaska, *Women and philanthropy*, p. 244.
28 *Ibid.*, p. 222.
29 Olive Anderson, 'Women preachers in mid-Victorian Britain: some reflexions on feminism, popular religion and social change' in *Historical Journal*, 12 (1969), pp. 481–2.
30 *Ibid.*, p. 408.
31 Earl Kent Brown, 'Women in church history: stereotypes, archtypes and operational modalities' in *Methodist History*, 18 (1980), p. 124.
32 For example, Reverend R. Knill, in his pamphlet *The influence of pious women in promoting a revival of religion* (Narrative Series No. 800, London, [1830?]), is not referring to any preaching function but is advocating the importance of visiting. He states, 'Is it not

cheering? Is not this the way to promote a revival?' (p. 3) Similarly, Reverend George Osborn makes no mention of preaching in his article 'The work of women in the church'. Apart from their traditional duties, women were urged to also begin welcoming strangers at church, conducting Bible classes for women and visiting. See *Wesleyan Methodist Magazine* (1881), pp. 30–4. Even modern research can be deceiving. Donald Lewis' article on 'women evangelists in early Victorian Britain' reproduces the confusion surrounding home mission work. Although the district visitors he describes were involved in evangelistic activity, it was purely on a one-to-one basis and as such cannot be classified as 'preaching'. See Lewis, '"Lights in dark places"'.

33 Brown, 'Women in church history', pp. 126–7.

34 There is an extensive literature on women and religion in seventeenth-century England. See Keith Thomas, 'Women and the civil war sects' in *Past and Present*, 13 (1958), pp. 42–62; Christopher Hill, *The world turned upside down* (London, 1972); Clare Cross, '"He-goats before the flocks": a note on the part played by some women in the founding of some Civil War churches' in *Popular Belief and Practice: Studies in Church History*, 8 (Cambridge, 1972), pp. 195–202; Phyllis Mack, 'Women as prophets during the English Civil War' in *Feminist Studies*, 8 (1982), pp. 20–45; Anne Laurence, 'A priesthood of she-believers: women and congregations in mid-seventeenth century England' in *Women and the Church: Studies in Church History*, 27 (Oxford, 1990), pp. 345–63; Phyllis Mack, *Visionary women: ecstatic prophecy in seventeenth-century England* (Berkeley and Los Angeles, 1992); Patricia Crawford, *Women and religion in England 1500–1720* (London, 1993).

35 2 Timothy 2:12. All biblical citations are from the *New International Version*.

36 Paul Chilcote, *John Wesley and the women preachers of early Methodism* (Metuchen, N.J. and London, 1991); Leslie Church, *More about the early Methodist people* (London, 1949), Chapter 5.

37 *Minutes of the Wesleyan Methodist Conference 1803* (1862 edn), p. 187.

38 This is particularly true in the American context. See Catherine A. Brekus, *Strangers and pilgrims: female preaching in America, 1740–1845* (Chapel Hill, 1998); Candy Gunther, 'The spiritual pilgrimage of Rachel Stearns, 1834–1837: reinterpreting women's religious and social experiences in the Methodist revivals of nineteenth-century America' in *Church History*, 65 (1996), pp. 577–95; Vicki Tolar Collins, 'Walking in light, walking in darkness: the story of women's changing rhetorical space in early Methodism' in *Rhetoric Review*, 14 (Spring 1996), pp. 336–54.

39 E. Dorothy Graham, 'Called by God: the female itinerants of early Primitive Methodism' (unpub. PhD diss., University of Birmingham, 1987); Idem, 'Chosen by God: the female travelling preachers of early Primitive Methodism' in *Proceedings of the Wesley Historical Society*, 49 (1993), pp. 77–95.

40 Wesley Swift, 'The women itinerant preachers of early Methodism', part 2 in *Proceedings of the Wesley Historical Society*, 29 (1953), pp. 76–8. After 1861 there were no other female itinerants until the 1890s, when a cluster of five women appear in the *Minutes*. See Oliver Beckerlegge, 'Women itinerant preachers' in *Proceedings of the Wesley Historical Society*, 30 (1956), pp. 182–4.

41 E.D. Graham, 'Chosen by God' PhD, pp. 250–75; Linda Wilson, 'An investigation into the decline of female itinerant preachers in the Bible Christian sect up to 1850' (unpub. MA diss., Cheltenham and Gloucester College of Further Education, 1992), pp. 17–18.

42 Deborah Valenze, 'Cottage religion and the politics of survival' in Jane Rendall (ed.), *Equal or different: women's politics 1800–1914* (Oxford, 1987), p. 55. For a fuller and more detailed analysis of these ideas, see Idem, *Prophetic sons and daughters: female preaching and popular religion in industrial England* (Princeton, 1985).

43 Anderson, 'Women preachers', p. 481.

44 Jocelyn Murray, 'Gender attitudes and the contribution of women to evangelism and ministry in the nineteenth century' in John Wolffe (ed.), *Evangelical faith and public zeal:*

evangelicals and society in Britain 1780–1980 (London, 1995), p. 109.
45 Pamela Walker, 'A chaste and fervid eloquence: Catherine Booth and the ministry of women in the Salvation Army' in Beverly Mayne Kienzle and Pamela J. Walker (eds), *Women preachers and prophets through two millennia of Christianity* (Berkeley, Los Angeles and London, 1998), p. 293.
46 See below pp. 126–32.
47 Pioneering work in this field has been conducted by David Hempton and Myrtle Hill, *Evangelical protestantism in Ulster society, 1740–1890* (London, 1992), Chapter 7; David Hempton, *The religion of the people: Methodism and popular religion c. 1750–1900* (London, 1996), Chapter 10; and Andrea Ebel Brozyna, *Labour, love and prayer: female piety in Ulster religious literature 1850–1914* (Belfast and Montreal/Kingston, 1999).
48 See Hempton and Hill, pp. 131–3; Rosemary Raughter, 'A natural tenderness: the ideal and the reality of eighteenth-century female philanthropy' in Maryann Gialanella Valiulis and Mary O'Dowd (eds), *Women and Irish history: essays in honour of Margaret MacCurtain* (Dublin, 1997), pp. 71–88.
49 Jacinta Prunty, *Dublin slums 1800–1925: a study in urban geography* (Dublin, 1997).
50 Hempton and Hill, p. 134; Hempton, *Religion of the people*, pp. 185–6. For a biographical account of Alice Cambridge, see C.H. Crookshank, *Memorable women of Irish Methodism in the last century* (London, 1882), p. 200. For an account of Anne Lutton's life, see Anne Lutton, *Memorials of a consecrated life* (London, 1882).
51 For an in-depth discussion of the role of women during the revival, see Janice Holmes, 'Lifting the curtain on popular religion: women, laity and language in the Ulster revival of 1859' (unpub. MA diss., Queen's Kingston, 1991), Chapter 4.
52 Thus, Miss Buck of Leicester preached in Londonderry in 1859 and a Miss Wakefield held revival meetings in 1897. See *Belfast News-Letter*, 3 October 1859, p. 2 and Brozyna, p. 148. Phoebe Palmer also preached in Ulster in 1859 and Catherine Booth made several preaching trips to the north.
53 Minutes of the Social Service Committee (Deaconess Guild), Vol. 2 (1913–37) (Presbyterian Historical Society, Church House Strong Room, Belfast).
54 Brozyna, p. 148.
55 1 Corinthians 14:34.
56 Reverend P.J. Jarbo, *A letter to Mrs Palmer in reference to women speaking in public* (North Shields, 1859), p. 2.
57 Reverend Robert Young, *North of England revivals. Prophesying of women* (Newcastle-on-Tyne, 1859), p. 5.
58 1 Timothy 2:11–14.
59 Young, *North of England*, p. 6.
60 Dwyer, *Christian work*, p. 86.
61 R. [George Railton], *Heathen England and what to do for it* (London, 1877), p. 124. A similar argument is made in Jessie McFarlane, *Scriptural warrant for women to preach the gospel* (London, n.d.), p. 6.
62 Mrs Fanny Grattan Guinness, *'She spake of him': recollections of the late Mrs Henry Dening* (London and Bristol, 1872), p. 246.
63 Quoted in Acts 2:17–21. The original prophecy can be found in Joel 2:28–9.
64 Kenneth Barker (ed.), *The NIV study Bible* (Grand Rapids, 1984), commentary on Exodus 7:1–2.
65 Judges 4.
66 2 Kings 22. Other women named as prophetesses include Miriam (Exodus 15:20), Naodiah (Nehemiah 6:14), Anna (Luke 2:36) and the four daughters of Philip (Acts 21:9).
67 For these descriptions of Phoebe and Priscilla, see Romans 16:1–3. Phoebe was probably a deaconess while Priscilla, along with her husband Aquila and Paul, founded the Christian church at Corinth.
68 W.R. Collett argued that Phoebe merely offered hospitality and that Priscilla only ever

gave private instruction. See Collett, *Woman's work*, pp. 8–9.

69 Reverend Arthur A. Rees, *Reasons for not co-operating in the alleged 'Sunderland revivals'* (Sunderland, 1859), p. 5.

70 O.W.L.A., *Some reasons why I do not sympathize with the Salvation Army* (London, 1882), p. 9.

71 Letter of James Gall, Jr in *The Revival*, 30 June 1864, p. 412.

72 'Women's ministry' in *Ibid.*, 20 November 1862, p. 233.

73 Rees, *Reasons*, pp. 9–10.

74 Harold Raser, *Phoebe Palmer: her life and thought* (Lewiston, NY, 1987), pp. 131–5.

75 Phoebe Palmer, *The promise of the father; or, a neglected speciality of the last days* (Boston, 1859), p. 36.

76 *Ibid.*, p. 1.

77 Anne Loveland, 'Domesticity and religion in the antebellum period: the career of Phoebe Palmer' in *The Historian*, 39 (1977), pp. 467–70. For a more sophisticated analysis of Palmer's domestic ideology, see Theodore Hovet, 'Phoebe Palmer's "altar phraseology" and the spiritual dimension of woman's sphere' in *Journal of Religion*, 63 (1983), pp. 264–80.

78 Armstrong, p. 16.

79 Rees, *Reasons*, pp. 5–17.

80 Jarbo, *Letter to Mrs Palmer*.

81 Young, *North of England*, p. 7.

82 Norman Murdoch, 'Female ministry in the thought and work of Catherine Booth' in *Church History*, 53 (1984), pp. 348–62.

83 Catherine Booth, *Female teaching: or, the Reverend A.A. Rees versus Mrs Palmer, being a reply to a pamphlet by the above gentleman on the Sunderland revival* (2nd edn, London, 1861), p. 30.

84 See *Female teaching*, p. 5 as to why women should avoid publicity; p. 23 for a spirited rejection of the 'moral superiority' argument; and p. 25 for a humorous rebuttal of Rees' claim that 'privacy is [a woman's] proper sphere'.

85 Catherine Booth, 'Female ministry; or, woman's right to preach the gospel' in *Papers on popular religion* (London, 1878), p. 111. The sentiments in this subsequent edition are not, I feel, a defining feature of Booth's thinking on this subject. For a detailed historiography of this pamphlet, see Walker, 'Devil's kingdom' PhD, pp. 64–5, footnotes 52, 53.

86 Grattan Guinness, *'She spake of him'*, p. 250.

87 Railton, *Heathen England*, p. 121.

88 Henry Chapman, 'Sisterhoods' in *Free Methodist*, 20 March 1890, p. 1.

89 'S.E.R. Wilson' in *Joyful News*, 16 December 1886, p. 1.

90 Jarbo, *Letter to Mrs Palmer*, pp. 3–4.

91 'Should women preach?' in *War Cry*, 21 January 1905, p. 12.

92 I.E. Page, 'Reverend F.D. Sanford in Bolton' in *King's Highway* (1886), p. 62.

93 'Nathaniel Wiseman' (pseud. of J.J. Ellis), *Elizabeth Baxter, saint, evangelist, preacher, teacher and expositor* (London, 1928), pp. 70–1.

94 'Northwich' in *Christian Mission Magazine* (1878), p. 260.

95 Anderson, 'Women preachers'.

96 Guinness, *'She spake of him'*.

97 'Swansea' in *The Revival*, 14 July 1864, p. 19.

98 J.V.B., *She walked with God, and was not, for God took her. Memorials of Mrs Bass* (London, [1881]), pp. 9, 24–5.

99 'A lady's labours in an agricultural district' in *The Revival*, 23 July 1863, p. 55.

100 'The ministry of women' in *Ibid.*, 7 June 1866, p. 317.

101 Gordon Forlong, 'Edinburgh: Mrs Thomson, Miss McFarlane and Richard Weaver' in *Ibid.*, 10 March 1864, p. 150.

102 'The Swansea magistrates and the gospel' in *Ibid.*, 25 August 1864, p. 118.
103 J.V.B., *She walked with God*, p. 21.
104 Gordon Forlong, 'Edinburgh' in *The Revival*, 10 March 1864, p. 150.
105 'Mrs Col. Bell in London' in *Ibid.*, 15 December 1864, p. 376.
106 'Edinburgh' in *Ibid.*, 18 August 1864, p. 101.
107 Geraldine Hooper Dening held meetings for prostitutes in a 'small room'. See Guinness, *'She spake of him'*, p. 23. Elizabeth Baxter began her public labours in the cottage of a poor woman. See Wiseman, *Elizabeth Baxter*, p. 70.
108 For an account of the Polytechnic meetings, see 'Sunday afternoon services at the Polytechnic' in *The Revival*, 5 July 1866, p. 11 and 'Preaching by ladies' in *Ibid.*, 11 October 1866, p. 204. For more details concerning the colourful career of Mrs Thistlethwayte (Laura Bell) and her relationship with Gladstone, see Horace Wyndham, *Feminine frailty* (London, 1929), pp. 33–61 and H.C.G. Matthew, *Gladstone, 1809–1874* (Oxford, 1988), pp. 157–8, 233, 237–42.
109 Anderson, 'Women preachers', p. 473.
110 'Miss Marsh and the navvies on the Metropolitan railway' in *The Revival*, 15 February 1866, p. 93. See also L.E. O'Rorke, *The life and friendships of Catherine Marsh* (London, 1917) and Marsh's own account in C[atherine] M. M[arsh], *English hearts and English hands; or, the railway and the trenches* (21st thou., London and Edinburgh, 1858).
111 Heasman, *Evangelicals*, Chapter 14; 'In memoriam: Mrs Daniell, of Aldershot' in *The Revival*, 28 September 1871, p. 11.
112 Anderson, 'Women preachers', p. 473.
113 This discussion has been summarised from Anderson, 'Women preachers', pp. 474–7.
114 Guinness, *'She spake of him'*, pp. 21–4.
115 Wiseman, *Elizabeth Baxter*, pp. 73–4, 89.
116 Reverend William Haslam, *'Yet not I': or, more years of my ministry* (London, 1882), pp. 161–74.
117 J.V.B., *She walked with God*, p. 21.
118 Guinness, *'She spake of him'*, pp. 4–5.
119 'Death of Mrs Dening' in *The Christian*, 15 August 1872, p. 12; 'The late Mrs Dening' in *Ibid.*, 22 August 1872, p. 8.
120 Anderson, 'Women preachers', p. 482.
121 The name of Booth's organisation changed with a confusing frequency. In 1867 it became the East London Christian Mission, a title shortened to The Christian Mission in 1870. 'Salvation Army' originated in 1878 and was officially adopted that same year. Cf. Robert Sandall, *The history of the Salvation Army* (3 vols., London, 1947–55), i, pp. 85, 99, 228, 286.
122 Quoted in Walker, 'Devil's kingdom' PhD, p. 23 from a letter written to Catherine's clergyman in 1855. See also Walker's footnote to this quote on p. 61 for the proper dating of this letter.
123 *Ibid.*, p. 255.
124 Bramwell Booth, *Echoes and memories* (London, 1925), p. 166.
125 W.T. Stead, *Catherine Booth* (London, 1900), pp. 214–16, 230–2; Bernard Watson, *A hundred years' war* (London, 1964), pp. 30–1; Catherine Bramwell-Booth, *Catherine Booth: the story of her loves* (London, 1970), p. 291.
126 Harold Begbie, *Life of William Booth, the founder of the Salvation Army* (2 vols., London, 1920), i, p. 255.
127 'Mrs Caroline Reynolds' in *War Cry*, 4 September 1886, p. 1.
128 R. [George Railton], *Twenty-one years Salvation Army. Under the generalship of William Booth* (London, 1887), p. 223.
129 Bramwell Booth, *Echoes*, p. 166.
130 'Annual meeting' in *Christian Mission Magazine* (1878), p. 246.
131 Christine Ward, 'The social sources of the Salvation Army, 1865–90' (unpub. MPhil

diss., Bedford College, University of London, 1970).

132 'Conference and annual meeting' in *Christian Mission Magazine* (1877), p. 173.
133 Typescript obituary of Annie Davis, n.d. (Salvation Army International Heritage Centre (SAIHC), Annie Davis Ridsdell file).
134 I am thinking of Mrs James Dowdle, Mrs Garner, Mrs Peter Hansen and Mrs Wilson, all of whom were respected for the work they did apart from their position as wives to station evangelists.
135 'Northwich' in *Christian Mission Magazine* (1878), p. 260.
136 *Jackdaw*, 7 November 1879, quoted in *Victorian Nottingham*, p. 28.
137 Railton, *Twenty-one years*, p. 103.
138 Typescript obituary of Annie Davis, n.d. (SAIHC, Annie Davis Ridsdell file).
139 Railton, *Twenty-one years*, p. 104.
140 *Ibid.*, p. 105.
141 Bramwell Booth, *Echoes*, p. 167.
142 'Congress of War' in *Christian Mission Magazine* (1878), pp. 229–30.
143 'Merthyr, the people' in *Ibid.*, p. 129.
144 H[enry] T. C[hapman], 'Sisterhoods and female evangelism' in *Free Methodist*, 26 June 1890, p. 7. Chapman is referring to a conversation he had with George Clegg.
145 Railton, *Twenty-one years*, p. 110.
146 Bramwell Booth, *Echoes*, p. 166.
147 The *Northern Daily Express* quoted in *The Salvationist* (1879), p. 98.
148 From the *Buchan Observer*, quoted in 'Scotland – Peterhead' in *The Revival*, 22 October 1863, p. 259. Supporters of this ministry regarded such comments as injurious to the work. When the revival which Miss Graham's presence had stimulated was still in full swing three weeks later, *The Revival* smugly stated that what was originally curiosity had now turned to 'deep earnestness'. Cf. 'Miss Graham's labours at Peterhead' in *Ibid.*, 17 December 1863, p. 395.
149 'Gateshead' in *The Salvationist* (1879), pp. 95–7.
150 'Aberdare' in *Christian Mission Magazine* (1878), p. 290.
151 'Rotherham' in *Ibid.*, p. 149.
152 'The month' in *Ibid.*, p. 98.
153 'Southwick' in *The Salvationist* (1879), p. 16.
154 'Congress of War' in *Christian Mission Magazine* (1878), pp. 234–5.
155 *Ibid.*
156 'Life of Mother Shepherd', part 3 in *War Cry*, 30 April 1887, p. 1.
157 'Poplar' in *Christian Mission Magazine*, p. 236.
158 *Ibid.*, p. 212.
159 'Coventry' in *Ibid.* (1878), pp. 104–5.
160 'Congress of War' in *Ibid.*, p. 229.
161 After a trial, charges of obstruction were dropped against Rose Clapham and Jane Smith in Barnsley. Cf. 'Barnsley' in *Ibid.*, p. 203. Louisa Lock and several other Mission workers were arrested at Pentre for obstructing the thoroughfare and sent to Cardiff Gaol for one night. This appears a largely symbolic effort by local magistrates to control Mission activity. It actually created a great deal of interest and tumult as thousands lined the streets to see Lock pass by on her way to prison. Even larger crowds gathered the next morning for her return. Cf. 'Imprisonment of Capt. Louisa Lock and three members of her corps' in *The Salvationist* (1879), pp. 261–5; 'Louisa Lock' in *War Cry*, 17 March 1881, pp. 1, 4.
162 Mrs Col. Kate Taylor in *Fighting in many lands: memories of veteran salvationists* (1st series, London, 1946), p. 27.
163 'Annual meeting' in *Christian Mission Magazine* (1878), p. 247.
164 Eileen Douglas, 'Major Rose: a tale of two continents', part 1 in *All The World* (July 1889), p. 303.

165 'Consett' in *Ibid.*, p. 262.
166 George Railton to William Booth, 13 October 1877 (SAIHC, Booth Correspondence).
167 'Stroud' in *The Salvationist* (1879), p. 320.
168 'Rotherham' in *Christian Mission Magazine* (1878), p. 149.
169 'Congress of War' in *Ibid.*, pp. 228–9.
170 'Leeds' in *The Salvationist* (1879), p. 76.
171 Ward, 'Social sources' MPhil., pp. 93–6.
172 Eileen Douglas, 'Major Rose: a tale of two continents', part 2 in *All The World* (September 1889), pp. 416–17.
173 Reverend W.H. Tindall, 'Try Women!' in *Joyful News*, 5 March 1885, p. 1.
174 Anglican sisterhoods were founded by Tractarians as early as 1844 and by 1875 there were 18 orders in 95 locations. Controversy over their status and the requirement of vows made the less formal deaconess institutes a more popular alternative. Among evangelicals, Reverend William Pennefather and his wife Catherine had established the Mildmay Deaconess Institute in 1860, which by 1899 had 250 workers. Wesleyans started their Wesleyan Deaconess Order in 1890 and by 1901 it was responsible for 54 deaconesses and 13 probationers. Both sisterhoods and deaconess institutes remained small and neither exercised any ministerial or leadership functions. Rather, they focused their energies on church work and basic nursing. There is a fairly extensive literature on these two movements. See Harriette Cooke, *Mildmay; or, the story of the first deaconess institution* (London, 1892); Zoë Fairfield (ed.), *Some aspects of the woman's movement* (London, 1915), Appendix 1; Alan Deacon and Michael Hill, 'The problem of "surplus women" in the nineteenth century: secular and religious alternatives' in Michael Hill (ed.), *A sociological yearbook of religion in Britain*, 5 (London, 1972), pp. 87–102; Martha Vicinus, *Independent women: work and community for single women 1850–1920* (Chicago, 1985), Chapter 2; Catherine Prelinger, 'The female diaconate in the Anglican church: what kind of ministry for women?' in Malmgreen (ed.), *Religion*, pp. 161–92; Brian Heeney, *The women's movement in the church of England 1850–1930* (Oxford, 1988); Jacqueline Field-Bibb, *Women towards priesthood: ministerial politics and feminist praxis* (Cambridge, 1991); Sean Gill, 'The power of Christian ladyhood: Priscilla Lydia Sellon and the creation of Anglican sisterhoods' in Stuart Mews (ed.), *Modern religious rebels: presented to John Kent* (Epworth, 1993), pp. 144–65; E. Dorothy Graham, 'The early deaconess evangelists: snapshots of their work' in Richard Sykes (ed.), *Beyond the boundaries: preaching in the Wesleyan tradition* (Oxford, 1998), pp. 87–115.
175 John Lenton, '"Labouring for the Lord": women preachers in Wesleyan Methodism 1802–1932. A revisionist view' in Richard Sykes (ed.), *Beyond the boundaries: preaching in the Wesleyan tradition* (Oxford, 1998), pp. 65–8.
176 For this interpretation, see Fairfield, *Woman's movement*, p. 222 and Field-Bibb, *Women towards priesthood*, pp. 24–5.
177 Lenton, p. 69.
178 Thomas Meadley, 'Thomas Champness – Joyful News centenary 1883–1983' typescript, 1982 (Cliff College Archives, Calver, C14). This was eventually published as *Kindled by a spark* (Rochdale?, 1983).
179 For the standard accounts of Champness' life, see Eliza Champness, *The life-story of Thomas Champness* (London, 1907); Josiah Mee, *Thomas Champness as I knew him* (London, 1906). For a general survey of *Joyful News*'s publishing history, see David Howarth, '"Joyful News" (1883–1963): some reflections' in *Proceedings of the Wesley Historical Society*, 44 (1983), pp. 2–15.
180 *Joyful News*, 5 March 1885, p. 1.
181 'Should women preach?' in *Joyful News*, 13 August 1885, p. 1.
182 The debate revolved around the desire of some, with 'views more in harmony with modern ideas', to expand the 1803 ruling to allow female preaching. A decision on the 'vexed question' proved impossible and Conference refused its sanction. See

'Conference sketches' in *Methodist Recorder*, 28 July 1885, p. 555.

183 Quoted in H.T. C[hapman], 'Sisterhoods and female evangelism' in *Free Methodist*, 26 June 1890, p. 7.

184 The Home was originally located at 24 Gladstone Road. In July 1889 it moved to Kingsley Place, also in Halifax. See *Joyful News*, 12 April 1888, pp. 1–2; 25 July 1889, p. 2.

185 'Joyful News Female Evangelists' Home, Halifax' in *Ibid.*, 29 March 1888, p. 1. The financial side of the Home was actually a partnership between Clegg and W.H. Greenwood, who had apparently contributed a substantial sum towards its maintenance. See *Ibid.*, 12 April 1888, p. 1. Miss Greenwood, one of the evangelists, could possibly have been his daughter.

186 Lists of appointments are no longer published in *Joyful News* and most of the 23 women still associated with the Home seem to retire. Some apparently do carry on an independent basis although references to their meetings continue to associate them with 'Mr Clegg's Home'. See references to Miss Ashford's meetings at Waddington and Hoyland Common in *Ibid.* for 1897: 7 January, p. 2 and 25 November, p. 4.

187 My calculations based on *Joyful News* accord exactly with Eliza Champness' estimate in *Life-story*, p. 259. Neither of us have included Susannah Cook in this total. Cook had been active as an evangelist before her association with Clegg and after 1897 returned to her independent work until 1902, when no further mention is made of her.

188 'The women publishers' in *Joyful News*, 24 March 1892, p. 1.

189 John Lenton suggests a figure of 107 women. However, he seems to have conflated the number of women in Clegg's home with those in Champness' Rugby home. Articles in *Joyful News*, however, would suggest that they were two quite distinct institutions, each with their own members. Taken together, according to my calculations, they should total 139. See Lenton, p. 74.

190 Mary Champness, 'The women's Joyful News Home' in *Ibid.*, 12 April 1900, p. 2.

191 For an account of the transfer, see the letter of Reverend Thomas Cook, the principal of the new institute, in *Ibid.*, 3 September 1903, p. 3. For accounts of the origins of Cliff College, see J.I. Brice, *The crowd for Christ* (London, 1934); D.W. Lambert, *What hath God wrought: the story of Cliff College 1904–54* (Chesterfield, 1954?); Amos Cresswell, *The story of Cliff* (Calver, 1983).

192 For example, Miss Hickman appears to have continued her evangelistic work on an independent basis. Cf. *Joyful News*, 23 July 1903, p. 3. Margaret Manley, however, became a Wesleyan deaconess. Cf. *Ibid.*, 5 November 1903, p. 3. Only Miss Coles was kept on in order to begin a work among young people and children. Cf. *Ibid.*, 3 September 1903, p. 1.

193 The campaigns were held in Ainsdale (March–April), Dumbarton (July), and Bootle, Liverpool (October). Cf. *Joyful News* for 1885: 19 April, p. 2; 30 April, p. 1; 9 July, p. 2; 16 July, p. 3; 22 October, p. 3.

194 Unfortunately, Miss Wilson's first name remains unknown and there is some confusion surrounding her initials. In the *Joyful News* article cited on p. 114, endnote 89, she is called 'S.E.R. Wilson', but I think this is a misprint. On one other occasion she is called 'S.C.R. Wilson' and more frequently she is referred to as 'C. Wilson'. I am assuming it is the same person because these references also identify her as 'of Carlisle'. See *Joyful News*, 25 November 1897; *The Christian*, 8 November 1894, p. 25.

195 J.G. Cooke, 'Black Hill and Shotley Bridge' in *Joyful News*, 5 March 1885, p. 3.

196 'Wesley Chapel, Haswell' in *Ibid.*, 20 October 1892, p. 4.

197 George Clegg, 'Lady workers wanted' in *Ibid.*, 24 November 1887, p. 4.

198 H.T. C[hapman], 'Sisterhoods and female evangelism'. Eliza Champness, however, describes the women as 'godly servant-maids and factory-lasses' who could not get into the city sisterhoods 'where women of gentle birth and better education were preferred'. Cf. Champness, *Life-story*, p. 259. At the moment I doubt the accuracy of her description.

199 Susannah Cook, the Superintendent of the Halifax Home, was 45 when it became

affiliated with Joyful News. The other three women, Mary Farnden, Clara Walker and Mary Jane Smith, were 29, 22 and 23 respectively when they joined the organisation. Cf. Census for Kingsley Place, Halifax, 1891 (Calderdale District Archives, Halifax); and Diary of Mary Jane Smith (later Norwell), May 1892–Feb. 1893 (Cliff College Archives, C25).

200 It is unclear whether or not these married women actually preached or if they just assisted their husbands.

201 Smith's mission in Collingborne ran from 25 September to 23 October 1892, while Branscombe's ran from 29 January to 10 February 1893, and Chard's from 12–24 February 1893.

202 Diary of Mary Jane Smith, 29 January 1893 (Cliff College Archives, C25).

203 H.T. C[hapman], 'Sisterhoods and female evangelism'. See Miss C. Wilson, 'An Appeal' in *Joyful News*, 16 December 1886, p. 1.

204 John Laws, 'Dunstan-on-Tyne' in *Joyful News*, 7 April 1887, p. 2.

205 W. Matthews, 'Moulton' in *Ibid.*, 2 June 1887, p. 4.

206 In this context Jones and Chapman are using 'sisterhoods' not in the strict sense of the term, but as a synonym for 'female evangelists' or 'a band of women workers'. See Alfred Jones, 'Connexional evangelism – the question of sisterhoods' in *Free Methodist*, 27 March 1890, p. 7.

207 Alfred Jones, 'Female ministries' in *Ibid.*, 18 December 1890, p. 3.

208 Diary of Mary Jane Smith, 2 May 1892 (Cliff College Archives, C25).

209 *Ibid.*, 27 September 1892.

210 *Ibid.*, 21 September 1892.

211 Not surprisingly, he went to hear Mrs Thistlethwayte preach at the London Polytechnic. See Matthew, *Gladstone*, p. 157.

CHAPTER FIVE

1 Kenneth Brown, *A social history of the nonconformist ministry in England and Wales 1800–1930* (Oxford, 1988).

2 Mark Smith, *Religion in industrial society: Oldham and Saddleworth 1740–1865* (Oxford, 1994), p. 215.

3 Tom Holland, *The story of my life* (with a foreword by William Nelson, n.p., [1914]), p. 37.

4 John Burnett, David Vincent, David Mayall (eds), *The autobiography of the working class: an annotated critical bibliography* (3 vols., Brighton, 1984–9), i, p. xxiv.

5 W.J. Willis, *From taproom to pulpit. Being a lecture by Mr W.J. Willis, evangelist, together with photographs of the lecturer, Mr Tom Holland, and the late Reverend David Kyles* (Darlington, n.d.), p. 6.

6 Rodney (Gipsy) Smith, *Gipsy Smith. His life and work, by himself* (London, 1903), pp. 10–20.

7 Holland, *Story of my life*, p. 6.

8 William Foster, *Praying Billy, the street preacher* (2nd edn, Rochdale, 1901), pp. 15–17.

9 Albert J. Mahomet, *From street arab to pastor* (Cardiff, 1901), pp. 18–24.

10 Holland, *Story of my life*, p. 19.

11 Reverend James Paterson, *Richard Weaver's life story* (London, 1897), pp. 36–8.

12 Reverend John Macpherson, *Henry Moorhouse, the English evangelist* (London, n.d.), p. 7.

13 Holland, *Story of my life*, p. 27.

14 Albert Mahomet's alcoholic parents forced him and his brother and sister onto their own resources, which included street acrobatics and thieving. Prior to Mahomet's entry into the workhouse, his brother had been arrested for thieving and sent to a reformatory.

See Mahomet, *Street arab*, pp. 9–14. Gipsy Smith sold clothespegs door-to-door and assisted his father when he played the fiddle in local pubs. See Smith, *Life and work*, pp. 25, 42.

15 Anon (ed.), *The life of Joshua Poole. With details of his conversion, and particulars of his subsequent career* (London, 1867), pp. 42–3, 61–5.

16 'England – British evangelists' in *The Revival*, 30 October 1862, p. 201.

17 Albert Shakesby, *From street arab to evangelist* (Hull, 1910), p. 167.

18 John E. Coulson, *The peasant preacher: memorials of Mr Charles Richardson, a Wesleyan evangelist* (2nd edn, London, 1866), pp. 12, 15.

19 *Ibid.*, p. 67.

20 Reverend John Barfoot, *A diamond in the rough: or, Christian heroism in humble life, being jottings concerning that remarkable peasant preacher, William Hickingbothan, of Belper, Derbyshire* (London, 1874), pp. 46–53. A similar story is told of Charles Richardson in Coulson, *Peasant preacher*, p. 33.

21 'Mr Shakesby tells his own life story' in *Mr Albert Shakesby after his conversion*, various essays and newspapers articles (n.p., n.d.), p. 6.

22 Reverend John Macpherson, *The Christian hero: a sketch of the life of Robert Annan* (London, 1867), pp. 14–17.

23 Reverend W. Wakinshaw, 'A Miracle of grace' in *Mr Albert Shakesby*, p. 12.

24 Willis, *Taproom to pulpit*, p. 21.

25 Paterson, *Richard Weaver*, pp. 54–6.

26 Henry Varley, Jr, *Henry Varley's life story* (London, 1916), pp. 57–61 for the controversy, p. 74 for the quote.

27 W.J.H. Brealey, *'Always abounding': or recollections of the life and labours of the late George Brealey, the evangelist of the Blackdown Hills* (London, 1889), pp. 219–20.

28 See Edmund Gosse, *Father and Son* (London, 1989 rept of 1907 orig edn); Max Wright, *Told in Gath* (Belfast, 1990) and Jeffrey Cox, *The English churches in a secular society: Lambeth, 1870–1930* (Oxford, 1992).

29 *Jubilee Year. Brief history of Merrion Hall, Dublin. 1863–1913* (Dublin, 1913), p. 9.

30 George Sails, *At the centre: the story of Methodism's central missions* (London, 1970), pp. 27–32.

31 Jonathan Ireland, *Jonathan Ireland, the street preacher. An autobiography* (London, n.d.), p. 24.

32 James Obelkevich has identified these as two of the main reasons why the Church of England failed in South Lindsey, 1830–75. See James Obelkevich, *Religion and rural society: South Lindsay 1825–1875* (Oxford, 1976), pp. 178, 181.

33 Reverend John Whittle, *'Owd Roger': Bible colporteur and Primitive Methodist lay preacher* (Blackburn, 1912), pp. 30, 39.

34 Reverend T. Mardy Rees, *Seth Joshua and Frank Joshua: the renowned evangelists* (Wrexham, 1926), p. 27.

35 A.L. Calman, *The life and labours of John Ashworth* (Manchester, 1875), p. 310.

36 John Wright, *Saved just in time. The history of my conversion* (London, n.d.), p. 25.

37 Samuel Thorne, *The Cornish wrestler; or, the life of Abraham Bastard* (3rd edn, London, [1880]), p. 14. The Bible Christian denomination was based in Cornwall and Devon, so it is more than likely that Bastard would come into contact with one of their female preachers. For a fuller discussion of female preaching among the Bible Christians, see Wesley Swift, 'The women itinerant preachers of early Methodism' in *Proceedings of the Wesley Historical Society*, part 1, 28 (1952), p. 94; part 2, 29 (1953), p. 76.

38 Whittle, *'Owd Roger'*, p. 42.

39 Isaac Watson, *The life story of Thomas Langton, of Malton, the Yorkshire evangelist* (Rochdale, 1895), p. 170.

40 For John Hambleton's work see 'John Hambleton at Aldershot' in *The Revival*, 12 November 1863, p. 316. For Middleton's see 'Mr Lancelot Middleton' in *'Joyful News'*

Banner of Hope (June 1892), p. 81.

41 [John Urquhart], *The life-story of William Quarrier. A romance of faith* (3rd edn, Glasgow and London, [1905]), p. 128.

42 Harold Murray, *Gipsy Smith: an intimate memoir* (Exeter, 1947), p. 27.

43 John Sharp, 'Juvenile holiness: Catholic revivalism among children in Victorian Britain', *Journal of Ecclesiastical History*, 35 (1984), p. 220.

44 'The Woolwich Boys' in *The Revival*, 18 May 1861, p. 157

45 *Ibid.*, 3 August 1861, p. 38.

46 *Ibid.*, 26 October 1861, p. 133. Similar groups also formed in Islington and Greenwich.

47 *Ibid.*, 30 July 1863, pp. 75–6.

48 Macpherson, *Christian hero*, p. 50.

49 R.C. Morgan, *The life of Richard Weaver, the converted collier* (London, 1861), pp. 36–8.

50 'Increased activity in the churches' in *Revival Advocate* (July 1858), p. 218.

51 'Theatre services for the working classes of London' in *The Revival*, 10 November 1860, p. 148.

52 'Newcastle-on-Tyne' in *Ibid.* 22 July 1869, p. 11.

53 'Evangelistic work at Brighouse' in *Ibid.*, 18 November 1869, p. 9.

54 William Booth, *Addresses by the Reverend William Booth, Mr W. Corbridge, and Mr E. Cadman, on 'Hallelujah Bands', and their work, with an introduction by Reverend T. Whitehouse* (Lye, 1891), p. 4.

55 Reverend Thomas Whitehouse, *Great awakening in the Black country; and an effort to reach the masses: with a brief sketch of the Hallelujah Band* (West Bromwich, 1875), p. 5.

56 Elijah Cadman in Booth, *Addresses*, p. 12.

57 A member of the Evangelization Society, *Preaching the gospel; or, evangelists and evangelization* (n.p., n.d.), pp. 11–12.

58 Irish Evangelization Society, *Occasional paper. November 1874* (Dublin, 1874), p. 16.

59 William John Taylor, *The life and work of the late William Taylor, the navvy* (with an intro. by Cpn W.E. Smith, Glasgow, 1892), p. 141.

60 Reverend Thomas Waugh, *Twenty-three years a missioner. Life-sketch lessons and reminiscences* (2nd edn, London and Rochdale, 1905), p. 66.

61 Henry T. Smart, *Thomas Cook's early ministry: with incidents and suggestions concerning Christian work* (London, 1892), p. 72.

62 J. Stephen Flynn, *Cornwall forty years after* (London, 1917), pp. 77–8. For a comprehensive and wide-ranging discussion of the role of local preachers within Methodism, see the articles in Geoffrey Milburn and Margaret Batty (eds), *Workaday preachers: the story of Methodist local preaching* (Peterborough, 1995).

63 Obelkevich, *Religion and rural society*, p. 223. See R.W. Ambler, *Ranters, revivalists and reformers* (Hull, 1989) pp. 43–4.

64 'Men wanted!' in *Joyful News*, 9 July 1885, p. 1.

65 Eliza Champness, *The life-story of Thomas Champness* (London, 1907), Chapter 18.

66 J.B. Brice, *The crowd for Christ* (London, 1935); Amos S. Cresswell, *The story of Cliff* (Calver, 1983).

67 Reference to the Primitive Methodist training home can be found in Denis Crane, *James Flanagan: the story of a remarkable career* (London, 1906), pp. 158–60. As of 1890, the UMFC had appointed only three connexional evangelists. Efforts to promote lay training had not been started. See *Free Methodist*, 8 May 1890, p. 10.

68 *The Revival*, 23 February 1861, p. 61.

69 'William Carter's work in South London' in *The Revival*, 24 September 1863, p. 201. For a full account, see William Carter, *The power of grace. Results of theatre preaching, extraordinary tea meetings, and mothers' meetings, in the south of London* (London, 1863); William Carter, *The power of truth: or, results of theatre preaching and extraordinary tea meetings in South London* (London, 1865).

70 Shaftesbury was an active supporter of Carter's work both in South London and in the

'theatre movement'. See 7th Earl Shaftesbury (Anthony Ashley Cooper), *Speech of the Rt. Hon. the Earl of Shaftesbury, in the House of Lords, February 24, 1860, on the holding of special religious services in theatres* (London, 1860).

71　For the full account of Weaver's experiences at Hollinwood, see Paterson, *Richard Weaver*, pp. 162–72.

72　Smith, *Life and work*, pp. 131–36, 144–48. See also David Lazell, *Gypsy from the forest* (Bridgend, 1997), pp. 49–54.

73　Smith, *Life and work*, p. 161.

74　*Ibid.*, p. 162.

75　Paterson, *Richard Weaver*, p. 172.

76　Crane, *James Flanagan*, p. 79. See also Samuel Horton, *From coal mine to pulpit: life story of James Flanagan* (London, 1938); R.W. Russell, *The life of James Flanagan* (London, n.d.).

77　The Forward Movement was an initiative within Wesleyan Methodism spearheaded by the Reverend Hugh Price Hughes. He believed Methodism needed to shift its focus from one concerned only with personal salvation to one which also dealt with the social condition of the individual. To this end, a number of urban missions were established in large English cities which sought to alleviate poverty as well as promote the gospel. See Philip S. Bagwell, *Outcast London: a Christian response* (London, 1987), pp. 6–7.

78　Crane, *James Flanagan*, p. 117.

79　Ella K. Crossley, *John B. Bayliffe: a twentieth century messenger of God* (London, 1952), p. 65.

80　Wright, *Thomas Langton*, p. 11.

81　William Carter (ed.), *Isaac Marsden, of Doncaster: his character, work, studies, experiences, and revivalistic achievements* (London, 1880), p. 6.

82　For a printed example of this custom, see Joshua Poole, *The extraordinary life story of 'Fiddler Joss', as told by himself, to a great public meeting at Surrey Chapel, the Reverend Newman Hall, presiding* (London, 1866). Thirty years later Henry Thorne gave his testimony to a woman's meeting during the Ramsgate United Mission. The testimony was entitled 'From the stage to the cross; or, the story of my life'. See *The Christian*, 3 April 1891, p. 22.

83　'England – British Evangelists' in *The Revival*, 30 October 1862, p. 201.

84　William Sampson did this because he knew it was considered unusual and would attract attention. See William Sampson, *Just in time* (London, 1902), p. 88.

85　'Mr Thomas Dinsdale, the "Hallelujah Preacher"' in *'Joyful News' Banner of Hope* (August 1892), p. 121.

86　Wright, *Saved just in time*, p. 12.

87　David Whiteley (ed.), *Illustrious local preachers* (Bradford, 1891), p. 209.

88　Flynn, *Cornwall*, pp. 79–80.

89　R.C. Morgan, *Richard Weaver*, p. 84.

90　William Hickingbotham was in the habit of addressing everyone about the state of their souls. See Barfoot, *Diamond in the rough*, pp. 88–107 for numerous examples.

91　'A story of an engine driver' in *The Revival*, 2 March 1861, p. 66.

92　Carter (ed.), *Isaac Marsden*, p. 8.

93　Crossley, *John B. Bayliffe*, p. 27.

94　Varley, Jr, *Henry Varley*, pp. 230–3.

95　*Ibid.*, pp. 207–8. Anti-Catholicism was a common theme in several of the biographies. See also Robert Flockhart, *The street preacher, being the autobiography of Robert Flockhart* (ed. Thomas Guthrie, Edinburgh, 1858).

96　Reverend G. Middleton, *Son of Thunder: or, a life sketch of Charles Bayliss, commonly called 'Ironsides'* (2nd edn, London, 1874), p. 98.

97　Moses Welsby ('Owd Mo'), *From coal-pit to Joyful News Mission* (5th edn, Rochdale,

n.d.), p. 67.
98 The quote is from the *Aberdeen Journal* and included in a report in *Revival Advocate* (May 1859), p. 530.
99 *The Revival*, 30 June 1860, p. 204.
100 *Ibid.*, 30 April 1863, pp. 205–6.
101 *Ibid.*, 21 January 1864, pp. 33–4.
102 *Ibid.*, 31 August 1865, p. 129.
103 'A defence of some rough evangelists' in *Ibid.*, 2 January 1869, p. 9.
104 'Five weeks among the Woolwich boys' in *Ibid.* 3 November 1860, p. 139.
105 Middleton, *Son of thunder*, pp. 32, 44.
106 'Connexional evangelism' in *Free Methodist*, 31 October 1895, p. 740.
107 William Booth, *How to reach the masses with the gospel* (London, 1872), p. 127.
108 'A defence of some rough evangelists' in *The Revival*, 2 January 1868, p. 9.
109 'Tunbridge Wells' in *Ibid.*, 8 March 1862, pp. 78–9.
110 Mahomet, *Street arab*, p. 99.
111 Middleton, *Son of thunder*, pp. 51–2; R.C. Morgan, *Richard Weaver*, p. 45.
112 John Walsh has some interesting ideas about the ritual nature of much of this popular violence. See John Walsh, 'Methodism and the mob' in *Popular Belief and Practice: Studies in Church History*, 8 (Cambridge, 1972), pp. 213–27
113 'Gladstone Music Hall, Leicester' in *The Revival*, 1 July 1869, p. 12.
114 William Corbridge in *Addresses*, p. 10.
115 Foster, *Praying Billy*, pp. 44–55.
116 Middleton, *Son of thunder*, p. 51.
117 Crane, *James Flanagan*, p. 85.
118 Middleton, *Son of thunder*, pp. 57–8, 61.
119 Crossley, *John B. Bayliffe*, pp. 24–5.
120 Willis, *Taproom to pulpit*, p. 23.
121 Carter (ed.), *Isaac Marsden*, p. 11.
122 Thorne, *The converted wrestler*, p. 28.
123 Welsby, *From coal-pit*, p. 88.
124 Wright, *Saved just in time*, pp. 25–6; Watson, *Thomas Langton*, pp. 144–8.
125 Welsby, *From coal-pit*, p. 106.
126 Whittle, *'Owd Roger'*, p. 62.
127 Robinson's reminiscences were attached to the back of Flockhart's own account. See Flockhart, *The street preacher*, p. 168.
128 Murray, *Gipsy Smith*, p. 10.
129 These opinions are taken from a press notice of Holland's mission in Darlaston, which was published in Holland, *Story of my life*, p. 49.

CHAPTER SIX

1 See the work of Callum Brown, 'Did urbanization secularize Britain?' in *Urban History Yearbook* (1988), pp. 1–14; Steve Bruce (ed.), *Religion and modernization: sociologists and historians debate the secularization thesis* (Oxford, 1992); Jeffrey Cox, *English churches in a secular society: Lambeth 1870–1930* (Oxford, 1982); Hugh McLeod, *Religion and irreligion in Victorian England: how secular was the working class?* (Bangor, 1993); and Stephen Yeo, *Religion and voluntary organisations in crisis* (London, 1976).
2 Surprisingly, little historical research has been devoted to an analysis of this Welsh revival. See Eifion Evans, *The Welsh revival of 1904* (Port Talbot, 1969) and Christopher Turner, 'Revivals and popular religion in Victorian and Edwardian Wales' (unpub. PhD diss., University of Aberystwyth, 1979). Recent surveys of modern Welsh history make only the briefest references to the 1904–5 revival. See John Davies, *A history of Wales*

(London, 1993), pp. 505–7; K.O. Morgan, *Rebirth of a nation: Wales 1880–1980* (Oxford, 1981), pp. 134–5.

3 See Kermit Staggers, 'Reuben A. Torrey, American fundamentalist, 1856–1928' (unpub. PhD diss., Claremont Graduate School, 1986) and Mark Toone, 'Evangelicalism in transition: a comparative analysis of the work and theology of D.L. Moody and his protégés, Henry Drummond and R.A. Torrey' (unpub. PhD diss., St Andrews, 1988).

4 For a helpful summary of some of the main features of a revival definition see Russell Richey, 'Revivalism: in search of a definition' in *Wesleyan Theological Journal*, 28 (1993), pp. 165–75.

5 John Kent, *Holding the fort: studies in Victorian revivalism* (London, 1978), p. 18.

6 J.C.H., 'Revivals' in *Evangelical Magazine* (1859), p. 699.

7 Reverend William Unsworth, 'What is a revival of religion?' in *Joyful News*, 23 August 1900, p. 4.

8 Anon., *Moody and Sankey, the new evangelists, their lives and labours; together with a history of the present great religious movement* (London, [1875]), p. 4.

9 Reverend Theodore Cuyler, 'The next revival' in *The Christian*, 19 November 1903, p. 11.

10 William Arthur, *May we hope for a great revival?* (London, 1859), p. 4.

11 There are numerous examples of this trend, some of which include William S. Allen, *Revivals of religion and how to bring them about* (Manchester, 1876), pp. 3–4, and the frequent references to local revivals in various Methodist periodicals such as *Joyful News* and the *Free Methodist*.

12 R.A. Torrey, *How to work for Christ. A compendium of effective methods* (London, 1893), p. 280.

13 Reverend Samuel Garratt, 'Revivals and missions' in *The Christian*, 14 August 1873, p. 8.

14 Dr I.C. Jones, 'Introduction' in Jessie Penn-Lewis, *The awakening in Wales and some of the hidden springs* (London, 1905), p. 5.

15 'The revival in Wales' in *The Christian*, 1 December 1904, p. 10.

16 William T. Stead, 'The revival in the west' in W.T. Stead, *Revival pamphlets* (London, 1905), p. 62. This work is sometimes titled *The revival of 1905* or *The coming revival*.

17 W. Monro Collings, 'The keynote of revival' in *The Christian*, 4 April 1895, p. 11.

18 Reverend William Unsworth, 'What is a revival of religion?' in *Joyful News*, 23 August 1900, p. 4 and W.Y. Fullerton, *F.B. Meyer: a biography* (London and Edinburgh, 1929), p. 40.

19 Henry R. Cripps, 'Are we ready for revival?' in *The Christian*, 22 August 1895, p. 6.

20 Cripps, however, does not include works such as starting prayer meetings or house-to-house visitation like other evangelicals did. See Reverend W. Percy Hicks, *Life story of Evan Roberts and stirring experiences in the Welsh revival* (London, 1906), p. 94 and R.A. Torrey, 'The Torrey-Alexander mission' in *The Christian*, 4 June 1903, p. 12.

21 'Prayer in connexion with revival' in *The Christian*, 3 September 1859, p. 41.

22 E.G.F., 'Revival' in *Ibid.*, 21 July 1892, p. 9.

23 John Bain, 'Prayer for revival answered' in *Ibid.*, 14 April 1892, p. 14.

24 'The history of American revivals' quoted in Hicks, *Life story*, p. 95.

25 *Ibid.*

26 R.A. Torrey, 'The place of prayer in revival' in R.A. Torrey (ed.), *How to promote and conduct a successful revival. With suggestive outlines* (London, 1901), p. 28.

27 Torrey, *How to work*, pp. 284–6.

28 'The Torrey-Alexander Mission' in *The Christian*, 4 June 1903, p. 12.

29 *The Revival*, 10 September 1859, p. 53 and *The Christian*, 21 July 1892, p. 9. In the latter, E.G.F. remarked, 'Alas, our churches resemble too much the dry bones in Ezekiel's vision. There is no lack of organizations and unions and guilds, but we want the living breath, and for this we must pray specially.'

30 Reverend H.W. Williams, 'The means of securing a revival of religion' in *Wesleyan Methodist Magazine* (1881), p. 94.

31 Reverend R.W. Dale, 'The Holy Spirit in the conversion of men' in *The evangelical revival and other sermons* quoted in *Ibid.*, p. 96.

32 Reverend J. Idrisyn Jones, 'Is a revival at hand?' in *The Christian*, 17 March 1892, p. 10.

33 This idea is from an article of a similar nature by William Blake, 'May we expect a revival?' in *Ibid.*, 21 April 1892, p. 12.

34 David Bebbington, *Evangelicalism in modern Britain: a history from the 1730s to the 1980s* (London, 1989), pp. 145–6.

35 This controversy erupted when Spurgeon accused the Baptist Union of 'downgrading' traditional evangelical doctrines like those relating to the atonement, scripture, sin and hell. He eventually seceded from the Union in protest. See Gerald Parsons, 'From Dissenters to Free Churchmen: the transitions of Victorian Nonconformity' in Gerald Parsons (ed.), *Religion in Victorian Britain* (5 vols., Manchester, 1988, 1997), i (*Traditions*), p. 107.

36 'The "Daily News" on the religious census' in *British Weekly*, 24 December 1886, p. 2.

37 Reverend Canon H. Scott Holland quoted in 'Symposium on the religious census of London' in *Daily News*, 16 July 1903, p. 8.

38 John Brash, 'Why does Christianity fail?' in *King's Highway* (1890), pp. 112–13.

39 Reverend R.W. Dale, *The old evangelicalism and the new* (London, 1889), pp. 20, 28.

40 'After fifty years' in *The Christian*, 12 April 1984, p. 10.

41 Harold Murray, *Sixty years an evangelist: an intimate study of Gipsy Smith* (London and Edinburgh, 1937), p. 52.

42 Reverend Elder Cumming, 'The religious condition of the people – no. II' in *The Christian*, 7 January 1892, p. 9.

43 Eliza Champness, *The life-story of Thomas Champness* (London, 1907), pp. 263–72.

44 Reverend Thomas Phillips, 'The drink traffic and spiritual revival' in *The Christian*, 16 June 1904, p. 11.

45 Reverend William Ross, 'Revival our greatest need' in *The Christian*, 12 January 1893, p. 9.

46 Richey, 'Revivalism', pp. 168–9.

47 'Come, thou south wind!' in *The Christian*, 14 April 1892, p. 8.

48 Richey, 'Revivalism', p. 169.

49 Reverend Samuel Garratt, 'The revival of 1859' in *The Christian*, 5 April 1894, p. 10.

50 'Thanksgiving for blessing since 1859' in *Ibid.*, 15 March 1894, p. 9.

51 For categorisations of evangelistic work in Ireland as 'revival' see *Ibid.*, 23 February 1893, p. 20. Gordon Forlong published an article about revivals in mid-century Scotland in *Ibid.*, 14 March 1895, p. 11 and excerpts from the 1859 edition of *The Revival* were reprinted in *Ibid.*, 23 February 1893, p. 20.

52 Eric Hobsbawm, 'Inventing traditions' in Eric Hobsbawm and Terence Ranger (eds), *The invention of tradition* (London, 1992), p. 1.

53 *Ibid.*, p. 2.

54 Bessie Howieson, 'The Irish revival of '59' in *The Christian*, 13 June 1895, p. 18.

55 Martin Hope Sutton, 'The revival of 1859. Some of its fruits' in *The Christian*, 4 July 1895, p. 16.

56 For details of Paton's conference, see *The Christian*, 24 March 1892, p. 8. Notice of the Thanksgiving meetings is in *Ibid.*, 15 March 1894, p. 9 and 9 May 1895, pp. 10–11. The Dundee conference is recorded in *Ibid.*, 27 September 1894, pp. 12–13. The long-standing Dublin Believers' Meeting devoted its 1891 annual conference to 'a call to prayer for a spiritual revival'. See *Ibid.*, 11 June 1891, p. 21.

57 Christian workers of the female persuasion were asked to submit written reminiscences because, as one organiser put it 'few women's voices [were] equal to so large a hall'. See 'Day of thanksgiving' in *Ibid.*, 22 March 1894, p. 8.

58 'Thanksgiving meetings' in *Ibid.*, 9 May 1895, p. 11.
59 *Ibid.*, p. 10.
60 'The Welsh revival' in *The Times*, 13 February 1905, p. 9.
61 'Messrs Moody and Sankey in Glasgow' in *Glasgow Herald*, 9 February 1874, p. 4.
62 J. Kennedy MacLean, *Torrey and Alexander: the story of their lives* (London, 1905), p. 63.
63 See William Booth, *Addresses by the Reverend W. Booth, Mr W. Corbridge, and Mr E. Cadman, on 'Hallelujah Bands', and their work* (Lye, 1891) and Reverend Thomas Whitehouse, *Great awakening in the Black Country; and an effort to reach the masses: with a brief sketch of the Hallelujah Band* (West Bromwich, 1875).
64 'Reverend G. Warner among the Durham miners' in *Primitive Methodist*, 22 January 1885, p. 51.
65 'The revival in the Rhondda valley' in *South Wales Daily News*, 4 April 1879, p. 3.
66 See 'The Welsh revival' in *The Times*, 3 January 1905, p. 12.
67 'The religious revival in Wales' in *Ibid.*, 31 January 1905, p. 7. The author of these reports, Dr J. Morris Jones, however, later claimed he had said no such thing. See 'The revival in Wales' in *Ibid.*, 11 February 1905, p. 8.
68 There are numerous accounts of Evan Roberts' life and activities. See Evans, *Welsh revival*; Hicks, *Life story*; W.T. Stead, *Revival*, pp. 41–54; and Arthur Goodrich et. al., *The story of the Welsh revival as told by eyewitnesses together with a sketch of Evan Roberts and his message to the world* (Chicago, 1905).
69 'The work in Wales' in *The Christian*, 11 May 1905, p. i.
70 *Western Mail* quoted in 'The Welsh revival' in *Ibid.*, 24 November 1904, p. 24; and Goodrich, *Story of the Welsh revival*, p. 42.
71 Stead, *Revival*, p. 29.
72 'The Welsh revival' in *The Times*, 3 January 1905, p. 12.
73 Henry T. Smart, *Thomas Cook's early ministry* (London, 1892), pp. 71–80. Reverend Thomas Cook was the first Wesleyan connexional evangelist, appointed in 1882 and responsible to the Home Missionary Committee Secretary.
74 Reverend D. M. Phillips, Tylorstown in *British Weekly*, quoted in Goodrich, *Story of the Welsh revival*, p. 85.
75 *Ibid.*, p. 77.
76 'The Torrey-Alexander Mission' in *The Times*, 8 February 1905, p. 7.
77 Letter from 'Churchman' in *Irish Times*, 4 March 1904, p. 6.
78 Letters of Reverend Hugh Chapman and Reverend Charles Harford, 'The Torrey-Alexander Mission' in *The Times*, 9 February 1905, p. 9.
79 Price's letter to the *Western Mail* is quoted in full in Reverend J. Vyrnwy Morgan, *The Welsh religious revival, 1904–5: a retrospect and a criticism* (London, 1909), pp. 141–5.
80 'Native-born Cymro', and 'The religious revival in Wales' in *The Times*, 4 February 1905, p. 8.
81 'The Welsh revival' in *Ibid.*, 3 January 1905, p. 12.
82 'Steps towards reality' in *Christian World*, 22 January 1890, p. 64.
83 'Congregationalism in 1890' in *The Independent and Nonconformist*, 2 January 1890, p. 6.
84 Reverend K. C. Anderson, 'Revival and intellectual reaction' in Reverend T. Rhondda Williams (ed.), *The true revival versus Torreyism* (2nd edn, London, 1905), p. 16.
85 James M. Dixon, *Messrs Moody and Sankey: a peep behind the curtain* (n.p., 1878), p. 2.
86 'Torrey-Alexander mission' in *Irish Times*, 17 March 1904, p. 7.
87 [William Sampson], *Strange but true. Experiences of William Sampson, the Cornish evangelist* (London, 1894), p. 58.
88 Geoffrey Rowell, *Hell and the Victorians* (London, 1974), p. 13.
89 Bebbington, *Evangelicalism*, pp. 144–5.
90 John Page Hopps, *Mr Moody's late sermon on hell. A lecture* (Glasgow, 1874), p. 2.

91   A.H. Moncur Sime, 'Dr Torrey's idea of eternal torment' in Williams (ed.), *Torreyism*, p. 50.
92   Bebbington, *Evangelicalism*, p. 145 and Charlotte E. Woods, *Memoirs and letters of Canon Hay Aitken* (London, 1928), pp. 70–81.
93   'Torrey-Alexander mission' in *Irish Times*, 17 March 1904, p. 7.
94   Bebbington, *Evangelicalism*, p. 141.
95   Stead, *Revival*, p. 8.
96   *Ibid.*, pp. 3–8.
97   Frederic Whyte, *The life of W.T. Stead* (2 vols., London, 1925), i, pp. 159–84.
98   *Ibid.*, p. 325 ff. Stead compiled these messages into two volumes. See Julia [Julia A. Ames], *Letters from Julia; or, light from the borderland* (transmitted by W.T. Stead, London, 1898) and Idem., *After death: a personal narrative* (ammanuensis W.T. Stead, ed. by Estelle Stead, London, 1914).
99   He wrote articles for the *Daily Chronicle* and the *Christian World*, and gave an interview to the *Methodist Times*. All three of these articles are reprinted in Stead, *Revival*, pp. 23–40.
100 Stead, *Revival*, p. 149.
101 'London for Christ' in *The Christian*, 27 March 1891, pp. 18–19.
102 'The Welsh revival' in *The Times*, 3 January 1905, p. 12.
103 'The religious revival in Wales' in *Ibid.*, 24 January 1905, p. 8.
104 'The revival in Wales' in *Ibid.*, 6 February 1905, p. 8.
105 'The revival in Wales' in *Ibid.*, 16 January 1905, p. 8.
106 Silas Henn, 'Means for promoting a revival of religion' in *Revival Advocate* (January 1859), p. 384.
107 Reverend William Unsworth, 'What is a revival of religion?' in *Joyful News*, 23 August 1900, p. 4. For other examples, see Reverend Newman Hall, 'Prayer and revival' in *The Christian*, 5 April 1894, p. 11; Torrey, *How to promote*, pp. 15–17.
108 Champness, *Life-story*, pp. 218–26.
109 H[enry] T. C[hapman], 'A glorious revival at Leeds' in *Free Methodist*, 6 February 1890, pp. 13–14.
110 J. Stapleton, 'How to get a revival' in *Joyful News*, 16 September 1897, p. 4.
111 Stead, *Revival*, pp. 94–6. Other evangelists, like Gipsy Smith, also used decision cards. See Murray, *Sixty years*, pp. 57–60.
112 W.R. Ward, 'The evangelical revival in Britain' in Sheridan Gilley and W.J. Shiels (eds), *The history of religion in Britain* (Oxford, 1994), p. 252.
113 There are numerous instances of Roberts' harangues. See *The Times*, 10 January 1905, p. 9; 16 January 1905, p. 8; 24 January 1905, p. 8. Reverend Peter Price also referred to what he called Roberts' 'bad temper' in Morgan, *Welsh religious revival*, p. 145.
114 Edward Storrow, 'Button-holding' in *The Christian*, 1 October 1891, p. 9.
115 *The Christian* ran a series of articles describing the theory behind aggressive work and offering practical advice on how to do it. D.M. Drysdale, 'Aggressive work' in *Ibid.*, 16 November 1893, p. 16, and subsequent issues.
116 'A girl minister' in *Christian Mission Magazine* (1878), p. 120.
117 Garratt in *The Christian*, 5 April 1894, p. 10.
118 Anderson in Williams (ed.), *Torreyism*, p. 80.
119 'Testimony of David Dickie' in *Ibid.*, p. 84.
120 For these criticisms in a local context, see the correspondence sparked by Torrey's mission in Dublin in *Irish Times*, 5 March 1904, p. 9 and 7 March 1904, p. 6.
121 Reverend G. Campbell Morgan, 'The lesson of the revival' in Goodrich, *Story of the Welsh revival*, p. 50.
122 Torrey, *How to promote*, p. 5.
123 Reverend J.A. Watts in *Free Methodist*, 21 November 1895, p. 783.
124 Woods, *Canon Hay Aitken*, p. 206.

125 *Ibid.*
126 Murray, *Sixty years*, pp. 104–5.
127 *Ibid.*, p. 43.
128 F.M. Davenport, *Primitive traits in religious revivals: a study in mental and social evolution* (New York, 1905), pp. 213–4.
129 Bebbington, *Evangelicalism*, pp. 151, 162.
130 Dr A. Lowrey, 'Holiness and revivals' in *Primitive Methodist*, 22 January 1885, p. 55.
131 Reverend I.E. Page, *The revival we need. A revival of scriptural holiness* (London, 1871), p. 6.
132 See, for example, the meetings conducted by Reverend Thomas Cook, described in *King's Highway* (1886), pp. 133–4 and 231–7.

CONCLUSION

1 Reverend R.W. Dale, *The old evangelicalism and the new* (London, 1889), pp. 20–5.

Bibliography

MANUSCRIPTS

Bolton Central Library Archives, Bolton
  Bolton Evangelical Revival Committee, 1860. Visitation Reports, FZ/6/1–16.
British Library
  Booth Papers. Vol. V–VIII. Letters of Catherine Booth, Ad. Mss 64803–64806.
Cliff College, Calver, Derbyshire
  Folder of letters from Reverend Thomas Champness, 1896–1905, C1.
  Letters from Reverend Thomas Champness, mainly to Ernest C. Cooper, 1893–6, C2.
  Thomas D. Meadley, 'Thomas Champness – Joyful News Centenary 1883–1983' (Joyful News Bookroom, 1982), typescript, C14.
  Eliza Champness, 'The story of the Joyful News mission', Rochdale, January 1899, typescript, C17.
  Diary of Mary Jane Smith (later Norwell), C25.

Lambeth Palace Library, London
  Tait Correspondence. Letters to Archbishop A.C. Tait, vols. 94, 209.
Methodist Archives and Research Centre, John Rylands Library, Manchester
  Diary of Billy Bray.
Moody Bible Institute, Chicago, Illinois
  Letters of Mrs D.L. Moody. Letters to D.L. Moody, filing drawer 22.
  Diary of Emma Revell Moody, filing drawer 23.
  Uncatalogued volumes of D.L. Moody's letters, 13 vols., Vol. 1: 1854–79, Vol. 2: 1879–86.
Oberlin College Archives, Oberlin, Ohio
  Charles Grandison Finney Papers. Correspondence, Series I and II.
Presbyterian Historical Society, Belfast
  Minutes of the Social Services Committee (Deaconess Guild), Vol. 2, 1913–37 (located in the Strong Room).
Public Records Office of Northern Ireland, Belfast
  Armour Papers, D.1792/A2.
  Diary of the minister of Kilwarlin Moravian Church, Kilwarlin, Co. Down, MIC 1F/2A.
Representative Church Body Library, Dublin
  Correspondence of Reverend Edward Adderly Stopford, Archdeacon of Meath, 1844–72, 77/1–3.
Rochdale Central Library Archives, Rochdale
  Commercial and Trade Directory, 1888–1916.
  1891 Census for Castleton Hall.
Rossendale Collection, Rawtenstall District Central Library
  Haslingden Gospel Mission minute books, 1890–1983, Rc 289.9 HAS.
Salvation Army International Heritage Centre, London
  Booth Correspondence, 1871–1881.
  Notes of a lecture on life story, Elijah Cadman file.
  Letters from George Scott Railton. Female Ministry file, Josiah Taylor file.
  George Scott Raliton, 'What ought a woman to do?', 1882, typescript, Female Ministry file.

DENOMINATIONAL AND INSTITUTIONAL

Methodism

General minutes made at the … annual conference … of the Primitive Methodist Connexion, 1860. London, 1860.
Minutes of the proceedings of the … United Methodist Free Churches. London, 1859.
Minutes of the … Methodist New Connexion conference. 1859.
Minutes of the … Wesleyan Methodist Conference. 1803 (1862 edn).

Hansard's parliamentary debates ... 3rd series 1875. Vol. CCXXV. London, 1875.

Evangelical Alliance

Conference for Promoting Christian Union. *A brief statement of the proceedings of the Conference in Liverpool for promoting Christian union, and of the object of the proposed Evangelical Alliance.* London, 1845.
Conference on Christian Union. *Held in Liverpool on Wednesday the 1st of October, 1845. And subsequent days.* Liverpool, 1845.
The Evangelical Alliance for the promotion of Christian union. *A brief statement of its objects, basis and results.* London, 1859.
The Evangelical Alliance: its aims and operations. London, 1861.
Anon (ed.). *Present aspects of the Irish revival. Being papers read at the 13th conference of the Evangelical Alliance, held at Nottingham, 1860.* London, 1861.
Proceedings of the 13th conference of the Evangelical Alliance.
Report presented to the 13th annual conference, held in Belfast, September 1859. With a list of subscribers. London, 1860.
Report presented to the 14th annual conference, held in Nottingham, October 1860. With a list of subscribers. London, 1861.
Transactions of the 13th annual conference, held at Belfast, September 20–24, 1859. London, 1859.

Evangelical Free Church

Proceedings of the First National Council of the Evangelical Free Churches (the Fourth Free Church Congress) held at Nottingham, March 10–12, 1896. London, 1896.

Irish Evangelization Society

Occasional Paper. November 1874. Dublin, 1874.

North London Deaconess' Institution

The Second Annual Report and balance sheet of the North London Deaconess' Institution. London, 1863.
The Seventh Annual Report and balance sheet of the North London Deaconesses' Institution. London, 1868.

Open Air Mission

Reports of the Open Air Mission. 1854–7, 63, 1878–9.

Salvation Army

Reports of the Salvation Army
  The advance of the Salvation Army (1880, 1886).
  All about the Salvation Army (1882).
  The Salvation war (1883).
  All about the Salvation Army (1888).
  F. Booth-Tucker, *A Year of Grace: being a sketch of the advance of the Salvation Army, 1893–4* (London, 1894).

PERIODICALS

Magazines

All the World
Banner of Holiness
Baptist Magazine
Bible Christian Magazine
British Evangelist
Christian Standard (ed. J. Grant)
Christian Standard (ed. W. Threadgold)
Christian World Magazine and Family Visitor
The Congregationalist
The Deliverer
East London Evangelist
  (later *Christian Mission Magazine*, *The Salvationist*, *War Cry*)
Evangelical Christendom
Experience
Holiness Advocate
The Intercessor
Joyful News 'Banner of Hope'
King's Highway
The Lancet
Life of Faith
Literary Guide and Rationalist Review
Methodist New Connexion Magazine
Penuel
Primitive Methodist Magazine
Primitive Methodist Quarterly Review
Quarterly Review (London)
The Revival
  (after 1870 *The Christian*)
Revival Advocate and Record of the Churches
The Revivalist (London, Louth and Hull)

Times of Blessing
Union Magazine for Sunday School Teachers
United Methodist Free Churches Magazine
Wesleyan Methodist Magazine

Newspapers

Armagh Guardian
Ballymena Observer
Belfast Daily Mercury
Belfast News-Letter
British Messenger (Stirling)
British Standard (London)
British Weekly
The Christian (London)
Christian World (London)
Church Times
Coleraine Chronicle
Daily Express (Dublin)
Daily News (London)
Daily Telegraph (London)
Dublin Evening Mail
Flag of Ireland (Dublin)
Freeman's Journal (Dublin)
Free Methodist (London)
Glasgow Herald
Illustrated London News
Irish Evangelist (Dublin)
Irish Times (Dublin)
Joyful News (Bacup, Stockport)
Leeds Mercury
Londonderry Standard
Manchester Guardian
Medical Times and Gazette (London)
The Methodist (London)
Methodist Evangelist
The Methodist Recorder (London)
Morning Advertiser (London)
Morning Chronicle (London)
The Nation (Dublin)
Newcastle Chronicle
The Nonconformist and Independent (London)
North British Daily Mail (Glasgow)
Northern Whig (Belfast)

Pall Mall Gazette (London)
Portadown Weekly News
The Primitive Methodist
Public Opinion (London)
Punch (London)
The Record (London)
Revival Times (London)
Saturday Review (London)
Scottish Guardian (Glasgow)
South Wales Daily News (Cardiff)
The Spectator (London)
The Times (London)
War Cry (London)
The Watchman and Wesleyan Advertiser
Wesleyan Times (London)
Western Mail (Cardiff)

OTHER PRINTED SOURCES

Pamphlets

A., O.W.L. *Some reasons why I do not sympathize with the Salvation Army.* London, 1882.
Adams, Reverend David. *The revival at Ahoghill.* Belfast, 1859.
Aitken, Reverend W.H.M.H. *Mr Aitken: his mission to Dublin and his gospel. (Taken from the 'Church Advocate' of February 1, 1884, with notes added).* Dublin, 1884.
——. *Reminiscences of the eleven days' mission held at Swansea, in October 1874, being notes of sermons, etc. ...* London, 1874.
Alexander, James Waddell. *Revival lessons.* Edinburgh, 1859.
Allen, William Shepherd. *Revivalism.* Manchester, 1868.
——. *Revivals of religion and how to bring them about.* Manchester, 1876.
Anon. *Brief history of Merrion Hall, Dublin. 1863–1913.* Dublin, 1913.
Anon. *The great revival. Where is it? What is it? Is it needed here? How may it be obtained?* Nottingham, 1859.
Anon. *The late revival in Ireland in its connexion with religious efforts in London; or, addresses delivered to the missionaries of the London City Mission, by recent visitors to the scene of revival there.* London and Edinburgh, 1860.
Anon. *Merrion Hall Dublin. Centenary. One hundred years of witness, 1863–1963.* N.p., n.d.
Anon. *Shall there be a revival of religion?* Brighton and London, 1859.
Anon (ed.). *Testimony to the Lord's reviving work in Wales, Scotland, Ireland, and Syria, being addresses delivered in Freemason's Hall in the first week of January, 1865.* London, 1865.

Anon. *What doth hinder a great revival?* London, 1861.

Antliff, William. *Woman, her position and mission. A lecture delivered in various places.* 3rd edn, London, 1864.

Armstrong, Miss I.T. *Plea for modern prophetesses.* Glasgow, 1866.

Arthur, Reverend William. *Revival tracts.* London, 1859–60.
  includes: *May we hope for a great revival?*
      The conversion of all England.
      Did Christ die for all?
      Beginning of a great revival: Connor.
      The revival in Ulster: Ahoghill and Ballymena.
      Beginning of a great revival: Ballymena and Coleraine.
      Free, full and present salvation.
      Only believe.

——.*The revival in Ireland.* Abridged from *The Eclectic* (1860), pp. 104–12.

Bell, Reverend Thomas. *Notes on the revival at Newtownards: a letter to James Douglas.* Edinburgh, 1859.

Bolton, Philip. *The revival movement and the way of salvation explained.* London, 1859.

Booth, Catherine. *Female teaching: or, the Reverend A.A. Rees vs. Mrs Palmer, being a reply to the pamphlet by the above gentleman on the Sunderland revival.* 2nd edn, London, 1861.

Booth, William. *Addresses by the Reverend William Booth, Mr W. Corbridge and Mr E Cadman on 'Hallelujah Bands', and their work, with an introduction by Reverend T. Whitehouse.* Lye, 1891.

Brown, Reverend David. *On united and universal prayer throughout the church of God. Being a paper read at the 13th conference of the Evangelical Alliance, held at Nottingham, 1860.* London, 1861.

Bruce, Reverend John. *The revivals and the church.* Edinburgh, 1859.

Bunton, William. 'A visit to Dr Palmer's meetings at the Wesleyan Chapel, 1860', reprinted in *Cake and Cockhorse: the magazine of the Banbury Historical Society,* 8 (1966), pp. 75–7.

Bushnan, J. Stevenson. *Religious revivals in relation to nervous and mental diseases.* London, 1860.

Cardwell, John R. *The ministry of women: a careful comparison of the teaching of the word of God, with present day theories.* Glasgow, n.d.

Carson, James C.L. *Three letters on the revival in Ireland.* Coleraine, 1859.

——. *Additional letters on the revival in Ireland.* London, 1877.

Champness, Reverend Thomas. *Shall Methodism attack the world on 'Joyful News' lines? Being a letter to John Wesley's children by Thomas Champness.* Rochdale, 1888.

A Clergyman of the United Church of England and Ireland. *A tract intended to convey correct notions of conversion according to the sense of Holy Scripture.* Belfast, 1859.

Collett, W.R. *Women's work in the church.* Norwich, 1863.

A Converted Deist. *The revival at St Ives, Cornwall: being a full report of the revival services conducted by the Reverend William, and Mrs Booth*. London, 1862.

Cropp, Reverend John. *Remarks arising from a visit to the north of Ireland, during the revival, September, 1859*. London and Belfast, 1860.

Cuckson, Reverend John. *Religious excitement, a sermon on the Moody & Sankey revival, preached in the Unitarian Church, Newhall Hill, on Sunday, January 31, 1875*. Birmingham, 1875.

Dale, Reverend R.W. *The day of salvation: a reply to the letter of the Archbishop of Canterbury, on Mr Moody & Mr Sankey*. London and Birmingham, 1875.

——. *Mr Moody and Mr Sankey*. London, 1875.

Davies, Reverend John. *Times of refreshing: the revival required at the present crisis*. Gateshead, 1859.

Dixon, James. *Messrs Moody and Sankey: a peep behind the curtain*. N.p., 1878.

Dobbin, Reverend O.T. *Conversion: what it is not and what it is. A sermon on revivals, delivered in the parish church of Ballivor, on Sunday, August 7, 1859*. Dublin and London, 1859.

Gibson, Reverend William. *Present aspects of the Irish revival. A paper read at the 13th conference of the Evangelical Alliance, held at Nottingham, October 1860*. London, 1860.

Goodrich, Arthur et. al. *The story of the Welsh revival as told by eyewitnesses together with a sketch of Evan Roberts and his message to the world*. Chicago, 1905.

Grant, James. *Personal visit to the chief scenes of the religious revivals in the north of Ireland ... Reprinted, with additions from the 'Morning Advertiser'*. London, 1859.

Hammond, W.A. *From darkness to light*. London, 1894.

Holyoake, M. *The afterglow gleamings from the Welsh revival*. London, 1907.

Hopps, John Page. *Mr Moody's late sermon on hell. A lecture*. Glasgow, 1874.

Jackson, Reverend L.W. *A few impressions, by an eyewitness, of D.L. Moody's meetings at Leicester in 1884*. Typescript, Croydon, 1942.

James, Reverend John Angell. 'The bearing of the American revival on the duties and hopes of British Christians' in Charles Reed and J. A. James, *On religious revivals. Two paper read by request at the annual meeting of the Congregational Union*. London, 1858.

——. *On the revival of religion*. London, 1858.

——. *Revival of religion: its principles, necessity, effects*. London, 1859.

Jarbo, Reverend P.J. *A letter to Mrs Palmer, in reference to women speaking in public*. North Shields, 1859.

Kennedy, Reverend John. *Hyper-evangelism. Another gospel, though a mighty power. A review of the recent religious movement in Scotland*. 7th edn, London, 1875.

King, Reverend Francis. *Revivals in religion, with some cautions concerning them, being a lecture, delivered in the scriptural schools, Newry*. Newry, 1859.

Knill, Reverend R. *The influence of pious women in promoting a revival of religion* (Narrative Series No. 800, London, 1830).

Knox, Reverend Robert; Seaver, Reverend Charles; and McCosh, Prof. James. *Religious revivals in the north of Ireland*. Dublin, 1859.

A London Physician. *Emotional goodness; or Moody and Sankey reviewed. The people go mad through religious revivals*. London, 1875.

Lorimer, Reverend John. *The recent great awakening in America, and the lessons which it suggests*. Glasgow and London, 1859.

McFarlane, Jessie. *Scriptural warrant for women to preach the gospel*. Peterhead, n.d.

McIlwaine, Reverend William. *Revivalism reviewed*. Belfast, 1859.

McVicker, J.G. *The revival of 1859*. London, [1898].

Macgill, Reverend Hamilton. *On the present revival of religion in Scotland. A paper read at the conference of the Evangelical Alliance, held at Nottingham, October 1860*. London, 1860.

Massie, James. *Revivals in Ireland: facts, documents and correspondence*. Part 1. London, 1859.

——. *A visit to the scenes of revival in Ireland. The origin, progress and characteristics of the work of 1859*. Parts 2 and 3. London, 1859.

Maynard, John. *The philosophy of revivals*. London, 1867.

Middleton, Lancelot. *The Bible idea of revival; or Isaiah's prophecy spiritualized. A special mission address*. London and Bacup, 1889.

Miller, Walter. *Messrs Moody and Sankey weighed again: being a reply to Mr Leigh's 'Messrs Moody and Sankey weighed in the balances and found wanting'*. London, 1875.

Moore, Reverend Samuel. *The history and prominent characteristics of the present revival in Ballymena and its neighbourhood*. Belfast, 1859.

Morgan, Reverend James. *Thoughts on the revival of 1859*. Belfast, 1859.

Protestant Dissenter. *The Moody and Sankey humbug: recent ridiculous religious(?) revivals rationally reprobated*. London, 1875.

Nixon, Reverend William. *An account of the work of God at Ferryden. With illustrated cases*. London, 1860.

An Old Missioner. *Real revivals*. London, 1916.

Page, Reverend I.E. *The revival we need. A revival of scriptural holiness*. London, 1871.

Popham, J.K. *Moody and Sankey's errors versus the scriptures of truth*. Liverpool, 1875.

A Priest of the Church of England. *The London mission of 1874. A protest against a theory of 'conversion', as preached by some 'missioners'*. London, 1874.

Prime, Samuel Irenæus. *The power of prayer, illustrated in the wonderful displays of Divine grace at the Fulton St., and other meetings in New York*. Edinburgh, 1859.

Rees, Reverend A.A. *Reasons for not co-operating in the alleged 'Sunderland revivals'*. Sunderland, 1859.

Salmon, Reverend George. *Evidence[s] of the work of the Holy Spirit. A sermon preached in St Stephen's Church, Dublin, on Sunday, July 3, 1859. With an appendix on the revival movement in the north of Ireland*. Dublin, 1859.

Saphir, Adolph. *Means of revival from spiritual lukewarmness*. London, 1875.

Scott, Benjamin. *The revival in Ulster: its moral and social results*. London, 1859.

Scott, Reverend Robinson. *The American revival: its facts and lessons. A lecture, delivered in the Centenary Chapel, Dublin*. Dublin, 1860.

Seaver, Reverend Charles. *Religious revivals: two sermons, preached in St John's Church, on Sunday, 10th July*. Belfast, 1859.

Sexton, Dr George. *An impartial review of the revival movement of Messrs Moody and Sankey*. London, 1875.

Shaftesbury, 7th Earl (Anthony Ashley Cooper). *Speech of the Rt. Hon. the Earl of Shaftesbury, in the House of Lords, February 24, 1860, on the holding of special religious services in theatres*. London, 1860.

Small, Reverend James Grindlay. *Restoration and revival; or, times of refreshing*. London, 1859.

Stead, William T. *Revival pamphlets*. London, 1905.
    includes: *The revival in the west.*
               The Torrey and Alexander mission.
               The missions of the National Free Church.
——. *The coming revival: what I have seen and what I hope to see*. London, 1905.

Steane, Reverend Edward (ed.) *The Ulster revival, in its religious features and physiological accidents. Papers read to the conference of the Evangelical Alliance in Belfast, September 22, 1859*. London, 1859.

Stopford, Reverend E.A. *The work and the counterwork; or, the religious revival in Belfast*. Belfast and Dublin, 1859.

Talbot, Reverend Edward (Bishop of Southwark). *The Lord's servant blind and deaf: a sermon on England's call to evangelization*. London, 1909.

[Tarbet, W.] *The revivals of the latter day*. London, [1860].

Thomas, Reverend John. *Sunshine on the 'hills', being a narrative of a revival of the Lord's work at Tredegar, during the visitation of the cholera in the year 1866*. London, n.d.

Venn, Reverend John. *The revival in Wales. A paper read at the conference of the Evangelical Alliance, held at Nottingham, October 1860; with subsequent additions*. London, 1860.

Voysey, Reverend C. *Reverend C. Voysey on Messrs Moody & Sankey. The fallacy of their gospel exposed*. London, 1875.

Wallace, Reverend Robert. *Notes and recollections of a fortnight's tour in the North of Ireland, in the month of August, 1859. With reflections on the work of religious revival in that land*. London, 1859.

A Welseyan Preacher. *Revivalism, its nature, importance, and means of attainment*. London, 1857.

West, Reverend Francis A. *A pastoral letter on the revival of religion: addressed especially to Methodists*. Leeds, 1843.

Whitehouse, Reverend Thomas. *Great awakening in the Black country; and an effort to reach the masses: with a brief sketch of the Hallelujah Band*. West Bromwich, 1875.

Williams, Reverend A. *Weak Points in Mr Moody's teaching*. Kingston-on-Thames and London, 1875.

Young, George Edward. *Bringing in revival. Some practical suggestions and appeals* … 3rd edn, London, 1913.

Young, Reverend Robert. *North of England revivals: prophesying of women*. Newcastle-on-Tyne, 1859.

Biographies, collective biographies, and autobiographies

W.H.M.H. Aitken. Woods, Charlotte. *Memoirs and letters of Canon Hay Aitken*. London, 1928.

John Allen. Railton, G.S. *The salvation navvy*. London, 1880.

Robert Annan. Macpherson, Reverend John. *The Christian hero: a sketch of the life of Robert Annan*. London, 1867.

William Arthur. Stephenson, Thomas B. *William Arthur, a brief biography*. London, 1907.

——. Taggart, Norman. *William Arthur: first among Methodists*. London, 1993.

John Ashworth. Calman, A.L. *The life and labours of John Ashworth*. Manchester, 1875.

Matilda Bass. B., J.V. *She walked with God, and was not, for God took her. Memorials of Mrs Bass*. London, 1881.

Abraham Bastard. Thorne, Samuel Ley. *The Cornish wrestler; or, the life of Abraham Bastard*. 3rd edn, London, [1880].

Elizabeth Baxter. 'Wiseman, Nathaniel' (or J.J. Ellis). *Elizabeth Baxter, saint, evangelist, preacher, teacher and expositor*. London, 1928.

Michael Paget Baxter. 'Wiseman, Nathaniel' (or J.J. Ellis). *Michael Paget Baxter, clergyman, evangelist and philanthropist*. London, 1923.

John Bayliff. Crossley, Ella. *John B. Bayliffe*. London, 1952.

Charles Bayliss. Middleton, George. *Son of thunder, or a life sketch of Charles Bayliss, commonly called 'Ironsides'*. 2nd edn, London, 1874.

S.A. Blackwood. Blackwood, Stevenson Arthur. *Some records of the life of Stevenson Arthur Blackwood, K.C.B. Compiled by a friend and edited by his widow (Harriet S. Blackwood)*. London, 1896.

P.P. Bliss. Whittle, W.D. and Guest, W. *P.P. Bliss, his life and work*. London, 1877.

A.A. Bonar. Bonar, Reverend Andrew A. *Diary and life, edited by his daughter Marjory Bonar*. Reprint, n.p., 1960, of orig. edn, London, 1894.

Bramwell Booth. Booth, Catherine Bramwell. *Bramwell Booth*. London, 1933.

Catherine Booth. Bramwell-Booth, Catherine. *Catherine Booth: the story of her loves*. London, 1970.

——. Stead, William T. *Mrs Booth of the Salvation Army*. London, 1900.

——. Tucker, Frederick St George de L. Booth. *The life of Catherine Booth*. 2 vols., London, 1893.

William Booth. Begbie, Harold. *Life of William Booth, the founder of the Salvation Army*. 2 vols., London, 1920.

——. Stead, W.T. *General Booth: a biographical sketch*. London, 1891.

Billy Bray. Bourne, Frederick W. *The King's son; or a memoir of Billy Bray*. Reprint, London, 1958 of 1937 edn.

George Brealey. Brealey, W.J.H. *'Always abounding': or, recollections of the life and labours of the late George Brealey, the evangelist of the Blackdown Hills*. London, 1889.

Elijah Cadman. Wallis, Humphrey. *The happy warrior: the life story of Commissioner Elijah Cadman*. London, 1927.

Hodgson Casson. Steele, Allen. *Christianity in earnest as exemplified in the life and labours of the Reverend Hodgson Casson*. London, 1853.

Thomas Champness. Champness, Eliza. *The life story of Thomas Champness*. London, 1907.

——. Mee, Josiah. *Thomas Champness as I knew him*. London, [1906].

Thomas Collins. Coley, Reverend Samuel. *The life of the Reverend Thomas Collins*. 2nd edn, London, 1869.

Thomas Cook (Baptist). Pudney, John. *The Thomas Cook story*. London, 1953.

Thomas Cook (Methodist). Cook, Vallance. *Thomas Cook, evangelist, saint. An appreciation*. 2nd edn, London, 1914.

——. Smart, Henry T. *The life of Thomas Cook, evangelist and first principal of Cliff College, Calver*. London, 1913.

——. ——. *Thomas Cook's early ministry: with incidents and suggestions concerning Christian work*. London, 1892.

William Crister. Everett, James. *The Walls End miner; or, a brief memoir of the life of William Crister*. 3rd edn, Manchester, 1850.

Mary Ann Davey. *Told for a memorial. The story of Mary Ann*. London, 1886.

Rosina Davies. Davies, Rosina. *The story of my life*. Llandyssul, 1942.

Emma Davis. Parr, James Tollefree. *Sister Annie: the angel of Blackfriars: or, the sister with the shining face*. 2nd edn, London, 1914.

Geraldine Hooper Dening. Guinness, Fanny. *'She spake of Him': being recollections of the loving labours and early death of the late Mrs Henry Dening*. London and Bristol, 1872.

James Dowdle. Railton, George. *Commissioner Dowdle: the saved railway-guard*. London, 1901.

Henry Drummond. Simpson, James Young. *Henry Drummond*. Edinburgh and London, 1901.

——. Smith, George Adam. *The life of Henry Drummond*. 11th edn, London [1902].

John Ellerthorpe. Woodcock, Henry. *The hero of the Humber; or, the history of the late John Ellerthorpe*. 2nd edn, London, 1880.

Charles Finney. Rosell, Garth and Dupuis, Richard (eds). *The memoirs of Charles G. Finney – the complete restored text*. Grand Rapids, MI, 1989.

——. Hardman, Keith J. *Charles Grandison Finney, 1792–1875: revivalist and reformer*. London, 1987.

James Flanagan. Crane, Denis (pseud.). *James Flanagan, the story of a remarkable career*. London, 1906.
———. Flanagan, James. *Saved! Yet so as by fire*. London, n.d.
———. ———. *Scenes from my life, both grave and gay*. London, 1907.
———. Horton, Samuel. *From coal mine to pulpit: life story of James Flanagan*. London, 1938.
———. Russell, R.W. *The life of James Flanagan*. London, 1920.
Robert Flockhart. Flockhart, Robert. *The street preacher; being the autobiography of Robert Flockhart*. Ed. by Thomas Guthrie, Edinburgh, 1876.
William Foster. Foster, William. *Praying Billy, the street preacher*. 2nd edn, Rochdale, 1901.
Alexander Fullerton. Fullerton, Alexander. *Fifty years an itinerant preacher: being reminiscences of fifty years in the Irish Methodist ministry*. Belfast, [1912].
Charles Garrett. Broadbent, James W. *The people's life of Charles Garrett*. Leeds, [1900].
John Gordon. Brewster, Margaret Maria. *John Gordon, of Pitlurg and Parkhill; or, memories of a standard-bearer. By his widow*. London, 1885.
Hay Macdowall Grant. Brewster, Margaret Maria. *Hay Macdowall Grant, of Arndilly: his life, labours and teaching*. London, 1877.
Walford Davis Green. *A brief memoir by his son, Walford Davis Green, M.P. With sermons selected ...* London, 1904.
Benjamin Gregory. Gregory, J.R. (ed.). *Autobiographical reflections. Edited, with memorials of his later life by his eldest son*. London, 1903.
Henry Griffiths. Wightman, Mrs Julia Bainbrigge. *Sunset on the line; or, the story of Henry Griffiths*. London, 1863.
Fanny Guinness. Guinness, Lucy. *Enter thou: pages from the life story of Fanny E. Guinness*. Regions Beyond Missionary Union, n.d.
———. Guinness, Michele. *The Guinness Legend*. London, 1990.
Edward Payson Hammond. Headley, Reverend P.C. *The reaper and the harvest; or, scenes and incidents in connexion with the work ... of Reverend Edward Payson Hammond, M.A.* New York and London, 1884.
———. Elis (pseud.) *Good will to men: a narrative of the evangelistic labours of Mr Edward Payson Hammond, and of the blessed results which attended them during his visit to Glasgow in the spring of 1861*. London, 1861.
Richard Hampton. Christophers, Samuel W. *Foolish Dick: a biography of Richard Hampton*. London, 1873.
William Haslam. Haslam, Reverend William. *From death into life: or, twenty years of my ministry*. London, 1894.
———. ———. *'Yet not I': or, more years of my ministry*. London, 1882.
Roger Haydock. Whittle, Reverend John. *Owd Roger: Bible colporteur and Primitive Methodist lay preacher*. Blackburn, 1912.
William Hickingbotham. Barfoot, John. *A diamond in the rough; or, Christian heroism in humble life, being jottings concerning that remarkable peasant preacher,*

William Hickingbotham, of Belper, Derbyshire. London, 1874.

Tom Holland. Holland, Tom. *The story of my life.* With a forward by William Nelson. N.p., [1914].

Henry Holloway. Holloway, Henry. *A voice from the convict cell; or, life and conversion of Henry Holloway. With an account of his trials and sufferings as an evildoer; also, the bright side of his life, and success as a preacher of the gospel among the working classes.* 3rd edn. Manchester, [1877].

Hugh Price Hughes. Hughes, Dorothea. *The life of Hugh Price Hughes.* London, 1904.

Russell Hurdich. 'Septima' (ie. —— Hurditch). *Peculiar people: an account of the religious experiences of C.R. Hurditch and his family.* London, 1935.

Jonathan Ireland. Ireland, Jonathan. *Jonathan Ireland the street preacher. An autobiography.* Ed. by John Smith. London, n.d.

Thomas Jackson. Potter, William. *Thomas Jackson of Whitechapel. A record of 50 years of social and evangelistic enterprise.* Liverpool, 1929.

Jacoby. Maclean, J. Kennedy. *Under two masters; the story of Jacoby, Dr Torrey's assistant.* London, 1905.

Charles Jeffries. Claughton, Lillian. *Charles H. Jeffries: from 'skeleton' to salvationist leader.* London, 1946.

Seth and Frank Joshua. Rees, Reverend Thomas Mardy. *Seth Joshua and Frank Joshua: the renowned evangelists.* Wrexham, 1926.

Gawin Kirkham. Cockram, Frank. *Gawin Kirkham: the open-air evangelist.* London, n.d.

Thomas Langton. Watson, Isaac Crowther. *The life story of Thomas Langton, of Malton, the Yorkshire evangelist.* Rochdale, 1895.

Peter Mackenzie. Dawson, Joseph. *Peter Mackenzie, his life and labours.* 3rd edn, London, 1896.

——. Davis, George W. 'Reverend Peter Mackenzie 1824–1895: preacher and lecturer' in *Scottish Methodism: the journal of the Scottish Branch of the Wesley Historical Society* 28 (1998), pp. 5–13.

Jessie McFarlane. G., H.I. *In memoriam. Jessie McFarlane: a tribute of affection.* London, 1872.

John McNeill. Gammie, Alexander. *Reverend John McNeill: his life and work.* London, 1933.

Albert Mahomet. Mahomet, Albert John. *From street arab to pastor.* Cardiff, 1901.

Isaac Marsden. Carter, William (ed.). *Isaac Marsden of Doncaster: his character, work, studies, experiences, and revivalistic achievements.* London, 1880.

——. Taylor, John. *Reminiscences of Isaac Marsden, of Doncaster.* London, 1883.

Catherine Marsh. O'Rorke, L.E. *The life and friendships of Catherine Marsh.* London, 1917.

Alexander Marshall. Hawthorne, John. *Alexander Marshall. Evangelist, author and pioneer.* London, 1929.

Duncan Matheson. Macpherson, Reverend John. *Life and labours of Duncan*

Matheson, the Scottish evangelist. London, 1871.

F.B. Meyer. Fullerton, William. *F.B. Meyer: a biography*. London and Edinburgh, 1929.

Parkinson Milson. Shaw, George. *The life of Reverend Parkinson Milson. [With extracts from his journals]*. London, 1893.

Dwight Lyman Moody. Anon. *The coming tribulation! Authentic and exhaustive account of the lives and labours of those American evangelists, D.L. Moody and Ira D. Sankey ... and a choice of the ... sacred songs and hymns sung by Mr Sankey*. London, 1875.

——. Anon. *Moody and Sankey*. London, 1875.

——. Anon. *Moody and Sankey, the new evangelists, their lives and labours; together with a history of the present great religious movement*. London, 1875.

——. Anon. *Narrative of Messrs Moody and Sankey's Labors in Great Britain and Ireland, with eleven addresses and lectures in full*. New edition. 2 parts, New York, 1875.

——. Barnwell, R. Grant. *Life of Moody and Sankey, the American evangelists. Together with scenes and incidents of the revival in Great Britain*. Philadelphia, 1875.

——. Batt, Reverend J.H. *Dwight L. Moody: the life work of a modern evangelist*. London, 1900.

——. Boyd, Reverend Robert. *The wonderful career of Moody and Sankey, in Great Britain and America*. New York, 1875.

——. Bradford, Gamaliel. *D.L. Moody, a worker in souls*. New York, 1927.

——. Chapman, Reverend J. Wilbur. *The life and work of Dwight Lyman Moody*. London, 1900.

——. Clark, Rufus Wheelwright. *The work of God in Great Britain: under Messrs Moody and Sankey, 1873 to 1875. With biographical sketches*. New York, 1875.

——. Daniels, Reverend W.H. *D.L. Moody and his work*. London, 1875.

——. The Editor of 'Church and Home'. *The great revival: being an account of the evangelistic labours, in the United Kingdom, of Messrs Moody and Sankey, with biographical sketches and original portraits*. London, 1875.

——. Findlay, James, Jr. *Dwight L. Moody: American evangelist, 1837–1899*. Chicago, 1969.

——. Fitt, A.P. and Moody, W.R. *Life of D.L. Moody*. London, 1900.

——. Hall, John and Stuart, George H. *The American evangelists, D. L. Moody and Ira D. Sankey, in Great Britain and Ireland*. New York, 1875.

——. Lobb, John. *Arrows and andecdotes by Dwight L. Moody: with a sketch of his early life, and the story of the great revival*. London, 1876.

——. Macpherson, Reverend John. *Revival and revival work. A record of the labours of D.L. Moody and I.D. Sankey, and other evangelists*. London, 1875.

——. Moody, Paul. *My father: an intimate portrait of Dwight Moody*. London, 1937.

——. Moody, William R. *The life of D.L. Moody*. Chicago, 1900.

——. ——. *The life of D. L. Moody*. London, 1930, 1937.

——. Morgan, Peter. '... *And some evangelists*'. London, 1956.

——. Nason, Reverend Elias. *The American evangelists, Dwight L. Moody and Ira D. Sankey, with an account of their work in England and America; with a sketch of the lives of P.P. Bliss and Dr Eben Tourjée*. Boston, 1877.

——. Peddie, Mrs Robert (ed.). *A consecutive narrative of the remarkable awakening in Edinburgh, under the labours of Messrs Moody and Sankey, the city ministers and Christian laymen*. London, 1874.

——. Pollock, J.C. *Moody without Sankey*. London, 1963.

——. Ross, William. *Dwight L. Moody, the prince of evangelists*. London, 1926.

Henry Moorhouse. Macpherson, Reverend John. *Henry Moorhouse, the English evangelist*. London, 1881.

G. Campbell Morgan. Murray, Harold. *Campbell Morgan, Bible teacher. A sketch of the great expositor and evangelist*. London, 1938.

David Morgan. Morgan, John James. *The '59 revival in Wales. Some incidents in the life and work of David Morgan, Ysbytty*. Mold, 1909.

R.C. Morgan. Morgan, George E. *'A veteran in revival'. R.C. Morgan: his life and times*. London, 1909.

——. ——. *Mighty days of revival: R.C. Morgan, his life and times*. London, 1922.

Hans Morrison. Coulter, Reverend John. *Hans Morrison, local preacher and Christian worker, being a sketch of the life and labours of Mr Hans Morrison, of Echlinville, Co. Down*. Belfast, 1899.

George Müller. Müller, George. *A narrative of some of the Lord's dealings with George Müller: written by himself*. 2 parts. London, 1837, 1841.

——. Müller, Mrs [Mueller, Susannah Grace]. *Preaching tours and missionary labours of George Müller (of Bristol)*. London, 1883.

John Murfitt. Gauntlett, S.C. *John Murfitt: from miner to major*. London, 1944.

William Murrish. Tyack, W.D. *The miner of Perran-Zabuloe; or, simple records of a good man's life*. London and Leeds, 1866.

John Oxtoby. Leigh, Harvey. *'Praying Johnny' or the life and labours of John Oxtoby*. London, 1855.

——. Shaw, George. *Life of John Oxtoby (Praying Johnny)*. London, 1894.

Phoebe Palmer. Oden, Thomas (ed.). *Phoebe Palmer: selected writings*. New York, 1988.

——. Palmer, Phoebe. *Four years in the old world*. 2nd thousand, New York, 1866.

——. ——. ——. 10th edn, Toronto, 1886.

——. Raser, Harold. *Phoebe Palmer: her life and thought*. Lewiston, NY, 1987.

——. Wheatley, Reverend Richard. *The life and letters of Mrs Phoebe Palmer*. New York, 1876.

William Pennefather. Braithwaite, Richard. *The life and letters of William Pennefather*. London, 1878.

Philip Phillips. Phillips, Philip. *Song pilgrimage around and throughout the world*. London, 1880.

Joshua Poole. Anon. *The life of Joshua Poole. With details of his conversion, and particulars of his subsequent career*. London, 1867.

——. Poole, Joshua. *The extraordinary life-story of 'Fiddler Joss', as told by himself, to a great pubic meeting at Surrey Chapel, the Reverend Newman Hall, presiding.* London, 1866.

John Preston. Gregory, Benjamin. *The poacher turned preacher, John Preston, of Yeadon.* London, 1896.

William Quarrier. [Urquhart, John]. *The life-story of William Quarrier. A romance of faith.* 3rd edn, Glasgow and London, [1905].

Reginald Radcliffe. Radcliffe, Jane. *Recollections of Reginald Radcliffe.* London, 1896.

Lord Radstock. Leskov, Nickolai. *Schism in high society: Lord Radstock and his followers.* Translated and edited by James Muckle. Nottingham, 1995 edn of orig. edn, St Petersburg, 1877.

James Hayes Raper. Hilton, J. Deane. *A brief memoir of James Hayes Raper. Temperance reformer, 1820–97.* London, 1898.

David Rea. Rea, Tom. *The life and labours of David Rea, evangelist. Largely written from his own manuscripts. Compiled by Tom Rea.* Belfast, 1917.

A.A. Rees. Brockie, William. *Memoirs of A.A. Rees, minister of the gospel at Sunderland.* London, 1884.

——. Everett, James. *The midshipman and the minister; the quarter deck and the pulpit.* London, 1867.

Henry Rees. Davies, Ann Marie. *Life and letters of Henry Rees.* Bangor, 1904.

Charles Richardson. Coulson, John E. *The peasant preacher: memorials of Mr Charles Richardson, a Wesleyan evangelist.* 2nd edn, London, 1866.

Evan Roberts. Hicks, Reverend W. Percy. *Life story of Evan Roberts and stirring experiences in the Welsh revival.* London, 1906.

——. Hughes, Gwilym. *Evan Roberts, revivalist, story of the Liverpool mission.* Dolgelley, 1905.

H.H. Roberts. Johnson, Cissie. *'H.H.R.': Henry Hosah Roberts, Cliff College evangelist.* London, 1948.

Ira D. Sankey. Sankey, Ira D. *My life and sacred songs.* 2nd edn, London, 1906.

Mrs James J. Scroggie. Scroggie, Dr W. Graham (ed.). *The story of a life in the love of God. Incidents collected from the diaries of Mrs James J. Scroggie.* London, 1938.

Richard Seager. Johns, Reverend J. *Richard M. Seager: the evangelist. His life story.* Rochdale, 1905.

Earl of Shaftesbury. Hodder, Edwin. *The life and work of the seventh Earl of Shaftesbuty, K.G.* 3 vols., London, 1886.

Albert Shakesby. *A collection of memoirs, magazine articles, revival reports concerning Albert Shakesby.* N.p., 1905.

——. Shakesby, Albert. *From street arab to evangelist: the life story of Albert Shakesby, a converted athlete.* Hull, 1910.

John Shaw. Colbeck, Alfred. *John Shaw of Pudsey.* 2nd edn, London, 1890.

Gipsy Smith. Smith, Gipsy. *Gipsy Smith. His life and work, by himself.* London, 1903.

——. Lazell, David. *From the forest I came. The story of Gipsy Rodney Smith.* London, 1970.

——. Idem. *Gypsy from the forest: a new biography of the international evangelist Gipsy Smith (1860–1947).* Bridgend, 1997.

——. Murray, Harold. *Sixty years an evangelist.* London, 1937.

——. ——. *Gipsy Smith, an intimate memoir.* Exeter, 1947.

——. Stead, W.T. 'The story of Gipsy Smith' in W.T. Stead, *Revival pamphlets* (London, 1905), pp. 115–60.

Gipsy Simon Smith. Smith, Gipsy Simon. *From hansom cab to platform.* Leytonstone, 1911.

Stanley Spencer. Spencer, Gilbert. *Stanley Spencer.* London, 1961.

W.T. Stead. Whyte, Frederick. *The life of W.T. Stead.* London, 1925.

Edward Sunners. Lund, Thomas W.M. *The moral of Edward Sunners' funeral. A sermon (on Acts 3:6).* Liverpool, 1866.

Kate Taylor. Taylor, Mrs Col. Kate. 'Reminiscences' in Anon. (ed.), *Fighting in many lands: memories of veteran salvationists.* 1st series. London, 1946.

William Taylor. Moore, Reverend C.G. *William Taylor of California (Bishop of Africa). An autobiography.* London, 1897.

William Taylor. Dixon, W. *A marvel of grace, the late William Taylor, 'The Navvy', evangelist for 25 years with the Evangelization Society.* 2nd edn, Strateaven, 1895.

——. Taylor, W.J. *The life and work of the late William Taylor, the Navvy.* With an introduction by Cpn W.E. Smith. Glasgow, 1892.

William Thompson. Pearse, Mark Guy (the elder). *The earnest evangelist and successful class leader. Memoir of William Thompson.* London, 1881.

R. A. Torrey. MacLean, J. Kennedy. *Torrey and Alexander: the story of their lives.* London, 1905.

——. ——. *Triumphant evangelism: the three years' mission of Dr Torrey and Mr Alexander in Great Britain and Ireland.* London, 1905.

Captain Trotter. Pennefather, Reverend William. *'To die is gain'; with a brief notice of Captain Trotter.* London, 1871.

James Turner. MacHardie, Elizabeth. *James Turner; or, how to reach the masses.* With an introductory note by R. Radcliffe. Aberdeen, 1875.

Henry Varley. Varley, Henry Jr. *Henry Varley's life story.* London, 1916.

Various. Harding, William Henry. *Revival Series (lives of religious leaders).* London, 1912–1915.
Richard Weaver.
The seventh Earl of Shaftesbury.
James Turner.
Duncan Matheson.
John MacGregor and Gawin Kirkham.

——. Hurd, F.H. *Earnest men: sketches of eminent Primitive Methodist ministers and laymen.* London, 1872.

———. Patterson, William M. *Men on fire and consecrated women also*. London, 1911.

———. Pearce, Joseph. *Burning and shining lights: a souvenir of Primitive Methodist radiant personalities*. Halesowen, 1935.

———. ———. *Dinna forget: Primitive Methodist soul-winning personalities*. Leominster, 1932.

———. Pickering, Hy. *Chief men among the brethren*. Reprint, Neptune, NJ, 1986, of orig. edn, London, 1918.

———. Shields, James. *Triumphs of grace*. Kilmarnock, [1920].

———. Whiteley, David (ed.). *Illustrious local preachers*. Bradford, 1891.

George Warner. Stephenson, J. *A man of faith and fire*. London, 1902.

George Warren. Barfoot, John. *Piety behind the plough; or, observations founded on the life and character of Mr George Warren*. London, 1864.

Mrs Sydney Watson. Watson, Mrs Sydney. *A village maiden's career. Life story of Mrs Sydney Watson*. 2nd edn, London, n.d.

Thomas Waugh. Waugh, Reverend Thomas. *Twenty-three years a missioner. Life-sketch lessons and reminiscences*. 2nd edn, London and Rochdale, 1905.

Richard Weaver. Morgan, R.C. *The life of Richard Weaver, the converted collier*. London, 1861.

———. Paterson, Reverend James. *Richard Weaver's life story*. Reprint, London, 1913 of orig. edn, London, 1897.

Edward Weeks. Wake, B. Barry. *Ned Weeks of Northhampton. Story of his life*. London, 1902.

Moses Welsby. Welsby, Moses ('Owd Mo'). *From coal pit to Joyful News Mission*. 5th edn, Rochdale, n.d.

Reverend F.A. West. Gregory, Reverend Benjamin. *Memorials of … F.A. West … and personal recollections by … Benjamin Gregory*. London, 1873.

Agnes Weston. *Our Blue Jackets. A narrative of Miss Weston's life and work among our sailors. By an eyewitness*. London, 1878.

Julia Bainbrigge Wightman. Fletcher, James M.J. *Mrs Wightman of Shrewsbury: the story of a pioneer in temperance work*. London, 1906.

———. Bullock, C. *Lives worth living: Prebendary and Mrs Wightman*. London, 1898.

George Williams. Williams, George. *Tales of the mystic way. Gospel incidents in the life of an Irish evangelist*. London, 1929.

W.J. Willis. Willis, W.J. *From taproom to pulpit. Being a lecture delivered by Mr Willis, evangelist, with photographs of the lecturer, Mr Tom Holland, and the late Reverend David Kyles*. Darlington, n.d.

John Wood. Wood, A. E. *A beloved disciple – John Wood*. London, 1920.

John Wright. Wright, John. *Saved just in time: the history of my conversion*. London, n.d.

Dinsdale Young. Murray, Harold. *Dinsdale Young: the preacher. An intimate sketch …* London, 1938.

Books

Arthur, Reverend William. *The tongue of fire: or, the true power of Christianity.* London, 1856.

Baillie, Reverend John. *The revival: or, what I saw in Ireland; with thoughts suggested by the same. The result of two personal visits.* London, 1860.

Bond, Reverend John. *How to fill our chapels: Wesleyan Methodism in 1885.* London, 1885.

Booth, Bramwell. *Echoes and memories.* London, 1925.

Booth, Catherine. *Papers on aggressive Christianity.* 10 parts, London, 1881.

——. *Papers on practical religion.* London, 1878.

Booth, William. *How to reach the masses with the gospel.* London, 1872.

——. *In darkest England and the way out.* London, 1890.

Carter, William. *The power of grace. Results of theatre preaching, extraordinary tea meetings and mothers' meetings, in the south of London.* London, 1863.

——. *The power of truth: or, results of theatre preaching and extraordinary tea meetings in South London.* London, 1865.

Clarke, Charles J. *Pioneers of revival.* London, 1939.

Cook, Reverend Thomas. *New testament holiness.* London, 1902.

Cooke, Harriette. *Mildmay; or, the story of the first deaconess institution.* London, 1892.

Dale, Reverend R.W. *The evangelical revival and other sermons.* London, 1880.

——. *The old evangelicalism and the new.* London, 1889.

Davenport, F.M. *Primitive traits in religious revivals: a study in mental and social evolution.* New York, 1905.

Davies, Reverend Evan (ed.). *Revivals in Wales: facts and correspondence supplied by pastors of the Welsh churches.* London, 1859.

Dwyer, Reverend John. *Christian work for gentle hands: thoughts on female agency in the church of God.* 3rd edn, London, 1873.

Fairfield, Zoë (ed.). *Some aspects of the woman's movement.* London, 1915.

Gall, James Jr. *The Carrubber's Close Mission: its planting and first fruits.* Edinburgh, 1860.

——. *The revival of pentecostal Christianity. The history of the Carrubber's Close Mission, with the twelve articles of the science of missions.* London, 1882.

——. *The science of missions.* Edinburgh and London, 1878.

Gibson, Reverend William. *The year of grace: a history of the Ulster revival of 1859.* 2nd edn, Edinburgh, 1860.

Graham, Reverend Charles. *The coming great revival; or, the church prepared for her Lord.* London, 1879.

Green, Walford and Morgan, J.H. *Methodist revival missions: a small handbook.* London, 1876.

Guinness, Henry Grattan. *Preaching for the million. Thirteen sermons on important subjects with a memoir of his life and ministry.* London, 1859.

Hamilton, Reverend William. *An inquiry into the scriptural character of the revival of 1859*. Belfast, 1866.

Henry, T. Shuldham. *Now and forever. Seven addresses … with hints on revival theology, by the editor (J. Offord)*. London and Plymouth, [printed, 1862].

James, Reverend John Angell. *Female piety; or, the young woman's guide through life to immortality*. 10th edn, London, 1864.

Johnson, Henry. *Stories of great revivals, with contributions from W.H.M.H. Aitken, Reverend F.B. Meyer, Reverend J. Stuart Holden, and Gipsy Smith*. London, 1906.

Key, Robert. *The gospel among the masses … 2nd edn*, London, 1872.

Lewis, Howell Elvet. *With Christ among the miners: incidents and impressions of the Welsh revival*. London, 1906.

Lewis, Jessie Penn. *The awakening in Wales and some of the hidden springs*. London, 1905.

M[arsh], C[atherine] M. *English hearts and English hands; or, the railway and the trenches*. 21st thousand, London and Edinburgh, 1858.

A Member of the Evangelization Society. *Preaching the gospel; or evangelists and evangelization*. N.p, n.d.

Middleton, Lancelot. *Mission addresses*. London, 1889.

Moody, D.L. *The Blood*. 1875.

——. *The London discourses of Mr D.L. Moody, as delivered in the Agricultural Hall and Her Majesty's Opera House*. London, 1875.

——. *Anecdotes and illustrations of D.L. Moody, related by him in his revival work*. Compiled by Reverend J.B. McClure. Wakefield, 1877.

——. *Anecdotes, incidents and illustrations*. London, 1898.

Morgan, Reverend J.Vrynwy. *The Welsh religious revival, 1904–5: a retrospect and a criticism*. London, 1909.

Murray, Harold. *Twixt Aldgate Pump and Poplar. The story of 50 years adventure in east London*. London, 1935.

Nelson, Reverend Isaac. *The year of delusion: a review of 'The year of grace'*. Belfast, 1860.

North, Brownlow. *'Yes or no!'* London, 1867.

[Palmer, Phoebe]. *The promise of the father; or, a neglected speciality of the last days*. Boston, 1859.

Pearce, Joseph. *Life changing evangelism*. London, 1936.

Phillips, Reverend Thomas. *The Welsh revival: its origin and development*. London, 1860.

Pierson, Reverend Arthur. *Evangelistic work in principle and practice*. London, 1888.

——. *Forward movements of the last half century*. New York and London, 1900.

——. *The revival of prayer*. London, 1903.

R. [Railton, George Scott]. *Twenty-one years Salvation Army. Under the generalship of William Booth*. London, 1887.

——. *Heathen England and what to do for it*. London, 1877.

Rees, Reverend Thomas. *Miscellaneous papers on subjects relating to Wales.* London, 1867.

Reid, Reverend William (ed.). *Authentic records of revival, now in progress in the United Kingdom.* London, 1860.

Richey, Reverend William. *Connor and Coleraine; or, scenes and sketches of the last Ulster awakening.* 2 vols., Belfast, 1870.

Sampson, William. *Just in time.* London, 1902.

——. *Strange but true. Experiences of William Sampson, the Cornish evangelist.* London, 1894.

Simpson, Reverend R.T. *Recollections of and reflections on the revival of 1859.* Dungannon, 1909.

Smith, Henry. *Ministering women: the story of the work of the sisters connected with the United Methodist Deaconess Institute, together with some account of the origin and history of the Institute.* London, 1913.

Smith, Reverend J. Denham. *Times of refreshing, illustrated in the present revival of religion.* Dublin, 1860.

Smith, Samuel. *Anecdotes, facts and biographical sketches connected with the great revival of the work of God in raising up and progressing the Primitive Methodist connexion.* Douglas, Isle of Man, 1872.

Smith, Cpn. W.E. *Address to evangelists.* London, 1874.

——. ——. 17th edn, London, 1903.

Stephenson, T. Bowman. *Concerning Sisterhoods.* London, 1890.

Thompson, Charles L. *Times of refreshing. A history of American revivals from 1740 to 1877, with their philosophy and methods.* Chicago, 1877.

Torrey, R.A. (ed.). *How to promote and conduct a successful revival. With suggestive outlines.* London, 1901.

——. *How to work for Christ. A compendium of effective methods.* London, 1893.

Vickers, James. *History of independent Methodism.* Bolton, 1920.

Watson, Reverend Dr John. *The inspiration of faith and other sermons.* London, 1905.

Weir, Reverend John. *The Ulster awakening: its origin, progress and fruit. With notes of a tour of personal observation and inquiry.* London, 1860.

Wightman, Julia Bainbrigge. *Haste to the rescue; or work while it is day.* London and Edinburgh, 1862.

Wilkinson, Reverend G. *Pentecost; or, the revival of the work of God.* London, 1867.

Wilkinson, William. *The revival in its physical, psychical and religious aspects.* London and Guildford, 1860.

Williams, T. Rhondda (ed.). *The true revival versus Torreyism.* 2nd edn, London, 1905.

John Wood. *The story of the Evangelization Society.* London, 1907.

Woodcock, Henry. *Wonders of grace; or, the influence of the Holy Spirit manifested in upwards of 350 remarkable conversions.* London, 1879.

Wyndham, Horace. *Feminine frailty.* London, 1929.

SECONDARY SOURCES

Books

Akenson, Donald H. *The Church of Ireland: ecclesiastical reform and revolution, 1800–85.* New Haven, NY, 1971.

Ambler, R.W. *Ranters, revivalists and reformers.* Hull, 1989.

Armitage, Rita. *Mission in the second city: the history of the Birmingham Methodist Central Mission 1887–1987.* [Birmingham], [1987].

Bagwell, Philip S. *Outcast London: a Christian response. The West London Mission of the Methodist Church 1887–1987.* London, 1987.

Bebbington, David. *Evangelicalism in modern Britain: a history from the 1730s to the 1980s.* London, 1989.

——. *The nonconformist conscience.* London, 1982.

Blakey, R.S. *The man in the manse.* Edinburgh, 1978.

Bradley, Ian. *The call to seriousness: the evangelical impact on the Victorians.* London, 1976.

Brekus, Catherine A. *Strangers and pilgrims: female preaching in America, 1740–1845.* Chapel Hill and London, 1998.

Brice, J.I. *The crowd for Christ.* London, 1934.

Brooke, Peter. *Ulster Presbyterianism: the historical perspective, 1610–1970.* Dublin, 1987.

Brown, Callum. *The social history of religion in Scotland since 1730.* London, 1987.

Brown, Kenneth. *A social history of the nonconformist ministry in England and Wales 1800–1930.* Oxford, 1988.

Brown, Terence. *The whole protestant community: the making of a historical myth.* Derry, 1985.

Brozyna, Andrea Ebel. *Labour, love and prayer: female piety in Ulster religious literature 1850–1914.* Belfast and Kingston/Montreal, 1999.

Bruce, Steve (ed.). *Religion and modernization: sociologists and historians debate the secularization thesis.* Oxford, 1992.

Burnett, John, Vincent, David, Mayall, David (eds). *The autobiography of the working class: an annotated critical bibliography.* 3 vols., Brighton, 1984–9.

Carson, J.T. *God's river in spate: the story of the religious awakening in Ulster in 1859.* Belfast, 1958.

Carwardine, Richard. *Transatlantic revivalism: popular evangelicalism in Britain and America, 1790–1865.* Westport, CN, 1978.

Chilcote, Paul Wesley. *John Wesley and the women preachers of early Methodism.* Metuchen, NJ and London, 1991.

Church, Leslie. *More about the early Methodist people.* London, 1949.

Clark, G.S. Kitson. *The making of Victorian England.* London, 1962.

Collier-Thomas, Bettye. *Daughters of thunder: black women preachers and their sermons, 1850–1979.* San Francisco, 1998.

Coad, F.Roy. *A history of the brethren movement.* Exeter, 1968.

Cox, Jeffrey. *The English churches in a secular society; Lambeth, 1870–1930.* Oxford, 1982.

Cresswell, Amos S. *The story of Cliff.* Calver, 1965.

Currie, Robert, Gilbert, Alan and Horsley, Lee. *Churches and churchgoers: patterns of church growth in the British Isles since 1700.* Oxford, 1977.

Currie, Robert. *Methodism divided: a study in the sociology of ecumenicalism.* London, 1968.

Curtis, L.P. *Apes and angels, the Irishman in Victorian caricature.* Newton Abbot, 1971.

Davies, E.T. *Religion in the industrial revolution in South Wales.* Cardiff, 1965.

———. *Religion and society in the nineteenth century.* Llandybie, 1981.

Davies, John. *A history of Wales.* London, 1993.

Davies, R., George, A.R., and Rupp, G. (eds). *A history of the Methodist church in Great Britain.* 2 vols., London, 1978.

Ditchfield, G.M. *The evangelical revival.* London, 1998.

Ellis, Robert. *Living echoes of the Welsh revival, 1904–5.* London, 1951.

Evans, Eifion. *The Welsh revival of 1904.* Glamorgan, 1969.

———. *When he is come: an account of the 1858–60 revival in Wales.* Bala, 1959.

Faverty, Frederic. *Matthew Arnold, the ethnologist.* New York, 1968.

Field-Bibb, Jacqueline. *Women towards priesthood: ministerial politics and feminist praxis.* Cambridge, 1991.

Flynn, J.Stephen. *Cornwall forty years after.* London, 1917.

Furlong, Monica. *A dangerous delight: women and power in the church.* London, 1991.

Gallagher, Robert H. *Pioneer preachers of Irish Methodism.* Belfast, [1965].

Garnett, Jane and Matthew, Colin (eds). *Revival and religion since 1700: essays for John Walsh.* London, 1993.

Gibbon, Peter. *The origins of Ulster unionism.* Manchester, 1975.

Gilbert, Alan. *The making of post-Christian Britain.* London, 1980.

———. *Religion and society in industrial England, 1740–1914.* London and New York, 1976.

Gill, Robin. *The myth of the empty church.* London, 1993.

Gilley, Sheridan and Shiels, W.J. (eds). *The history of religion in Britain.* Oxford, 1994.

Heasman, Kathleen. *Evangelicals in action.* London, 1962.

Heeney, Brian. *The women's movement in the Church of England, 1850–1930.* Oxford, 1988.

Helmstadter, Richard and Lightman, Bernard (eds). *Victorian faith in crisis. Essays on continuity and change in nineteenth-century religious belief.* London, 1991.

Hempton, David. *The religion of the people: Methodism and popular religion c.1750–1900.* London and New York, 1996.

———. *Religion and political culture in Britain and Ireland: from the Glorious Revolution to the decline of empire.* Cambridge, 1996.

Hempton, David and Hill, Myrtle. *Evangelical protestantism in Ulster society, 1740–1890*. London, 1992.

Hindmarsh, D. Bruce. *John Newton and the English evangelical tradition: between the conversions of Wesley and Wilberforce*. Oxford, 1996.

Hobsbawm, Eric and Ranger, Terence (eds). *The invention of tradition*. Cambridge, 1983.

Holden, Pat (ed.). *Women's religious experience*. London, 1983.

Holmes, R. Findlay. *Our Irish Presbyterian heritage*. Belfast, 1985.

Hoppen, Theo. *Ireland since 1800: conflict and conformity*. London, 1989.

Hylson-Smith, Kenneth. *Evangelicals in the Church of England, 1734–1984*. London, 1988.

Inglis, K.S. *Churches and the working classes in Victorian England*. London, 1963.

Jones, Rhys B. *Rent heavens – the revival of 1904. Some of its hidden springs and prominent results*. London, 1931.

Jones, Thomas. *Rhymney memories*. Gwasg Gomer, 1970.

Kent, John. *Holding the fort: studies in Victorian revivalism*. London, 1978.

Knight, Frances. *The nineteenth-century church and English society*. Cambridge, 1995.

Lambert, D.W. *What hath God wrought: the story of Cliff College 1904–54*. Chesterfield, [1954].

Larson, Rebecca. *Daughters of light: Quaker women preaching and prophesying in the colonies and abroad, 1700–1775*. New York, 1999.

Lewis, Donald. *Lighten their darkness: the evangelical mission to working-class London, 1828–60*. Westport, CN, 1986.

Long, Kathryn Teresa. *The revival of 1857–58: interpreting an American religious awakening*. New York and Oxford, 1998.

Luddy, Maria. *Women and philanthropy in nineteenth-century Ireland*. Cambridge, 1995.

McIlhiney, David. *A gentleman in every slum: Church of England missions in east London, 1837–1914*. Allison Park, PN, [1988].

MacInnes, John. *The evangelical movement in the highlands of Scotland, 1688 to 1800*. Aberdeen, 1957.

McIntosh, John R. *Church and theology in Enlightenment Scotland: the popular party 1740–1800*. East Linton, 1998.

McLeod, Hugh. *Class and religion in the late Victorian city*. London, 1974.

——. (ed.). *European religion in the age of great cities 1830–1930*. London and New York, 1994.

——. *Religion and irreligion in Victorian England: how secular was the working class?* Bangor, 1993.

——. *Religion and the working class in nineteenth-century Britain*. London, 1984.

McLoughlin, William. *Revivals, awakenings and reform*. Chicago and London, 1978.

Malmgreen, Gail (ed.). *Religion in the lives of English women, 1760–1930*. London, 1986.

Martin, William. *A prophet with honour*. New York, 1991.

Matthew, H.C.G. *Gladstone, 1809–1874*. Oxford, 1988.

Meadley, Thomas. *Kindled by a spark*. Rochdale?, 1983.

Mews, Stuart (ed.). *Modern religious rebels: presented to John Kent*. London, 1993.

Milburn, Geoffrey and Batty, Margaret (eds). *Workaday preachers: the story of Methodist local preaching*. Peterborough, 1995.

Moore, Robert. *Pitmen, preachers and politics: the effects of Methodism in a Durham mining community*. London, 1974.

Morgan, K.O. *Rebirth of a nation: Wales 1880–1980*. Oxford, 1981.

Murray, Ian H. *Revival and revivalism: the making and marring of American evangelicalism 1750–1858*. Edinburgh, 1994.

Noll, Mark, Bebbington, David W., and Rawlyk, George (eds). *Evangelicalism: comparative studies of popular protestantism in North America, the British Isles, and beyond 1700–1990*. New York and Oxford, 1994.

Obelkevich, James. *Religion and rural society: South Lindsey, 1825–75*. Oxford, 1976.

Obelkevich, James, Roper, Lyndal and Samuel, Raphael (eds). *Disciplines of faith: studies in religion, politics and patriarchy*. London, 1987.

Orr, J. Edwin. *The second evangelical awakening in Britain*. London and Edinburgh, 1949.

Owen, Alex. *The darkened room: women, power and spiritualism in late Victorian England*. London, 1989.

Paisley, Ian. *The 'fifty-nine': an authentic history of the great Ulster awakening of 1859*. Belfast, 1958.

Parsons, Gerald (ed.). *Religion in Victorian Britain*. 5 vols., Manchester, 1988–97.

Prochaska, Frank. *Women and philanthropy in nineteenth-century England*. Oxford, 1980.

Rack, Henry. *Reasonable enthusiast: John Wesley and the rise of Methodism*. London, 1989.

Rawlyk, George and Noll, Mark (eds). *Amazing grace: evangelicalism in Australia, Britain, Canada, and the United States*. Montreal and Kingston, 1994.

Rendall, Jane (ed.). *Equal or different: women's politics 1800–1914*. Oxford, 1987.

Robbins, Keith (ed.). *Protestant evangelicalism: Britain, Ireland, Germany and America, c. 1750–1950: Studies in Church History. Subsidia 7*. Oxford, 1991.

Roberts, Elizabeth. *Women's work 1840–1940*. Basingstoke, 1988.

Robertson, Darrel. *The Chicago revival, 1876: society and revivalism in a nineteenth-century city*. Metuchen, NJ, 1989.

Rowall, Geoffrey. *Hell and the Victorians*. London, 1974.

Sails, George. *At the centre: the story of Methodism's Central Missions*. London, 1970.

Sandall, Robert. *The history of the Salvation Army*. 3 vols., London, 1947–55.

Schenthler, Boyd Stanley. *Queen of the Methodists: the Countess of Huntingdon and the eighteenth century crisis of faith and society*. Durham, 1997.

Shaw, Jane and Kreider, Alan (eds). *Culture and the nonconformist tradition*. Cardiff, 1999.

Shaw, Thomas. *The Bible Christians, 1815–1907*. London, 1965.

———. *A history of Cornish Methodism*. Truro, 1967.

Shoemaker, Robert B. *Gender in English society 1650–1850: the emergence of separate spheres?* London and New York, 1998.

Smith, Mark. *Religion in industrial society: Oldham and Saddleworth 1740–1885*. Oxford, 1994.

Sullivan, Dick. *Navvyman*. London, 1983.

Swift, Rowland C. *Lively people: Methodism in Nottingham, 1740–1979*. Nottingham, 1982.

Thompson, David. *Nonconformity in the nineteenth century*. London, 1972.

Thompson, Dorothy. *British women in the nineteenth century*. London, 1989.

Thompson, E.P. *The making of the English working class*. Penguin edn, with postscript, London, 1980 of orig. edn, London, 1963.

Urdank, Albion. *Religion and society in a Cotswold vale, Nailsworth, Gloucestershire, 1780–1865*. Berkeley, CA, 1990.

Valentine, Simon Ross. *John Bennett and the origins of Methodism and the Evangelical Revival in England*. Lanham, MD and London, 1997.

Valenze, Deborah. *Prophetic sons and daughters: female preaching and popular religion in industrial England*. Princeton, NJ, 1985.

W.E. Vaughan (ed.). *A new history of Ireland* (11 vols., Oxford, 1982–95), V (*Ireland under the union, 1800–1870*).

Vicinius, Martha. *Independent women: work and community for single women, 1850–1920*. Chicago, 1985.

Watson, Bernard. *A hundred years' war: the Salvation Army, 1865–1965*. London, 1964.

Ward, W.R. *Faith and faction*. London, 1993.

———. *The protestant evangelical awakening*. Cambridge, 1992.

Watts, Michael R. *The Dissenters*. 2 vols., Oxford, 1995.

Weisberger, Bernard. *They gathered at the river: the story of the great revivalists and their impact upon religion in America*. Boston, 1958.

Werner, Julia Stewart. *The Primitive Methodist connexion*. Madison, WI, 1984.

Wickham, E.R. *Church and people in an industrial city*. London, 1957.

Wolffe, John. *The protestant crusade in Great Britain, 1829–1860*. Oxford, 1991.

Yeo, Stephen. *Religion and voluntary organisations in crisis*. London, 1976.

Articles

Ainsworth, A. 'Religion in the working-class community and the evolution of socialism in later nineteenth-century Lancashire' in *Histoire Sociale*, 10 (1977), pp. 354–80.

Altheide, David L. and Johnson, John M. 'Counting souls: a study of evangelical crusades' in *Pacific Sociological Review*, 20 (1977), pp. 323–48.

Ambler, R.W. 'From Ranters to chapel builders: Primitive Methodism in the south Lincolnshire fenland c.1820–1875' in *Voluntary Religion: Studies in Church History*, 23 (Oxford, 1986), pp. 319–31.

Anderson, Olive. 'Women preachers in mid-Victorian Britain: some reflexions on feminism, popular religion and social change' in *Historical Journal*, 12 (1969), pp. 467–84.

Baxter, John. 'The great Yorkshire revival 1792–6: a study of mass revival among the Methodists' in Michael Hill (ed.), *A sociological yearbook of religion in Britain*, 7 (1974), pp. 46–76.

Bebbington, David. 'The city, the countryside and the social gospel in late Victorian nonconformity' in *The church in town and countryside: Studies in Church History*, 16 (Oxford, 1979), pp. 415–26.

———. 'How Moody changed revivalism' in *Christian History*, 25 (Vol. IX, No. 1) (1990), pp. 22–5.

Beckerlegge, Oliver A. 'Women itinerant ministers' in *Proceedings of the Wesleyan Historical Society*, 30 (1956), pp. 182–4.

Bederman, Gail. 'The women have had charge of the church work long enough: the men and Religion Forward Movement of 1911–12 and the masculinization of middle-class protestantism' in *American Quarterly*, 41 (1989), pp. 432–65.

Billington, Louis. 'Female labourers in the church: women preachers in the northeastern United States, 1790–1840' in *Journal of American Studies*, 19 (1985), pp. 369–94.

———. 'Popular religion and social reform: a study of revivalism and teetotalism, 1830–50' in *Journal of Religious History*, 10 (1979), pp. 266–93.

———. 'Revivalism and popular religion' in Eric Sigsworth (ed.), *In search of Victorian values: aspects of nineteenth-century thought and society* (Manchester, 1988), pp. 147–61.

Billington, Rosamund. 'The dominant values of Victorian feminism' in Eric Sigsworth (ed.), *In search of Victorian values: aspects of nineteenth-century thought and society* (Manchester, 1988), pp. 116–30.

Brekus, Catherine A. 'Harriet Livermore, the pilgrim stranger: female preaching and biblical feminism in early-nineteenth-century America' in *Church History*, 65 (1996), pp. 389–404.

Briggs, J.H.Y. 'Charles Haddon Spurgeon and the Baptist denomination in nineteenth-century Britain' in *Baptist Quarterly*, 31 (1986), pp. 218–40.

Brown, Callum. 'Did urbanization secularize Britain?' in *Urban History Yearbook* (1988), pp. 1–14.

Brown, Earl Kent. 'Women in church history: stereotypes, archtypes and operational modalities' in *Methodist History*, 18 (1980), pp. 109–32.

Brown, Lindsay. 'The Presbyterians of County Monaghan', pt. 1 in *Journal of the Clogher Historical Society*, 13 (1990), pp. 7–54.

Bruce, Steve. 'Born again: crusades, conversions and brainwashing' in *Scottish*

Journal of Religious Studies, 3 (1982), pp. 107–23.

——. 'Modernity and fundamentalism' in *British Journal of Sociology*, 41 (1991), pp. 478–96.

——. 'Social change and collective behaviour: the revival in eighteenth-century Ross-shire' in *British Journal of Sociology*, 34 (1983), pp. 554–72.

Bruce, Steve and Wallis, Roy. 'Accounting for action: defending the common-sense heresy' *Sociology*, 17 (1983), pp. 97–110.

——. 'Network and clockwork' in *Sociology*, 16 (1982), pp. 102–7.

——. 'Rescuing motives' in *British Journal of Sociology*, 34 (1983), pp. 61–71.

Carwardine, Richard. 'The evangelist system: Charles Roe, Thomas Pulford, and the Baptist Home Missionary Service' in *Baptist Quarterly*, 28 (1979–80), pp. 209–25.

——. 'The religious revival of 1857–8 in the United States' in *Religious motivation: Studies in Church History*, 15 (Oxford, 1978), pp. 393–406.

——. 'The Welsh evangelical community and "Finney's revival"' in *Journal of Ecclesiastical History*, 29 (1978), pp. 463–80.

Cieszkowski, K.Z. 'Bendigo, the boxer' in *History Today*, 24, pt. 2 (1984), pp. 25–30.

Cott, Nancy. 'Young women in the second great awakening in New England' in *Feminist Studies*, 3 (1975), pp. 14–29.

Crawford, Michael J. 'Origins of the eighteenth-century evangelical revival: England and New England compared' in *Journal of British Studies*, 26 (October 1987), pp. 361–97.

Cross, Clare, '"He-goats before the flocks": a note on the part played by some women in the founding of some Civil War churches' in *Popular Belief and Practice: Studies in Church History*, 8 (Cambridge, 1984), pp. 195–202.

Davidoff, Lenore. 'Class and gender in Victorian England' in Judith Newton, Mary Ryan and Judith Walkowitz (eds), *Sex and class in women's history* (London, 1983), pp. 16–71.

Dayton, Donald and Dayton, Lucille. 'Women as preachers: evangelical precedents' in *Christianity Today*, 19, No. 17 (23 May 1975), pp. 882–5.

——. 'Your daughters shall prophesy: feminism in the holiness movement' in *Methodist History*, 14 (1976), pp. 67–92.

Deacon, Alan and Hill, Michael. 'The problem of "surplus women" in the nineteenth century: secular and religious alternatives' in Michael Hill (ed.), *A sociological yearbook of religion in Britain*, 5 (London, 1972), pp. 87–102.

Dews, D. Colin. 'Ann Carr and the female revivalists of Leeds' in Gail Malmgreen (ed.), *Religion in the lives of English women, 1760–1930* (London, 1986), pp. 68–87.

Digby, Anne. 'Victorian values and women in public and private' in T.C. Smout (ed.), *Victorian values: proceedings of the British Academy*, 78 (Oxford, 1992), pp. 195–215.

Donat, James. 'Medicine and religion: on the physical and mental disorders that accompanied the Ulster revival of 1859' in W.F. Bynum, Roy Porter and Michael Shepherd (eds), *The Anatomy of Madness* (3 vols., London and New York, 1985–8), III (*The asylum and its psychiatry*), pp. 125–50.

Dunn, Mary Maples. 'Saints and sisters: Congregational and Quaker women in the early colonial period' in Janet James (ed.), *Women in American religion* (Philadelphia, 1980), pp. 27–46.

Dunne, Tom. '"La trahaison des clercs": British intellectuals and the first home rule crisis' in *Irish Historical Studies*, 23 (1982), pp. 134–73.

Enright, William. 'Urbanization and the evangelical pulpit in nineteenth-century Scotland' in *Church History*, 47 (1978), pp. 400–7.

Evans, Eric. 'Some reasons for the growth of English rural anti-clericalism, c. 1750–1830' in *Past and Present*, 66 (1975), pp. 84–110.

Field, Clive D. 'The social composition of English Methodism to 1830: a membership analysis' in *Bulletin of the John Rylands University Library of Manchester*, 76 (1994), pp. 153–78.

——. 'The social structure of English Methodism: eighteenth – twentieth centuries' in *British Journal of Sociology*, 28 (1977), pp. 199–225.

——. 'A sociological profile of English Methodism, 1900–32' in *Oral History*, 4 (1976), pp. 73–95.

Gill, Sean. 'The power of Christian ladyhood: Priscilla Lydia Sellon and the creation of Anglican sisterhoods' in Stewart Mews (ed.), *Modern religious rebels: presented to John Kent* (Epworth, 1993), pp. 144–65.

Graham, E. Dorothy. 'Chosen by God: the female travelling preachers of early Primitive Methodism' in *Proceedings of the Wesley Historical Society*, 49 (1993), pp. 77–95.

——. 'The early deaconess evangelists: snapshots of their work' in Richard Sykes (ed.), *Beyond the boundaries: preaching in the Wesleyan tradition* (Oxford, 1998), pp. 87–115.

Gray, R.Q. 'Religion, culture and social class in late nineteenth and early twentieth-century Edinburgh' in Geoffrey Crossick (ed.), *The lower middle class in Britain* (London, 1977), pp. 134–58.

Green, S.J.D. 'Religion and the rise of the common man: mutual improvement societies, religious associations and popular education in three industrial towns in the West Riding of Yorkshire, c. 1850–1900' in Derek Fraser (ed.), *Cities, class and communication* (London, 1990), pp. 25–43.

——. 'The religion of the child in Edwardian Methodism: institutional reform and pedagogical reappraisal in the West Riding of Yorkshire' in *Journal of British Studies*, 30 (1991), pp. 377–98.

Gunther, Candy. 'The spiritual pilgrimage of Rachel Stearns, 1834–1837: reinterpreting women's religious and social experiences in the Methodist revivals of nineteenth-century America' in *Church History*, 65 (1996), pp. 577–95.

Hall, Basil. 'Two French contributions to the history of the revival' in Sidney Evans and Gomer M. Roberts (eds), *Cyfrol Goffa Diwygiad, 1904–5*

(Caernarfon, 1954), pp. 74–83.

——. 'The Welsh revival of 1904–5: a critique' in *Popular belief and practice: Studies in Church History*, 8 (Cambridge, 1972), pp. 291–301.

Hall, Catherine. 'Gender divisions and class formation in the Birmingham middle class, 1780–1850' in Raphael Samuel (ed.), *Peoples history and socialist theory* (London, 1981), pp. 164–75.

Harrison, Brian. 'Religion and recreation in nineteenth-century England' in *Past and Present*, 38 (1967), pp. 98–125.

Hempton, David. 'Bickersteth, bishop of Ripon: the episcopate of a mid-Victorian evangelical' in Gerald Parsons (ed.), *Religion in Victorian Britain* (5 vols., Manchester, 1988–97), IV, pp. 41–60.

——. 'Evangelicalism and eschatology' in *Journal of Ecclesiastical History*, 31 (1980), pp. 179–94.

——. 'For God and Ulster: evangelical religion and the Home Rule crisis of 1886' in Keith Robbins (ed.), *Protestant Evangelicalism: Britain, Ireland, Germany and America c.1750–c.1950. Studies in Church History. Subsidia 7* (Oxford, 1990), pp. 225–54.

——. 'Gideon Ouseley: rural revivalist, 1791–1839' in *The Church, Ireland and the Irish: Studies in Church History*, 25 (Oxford, 1988), pp. 203–14.

Hendrickson, Kenneth. 'Winning the troops for vital religion: female evangelical missionaries to the British Army, 1857–1880' in *Armed Forces and Society*, 23 (Summer 1997), pp. 615–34.

Hennell, Michael. 'Evangelicalism and worldliness, 1770–1870' in *Popular belief and practice: Studies in Church History*, 8 (Cambridge, 1972), pp. 229–36.

Hill, Myrtle. 'Ulster awakened: the '59 revival reconsidered' in *Journal of Ecclesiastical History*, 41 (1990), pp. 443–62.

Hillis, Peter. 'Presbyterianism and social class in mid-nineteenth century Glasgow: a study of nine churches' in *Journal of Ecclesiastical History*, 32 (1981), pp. 47–64.

Hovet, Theodore. 'Phoebe Palmer's alter phraseology and the spiritual dimension of woman's sphere' in *Journal of Religion*, 63 (1983), pp. 264–80.

Howarth, David. '"Joyful News" (1883–1963): some reflections' in *Proceedings of the Wesley Historical Society*, 44 (1983), pp. 2–15.

Jaffe, J.A. 'The "chiliasm of despair" reconsidered: revivalism and working-class agitation in County Durham' in *Journal of British Studies*, 28 (1989), pp. 23–42.

Kent, John. 'American revivalism and England in the nineteenth century' in *Papers presented to the Past and Present conference on popular religion*, 7 July 1966 (typescript), p. 14.

——. 'Feelings and festivals: an interpretation of some working-class religious attitudes' in H.J. Dyos and Michael Wolff (eds), *The Victorian city: images and realities.* (2 vols., London, 1973), II, pp. 855–71.

——. 'A late nineteenth-century nonconformist renaissance' in *Renaissance and renewal in church history: Studies in Church History*, 14 (Oxford, 1977), pp. 351–60.

Kent, J.H.S. 'The role of religion in the cultural structure of the later Victorian city' in *Transactions of the Royal Historical Society*, 5th series, 23 (1973), pp. 153–73.

King, William. 'Hugh Price Hughes and the British "social gospel"' in *Journal of Religious History*, 13 (1984), pp. 66–82.

Knoll, William. 'Women as clergy and laity in the nineteenth-century Methodist Protestant church' in *Methodist History*, 15 (1977), pp. 107–21.

Lambert, W.R. 'Some working-class attitudes towards organized religion in nineteenth-century Wales' in *Llafur*, 2 (1976), pp. 4–17.

Landsman, Ned. 'Evangelists and their hearers: popular interpretations of revivalist preaching in eighteenth-century Scotland' in *Journal of British Studies*, 28 (1989), pp. 120–49.

Lawless, Elaine. 'Piety and motherhood: reproductive images and maternal strategies of the woman preacher' in *Journal of American Folklore*, 100 (1987), pp. 469–78.

Lawrence, Anne. 'A priesthood of she-believers: women and congregations in mid-seventeenth century England' in *Women in the Church: Studies in Church History*, 27 (Oxford, 1990), pp. 345–63.

Lenton, John. '"Labouring for the Lord": women preachers in Wesleyan Methodism 1802–1932. A revisionist view' in Richard Sykes (ed.), *Beyond the boundaries: preaching in the Wesleyan tradition* (Oxford, 1998), pp. 58–86.

Lewis, Donald. '"Lights in dark places": women evangelists in early Victorian Britain, 1838–1857' in *Women in the Church: Studies in Church History*, 27 (Oxford, 1990), pp. 415–27.

Lovegrove, Deryck W. 'Unity and separation: contrasting elements in the thought and practice of Robert and J. Alexander Haldane' in *Voluntary Religion: Studies in Church History*, 23 (Oxford, 1986), pp. 155–66.

Loveland, Anne C. 'Domesticity and religion in the Antebellum period: the career of Phoebe Palmer' in *The Historian*, 39 (1977), pp. 455–71.

Luker, David. 'Revivalism in theory and practice: the case of Cornish Methodism' in *Journal of Ecclesiastical History*, 37 (1986), pp. 603–19.

McKee, W.J.H. 'The Ulster revival of 1859 and the development of Presbyterianism' in R.F.G. Holmes and R.B. Knox (eds), *The General Assembly of the Presbyterian Church in Ireland, 1840–1990: a celebration of Irish Presbyterian witness during a century and a half* (Coleraine, 1990), pp. 39–55.

MacLaren, A.A. 'Presbyterianism and the working class in a mid-nineteenth century city [Aberdeen]' in *Scottish Historical Review*, 46 (1967), pp. 115–39.

McLeod, Hugh. 'Class, community and region: the religious geography of nineteenth century England' in Michael Hill (ed.), *A sociological yearbook of religion in Britain*, 6 (1973), pp. 29–72.

——. 'Female piety and male irreligion? Religion and gender in the nineteenth century'. English typescript, 30 pp, of 'Weibliche foömigkeit, männlicher unglanbe?' in Ute Frevert (ed.), *Bürgerinnen und Jürger* (Göttingen, 1988).

——. 'New perspectives on Victorian working-class religion' in *Oral History Journal*, 14 (1986), pp. 31–49.

——. 'Urbanization and religion in nineteenth-century Britain' in Kaspar Elm and Hans Loock (eds), *Seelsorge und Diakonie in Berlin* (Berlin, 1990), pp. 63–80.

——. 'Varieties of Victorian belief' in *Journal of Modern History*, 64 (1992), pp. 321–37.

——. 'White collar values and the role of religion' in Geoffrey Crossick (ed.) *The lower middle class in Britain, 1870–1914* (London, 1977), pp. 61–88.

Mack, Phyllis. 'Giving birth to the truth: a letter by the Methodist Mary Taft' in *Scottish Journal of Religious Studies*, 19, No. 1 (1998), pp. 19–30.

——. 'Women as prophets during the English civil war' in *Feminist Studies*, 8 (1982), pp. 19–47.

Miller, David. 'Presbyterianism and "modernization" in Ulster' in *Past and Present*, 80 (1978), pp. 66–90.

Mitchell, Norma. 'From social to radical feminism: a survey of emerging diversity in Methodist women's organizations, 1869–1974' in *Methodist History*, 13 (1975), pp. 21–44.

Muirhead, I.A. 'The revival as a dimension of Scottish church history' in *Records of the Scottish Church History Society*, 20 (1980), pp. 179–96.

Murdoch, Norman. 'Female ministry in the thought and work of Catherine Booth' in *Church History*, 53 (1984), pp. 348–62.

Murray, Ian. 'Explaining evangelical history' in *Banner of Truth* (July 1994), pp. 8–14.

Murray, Jocelyn. 'Gender attitudes and the contribution of women to evangelism and ministry in the nineteenth century' in John Wolffe (ed.), *Evangelical faith and public zeal: evangelicals and society in Britain 1780–1980* (London, 1995), pp. 97–116.

Olsen, Gerald W. 'From parish to palace: working class influences on Anglican temperance movements, 1835–1914' in *Journal of Ecclesiastical History*, 40 (1989), pp. 239–52.

Owen, T.M. 'The "communion season" and Presbyterianism in a Hebridean community' in *Gwerin*, 1 (1956), pp. 53–66.

Pelling, Henry. 'Religion and the nineteenth-century British working class' in *Past and Present*, 27 (1964), pp. 128–33.

Price, D. 'A Victorian parson and his people: Rector Ffoulkes at Wigginton' in *Cake and Cockhorse: the magazine of the Banbury Historical Society*, 7 (1976), pp. 23–30.

Prochaska, F.K. 'Body and soul: Bible nurses and the poor in Victorian London' in *Historical Review*, 60 (1987), pp. 336–48.

Rack, H.D. 'Domestic visitation: a chapter in early nineteenth-century evangelism' in *Journal of Ecclesiastical History*, 24 (1973), pp. 357–76.

——. 'Survival and revival: John Bennet, Methodism and old dissent' in

Voluntary Religion: Studies in Church History, 23 (Oxford, 1986), pp. 2–23.

Raughter, Rosemary. 'A natural tenderness: the ideal and the reality of eighteenth-century female philanthropy' in Maryann Gialanella Valiulis and Mary O'Dowd (eds), *Women and Irish history: essays in honour of Margaret MacCurtain*. Dublin, 1997.

Richey, Russell. 'Revivalism: in search of a definition' in *Wesleyan Theological Journal*, 28 (1993), pp. 165–75.

Robson, Geoffrey. 'Between town and country: contrasting patterns of church-going in the early Victorian Black country' in *The Church in Town and Countryside: Studies in Church History*, 16 (Oxford, 1979), pp. 401–14.

——. 'The failures of success: working-class evangelists in early Victorian Birmingham' in *Religious Motivation: Studies in Church History*, 15 (Oxford, 1978), pp. 381–91.

Rosell, Garth. 'Sailing for the kingdom of God: Charles Finney and nineteenth-century transatlantic revivalism' in *Christian History*, 7 (1988), pp. 22–3.

Royle, E. 'The Church of England and Methodism in Yorkshire, c. 1750–1850: from monopoly to free market' in *Northern History*, 33 (1997), pp. 137–61.

Rule, John. 'Methodism, popular beliefs and village culture in Cornwall, 1800–50' in R.D. Storch (ed.), *Popular culture and custom in nineteenth-century England* (London, 1982), pp. 48–70.

Ryan, Mary. 'The power of women's networks' in Judith Newton, Mary Ryan and Judith Walkowitz (eds), *Sex and class in women's history* (London, 1983), pp. 167–86.

Sharp, John. 'Juvenile holiness: Catholic revivalism in Victorian Britain' in *Journal of Ecclesiastical History*, 35 (1984), pp. 220–38.

Sizer, Sandra. 'Politics and apolitical religion: the great urban revivals of the late nineteenth century' in *Church History*, 48 (1979), pp. 81–98.

Smout, T.C. 'Born again at Cambuslang: new evidence on popular religion and literacy in eighteenth-century Scotland' in *Past and Present*, 97 (1982), pp. 115–27.

Stark, Rodney and Bainbridge, W.S. 'Networks of faith: interpersonal bonds and recruitment to cults and sects' in *American Journal of Sociology*, 85 (1980), pp. 1376–95.

——. 'Of churches, sects and cults: preliminary concepts for a theory of religious movements' in *Journal for the Scientific Study of Religion*, 18 (1979), pp. 117–31.

Stark, Rodney. 'Social contexts and religious experience' in *Review of Religious Research*, 7 (1965), pp. 17–28.

Swift, Wesley. 'The women itinerant preachers of early Methodism', Parts 1 and 2 in *Proceedings of the Wesley Historical Society*, 28 (1952), pp. 89–94 and 29 (1953), pp. 76–83.

Taiz, Lillian. 'Hallelujah lasses in the battle for souls: working and middle-class women in the Salvation Army in the United States, 1872–1896' in *Journal of Women's History*, 9 (Summer 1997), pp. 84–107.

Thomas, Keith. 'Women and the civil war sects' in *Past and Present*, 13 (1958), pp. 42–62.

Thompson, David M. 'The churches and society in nineteenth-century England: a rural perspective' in *Popular belief and practice: Studies in Church History*, 8 (Cambridge, 1972), pp. 267–76.

Thorp, Malcolm R. 'Popular preaching and millennial expectations: the Reverend Robert Aitken and the Christian Society, 1836–40' in Malcolm Chase and Ian Dyck (eds), *Living and learning: essays in honour of J.F.C. Harrison* (Aldershot, 1996), pp. 103–17.

Tolar Collins, Vicki. 'Walking in light, walking in darkness: the story of women's changing rhetorical space in early Methodism' in *Rhetoric Review*, 14 (Spring 1996), pp. 336–54.

Turner, Christopher. 'Religious revivalism and Welsh industrial society, Aberdare in 1859' in *Llafur*, 4 (1984), pp. 4–13.

Twells, Alison. '"Happy English children": class, ethnicity, and the making of missionary women in the early nineteenth century' in *Women's Studies International Forum*, 21 (1998), pp. 235–45.

Valenze, Deborah. 'Cottage religion and the politics of survival' in Jane Rendall (ed.) *Equal or different: women's politics 1800–1914* (Oxford, 1987), pp. 31–56.

Vickery, Amanda. 'Golden age to separate spheres? A review of the categories and chronology of English women's history' in *Historical Journal*, 36 (1993), pp. 383–414.

Walker, Pamela. 'A chaste and fervid eloquence: Catherine Booth and the ministry of women in the Salvation Army' in Beverly Mayne Kienzle and Pamela J. Walker (eds), *Women preachers and prophets through two millennia of Christianity* (Berkeley, 1998), pp. 288–302.

Walker, R.B. 'The growth of Wesleyan Methodism in Victorian England and Wales' in *Journal of Ecclesiastical History*, 24 (1973), pp. 267–84.

Wallace, Anthony. 'Revitalization movements' in *American Anthropologist*, 58 (1956), pp. 264–81.

Walsh, John. 'Methodism and the mob in the eighteenth century' in *Popular belief and practice: Studies in Church History*, 8 (Cambridge, 1972), pp. 213–27.

——. 'Origins of the evangelical revival' in G.V. Bennett and J.D. Walsh (eds), *Essays in modern English church history* (London, 1966), pp. 132–62.

——. 'Religious societies: Methodist and evangelical 1738–1800' in *Voluntary Religion: Studies in Church History*, 23 (Oxford, 1986), pp. 279–302.

Ward, W.R. 'Power and piety: the origins of religious revival in the early eighteenth century' in *Bulletin of the John Rylands University Library of Manchester*, 63 (1980), pp. 231–52.

——. 'The relations of enlightenment and religious revival in central Europe and in the English-speaking world' in *Reform and Reformation, England and the Continent c. 1500–1750: Studies in Church History. Subsidia 2* (Oxford, 1979), pp. 281–305.

Welter, Barbara. 'The feminization of American religion: 1800–60' in Mary Hartman and Lois Banner (eds), *Clio's consciousness raised* (New York, 1974), pp. 137–57.

Williams, C.R. 'The Welsh religious revival, 1904–5' in *British Journal of Sociology*, 3 (1952), pp. 242–59.

Williams, E.M. 'Women preachers in the civil war' in *Journal of Modern History*, 1 (1929), pp. 561–9.

Wilson, Linda. '"Constrained by zeal": women in mid-nineteenth century nonconformist churches' in *Journal of Religious History*, 23 (June 1999), pp. 185–202.

——. 'Conversion amongst female Methodists, 1825–75' in *Proceedings of the Wesley Historical Society*, 51 (1997–98), pp. 217–25.

Winn, William. 'Tom Brown's schooldays and the development of "muscular Christianity"' in *Church History*, 29 (1960), pp. 64–73.

Withrington, D.J. 'The churches in Scotland c. 1870–1900: towards a new social conscience?' in *Records of the Scottish Church History Society*, 19 (1977), pp. 155–68.

——. 'Non-churchgoing in Scotland, c. 1750–1850: a preliminary survey' in *Records of the Scottish Church History Society*, 17 (1970), pp. 99–113.

Wolffe, John. 'The Evangelical Alliance in the 1840s: an attempt to institutionalise Christian unity' in *Voluntary Religion: Studies in Church History*, 23 (Oxford, 1986), pp. 33–46.

Yeo, Stephen. 'A new life: the religion of socialism in Britain, 1883–1896' in *History Workshop*, 4 (1977), pp. 5–56.

Unpublished theses

Carwardine, Richard. 'American religious revivalism in Great Britain, c. 1826–c.1863'. Unpub. D.Phil. diss., Oxford, 1974.

Chilcote, Paul Wesley. 'John Wesley and the women preachers of early Methodism'. Unpub. PhD diss., Duke University, 1984.

Graham, E. Dorothy. 'Called by God: the female itinerants of early Primitive Methodism'. Unpub. PhD diss., University of Birmingham, 1987.

Holmes, Janice. 'Lifting the curtain on popular religion: women, laity and language in the Ulster revival of 1859'. Unpub. M.A. diss., Queen's University at Kingston, 1991.

Morgan, P.B. 'A study of the work of American revivalists in Britain from 1870–1914, and of the effect upon organized Christianity of their work there'. Unpub. B.Litt. diss., Oxford, 1961.

Morrell, David J. 'Some aspects of revivalist and charismatic movements in England, 1800–62'. Unpub. M.Phil. diss., University of Manchester, 1987.

Pearson, Philip Chisholm. 'Wesleyan Methodism from 1850–1900 in relation to the life and thought of the Victorian age …'. Unpub. M.A. diss., University of Manchester, 1965.

Rice, Robert Jay. 'Religious revivalism and British Methodism, 1855–65'. Unpub. PhD diss., University of Illinois, 1979.

Roberts, Elizabeth. 'The working-class family in Barrow and Lancaster, 1890–1930'. Unpub. PhD diss., University of Lancaster, 1978.

Rule, J. 'The labouring miner in Cornwall, c. 1740–1870'. Unpub. PhD diss., Warwick University, 1971.

Scott, Albert. 'The Ulster revival of 1859'. Unpub. PhD diss., Trinity College Dublin, 1962.

Staggers, Kermit. 'Reuben A. Torrey, American fundamentalist, 1856–1928'. Unpub. PhD diss., Claremont Graduate School, 1986.

Toone, Mark J. 'Evangelicalism in transition: a comparative analysis of the work and theology of D.L. Moody and his proteges, Henry Drummond and R.A. Torrey'. Unpub. PhD diss., St Andrews', 1988.

Turner, Christopher. 'Revivals and popular religion in Victorian and Edwardian Wales'. Unpub. PhD diss., University of Aberystwyth, 1979.

Walker, Pamela. 'Pulling the devil's kingdom down: gender and popular culture in the Salvation Army, 1865–1895'. Unpub. PhD diss., Rutgers, 1992.

Ward, Christine. 'The social sources of the Salvation Army, 1865–90'. Unpub. M.Phil. diss., Bedford College, University of London, 1970.

White, John Wesley. 'The influence of North American evangelism in Great Britain between 1830 and 1914 on the origin and development of the ecumenical movement.' Unpub. D.Phil. diss., Mansfield College, Oxford, 1963.

Wilson, Linda. 'An investigation into the decline of female itinerant preachers in the Bible Christian sect up to 1850'. Unpub. M.Phil. diss., Cheltenham and Gloucester College of Further Education, 1992.

Index